Understanding Families

Understanding Families

DIVERSITY, CONTINUITY, AND CHANGE

George E. Dickinson
College of Charleston

Michael R. Leming
St. Olaf College

ALLYN AND BACON
Boston London Sydney Toronto

Series Editor: Karen Hanson
Production Administrator: Susan McIntyre
Editorial-Production Service: Editorial Inc.
Copyeditor: Jay Howland
Cover Administrator: Linda Dickinson
Manufacturing Buyer: Tamara McCracken

Library of Congress Cataloging-in-Publication Data

Dickinson, George E.
  Understanding families.

  Includes bibliographical references.
  1. Family—United States.   2. Marriage—United
States.   I. Leming, Michael R.   II. Title.
HQ536.D53   1989   306.85′0973   89-18252
ISBN 0-205-11901-8

Photo Credits
Page 1 Sculpture by Paul T. Granlund; photo courtesy of Primarius, Ltd. Page 11 Paul Conklin. Page 13 Frank Siteman. Page 27 Frank Siteman. Page 35 Photo courtesy of St. Olaf College. Page 37 Frank Siteman. Page 51 Frank Siteman. Page 55 Frank Siteman. Page 65 Sculpture by Paul T. Granlund; photo courtesy of Primarius, Ltd. Page 71 Photo courtesy of the Library of Congress. Page 74 Eugene Gordon. Page 80 Photo courtesy of the Library of Congress. Page 83 Photo courtesy of the Library of Congress. Page 93 © The Christian Science Monitor. Photo by R. N. Matheny. Page 94 Frank Siteman. Page 102 Frank Siteman. Page 107 Frank Siteman. Page 119 © The Christian Science Monitor. Photo by Neal Menschel. Page 127 Frank Siteman. Page 130 Frank Siteman. Page 135 Frank Siteman. Page 155 Frank Siteman. Page 160 Frank Siteman. Page 165 Sculpture by Paul T. Granlund; photo courtesy of Primarius, Ltd. Page 169 Frank Siteman. Page 188 Frank Siteman. Page 196 © The Christian Science Monitor. Photo by Patrick McArdell. Page 199 © The Christian Science Monitor. Photo by Neal Menschel. Page 200 Frank Siteman. Page 209 (left) Frank Siteman; (right) AP/Wide World Photos. Page 211 Frank Siteman. Page 217 AP/Wide World Photos. Page 240 Frank Siteman. Page 242 Talbot Lovering. Page 247 Sculpture by Paul T. Granlund; photo courtesy of Primarius, Ltd. Page 253 (left) Frank Siteman; (right) Robert Harbison. Page 261 Frank Siteman. Page 277 © The Christian Science Monitor. Photo by T. A. Hoffman. Page 281 Photo courtesy of St. Olaf College. Page 284 Paul Conklin. Page 289 Frank Siteman. Page 300 Frank Siteman. Page 304 Frank Siteman. Page 307 (left) Frank Siteman; (right) Frank Siteman. Page 310 Frank Siteman. Page 318 Frank Siteman. Page 323 Sculpture by Paul T. Granlund; photo courtesy of Primarius, Ltd. Page 331 Frank Siteman. Page 336 Frank Siteman. Page 345 Frank Siteman. Page 358 Robert Harbison. Page 367 Frank Siteman. Page 371 Robert Harbison. Page 374 Robert Harbison. Page 384 Frank Siteman. Page 393 Frank Siteman. Page 399 Sculpture by Paul T. Granlund; photo courtesy of Primarius, td. Page 408 Frank Siteman. Page 411 © The Christian Science Monitor. Photo by Peter Main.

Printed in the United States of America

10 9 8 7 6 5 4 3 2 1   94 93 92 91 90 89

Contents

Preface

Since almost everyone is involved to some extent with family situations, you may think of the study of family as a "commonsense science." Being involved with a situation, however, does not make a person an expert. In fact, our subjectivity tends to overcome objectivity. *Understanding Families: Diversity, Continuity, and Change* will make you aware of different marriage and family forms; alert you to diversity in the family; stress that different does not necessarily mean better or worse but simply different; and place the family in sociological, historical, and cross-cultural perspective. The book focuses, too, on current and emerging social trends affecting American families.

This book is written on the premise that becoming aware of potential crises in the family will help you actually to cope with problems when they arise. Knowledge of social problems will alert you to the fact that you are not the only one facing such problems; it will also help you to be more supportive of others as they attempt to cope.

Each chapter concludes with a review of important points from the chapter, discussion questions, and annotated suggested readings. Short articles (boxed readings) appear throughout the book. These human interest reports give diversity to the format, present application materials, and provide food for thought. A glossary of key terms is at the end of each chapter; references for all chapters are at the end of the book.

Though we collaborated throughout the twenty-four months of writing this book, a division of labor was established from the outset. Chapters 4, 6, 7, 9, 10, 11, 12, 13, and 16 were primarily the responsibility of George Dickinson. Michael Leming was responsible for chapters 1, 2, 3, 5, 8, 14, 15, 17, and the Appendix. Thus, if you occasionally encounter a reference to "I" in a chapter, the first person singular refers to the primary author of that particular chapter. It is our hope that these personal anecdotes throughout the text will give a more personal touch to the chapters and make the reading seem less "textbookish."

Understanding Families: Diversity, Continuity, and Change is written with the assumption that many readers will have no other sociology, or perhaps social science, courses. Therefore, we wish to introduce you to the ways a social scientist conducts research. Part One is about "studying the family." Chapter 1 discusses how various social science disciplines might approach the topic of family. Chapter 2 presents families in cross-cultural perspective. The last chapter in Part One introduces "Theoretical Orientations to Research in Family Sociology." In addition to the theory and research presented in Chapter 3, an illustration in the Appendix will walk you through a research study.

Part Two looks at social change and families. Chapter 4 examines social and historical roots of American families. Gender roles in the context of family life are the subject of Chapter 5. Subcultural variations families in six ethnic American groups are discussed in Chapter 6—black, Jewish, Mexican, Italian, Chinese, and Japanese. Social class and American families is the topic of Chapter 7.

The institution of marriage is the theme of Part Three. Chapter 8 (mate selection), Chapter 9 (issues in human sexuality), and Chapter 10 (marriage and marital issues) include discussions of dating, love, cohabitation, sex education, birth control, sexually transmitted diseases, sexual dysfunctions, communication in marriage, and marital satisfaction.

Part Four, on the institution of family, follows a life-cycle approach and has chapters on the parenting years (Chapter 11), the middle years (Chapter 12), and the retirement years (Chapter 13). Among topics treated are feminists' views on motherhood, parents versus peers, grandparenting, and marital quality in later life.

The crises of divorce (Chapter 14), death (Chapter 15), and family violence (Chapter 16) are presented in Part Five. Discussions include the whys of divorce, resingling, remarriage, explaining death to children, sexual abuse, and physical abuse of children, parents, spouses, and elders.

Understanding Families: Diversity, Continuity, and Change concludes with Part Six and the Epilogue (Chapter 17). This final chapter sums up important points from our study of American families and looks ahead to changes the future may bring. Topics include the AIDS crisis, the expanding size of the elderly population, and the day care crisis in America.

This book represents not a "how-to" cookbook approach to marriage and family but an approach evolving from theoretical frameworks and empirical research. *Understanding Families: Diversity, Continuity, and Change* is designed primarily for undergraduate students. It is our hope that this book will stimulate your interest in marriage and family relationships.

As chapters of this book were written, they were reviewed by several professionals teaching marriage and family and sociology of the family. The reviewers provided very helpful suggestions toward this final product. Reviewers of the book were Ben Aguirre (Texas A&M University), Judy Aulette (University of North Carolina at Charlotte), H. Hugh Floyd (University of New Orleans), Martha E. Giminez (University of Colorado at Boulder), Jane Hall (Western Carolina University at Cullowhee), Michael Irwin (Louisiana State University), Ross Klein (Iowa State University), John Middleton (State University of New York at Plattsburgh), Jack W. Sattel (Normandale Community College in Minnesota), and Constance L. Shehan (University of Florida). We are grateful to them for their contributions.

Computers, like marriages and families, do not always have complete compatibility. We wish to extend a word of appreciation to Robert E. Tournier and Daniel P. Dickinson for technical assistance in making our personal computers communicate in an understandable way.

We also acknowledge the professional guidance of our acquisitions editor, Karen Hanson, for her able contributions in the completion of this book. We are grateful to Judy Langemo for acquiring permissions for the book. Finally, special thanks to Susan McIntyre, production editor, and Jay Howland, copyeditor, for overseeing the manuscript's transformation into book form.

Understanding Families

PART ONE

Studying the Family

Introduction: Why Study the Family?

◆ *Families then and now serve as the locus of our most intense, highly charged, and important human relationships. Indeed, many have argued that as the alienation and impersonality of the modern public world, including the pressures of market society, have increased, the family's function as a haven and a reminder that human beings can transcend cash exchange relationships has been enhanced. The family today is both a resilient and a vulnerable institution.* *

Recently, I saw a television news report on the popularity of walking as a form of exercise. The television reporter interviewed a man who taught courses on techniques of walking. Even though most of the students in his class were in mid-life, they did not find it strange that they had paid fifty dollars to be told to "put one foot in front of the other." To my way of thinking, this reporter had just provided good evidence for P. T. Barnum's statement that "there's a sucker born every minute."

When I was in college, I think that my parents had the same response to the news that I was taking a course dealing with marriage and family living. They had probably assumed that my twenty years of family living had given me adequate insights into the topic. Furthermore, I suspect that they wished that I had spent their money more judiciously.

My motivations for taking this course were many. First, it was a popular course on campus and many of my friends were enrolled

---

*Jean Bethke Elshtain, *Public Man, Private Woman: Women in Social and Political Thought* (Princeton, N.J.: Princeton University Press, 1981), 131.

in the class. Second, I had an intrinsic interest in many of the topics I thought might be covered. Third, I had become interested in the discipline of sociology and wanted to find out what insights into the family might be gleaned from a sociological perspective. Finally, I was in the process of developing a relationship with a female friend and was interested in taking a course that might prove to be of practical utility.

Like the recreational walkers, in the process of taking the family course I discovered that family behavior is more complex than I had realized and that "doing what comes naturally" is a poor substitute for systematic study and analysis. In fact, I found that the course was a liberating experience.

This book is about the family as a social institution. Yet readers ought to be suspicious of any book that claims to impart knowledge concerning *the* family. One does not have to survey the family backgrounds of many friends before one realizes that there are many different types of American families. There are couples with and without children, there are siblings living together without parents, there are single parents living with children, there are blended families (stepparents and stepchildren), there are foster families and families created by adoption, and there are three-generation families. You probably can name friends or relatives who are examples of each of these common American family forms. Yet people still speak of *the* American family, as if American families were of only one type.

Furthermore, how can one really understand any American social institution if America is all that one knows? In order truly to appreciate the many forms and functions of American families, it is helpful to make comparisons with other cultural pathways or traditions governing marriage and family relationships.

As we attempt to describe and to promote understanding of the many family patterns found in the United States, we will make use of **ideal types** as an analytical and methodological tool. The concept of the **ideal type** was developed by Max Weber, a German sociologist of the early twentieth century. For Weber, ideal types were logical constructs that might not have concrete counterparts in the observable world. For example, it is possible to conceptualize two ideal types of mate selection: free mate selection, where couples arrange their own marriages without influence from their family members, and arranged marriages, where other family members totally control the mate selection process. For most, if not all, societies, mate selection procedures may be classified along a continuum with these two types as polar extremes. According to Eshleman (1985:5):

> An ideal-type construct performs several basic functions: 1) it
> provides a limiting case with which concrete phenomena may

be contrasted; 2) it provides for the analysis and measurement of social reality; and 3) it facilitates classification and comparison.

In this book we will present many research findings from the field of sociology and from other social sciences to help you understand the family as a social institution. We will also attempt to put contemporary American families in an historical, cross-cultural, and subcultural perspective. Finally, in providing an awareness of various family forms, we hope to show that "different" does not necessarily mean bad or good and that family behavior can be evaluated only in reference to its social context.

A SOCIAL SCIENCE APPROACH TO THE FAMILY

Most recent presidential administrations have claimed that the family is a pivotal institution in American society and that social legislation should help to strengthen family life. If the president of the United States asked you to create a task force to strengthen family life and gave you funds to secure consultants with expertise in issues related to the family, what do you think would be the academic backgrounds of these people?

Your immediate response might be limited to a small number of academic disciplines—family studies, sociology, and psychology. Yet the number of disciplines dealing with family-related issues is quite large. Among the natural sciences, biology, medicine, public health, epidemiology, and genetics specialize in the physical organism and its growth, maturation, reproduction, and disintegration; these factors influence and are affected by the family as a social system. The humanities' disciplines of history, religion, literature, law, and philosophy also address the family as a unit of analysis and a subject of concern. And social and applied sciences—sociology, political science, psychology, social psychology, anthropology, child development, family studies, counseling, economics, demography, social gerontology, social work, public health, history, and geography—are all concerned with the interpersonal relationships within the family social system and how these relationships interact with sociocultural factors in the social environment. While this book will draw upon research done in many different disciplines, the primary focus will be on research generated by social scientists—especially sociologists.

The family cannot be studied in isolation from its social context. Political, economic, religious, cultural, and educational factors all influence the structure and function of the family. As this cartoon shows, family values may seem incongruous until we look beyond them to the forces that shaped them. (© 1976 Ron Cobb. All rights reserved. From *Cobb Again.* Wild & Woolley, Sydney, Australia.)

The Social Sciences as Sciences

To say that the social sciences are "scientific" may be to open a can of worms on most college campuses. Natural science students and faculty cannot believe such blasphemy would be spoken by educated people. How, they ask, can disciplines as imprecise as sociology, psychology, political science, and economics be recognized as scientific endeavors? Yet George C. Homans (1967:7) in *The Nature of Social Science* claims that any science has two basic jobs: discovery and explanation. By the first we judge whether a discipline is a science; by the second, how successful a science it is. The first job is to state and test more or less general relationships between **empirical,** or observed, events of nature. The second is to devise theories to explain these relationships. A scientific explanation will tell us why, under a given set of conditions, a particular phenomenon will occur (Homans 1967:22). In the process of discovery, the scientist attempts to formulate general statements concerning empirical variables that can be verified by systematic observation.

Even though the claim has often been made that the social sciences are different from the other sciences because they use a radically different research technique, Richard Rudner (1966:5) contends that in fact both the natural and social sciences use the same empirical methodology, an empirical methodology based on observation and reasoning, not on supernatural revelation, intuition, appeals to authority, or personal speculation. This is the basis for George C. Homans's (1967:4) assertion that the social sciences are scientific.

> *What makes a science are its aims, not its results. If it aims at establishing more or less general relationships between properties of nature, when the test of the truth of a relationship lies finally in the data themselves, and the data are not wholly manufactured—when nature, however stretched out on the rack, still has a chance to say "No!"—then the subject is a science. By these standards all the social sciences qualify.*

Sociology and the Other Social Sciences

Sociology has been defined in many ways. We define **sociology** as the scientific study of human interaction. Let's look at the two halves of this definition: (1) sociology as a scientific endeavor, and (2) human interaction as the subject of investigation.

As a science, sociology aims both to discover empirical regularities and to explain these regularities through references to empirical **propositions,** or statements of relationship. The goal of sociology is to produce a body of knowledge that will not only provide an understanding of the causal processes influencing human interaction but enable the sociologist to predict future social behaviors.

Sociology shares with the other social sciences the scientific **epistemology,** or study of knowledge, and a concern for understanding human interaction. As with any other science, the success of sociology is judged by the explanatory power and predictive ability of the body of knowledge produced by research efforts within the discipline.

As a study of human interaction, sociology focuses less on the internal workings of the individual than on relationships among individuals and groups of individuals. As a discipline, sociology is not concerned with the behavior of other nonhuman animals. While it might be interesting to develop **hypotheses,** or tentative theories, concerning human behavior from animal studies, the final test of these propositions must refer to data on human interaction. For example, a family sociologist may be interested in comparisons of baboon and human family structures, but would be unlikely to make inferences to human interaction based upon studies of baboon behavior. In medical and psychological research, by contrast, scientists typically make statements about human physiology based on data collected on other animals. This is necessary because of the ethical problems involved in experimentation on human subjects.

The social and behavioral sciences of history, anthropology, cultural geography, political science, economics, psychology, and sociology are unified by both their subject matter and method of investigation. The focus may vary, but the essential concern with the social life of humans is central to each. The techniques of investigation within disciplines may also vary, but the empirical epistemology is employed by all social sciences.

History History has traditionally emphasized the temporal sequences of human affairs, recounting and cataloging the events and experiences of a society. History seeks to describe how the present has grown out of the past and is likely to influence the future (Himes 1968:5). Thus, while the family historian typically studies social circumstances of the past in order to make causal inferences to family trends in the present and future, the sociologist is more inclined to study contemporary and social interaction with the intent of explaining past social regularities and predicting future social situations related to family issues.

An excellent example of an historical work on the family is Edmund S. Morgan's (1966) *The Puritan Family: Essays on Religion and Domestic Relations in Seventeenth-Century New England.* In this book Morgan gives a social history of the American family in colonial times and explains the family as a social system within an historical context. Topics covered include marriage relationships, parent-child interaction patterns, the family and the church, household management, and the family in the social order.

More recently, the distinctions between history and sociology have become more blurred as social historians have sought to make statements of social causation based on social scientific studies of contemporary history. Furthermore, within the sociology of the family, historical sociology has become a major methodological research trend.

Anthropology Cultural anthropologists are concerned chiefly with the concept of **culture,** defined broadly as a shared design for living. Culture is humanly constructed and socially transmitted; culture guides the actions of individuals in groups. Anthropologists have discovered in their ethnological field studies that "there is no conceivable human action which custom has not at one time justified and at another condemned" (Krutch 1929). Until recently, cultural anthropology had stressed the study of so-called primitive societies. Today many anthropologists have turned their attention to contemporary societies, and much of their research has been in the United States. Michael Irwin, professor of sociology at Louisiana State University (1988), further differentiates these two disciplines by adding the following points:

1. *Anthropology tends to emphasize culture and sociology tends to emphasize social structure.*
2. *Sociology has tended to focus on advanced agrarian and industrial societies, while anthropologists have tended to study preliterate societies.*
3. *These differences in orientation have resulted in the development of very different research approaches. Anthropology developed techniques appropriate to the study of small and often remote societies (field research) and sociology has tended to employ survey research techniques.*
4. *In recent years anthropologists have applied their research approaches and techniques to the study of industrial societies. As a result the division of labor between the two disciplines has blurred; however, the research orientations between sociology and anthropology are quite different.*

An example of a contemporary anthropological study of the black family is Carol B. Stack's (1974) *All Our Kin: Strategies for Survival in a Black Community.* Stack demonstrates the importance of "kith and kin" networks as supporting structures for black families as they attempt to survive in urban conditions of severe economic deprivation. This important research illustrates the collective adaptations to poverty of men, women, and children within the sociocultural network of the urban black family through alliances of individuals trading and exchanging goods, resources, and child care. These reciprocal exchanges and mutual dependency among kin and non-kin groups create a definition of "kin" that is broader and more inclusive than most Americans' view of family boundaries. However, it is only through this extended form of family life that the people are able to survive.

In some ways it is difficult to distinguish sociologists from modern cultural anthropologists. Like anthropologists, comparative sociologists emphasize the important influences of culture as they attempt to describe and analyze the interrelationships among the five basic social institutions of family, religion, economics, education, and government.

Geography Geography is concerned with describing and interpreting the influence of physical and cultural environments upon human social behavior. Geographers often emphasize factors such as climate, topography, soil, natural resources, opportunities for migration, and spatial mobility in their analyses of social and cultural behavior patterns. Today, it is not uncommon for urban geographers, sociologists, human ecologists, demographers, archaeologists, social workers, and civil engineers to work together with city and rural authorities as they study the impact of urban planning and community development upon family life. Family sociologists with a special interest in demography, rural and urban sociology, and the sociology of the community share many research interests with cultural geographers whose focus of analysis is the family.

Political science Political science is concerned with power, authority, and government. Political scientists study such issues as party politics, comparative governmental structures, international relations, social policy, political opinion, the process of governing, the nature and execution of social control agencies, legal institutions, and the legitimation of power.

The differences between political science and sociology are not always clear. In general, political scientists investigate social interaction in political and governmental situations mainly to explore the flow of power. Sociologists, on the other hand, investigate social interaction in a somewhat larger variety of situations and study a number of characteristics of social interaction including, but not limited to, issues of authority and power (Gouldner and Gouldner 1963:16). Political scientists and political sociologists with an interest in the family will be most concerned with issues such as the division of power within the family, the role of the family in political socialization, and the influence of social and public policy upon the family as a social institution.

An example of a political scientist's thinking about the family can be found in George Will's *Statecraft as Soulcraft: What Government Does*. In this book Will (1983:151) contends that the central government has taken away much of the legitimate power and influence formerly vested in the family. It was the family (along with the church, voluntary associations, and town governments) that promoted communitarian values and tempered individualism in the United States. From Will's perspective, social policy legislation needs to restore these values and refocus America's overemphasis upon

As a social institution, the family is affected by social and political movements in the larger society. The changing role of women, advances in medical technology, and the struggle for better housing, food, and education all affect the family.

individualism. For this reason, Will believes that social policy legislation should discriminatingly, but energetically, strengthen the family as a social institution. Accordingly, Will argues for a welfare system that supports rather than disintegrates families—which he calls the "little platoons" or basic units of government.

Economics Economics is regarded by many as the most advanced of the social sciences. Economics is concerned with the creation, use, acquisition, transfer, and exchange of economic values and materials. Most economists are interested in specific results of human interaction—especially those results measured in terms of material value, such as wages or the cost of goods.

One of the best examples of family analysis from the discipline of economics is found in the work of Gary S. Becker, professor of economics at the University of Chicago. In his book *A Treatise on the Family* (1981), Becker analyzes the family as a "little factory"— a multiperson corporation that utilizes its members' market goods, time, skills, and knowledge to produce meals, health, skills, children, and self-esteem. Becker's systematic analysis of the family assumes that behaviors of different individuals are coordinated by explicit and implicit markets and that people act to maximize their rewards in the marketplace. From a microeconomic perspective, Becker offers an explanation for such diverse family issues as mate selection, time allocation to child care and careers, family inheritance patterns, allocation of resources within the family, and divorce.

Sociologists, too, are interested in the distribution of wealth and the manner in which it affects social functioning, social inequality, and status rankings. Sociologists focus on the interrelationships among the primary social institutions of economics, politics, religion, family, and education. In the study of human beings as family members, it is obvious that economic factors will influence interaction patterns. However, while economic issues are central to the economist, they are only one of several sets of variables of interest to family sociologists.

Psychology Psychology has been formally defined as the science of the behavior of living organisms, both animal and human, with an emphasis on the study of individual behavior and its relationship to environmental stimuli (Theodorson and Theodorson 1969:321). If environmental stimuli are considered to include social institutions and structures, then psychology could be viewed as encompassing sociology. However, most would consider psychology as being primarily focused on the individual. From this perspective, psychology is more specialized than sociology.

Social psychologists, who find their intellectual roots in both sociology and psychology, study the experience and behavior of the individual in relation to others—others in large and small groups, institutions, and organizations. More psychologically oriented social psychologists will emphasize intraindividual variables such as perception, personality, memory, motivation, drives, and phobias. Sociologically inclined social psychologists will emphasize interindividual variables such as prejudice, social status, definitions of situations, social roles, social norms, and meanings or definitions of self.

An important example of psychological research on the family is the work of Diana Baumrind dealing with general styles of child rearing and their effects. According to Baumrind (1967), there are three basic styles of parenting—authoritarian, permissive, and authoritative—each having different effects. *Authoritarian* parents stress blind obedience to parental rules. They seldom reinforce behavior positively with praise, and they are somewhat aloof from their children. At the other end of the continuum of parental styles are *permissive* parents, who provide their children with few rules or standards of conduct. Many would categorize children raised in these

Authoritarian parenting tends to emphasize a chain of command within the nuclear family; traditionally, older males are vested with more authority than other family members, although females may take this role as well.

homes as undisciplined. *Authoritative* parents are in the middle of the parenting continuum. They provide their children with rules and set limits for behavior, but they are flexible in enforcing these standards. They are open to considering exceptional circumstances and tend to run their families in a more democratic, rather than dictatorial, manner.

A distinction sometimes drawn between sociology and psychology is that the former is concerned with the group and the latter with the individual. In fact, however, sociologists are interested in the relationship between the group and the individual, and psychologists are interested in more than what happens within the individual. Both family sociologists and psychologists are interested in the way the actions of individuals are influenced by and have an impact upon the family.

In summary, it is not easy to distinguish sociology from other social sciences. Sociology and the other social sciences with an interest in the family share a commitment to the scientific method and to the jobs of describing and explaining human social interaction. Family sociologists employ many research techniques—among them the historical and comparative approaches, qualitative methodologies involving field studies and unobtrusive techniques, and survey and experimental research designs—that will at various times overlap all of the other social sciences. Sociologists, however, are also uniquely interested in the relationships between these disciplines. Pitirim Sorokin (1947:7) makes this point emphatically:

> *Sociology sees generic social phenomena appearing in prac-*
> *tically all social processes: economic, political, artistic, reli-*
> *gious, philosophical. The same is true of such social processes*
> *as competition and exploitation, domination and subordina-*
> *tion, stratification and differentiation, solidarity and antago-*
> *nism, and so forth. Each of these processes appears not only*
> *in single compartments (of the social order as a whole) but in*
> *practically all compartments of sociocultural life, and as such*
> *requires a (separate) study of its generic form(s). Such a study*
> *transcends the boundary of any compartmentalized discipline.*

In Chapter 3 we will describe more fully the scientific nature of family sociology by exploring in detail the major theoretical perspectives within the discipline. We will also describe and discuss the process by which sociologists provide empirical evidence in order to test the validity of their explanations for marriage and family behavior.

WHY STUDY THE FAMILY FROM A SOCIOLOGICAL PERSPECTIVE?

In the beginning of this chapter, I mentioned my reasons for taking a course in the sociology of the family. After teaching family sociology for more than fifteen years, however, I have discovered some even more important reasons for pursuing a sociological perspective on the family.

First, while the primary goal of your course is not to make you a better family member, you may still find that the sociological perspective gives you valuable insights into your own life and the lives of the members of your family. For example, as you read about the history of families in the United States and begin to comprehend social class and ethnic variations in American families, you may gain a new appreciation for your own life experiences as well as for those of your grandparents, parents, and friends. As you consider how gender affects the socialization process relative to roles within the family, you may begin to grasp more fully how your personal identity is a function of the social context in which you were raised. Furthermore, as you study marriage and family issues over the life cycle, you may attain a more objective perspective on your future and on some of the decisions you may have to make.

Second, in order to understand U.S. society it is important to understand this nation's many forms of family systems. A course in the sociology of the family provides insights into the complex relationship between family social systems and the larger society.

Third, most people are interested in comprehending and adapting to social change. The sociological perspective emphasizes that social and cultural change tends to manifest itself in family systems. Consider the changes that took place in families in the 1970s and 1980s because of the influence of the women's movement and increased participation of mothers in the work force. These social changes caused many Americans to rethink family values and consider modifications or adjustments in their own family structures. On the other hand, it is important to recognize that family systems also influence other aspects of American society and culture.

Fourth, sociology students will want to take a course in the sociology of the family because it is an important and interesting area of study within the discipline. Family sociology provides the student with an opportunity to investigate the meaning and application of most of the important sociological concepts. Of interest to the area of applied sociology is the fact that many public policy debates involve discussions of "how to preserve and achieve family values." Family sociology has much to contribute to this dialogue.

A final reason for taking a course in the sociology of the family is to realize the difficulties and constraints of various family structures before becoming personally involved in them. It is better to consider the advantages and disadvantages of bearing and raising children than to make an uninformed decision, or to leave such an important determination to chance and later be forced to deal with an unanticipated outcome. We wish to help students become aware of the many options and choices open to them regarding marriage and family structures.

ORGANIZATION OF THIS BOOK

Six general themes are addressed in this book. The first part concerns theoretical, methodological, and cross-cultural perspectives on the family. Part Two is about sociocultural changes and their impact on the family as a basic social institution in the United States. We will examine the influence of ethnicity and class upon various American family structures. Parts Three and Four take a life-cycle perspective in describing changes in the institutions of marriage and family. Part Five is concerned with crises in families—divorce, death, and family violence. The final part of the book examines some practical applications of the sociology of the family for daily living. We will also consider three major national issues now facing U.S. families and discuss the need for social policy to address these issues in the 1990s.

Throughout this book we encourage the reader to view the American family as diverse and always undergoing modification. The family is continually adapting to changes in the larger social structure. Individuals should not see themselves, however, as merely passive agents in this relationship between the larger society and the family. Individuals have the ability to become the continual creators and coproducers of their own family structures. In this capacity, they can influence the institution of the family in the larger society.

CHAPTER REVIEW

- Within U.S. society there are many different types of family structures.
- In order to understand the family we must view it within its social context.
- Scientific propositions are statements concerning relationships between empirical variables. These statements usually take a causal form.
- The social sciences are scientific because they use the empirical method to attempt to generate statements of relationship concerning empirical variables.
- The social sciences are unified by their subject matter, method of investigation, and the methodological challenges they face.

DISCUSSION QUESTIONS

1. Why is it difficult to discuss *the* American family?
2. What do you feel is the most appropriate way of evaluating the legitimacy of various family structures and forms found within the United States?
3. Why are the social sciences scientific? What is the relationship between discovery and explanation in any science?
4. What is the relationship between sociology and the other social sciences?
5. How can one benefit from taking a course in the sociology of the family?

GLOSSARY

culture: The way of life of a social group, including all of its material and nonmaterial products that are transmitted from one generation to the next.

empirical: Knowledge based on observation, experience, or experimentation.

epistemology: The study or theory of knowledge—its origin, nature, and/or limits.

hypothesis: A statement of relationship between two or more theoretical concepts.

ideal type: An abstract description constructed from a number of real cases in order to reveal their essential features.

proposition: A statement of relationship between two or more empirical variables.

sociology: The scientific study of human interaction.

SUGGESTED READINGS

Eshleman, J. Ross. 1988. *The Family: An Introduction.* 5th ed. Boston: Allyn and Bacon.

Leslie, Gerald R., and Sheila K. Korman. 1989. *The Family in Social Context.* 7th ed. New York: Oxford University Press.

Reiss, Ira L., and Gary R. Lee. 1988. *Family Systems in America.* 4th ed. New York: Holt, Rinehart, and Winston.

Three well-researched textbooks emphasizing a sociological perspective on the family with some discussions of other social scientific research dealing with marriage and family issues.

Families in Cross-Cultural Perspective

◆ *There is no conceivable human action which custom has not at one time justified and at another condemned.**

When people are socialized into a particular society or group they tend to take their own culture's institutions for granted as indisputable social forms. American teenagers could not even imagine asking their parents to arrange for them to marry someone with whom they were unacquainted and not "in love." By the same token, most Americans would think a woman was crazy if she asked her husband to take a second wife as a means of raising her own social status. Yet both these situations happen every day in many cultures of the world, and the people of these cultures would not have it any other way.

Social institutions such as marriage and family relationships are created by human beings as practical ways of meeting their basic needs. People find workable patterns, which then become institutionalized through repetition into standardized customs. Peter Berger (1969:3) contends that while social institutions are nothing but human products, they continuously influence and affect their producers. It is within the society, and as a result of social processes, that the individual becomes a person, that he or she attains and holds onto an identity and carries out the various projects that constitute his or her life.

Berger's statement reflects the essential dialectical character of social living: Human beings are both the creators and the products

---

*Joseph Wood Krutch, "The Genesis of a Mood," 1929.

of the society. According to Berger (1969:3), this dialectical relationship consists of three processes: externalization, objectivation, and internalization. **Externalization** is the process whereby human beings construct their social world. This process includes the constructions of symbols (systems of meaning), society, culture, and all forms of social institutions. In the process of **objectivation** the socially constructed world takes on a reality of its own independent of its creators. For example, when I was preparing this book, my wife and I had three children aged eleven, eight, and six. Up to that point in their lives, we had had a great deal of control over the socialization process that shaped them as social beings; but we could see that they were already attaining a status of independence over which we had more limited influence. As another example of the externalization-objectivation process, when my wife and I were first married, we established (externalization) family norms, traditions, a system of division of household chores. Some of these behavioral patterns had been established in the families in which we had been raised, but others were of our own creation. Today I find that we continue to act in accordance with this "family script" that we "wrote" in 1970. Certainly we are free to change, but we both feel comfortable with this taken-for-granted social order.

According to Berger, **internalization** is the process of reappropriation by human beings of the reality that has been externalized and objectified. Internalization transforms the objective structure of the social world into the structure of the individual's subjective consciousness. Berger cites two examples of internalization. One example: Humans invent or create a language and then find that both their thoughts and the way they speak are dominated by its grammar. Another example: An individual not only performs the role of father but *becomes* a father, in terms of whatever "being a father" implies for the society in question. Berger (1963:13–14) summarizes the relationship between the objective social world and the subjective understanding of personal identity:

> *The individual's own biography is objectively real only insofar as it may be comprehended within the significant structures of the social world. Society assigns to the individual not only a set of roles but a designated identity.*

The process of creating a social world is above all, then, an ordering of experience for individuals and groups of individuals. In a concrete form, personal and social order is brought about through the process of institutionalization—order exists in society because there are institutions. From a sociological perspective, social institutions exist within every society because they are the inevitable product of social interaction and because they are functionally necessary.

The family, as a basic social institution, shapes and structures the activity of people in a manner that helps them realize the values and goals they have internalized from their culture. The family is an institution found in every society and performs the following fundamental tasks:

1. Creates and cares for new members of society.
2. Provides the basic subsistence requirements for individuals.
3. Is the agent of primary socialization of children, imparting society's meanings and values.
4. Is the primary agent of social control.
5. Meets periodically to carry out ritualized activities which reaffirm the ultimate value system of the society.

Social institutions constitute the cement, firm yet pliant, that allows society to cohere, change, and endure. This explains why we find some form of familial, political, economic, educational, and religious institutions in every human society. But even though social institutions function as essential integrative, conservative, and group-sustaining devices, they differ enormously from one society to another.

Let's look at the family from a cross-cultural functional perspective, as a way of understanding every family's structural interdependence with the culture and society of which it is a part. In every culture, basic social institutions create the societal context for the familial institution.

TYPES OF FAMILIES

From anthropology we learn that there are two general types of families—nuclear families and composite families. The **nuclear family** consists of a married couple (parents) and their offspring (children born to or adopted by this couple). The nuclear family is sometimes referred to as a conjugal family, because primary emphasis is placed upon the marriage (husband-wife) relationship rather than upon relationships with blood relatives. Some sociologists and anthropologists make distinctions between nuclear and conjugal families, however. They point out that a conjugal family must include a husband and a wife, whereas a nuclear family may consist of any two or

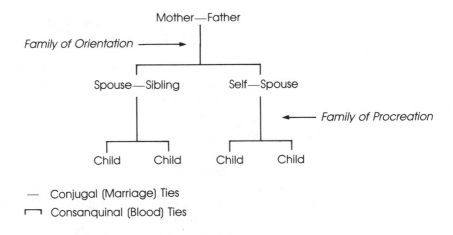

— Conjugal (Marriage) Ties

⌐⌐ Consanquinal (Blood) Ties

Figure 2.1 Families of Orientation and Procreation

more persons related to one another by blood, marriage, or adoption, assuming they are of the same or adjoining generations (Eshleman 1985).

There are two types of nuclear or conjugal families. The first is the **family of orientation**—the family in which one is socialized as a child. The second is the **family of procreation,** or the family one initiates as an adult in order to create a conjugal bond and/or produce children. You can see that individuals over the course of their lives are typically members of overlapping nuclear families of orientation and procreation (see Figure 2.1). In U.S. society individuals leave their family of orientation in order to establish their family of procreation. Yet each person continues to have obligations to his or her parents and siblings (family of orientation) throughout life. Furthermore, through divorces and remarriages it is possible to have many families of orientation and procreation. For many Americans, it is often problematic just to "be home with the family for the holidays."

The **composite family,** the second general type of family, consists of two or more nuclear families. Composite families can be created by either conjugal (marriage) ties or consanguinal (blood) ties. Conjugal composite families are usually referred to as **polygamous families**—where either the husband or the wife has multiple spouses. **Consanguinal** composite families or **extended families** consist of blood relatives (beyond nuclear family members) living together in a single household. From a global point of view, the most common form of extended family is the three-generation family of grandparents, parents (with or without siblings), and children. In this next section we will discuss different types of polygamous and extended families.

Polygamous Families

When two nuclear families share a common spouse, the composite family created is referred to as a polygamous family. There are two forms of polygamy: polygyny and polyandry. **Polygyny** is the practice of a man taking two or more wives. According to George Murdock's (1957) classification of world cultures, 79 percent of the known cultural groups of the world (that is, 79 percent of societies, not of people) view polygyny as the preferred form of marriage. However, even in cultures where polygyny is preferred and practiced, monogamy is usually the most common form of marriage. The reason is that there are similar numbers of males and females in most societies; besides, most men cannot afford multiple spouses. With a balanced **sex ratio,** or ratio of males to females, multiple spouses simply won't be available for most of the males in the society. The Bahaya of Tanzania provide an interesting example of a polygynous society.

The Bahaya of Bukoba

Despite the many changes in recent years due to the influence of Christian and Islamic missionary efforts in an independent nation once formally controlled by German and British colonial rule, the Bahaya [of Tanzania] are still predominantly a polygynous society. The number of wives to a single man ranges between hundreds for kings—who never know by face and name all of their many wives and hundreds of children—to some tens of wives for chiefs and rich men, to two or three wives for many of the commoners. (As in most polygynous societies, the largest number of commoners only have one wife.)

The practice of polygyny among the Bahaya has been supported by a number of factors including economics, religion, and an unbalanced sex ratio created by persistent tribal wars and the use of capital punishment for many crimes. However, it may be surprising to learn that even in the absence of war or any crimes at all, tribal leaders (kings) saw to it that women greatly outnumbered men.

Occasionally some king might decide to "enjoy" seeing a stream of blood flowing down a slope. Therefore a number of men would be lined up, and one by one, they would be beheaded by soldiers wielding swords. Usually, the affair would not stop before the "stream of blood" reached a certain point at the foot of the hill. To the king, and his queens, this brutality was more than pleasing. In this action the king proved how powerful and great he was, while at the same

When American males contemplate what it might be like to be polygynous, a likely first impression might involve the sexual benefits of having many wives. When a male in a polygynous society contemplates taking an additional wife, however, his thoughts will turn to the responsibility of supporting many wives and their children and the impact of this new wife upon his status in the community. The "sexual benefits" of polygyny can be secured in other ways not requiring additional responsibilities.

Furthermore, one must remember that not all wives are freely chosen. In societies where polygyny is practiced, men may acquire wives through arranged marriages, exchange, inheritance, service, wife capture through warfare, or self-arranged marriages. In arranged marriages a man's kin may acquire a "suitable" mate for him and assist him over a period of time in raising the bride's price or dower. In circumstances like these it is common for the new wife to be many years younger than the husband. In some polygynous societies, a son may inherit one of his father's wives (not his biological mother). In these cases it is likely that the inherited wife may be older.

The ancient Hebrews, who practiced polygyny, had a custom of the **levirate marriage**—the preferred mate for a childless widow is her deceased husband's brother or other male relative. In the Bible, the book of Ruth describes the levirate marriage of Ruth to Boaz—her "kinsman redeemer." To inherit a wife is a family responsibility not unlike raising an orphaned relative. Clearly, not all wives are equally desirable, and additional wives can create added responsibilities.

Polyandry, a second form of polygamy, is the practice of a number of males sharing the responsibilities of a single spouse. Polyandry is very rare. It is practiced by just 7 percent of the world's cultures; and without exception these are cultures having few economic or physical resources, where the people struggle for daily subsistence. Polyandry provides these preliterate societies with relatively low birth rates while still providing males a modicum of sexual gratification. Polyandry does require an unbalanced sex ratio (ratio of males to females) where males outnumber females. In polyandrous cultures males are more highly valued than females and the society invests fewer resources in females; thus there is higher female mortality, especially among infants. Female **infanticide** (the killing of babies) is also practiced on occasion.

Wives in polyandrous cultures should not be thought of as possessing male harems. Whereas in polygynous cultures multiple spouses can increase the polygynous man's power and prestige, the same is not true of women in polyandrous societies. In fact the authority and status of women in polyandrous societies is extremely poor. As the reading below illustrates, even polygyny provides relatively higher social standing for women than polyandry.

The Adult Female in Toda Society

The Todas were a pastoral, polyandrous Indian tribe of five or six hundred members in the plains of South India. They became culturally assimilated in the second half of the twentieth century. The Toda family was a composite of several nuclear, husband-wife marriages where one female is married to numbers of brothers and to which are added the offspring and, usually, the parents of the brothers. This form of marriage is called fraternal polyandry, and the family form is patrilocal, composite, and extended in the sense that brothers usually do not leave their families of orientation to marry.

Relative to the polygynous society, a much more subservient and subordinate role is played in the polyandrous Toda society by the female. Inasmuch as the ceremonial of the dairy has a predominant place in the lives and thoughts of the people, the exclusion of women from any share in this ceremonial has produced an almost insuperable status differential. Moreover, such biological functions as menstruation and childbearing have had associated with them ideas of impurity—even extending to the seclusion hut the same uncleanliness imputed to a corpse. The women are further made aware of their inferior status by the fact that they may not cook food in which milk or milk products are used. Finally, not only must women avoid the sacred dairies and stay out of the front portion of the hut where the husbands churn the buttermilk, but the Toda women must walk only on certain paths, taking special pain to avoid those traversed by the buffalo.

The patrilocal rule (which requires that a bride lives with or near her husbands' kin) becomes a pivot around which many relationships favorable to the male revolve. Since the bride moves into the house and village of her husband and his clan, it is possible for the patrilineal sib to exclude her from participating in a variety of activities such as property holding, dairying, herding, family decisions, the naming of males, matters pertaining to migration, building, divining, sorcery, and to a considerable extent the privilege of staying mated to the same person or groups of persons.

On the positive side, Toda women, despite the high incidence of sexual contacts, do not seem overburdened with childbearing nor saddled with an impossible set of household duties and social obligations. Toda women are responsible to perform the following household chores: pounding grain, sweeping, cleaning, and sewing. Once such tasks have been accomplished, the women have considerable leisure and personal freedom. Few societies provide the leisure and freedom accorded the Toda women. Also, because there is no way for a Toda female to compete with males, one basis for marital tension is eliminated. Consequently, Toda women reflect an attitude of equanimity and good will.

Although Toda women are in an obviously subordinate role, it does not seem to depress them. They are not without a sense of vanity, for much of their leisure time is spent in curling and greasing their abundant black hair. They cherish ornaments and only they tattoo themselves—on the neck, chest, and shoulders. Furthermore, the imbalance of the sexes (more males than females) has assured marital unions for virtually all Toda women meaning that few, if any, Toda women have gone through life deprived of either variety or number of sexual contacts.

Source: Stuart A. Queen and Robert W. Habenstein, *The Family in Various Cultures*, 3d ed. (Philadelphia: J. B. Lippincott Company, 1967), pp. 34–35. Copyright © 1961, 1967, 1974 by Harper & Row, Publishers, Inc. Reprinted by permission of the publisher.

Extended Families

Even in the absence of plural marriages, societies practicing monogamy (George Murdock [1957] claimed that 14 percent of the world's cultural groups have monogamy as their preferred form of marriage) may foster consanguinal composite families as a societal norm—that is, extended families consisting of groups of nuclear families brought together by blood relationships. The most common of all extended families is the traditional three-generation agrarian family with married siblings and their biological or adopted parents. The traditional three-generation family consists of at least one family of orientation and two or more families of procreation. The entire diagram of Figure 2.1 illustrates the structure of such a family. This form is typically **patrilocal:** most often, married sons live with or near their parents. Traditional Chinese, Japanese, and Korean societies, as well as the

Extended, patriarchal Italian American families are common in the United States, especially in areas like Boston's North End or Baltimore's Little Italy, where traditional family structures are engendered by a close-knit ethnic community. Family loyalty and sharing may be emphasized by large family gatherings for meals or celebrations.

ancient Hebrews, established this type of composite family as normative. Americans are familiar with the Ewing family of the television show "Dallas" as a contemporary fictional example of the traditional extended family.

Occasionally only one married offspring lives with his or her parents, spouse, and children. This kind of extended composite family is referred to as a **stem family.** A stem family can come into being for any of a number of reasons. In some societies where the extended three-generational family with married siblings is the cultural ideal, particular circumstances make it impossible for all the married adult siblings to live together. For example, the land on which the family lives may not sustain an extended family of this size, or there may be only one married child. Another reason for the emergence of a stem family may be the financial or emotional needs of older parents and/or adult married children who would otherwise live separately. The Waltons, of television fame, were a stem family of this type.

The third type of extended family is the **joint family.** The joint family is a two-generation family consisting of married siblings, their spouses, and their children. This type of family unites two or more families of procreation in a family structure similar to that of the polygamous family. The major difference between these two structures is that the joint family is brought together by the sibling bond, while the polygamous family is created by conjugal bonds. The joint family of India is a good illustration of the structure and function of the joint family model.

The Joint Family of India

The joint family is the traditional family in which adult brothers live together with their respective families of procreation. In addition to maintaining a common residence, they hold property in common and assume joint responsibility for the education of younger siblings.

This Indian joint family actually is characteristic of just one stage in the life cycle, with persons typically passing through several stages in their lifetime. The process begins when the sons remain in the parental home following their marriage. While the father is alive, the Indian family does not differ significantly from other extended families. Following the father's death, the true joint family comes into existence when the brothers keep the extended household intact. This joint family is preserved until all the younger siblings are educated and married, at which time, the brothers split off their families of procreation and divide the family property among them. Thus, for a time, nuclear units exist separately. Soon, however, the sons of the brothers are ready for marriage and the process begins again.

Source: Gerald R. Leslie and Sheila K. Korman, *The Family in Social Context,* 6th ed. (New York: Oxford University Press, 1985), pp. 34–35.

There are many differences between the composite family (both polygamous and extended) found in most cultures of the world and the isolated nuclear family that is the predominant family structure in the United States. Perhaps the most important difference is the relative emphasis placed upon individual rights versus the welfare of the group. Societies with composite family structures tend to minimize the importance of the individual in favor of the welfare of the family unit, clan, and/or larger society. Typically, individual ownership is greatly limited because property is owned by the extended family or clan. As an example, the language of the Bahaya of Bukoba does not have any words for "my" or "mine," because the family or clan owns everything. In fact one calls one's mother, her sisters, and one's father's co-wives by the same term meaning "our mother."

In a composite family, the value of the individual is determined by status of the family and his or her position within it. Furthermore, individuals living in cultures with composite families are more likely to pursue group goals than to aspire to individual accomplishments. Within this context, individual accomplishments are important chiefly because they increase the status of the group.

Cultures with a predominance of isolated nuclear families, by contrast, tend to emphasize private ownership, the rights of individuals, and personal achievements. Individuals in these cultures are encouraged to "do their own thing," "be their own best friend," and "cooperate with others in achieving personal goals."

LINEAGE SYSTEMS AND KINSHIP BEHAVIORS

While composite families place more emphasis upon relationships with members of one's own kinship group, societies organized around the conjugal family (or the isolated nuclear family) do not ignore kinship rights and obligations. The issue in both types of societies becomes "who is a member of my family?" This question may seem to have an obvious answer from an American point of view, but a different obvious answer emerges among people socialized in cultures with other family structures.

Who are the members of *your* family? I suppose that your answer might include your father, mother, brother, and sister. Perhaps you might even mention your grandparents, aunts, uncles, cousins, nieces, nephews, brothers-in-law, and sisters-in-law. But what about your great-aunt's daughter and her husband? Would they be invited to your house for Thanksgiving dinner? Are they likely to inherit your personal or real property? You may not even know the names of this couple. Yet among the Hopi of northern Arizona, you would live very near to this couple and call the woman "mother" and the man "mother's brother."

Every society develops an institutionalized method for reckoning kinship and lineage descent. Rules of descent, according to Leslie and Korman (1985:42), define the family as a social group in contrast to the family as a biological group. These rules determine for individuals who among the myriad of biological kin they will regard as relatives.

There are two general types of lineage descent—unilineal descent and multilineal descent. **Unilineal descent** traces lineage through the relatives either of the mother or of the father. The most common form of unilineal descent is **patrilineal descent,** where a person's primary kinship rights and obligations are to the biological relatives

Within the matrisib, female siblings will live and work together for their entire lives.

of his or her father. Typically, the biological "family" (or **patrisib**) will include only the adult male relatives of one's father, the wives of these male relatives, and any of the father's unmarried female relatives. With patrilineal descent, a wife marries into her husband's family (patrisib), and their children become members of this group. **Matrilineal descent,** the other type of unilineal descent, traces relationships through common female ancestors. While matrilineal descent is much less common, where it does exist the family group (or **matrisib**) consists of all females (married or not) and their children. Notice that unlike patrilineal descent, matrilineal descent does *not* usually include male spouses in the matrisib.

Leslie and Korman (1985:42) point out that unilineal systems of descent do not correspond to the facts of biological relationship, because the kin of one parent are affirmed while the relatives of the other are ignored. However, while one set of kin takes priority, people in each system are not ignorant of the ties to the other set of relatives and have a modicum of rights and responsibilities associated with them.

The second general type of rule of descent is **multilineal descent.** The most common form of this type of rules of descent is **bilateral** (or **bilineal) descent.** Bilateral descent is the type of kinship reckoning most common in the United States, where one traces one's lineage through both male and female parents. Since all biological and conjugal kin are included, individuals theoretically have twice as many relatives as those in societies practicing unilineal descent. However, in the United States we tend to limit the number of kin by including only "close" relatives—parents, grandparents, siblings, aunts, uncles, and the spouses and children of these people. As a practical matter, in a multilineal society each person actually has fewer persons he or she regards as "family" and correspondingly experiences fewer obligations and rights as a result of these kinship ties.

A second type of multilineal descent is **double descent.** Double descent, an extremely rare form of kinship reckoning, includes only the female relatives on the mother's side and the male relatives on the father's side. As in bilateral descent, the only people who have exactly the same set of kin as oneself are one's siblings. This fact makes the relationships among the large number of persons in the kinship group less stable than those in unilineal kinship systems.

While there are many differences among the various forms of descent rules, numerous similarities also exist among kinship behaviors in various cultures. First, people acknowledge individuals whom they reckon as kin by employing kinship terms. According to Stephens (1963:75),

> *Each society groups all genealogical ties into a few classes of kin relationship by recognizing a few of the distinctions between kin but ignoring most possible distinctions. Some of the main distinctions on which classificatory kin terms are based are: 1) generation ("cousin" versus "uncle" or "nephew"); 2) gender ("uncle" versus "aunt"); 3) consanguinity versus affinity ("cousin" versus "brother-in-law"); and 4) lineality (mother's kin versus father's kin).*

Second, every society institutionalizes a set of rights and obligations between kinsmen. If an individual is a member of your "family" or kin group, you can expect certain privileges as well as duties or obligations resulting from that relationship. These rights and duties make up a set of cultural norms that rule kinship behavior among relatives. Stephens (1963:85) describes the following four general types of kinship behavior found in most cultures: deference, avoidance, joking, and informality.

Deference is a general posture of respect, submissiveness, and obedience. Deference relationships are most often apparent between people of different ages. A child is expected to respect and mind her grandparents, a younger sibling may be expected to defer to his older sister. In some cultures, too, women are taught to show deference to men of their same age as well as to older men. Deference behavior is found in relationships where people consider themselves to be of unequal status.

Avoidance implies a quality of formality in the relationship. It also involves a cultural restriction on intimacy and the spontaneous expression of emotion or sentiment. Unlike the deference relationship, avoidance relationships imply not necessarily inferiority of members but rather an expectation of formality where a certain degree of social distance exists.

Avoidance relationships are most often found among people who are related only through marriage (in-laws) and are of the opposite sex. A familiar example in U.S. culture is the relationship between a son-in-law and his mother-in-law; and this avoidance relationship occurs in other cultures too. In many traditional Arab cultures a man is not allowed to talk directly to his mother-in-law or to look at her uncovered face. Stephens (1963:87) describes the following avoidance rules for the Baganda of Africa: "A man and his mother-in-law can't touch each other, can't look eye to eye, can't eat together, can't converse alone, and can't eat each other's leavings."

Joking is a kinship behavior that can involve belittling, sarcasm, sexual kidding, and mild physical violence. It is most apparent in sibling rivalry and teasing but also exists between adults and younger relatives and between in-laws. A well-known joking behavior found in the United States is the bachelor party before a wedding. Brothers of the groom and/or close friends **(fictive kin)** are expected to throw a party where they try to get the groom drunk and engage in excessive sexual kidding, sarcasm, or practical jokes. Margaret Mead (1935) gives the following example of joking behavior among the Mundugumor of New Guinea:

> So a Mundugumor child is taught that everyone who is related to it as mother's brother, father's sister, sister's child of a male, brother's child of a female, and their spouses, is a joking relative with whom one engages in rough-house, accusations of unusual and inappropriate conduct, threats, mock bullying, and the like. If a man meets his father's sister, he slaps her on the back, tells her she is getting old, and will die soon.
>
> In Mundugumor everyone must be continually on the alert and ready to respond with the appropriate joking behavior. A failure to joke is more serious than a failure of an American to greet properly an acquaintance on the street.

Stephens (1963:92) concludes his discussion of joking behavior with the following words. "Like deference and avoidance relationships, joking relationships are patterned. They involve behavior that is culturally standardized, predictable, and specified as 'proper behavior' between a given pair of relatives. The form the joking takes often seems quite stereotyped."

The final form of kinship behavior is **informality.** If you consider someone as "family" you are obliged to treat this person in a warm, friendly, and relaxed manner. You are also expected to show hospitality and provide aid for family members in need. Should you be traveling to Europe next summer, your grandmother might tell you to look up a cousin in Norway whom she has not seen in thirty years. If you called this woman when you arrived in Oslo, she would be expected to invite you over for a visit—anything less would be an offense to your grandmother. Informality, like all the other forms of kinship behavior, involves reciprocal expectations of rights and obligations between specific members of kin groupings.

RULES OF INHERITANCE

While rules of inheritance are related to the lineage system and rules of descent, they are much more complex. Rules of inheritance specify the culturally appropriate individual or group who will gain jurisdiction over or ownership of real or personal property.

In most societies property is held by the clan or "sib." When ownership passes to individuals, it is typically males who inherit. In patrilineal societies property flows through the male line of inheritance, while in matrilineal societies males in the female lineage group become rightful heirs.

However, this situation may become complicated for two reasons. First, some possessions such as clothing, ornaments, and tools are used only by the members of one sex and are therefore transmitted in a gender-appropriate manner (Leslie and Korman 1985:44). The second complicating factor is that not all heirs inherit equally. Usually women (daughters and spouses) inherit less or not at all. Also, a person's place in the birth order will affect the portion he or she receives as an inheritance. **Primogeniture** is the custom whereby the oldest son inherits all or a disproportionate part of the property, and **ultimogeniture** is the practice where the youngest son is favored.

RESIDENTIAL GROUPINGS

The primary building block of all other more elaborate family structures is the conjugal or nuclear family. This group is always a residential unit. However, the choice of the place of residence will be culturally mandated and influenced by the nature of the structure of the family in the respective society.

Societies which are polygynous and patrilineal usually practice **patrilocal residence.** With patrilocality the couple and their children live with, or near, the family of the husband. Occasionally, the male will work for his father-in-law for a period of time as a form of bride's price (dower) and then return with his family to his family's place of residence. This special patrilocal residential pattern is called **matri-patrilocal.** A Biblical example of matri-patrilocal residence is found in Genesis, chapter 29, where Jacob works for fourteen years as a bride's price for Laban's daughters Leah and Rachel.

Most matrilineal societies practice **matrilocal residence,** where a man takes up residence with his wife and the members of her matrisib. A rare form of matrilocal residence is the practice of the couple living with the maternal uncle of the bride (mother's brother). This practice is called **avunculocal residence.**

Many other societies allow the newly married couple the freedom to choose which set of relatives they wish to live with or near. This system of residence is referred to as **bilocal.** Bilocal residence ensures that the family of procreation will not be left without assistance from members of the larger kinship unit. The couple's decision regarding where they will live will be determined by the following factors: the strength of the personal ties between the couple and their respective parents, the relative wealth of each set of parents and their power in the community, and the parents' need for assistance from the young couple (Leslie and Korman 1985:44). The family structure in Mexico tends to promote bilocal families.

Notice that each of the three residential groupings described above—patrilocal, matrilocal, and bilocal—tends to promote composite extended families and favors a consanguinal family structure. These types of residential groupings also tend to place more emphasis upon the kinship unit than upon the personal needs and desires of individuals. Consequently, group ownership of property and group family decision making are probable outcomes of these residence patterns.

The last type of residential grouping is **neolocal residence.** In neolocal residence the new family of procreation lives apart from the families of orientation of both the bride and the groom. This is the residential pattern practiced in most nonagrarian areas in the United States and other industrial societies. In the United States, the isolated neolocal nuclear family structure reflects the limited importance we place upon the larger kinship network. One year, for example, I asked my brother if he planned to celebrate Christmas at our parents' house. He replied, "No, this year we plan to stay at home with our family." For him, the neolocal nuclear family was his "real" family.

In conclusion, consider the following statement by Leslie and Korman (1985:45):

In patriarchal societies, authority and decision making is vested primarily in males, especially older males. Religious and political institutions may further promote patriarchy.

It is probably apparent that there are certain logical associations (1) among patrilineal descent, patrilineal inheritance, and patrilocal residence and (2) among matrilineal descent, matrilineal inheritance, and matrilocal residence. Murdock concluded that patrilocal residence is associated with polygyny, warfare, slavery, and an economy that depends on the chase rather than on collecting. Matrilocal residence is favored by the development of agriculture in what previously was a hunting and gathering economy and by the ownership of land by women. Bilocal residence is accompanied by a migratory life in unstable bands and, at a higher economic level, by approximate equality of the sexes in the ownership of property. Finally, neolocal residence is associated with approximately equal economic contributions by men and women, monogamy, extensive poverty, and individualism.

FAMILY AUTHORITY

As we have discussed family structures in a cross-cultural perspective, we have noted that males enjoy a favorable position in most cultures. Most of the societies of the world have the following as family norms: composite polygynous extended family, patrilineal descent, and patrilocal residence. This structural situation tends to strengthen the power and authority of males within the society and within the family. When the males of the culture are invested with greater authority, the family structure is classified as being **patriarchal.** Most of the dominant historical cultures have been patriarchal. Males have enjoyed a favorable position with regard to power, authority, and decision making in the traditional cultures of the Greeks, Romans, Hebrews, Chinese, and Japanese. However, the relationship between family structure and patriarchal governance is more complex than what we have indicated. In reality, the relationship is probably symmetrical—patriarchal governance promotes family structures that favor males, and male-oriented family structures promote patriarchies.

But why do males possess authority more often than their female counterparts? A common answer to this question cites the male's ability to dominate women physically. However, not all males in positions of authority enjoy this advantage of strength over the women in their society. Consequently, a socially constructed legitimation of patriarchy must reinforce the biological advantage that most males experience. This topic will be discussed in more detail in Chapter 5.

While some families in the United States and elsewhere have been described as being **matriarchal** (women achieving dominance over men), anthropologists have never discovered a society where authority and power are vested in women as a cultural norm. As we discussed earlier, there are societies which are matrilineal, matrilocal, and polyandrous, but even in these societies, power and authority are chiefly vested in males. The matrilineal, matrilocal Hopi of northern Arizona designate the oldest male of the matrisib—the mother's brother—as the chief leader and decision maker, although older females are not without influence and authority. Older females in highly patriarchal societies such as traditional China and Japan also possess some authority. Furthermore, given the fact that life expectancy is greater for females, a woman is often likely to become a widow and the oldest member in the kinship unit. As the oldest, the woman will become influential in family decision making. However, while females are not without influence, primary authority and power reside in the male members of society.

In contemporary U.S. society patriarchal family structure is being replaced by the **egalitarian** family. The egalitarian family is one in which the husband and wife share power and authority. This type of family authority has emerged because women have increased their participation in the work force and because their levels of educational attainment parallel those of men. In the United States today, more than 50 percent of women with preschool children are working full or part time. Furthermore, women are slightly more likely to

Egalitarian families require much role sharing and joint decision making. Both partners enjoy equal respect, authority, and responsibility within the family.

graduate from college than men. As a consequence, it has now become normative for the American family to be egalitarian—especially for middle-class families. As the status of women gradually rises around the world, there is pressure to replace patriarchal rule with egalitarian family decision making. The international women's movement reflects this trend.

CONCLUSION

In this chapter we have viewed the family from a cross-cultural perspective in order to show how family behavior of individuals emerges from a sociocultural context. Individuals are influenced by the social setting of which they are a part; yet social institutions are nothing but human products arising out of social interaction.

Family institutions exist in all societies because they meet essential needs. Family institutions take many different forms in various cultures. And while the values and social structures of the larger society affect the family as one social institution, the way in which the family is structured also has an impact upon the culture of which it is a part.

Most of us are comfortable with the norms and values supporting the American family structure. Yet we know that the structure and functions of social institutions will have both positive and negative effects. For example, if a society places a strong emphasis upon the nuclear family of procreation, the elderly in the society are likely to become structurally isolated. On the other hand, a society organized around the extended family tends to minimize the importance and worth of the individual.

It is important for each of us to understand that while we are influenced by the structures in our culture, we are not determined by them. In the United States specifically, we are free to initiate family structures that will serve our needs as we understand them. As we gain an appreciation for the lifestyles of others in cultures that differ from our own, we can find the courage necessary to choose from among the myriad of options those courses of action that maximize fulfillment for ourselves and for those who are important to us.

In the words of Joan Huber (1981:234–35):

A person who maintains a self-definition with no social support is mad; with minimum support, a pioneer, and with broad support, a lemming. Most of us are lemmings. We accept or change our ideas about rights and duties only when we perceive social support for doing so.

CHAPTER REVIEW

- Social institutions are created by human beings as practical ways of meeting their basic needs.
- The process of creating a social world is, above all, an ordering of experience for individuals and groups of individuals. In a concrete form, personal and social order is brought about through the process of institutionalization—order exists in society because there are institutions.
- There are two general types of families—nuclear families and composite families. Families of orientation and families of procreation are the two types of nuclear families.
- Families become composite through conjugal (marriage) and consanguinal (blood) bonds.
- Polygyny and polyandry are the two types of polygamous (or plural) marriages. Seventy-nine percent of the world's societies prefer polygyny. Polyandry is rarely practiced and is most likely to be found among people who struggle to meet the minimum requirements for daily subsistence.
- There are three types of extended families (composite consanguinal

families)—traditional three-generation families, stem families, and joint families. Composite families place more emphasis upon group welfare than upon individual rights and accomplishments.

- There are two general types of lineage descent—unilineal descent and multilineal descent. Patrilineal and matrilineal descent are the two forms of unilineal descent, while bilateral and double descent are the two forms of multilineal descent. Most of the world's cultures prefer patrilineal kinship reckoning.
- All cultures require that people acknowledge individuals whom they regard as kin with special kinship terms. The following four types of institutionalized kinship behaviors occur in most of the cultures of the world: deference, avoidance, joking, and informality.
- All cultures create inheritance rules that specify societally approved heirs. These rules reflect the kinship reckoning system of each culture.
- Universally the nuclear family is a residential unit. The choice of its place of residence is always culturally mandated and influenced by the nature of the structure of the family in a society.
- From a cross-cultural perspective, most families have a patriarchal authority structure. However, while no societies have matriarchal family structures as a cultural ideal, even in patriarchal families women are not without influence. The international women's movement reflects a trend away from patriarchy in favor of egalitarian family structures.

DISCUSSION QUESTIONS

1. We often hear it said that the family is dying in the United States. Is this possible? That is, could a society exist without any family structure?
2. Is there a "natural" or "normal" way of constructing the family as a social institution? Are some structures more "normal" than others?
3. Given the discussion of family structure contained within this chapter, describe the structure of the American family with respect to conjugal system, kinship reckoning, descent rule, residential grouping, and authority structure. How much agreement is there in the United States with regard to values which support the structure you have described?
4. With widows greatly outnumbering widowers in the United States, would you favor polygyny after sixty as a solution to the problems faced by older Americans? Do you think that polygyny could be introduced successfully in age-segregated communities of older Americans? Why or why not?
5. How do divorce, remarriage, and blended families create composite families in the United States? How are these experiences changing the "ideal" family structure for Americans?
6. Americans value individualism and emphasize personal achievement, individual rights, and privacy. How do these values influence the structure of the American family? What are some of the negative results of these values?

7. Compare the advantages and disadvantages of unilineal and multilineal kinship reckoning. If your family practiced patrilineal descent, how might your life be different?
8. Who benefits from the cultural value placed upon neolocal residence? What are the disadvantages of this practice? Discuss examples of bilocal residence that you know of that seem to provide family stability for the individuals involved.

GLOSSARY

avoidance: A type of kinship behavior that implies a quality of formality.

avunculocal residence: The residence pattern where the bride and groom live with, or near, the bride's mother's brother. Occurs very rarely in matrilineal societies.

bilateral or bilineal descent: The form of kinship reckoning in which lineage is traced through both parents' sets of relatives.

bilocal residence: The residence pattern where the couple may choose to live with or near the family of either the bride or the groom.

composite family: A family of residence consisting of two or more nuclear families tied by either conjugal or consanguinal bonds.

conjugal family: The family in which primary emphasis is placed upon the husband-wife relationship.

consanguinal family: The family in which primary emphasis is placed upon blood relationships between relatives.

deference: A type of kinship behavior that involves a general posture of respect, submissiveness, and obedience.

double descent: The form of kinship reckoning in which lineage is traced only through the female relatives on the mother's side and the male relatives on the father's side.

egalitarian authority: A family structure where decision making and power are shared equally by adult male and female family members.

extended family: A family that includes more than two generations of family members living together.

externalization: The process whereby human beings construct their social world.

family of orientation: The family in which one is socialized as a child—consisting of one's parents and siblings.

family of procreation: The family one initiates as an adult (through marriage) in order to produce children.

fictive kin: Members of one's friendship group who are regarded and treated as family members.

infanticide: The killing of babies.

informality: A type of kinship behavior that treats family in a warm, friendly manner.

internalization: The process whereby human beings appropriate socially constructed meanings of culture as part of their own personal identity.

joint family: The composite family created when two or more adult siblings live together with their respective families of procreation.

joking: A type of kinship behavior that involves belittling, sarcasm, sexual kidding, and mild physical violence.

levirate marriage: A form of polygyny where the preferred mate for a childless widow is her deceased husband's brother or other male relative.

matri-patrilocal residence: A form of patrilocal residence where the bride and groom live with or near the bride's family for a period of time before making permanent residence with the family of the groom.

matriarchal authority: A form of family authority where primary authority and decision making is vested in females.

matrilineal descent: A unilineal kinship reckoning that includes only people related through common female ancestors—females (married or not) and their children.

matrilocal residence: The residence pattern where the bride and groom live with or near the family of the bride.

matrisib: The group of matrilineal kin who are related through common female ancestors.

multilineal descent: Descent determined equally by the mother's and the father's kinship. Bilateral descent and double descent are the two forms of multilineal descent.

neolocal residence: The residence pattern where the bride and groom live independently and separately from either set of relatives.

nuclear family: A family consisting of a husband, a wife, and their biological or adopted children.

objectivation: The process whereby the socially constructed world takes on a reality of its own independent of its creators.

patriarchal authority: A form of family authority where primary authority and decision making is vested in males.

patrilineal descent: A unilineal kinship reckoning that includes only the male relatives of one's father, the spouses of these adult male relatives, and any unmarried females.

patrilocal residence: The residence pattern where the bride and groom live with or near the family of the groom.

patrisib: The group of patrilineal kin who are related through common male ancestors.

polyandry: A female having more than one husband.

polygamous family: A family where either a male or a female has more than one spouse.

polygyny: A male having more than one wife.

primogeniture: The system of inheritance in which the eldest son inherits all or the largest share of the estate.

sex ratio: The number of males per 100 in a given population.

stem family: A three-generational household consisting of an older couple, one of their married children, and their grandchildren.

ultimogeniture: The system of inheritance in which the youngest son inherits all or the largest share of the estate.

unilineal descent: Kinship determined exclusively by either the mother's kin or the father's kin. Patrilineal and matrilineal descent are the two forms of unilineal descent.

SUGGESTED READINGS

Queen, Stuart A, Robert W. Habenstein, and Jill S. Quadagno. 1985. *The Family in Various Cultures.* 5th ed. New York: Harper and Row, Publishers. *Outstanding cross-cultural treatment of family structures and functions through the use of ethnographies.*

Kephart, William M. 1987. *Extraordinary Groups.* New York: St. Martin's Press. *Comparative study of American subcultural variations in family structures and functions. Much of the work deals with historical and contemporary social movements affecting subcultural groups and their family systems.*

Theoretical Orientations to Research in Family Sociology

♦ *An argument against the empirical method: Some haystacks don't have any needles.**

In Chapter 1 we discussed why one would want to study the family from a sociological perspective. We also explored the relations of family sociology to the other social scientific disciplines concerned with the study of marriage and family relationships. In this chapter we will elaborate on the way in which sociologists of the family do the two basic jobs of science—discover relationships between social variables and provide explanations for these discoveries. The first task entails empirical research or systematic observation of family behaviors. The second task calls for the construction of theories to explain these behaviors. We will begin this chapter with a consideration of this latter topic.

---

*e.e. cummings

DEVELOPING SCIENTIFIC THEORIES

The goal of any scientific research is to produce a body of knowledge that will help the researcher present circumstances and predict future events. A **theory** is a tool for building knowledge: an explanation of phenomena through a system of empirical propositions. The three basic components of every scientific theory are (1) a conceptual scheme, (2) a set of propositions stating relationships between properties or variables, and (3) a context for verification.

The Conceptual Scheme

The **conceptual scheme** consists of descriptive concepts and operative concepts. **Descriptive concepts** tell us what the theory is about. In 1958 Robert Winch developed a theory of mate selection in which he claimed that people are likely to marry individuals with similar social backgrounds but dissimilar personality types. Winch further claimed that individuals will marry persons who are most likely to satisfy their psychological needs and complement their own personalities. In Robert Winch's theory of mate selection, the primary descriptive concepts are "personality needs" and "field of eligibles." Personality needs are personal traits complementary to (or the opposite of) those of the person choosing a mate. The "field of eligibles" includes persons who share social background characteristics with the individual. Typically this field is made up of persons of the same or similar religion, educational background, age, social class, and ethnicity.

    Operative concepts are the variables that make up the propositions. Variables are concepts that can take on two or more values. Operative concepts include both theoretical concepts and observables (Willer and Webster 1970). **Theoretical concepts** provide the vocabulary for a theory. They are abstract concepts and not immediately verifiable by direct sensory observation. For example, for his analysis of mate selection in middle-class America, Winch was concerned with social rules or **norms** that required individuals to marry **endogamous** persons—persons with whom they shared many group memberships. Winch claimed that these endogamous norms defined the "field of eligibles" for individuals in the marriage market. It was Winch's contention that within this field of eligibles, a person would select a mate with a complementary personality type, thus providing the greatest promise of need gratification. The theoretical concepts of endogamy, personality type, and need gratification are all abstract concepts and are not directly observable by the researcher.

In contrast, **observables** are concepts (or empirical variables) that are immediately susceptible to direct sensory observation. **Operational definitions** convert theoretical concepts into observables by defining theoretical concepts in terms of indicators by which these concepts may be uniformly observed. For example, Winch's theory of endogamy says that one's field of eligibles will include individuals of similar socioeconomic status. The observables of occupational prestige, family income, and number of years of formal education often serve as indicators for the theoretical concept "socioeconomic status."

The System of Propositions

In addition to the conceptual scheme, a theory must possess a system of **propositions,** or statements of relationship between variables. The system of propositions serves to bring together and interrelate the concepts of the theory. These propositions will usually vary with regard to generality. The most general or abstract propositions are called higher-order propositions. The less general or lower-order propositions are called *empirical* propositions; these are based on actual observation or experience.

Let's consider a set of propositions related to Winch's theory of mate selection. The following propositions are ordered, they are interrelated, and they encourage the drawing of inferences:

Most Abstract Proposition

Mate selection is governed by rules of social endogamy and the quest for complementary psychological traits.

Abstract Propositions

People are most likely to marry a spouse with similar social background in the following areas: religious preference, socioeconomic status, ethnicity and race, age, and place of residence.

People are most likely to marry a spouse with dissimilar personality needs.

Concrete Propositions (Empirical Propositions)

Social similarities

Jews, Roman Catholics, Amish, and Mormons are most likely to marry persons who share their religious preference.

There is a strong correlation between the ages of the marriage partners.

There is a strong correlation between years of formal education of the marriage partners.

Blacks and Orientals are more likely to marry members of their racial group.

Psychological dissimilarities

Marriage partners are more likely to be complementary with regard to the following personality needs: achievement, autonomy, dominance, nurturance, status aspiration, anxiety, emotionality, vicariousness, and status striving.

All levels of propositions making up a theory are important. The most concrete propositions are important because without them theories cannot be evaluated by empirical data—the essential test of any scientific theory. However, one of the goals of theory is to employ the smallest number of proportions necessary to explain the **dependent variable,** or phenomenon whose changes the theory tries to explain. (Chafetz 1978). Abstract statements enable theories to explain an aspect of reality in a **parsimonious** manner—i.e., with brevity, conciseness, and succinctness.

The Context for Empirical Verification

All scientific theories must have a context for verification—that is, they must be empirically testable to be valid. Empirical data must determine the truth or falsity of the propositions that make up the theory. Since, after all, a proposition is a truth-asserting statement, empirical research can verify whether or not the statement is true.

However, not all propositions need to be verified through direct observation. Richard Braithwaite (1953:17–18) points out that one of the main reasons for organizing scientific propositions into a **deductive system**—where concrete statements can be derived from and provide evidence for more abstract statements—is that direct evidence for any of the empirical propositions of the theory will also provide indirect support for the untestable abstract propositions. Empirical evidence for any part of the theory will help establish the theory as a whole.

The most concrete propositions (the empirical propositions) of the theory, derived from the more abstract propositions, thus become **hypotheses** (tentative statements) to be evaluated by scientific investigation. If we can demonstrate the truth of these statements with empirical evidence, we can say by **theory inference** that indirect evidence exists for the more abstract propositions that cannot be evaluated by sensory data. Therefore, if a scientific theory consists of propositions with a deductive structure, then the truth or falsity of the entire theory can be inferred by empirical research. (In reality, a theory can never be *proved* in any final sense. Rather, empirical evidence either disconfirms a theory or does not disconfirm it.) The scientific status of the theory will depend on the quality and reliability of the objective evidence for the empirical propositions. And the usefulness of the theory will rest upon the parsimony of its set of propositions.

Let's return to our example: Winch's theory of mate selection based upon complementary needs. Unfortunately, the empirical evidence provided by many research studies does not provide sufficient empirical support to confirm this theory (see Chapter 8 for a review of these research studies). What seems to be a more accurate explanation of mate selection is that similarity exists in both the social backgrounds and the personality types of married couples. Furthermore, couples sharing personality characteristics are likely to experience greater marital satisfaction than extremely dissimilar couples.

To summarize, scientific theories have three components—a conceptual scheme, a system of propositions, and a context for verification. The model of a suspension bridge (Figure 3.1) serves as a good illustration of the relationship among the three components of scientific theory. Bridges are constructed out of girders and rivets and tied into both banks of the river. Likewise, a theory consists of concepts ("rivets") and propositions ("girders") tied into an empirical base of support. It is the relationship among the components that makes a bridge or a theory. A disorganized pile of girders and rivets does not equal a bridge. Likewise, concepts, propositions, and observations must mutually reinforce and support each other in order to constitute a scientific theory.

FIGURE 3.1 The Relationship between a Bridge and Scientific Theory

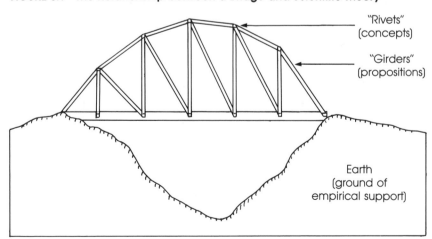

"Rivets" (concepts)

"Girders" (propositions)

Earth (ground of empirical support)

THEORETICAL PARADIGMS WITHIN THE BODY OF
SOCIOLOGICAL KNOWLEDGE

A body of scientific knowledge is a collection of statements of relationship (or propositions) for which there is empirical evidence. This body of knowledge may be organized in two ways. The first is the unsystematic collection of all research studies dealing with a particular content area published in research periodicals. For example, one might expect to find studies on mate selection published in a broad range of sociological and psychological journals. However, one would be most likely to find them in one of the following periodicals: *The Journal of Marriage and the Family, The Journal of Family Relations, The International Journal of Sociology of the Family, Journal of Marriage and Family Counseling, The American Sociological Review, The American Psychological Review, Human Organization, The Journal of Social Psychology,* and *The Journal of Abnormal and Social Psychology.* Research findings are there for all who will make use of them, although the only organization of these findings is in the theoretical frameworks of other research investigations and textbooks that cite these studies.

The second method by which a body of knowledge can be organized is through a theoretical **paradigm**. According to George Ritzer (1975:7),

> *A paradigm is a fundamental image of the subject matter within a science. It serves to define what should be studied, what questions should be asked, how they should be asked, and what rules should be followed in interpreting the answers obtained. The paradigm is the broadest unit of consensus within a science and serves to differentiate one scientific community (or sub-community) from another. It subsumes, defines, and interrelates the examples, theories, methods, and instruments that exist within it.*

Research studies sharing general commitments to methodological techniques, research assumptions, and levels of analysis are brought together to form theoretical paradigms.

Sociology, like most other scientific disciplines, is a multiparadigm science. While there is much debate over the number of paradigms existing within the field of sociology, all sociologists would agree that no single paradigm is dominant within the discipline. Paradigms are further divided into subparadigms or theoretical orientations. Examples of these theoretical traditions (discussed later in this chapter) include structural-functional theory, conflict theory, symbolic interaction theory, and social exchange theory.

Ritzer (1975) divides sociological knowledge into three basic paradigms—social factist, social definitionist, and social behavioralist. The social behavioralist paradigm, influenced by the work of B.F. Skinner, deals largely with psychological issues, and will be not discussed here. The social factist and definitionist approaches are the two central paradigms within the discipline of sociology and serve to organize contemporary sociological knowledge related to marriage and family issues. The social factist paradigm is generally concerned with group actions and societal structures; the social definitionist has as its focus the behavior, attitudes, meanings, and values of individuals. For the purpose of simplicity, we will discuss these two general paradigms as well as four subparadigms: structural-functional theory, conflict theory, symbolic interaction theory, and social exchange theory.

THE SOCIAL FACTIST PARADIGM

Emile Durkheim was the primary exponent of the social factist paradigm. In attempting to differentiate sociology from social philosophy, Durkheim defined the discipline as the study of social facts. For Durkheim (1964) social facts are "any way of doing things (fixed or not) which are capable of exercising restraint upon the individual." He advocated that sociologists should study social facts *as if* they were things. To accomplish this end, Durkheim (1964) formulated the following four guidelines in his *Rules of the Sociological Method* (originally published in 1895): (1) All preconceptions must be eradicated. (2) The subject matter for sociological research must be social facts directly observed. (3) Social facts must be viewed as a product of group experiences and not individual actions. (4) The cause of any given social fact must be sought in its preceding social facts.

The social factist paradigm emphasizes group actions and societal structures. This point emerges in Emile Durkheim's (1964) claim that "society is a social system which is composed of parts which, without losing their identity and individuality, constitute a whole which transcends its parts." From the social factist point of view, in other words, a particular nuclear family cannot be reduced merely to a collection of individuals—social phenomena have a reality of their own. Therefore, sociological research from the social factist perspective will study group-related phenomena (family systems, family structures, marriage **dyads** or two-person groups) rather than behaviors of particular individuals.

Durkheim advocated the use of historical and comparative methods in sociological research. An example of this type of family research might be comparison of the size, structure, and function of colonial families of Concord, Massachusetts, with the same attributes of contemporary families from the same city. Unlike Durkheim, many contemporary social factists employ surveys to do their research. The use of the survey technique creates a problem for some; as George Ritzer (1975:27) says, "How can one study social facts (families) by asking individuals questions?" Another way to look at this issue, however, is to consider the relationship between forests and trees. One can study forests in the United States and describe their sizes and distribution, their rates of reproduction, morbidity, and mortality, and the impact of acid rain upon them. But to understand a forest adequately, one must look at a few trees. The same may be true of families and individuals.

Subsumed under the social factist paradigm are the subparadigms of structural-functional theory and conflict theory. Structural-functional theory seeks to explain the persistence of social facts, social institutions and structures, and the stability of society. Conflict theory focuses upon the competition among the various parts, institutions, and/or structures within a given society and the coercive forces that cause societies to perpetuate themselves at times and change at others.

Structural-Functional Theory

Structural-functionalists view society as a social system of interacting parts. The family as a social institution is analyzed from two perspectives:

1. How does the family contribute to the maintenance of the larger social system?
2. In what ways is the social institution of the family (as well as a given nuclear family) affected by its relationship to the larger social system?

Functionalists are interested in positive and negative (eufunctional and dysfunctional) results of social interaction as well as the intended and unintended (manifest and latent) consequences of social conduct. A parent's working at two full-time jobs is eufunctional in that the family income is increased but dysfunctional in that the parent's time with the family is limited. A manifest function of attending a wedding is to support the couple as they begin a new family, but a latent function of attending a wedding is to strengthen the relationships within and between kinship and friendship groups.

Functional theorists stress the interdependency of social institutions. In the United States religious and family institutions are mutually reinforcing.

If a structural-functionalist were interested in the function of parent-child relationships throughout the family life cycle, she or he might investigate the following questions:

1. How do children affect marital satisfaction over the life cycle?
2. How do children help to promote relationships among kinship groups (grandparents, aunts and uncles, cousins, etc.)?
3. How do children contribute to and/or affect the relationships among families in a neighborhood?
4. How does the number of children affect family interaction patterns and group cohesiveness?
5. What is the role of children in supporting the elderly as they adjust to retirement roles?
6. Does the presence of a parent-child relationship facilitate recovery from bereavement in the death of a spouse?

Conflict Theory

While structural-functional theory focuses upon the issue of societal maintenance and social equilibrium, conflict theory is concerned primarily with issues related to social change and disequilibrium. Conflict theorists focus upon competition, conflict, and dissension resulting from individuals and groups competing over limited societal resources.

Because of this emphasis on social change, conflict theorists studying marriage and family issues attempt to understand the role of the spouse or family member in promoting family disintegration and/or change. Conflict theorists are likely, too, to view dominant family members as promoting family stability through the use of coercion and the exercise of power and authority. On the other hand, structural-functional theorists would claim that the primary mechanism of social control is the socialization process, which creates consensus within the family relative to shared values, goals, and norms.

Returning to our example of parent-child relationships throughout the family life cycle, a conflict theorist might investigate the following questions:

1. How do children interfere with marital satisfaction over the family life cycle?
2. What role conflicts are created at the birth of the first child for married couples who must now take on parental roles?
3. How do children contribute to conflicts between adults in the neighborhood?
4. What are the problems created by the presence of children in the relationships between the couple and the members of their kinship and friendship groups?
5. How do particular parent-child relationships contribute to increased competition for affection among family members?
6. How do children contribute to increased competition for scarce financial resources of the family?
7. How does the death of a parent create sibling rivalry among the children, and how does the death of a child create marital problems for the parents?

THE SOCIAL DEFINITIONIST PARADIGM

The social definitionist paradigm differs from the social factist paradigm at two crucial points. The first is that the definitionist would contend that the essential feature of society is its subjective character. Social facts do not have any inherent meaning other than that which humans attribute to them. W.I. Thomas argues that if people define situations as real, they will be real in their consequences. This argument is a basic premise of the social definitionist paradigm. This principle totally rejects Durkheim's *Rules of the Sociological Method*, which would restrict sociology to the study of *objective* social facts. The social definitionist would contend that all social facts are subjective.

The second distinguishing feature of the social definitionist paradigm is the methodological unit of analysis—the individual. The definitionist will emphasize individual behavior over group actions and societal structures.

George Ritzer (1975:85–86) rightly credits the writing of Max Weber as the exemplar of the social definitionist paradigm. The essence of Weber's analysis of social action was the *meaningful action of individuals.* Weber (1966:88) defines social action as human behavior to which the acting individual attaches subjective meaning and which takes into account the behaviors of others.

Weber advocated "interpretative understanding" (*Verstehen*) as the research methodology for investigating social action. The interpretative understanding approach requires the researcher to develop an empathy for the subjects he or she studies. At times this will require the investigator to enter the subjective world of the subject by participating in this person's life experience. A Native American proverb encourages us not to judge the behavior of others until we have walked a mile in their moccasins. Similarly, interpretative understanding attempts to describe and explain social behavior from the perspective of the actors' subjective intentions for that behavior. Today, contemporary sociologists utilize the *Verstehen* approach as they employ "participant observation" research techniques.

Two theoretical traditions that can be seen as implied by the social definitionist paradigm are symbolic interaction theory and social exchange theory.

Symbolic Interaction Theory

Symbolic interaction theory is summarized by the following statement: "Behavior of the individual is in response to symbols (or meaning) relative to an audience and a situation" (Vernon and Cardwell 1981). In other words, human interaction is mediated through socially constructed meanings; people interact with each other based on their understanding of the meanings of social situations and their perceptions of what others expect of them within these situations. Stressing the symbolic nature of social interaction, Jonathan Turner (1985:32) says:

> *Symbols are the medium of our adjustment to the environment, of our interaction with others, of our interpretation of experiences, and of our organizing ourselves into groups.*

From the symbolic interactionist perspective, human beings are autonomous agents whose actions are based upon their subjective understanding of society as socially constructed reality. Randall Collins (1985:200) makes this point:

> *Each individual projects himself or herself into various future possibilities; each one takes the role of the other in order to see what kind of reaction there will be to this action; as a result each aligns his or her own action in terms of the consequences he or she foresees in the other person's reactions. Society is not a structure, but a process. Definitions of situations emerge from this continuous negotiation of perspectives. Reality is socially constructed. If it takes on the same form over and over again, it is only because the parties to the negotiation have worked out the same resolution and because there is no guarantee that they cannot do it differently next time.*

If one were to study parent-child relationships throughout the family life cycle from the perspective of symbolic interactionism, the following questions might be investigated:

1. How and why do parents tend to identify symbolically with their children's accomplishments and/or failures?
2. How do children function as "significant others" or "social audiences" for parents?
3. How do parental roles stabilize the parent's conception of self over the family life cycle?
4. What are the various cultural meanings attributed to children, and how do these meanings affect patterns of family interaction?
5. As parents socialize children, in what ways do they also internalize society's values and norms for themselves?
6. How does a child leaving home, or the death of a child, diminish conceptions of self for parents?

Social Exchange Theory

There are two traditions followed by social exchange theorists. The first is consistent with principles of behavioral psychology; it focuses on how human behavior is rewarded or punished by the behavior of other persons. Willard Waller's (1951) theory of mate selection and the "principle of least interest" is in this tradition. Waller studied dating on American college campuses and concluded that men were more likely to invest themselves financially and emotionally in relationships with women in order to gain physical affection, while women were more likely to become sexually involved in order to receive attention and commitment from the males. Waller claimed that the person

In the process of mate selection, couples are involved in exchange relationships whereby they give and receive physical, emotional, and social rewards. Social exchange theorists might describe wedding or engagement rings as symbolic rewards.

with the least interest in continuing the relationship was able to control the relationship and exploit the other partner.

The second type of social exchange theory is that which has been influenced by the work of Peter Blau (1964) and is committed to many of the assumptions held by symbolic interactionists and by the social definitionist paradigm as a whole. Social exchange theorists of this type would contend that human behavior consists of subjective and interpretative interaction with others that attempts to exchange both symbolic and nonsymbolic rewards. It is important that such social exchange involves reciprocity so that each interacting individual receives something *perceived* as equivalent to that which is given.

From this perspective, individuals will continue to participate in social situations as long as they perceive that they derive equal benefits from their participation. For example, the social exchange theorist would contend that an abused spouse will stay in a violent marriage because she or he perceives that even a bad marriage is better than the alternative. If this perception changes, the relationship may end.

Social exchange theorists would also point out that specific rewards (status, esteem, love, money, etc.) may be more applicable in one exchange than in another and may have differing values for each participant (Eshleman 1985). A spouse who tolerates an alcoholic and the alcoholic partner may both find benefit in a relationship when each one feels that he or she is needed.

Using our example of parent-child relationships throughout the family life cycle, a social exchange theorist would be interested in the following research questions:

1. Why do parents take on the additional responsibilities of raising children?
2. What rewards and costs are involved in the parent-child relationship?
3. Do husbands and wives receive different rewards from the parent-child relationship?
4. If a child becomes a financial and/or emotional burden, do the parents become less satisfied with the parent-child relationship?
5. In what ways do families attempt to deal with rivalries between siblings for parental attention or affection?
6. Are adult children who care for their elderly parents more likely to receive a greater share of their parents' inheritance than those children who do not participate in the terminal care?

INDUCTIVE AND DEDUCTIVE APPROACHES TO THEORY CONSTRUCTION

Scientific theories can be expanded by employing both inductive and deductive strategies. **Induction** is the logical process by which generalizations are inferred from specific observations. In an inductive process, researchers will provide evidence for the support of a number of concrete statements. By combining these statements one can form general conclusions that summarize the significance of all the empirical statements in one or more abstract propositions. For example, if one were to discover that emotional well-being was considerably better among elderly people who were married, owned pets, and/or were involved in social organizations, then one might infer that social relationships have a positive effect upon emotional well-being. This parsimonious explanation is an addition to the body of scientific knowledge concerning the mental health of older people.

Deduction, or deductive reasoning, as we discussed earlier, is the process of reasoning from general statements to concrete situations. Deduction is important in theory building because specific hypotheses and scientific predictions are derived from abstract propositions. For example, if emotional well-being is a function of social relationships, we can hypothesize or predict that elderly people who frequently interact with neighbors, friends, and/or family members will have better emotional states than older people who do not.

As you can see, the processes of induction and deduction interact and, in so doing, contribute to theory building. Induction will provide new abstract statements from which one can deduce additional hypotheses to be verified by empirical research. Once verified, empirical propositions serve as the source from which parsimonious explanations are inferred.

Warnings for Interpreting Research

1) Don't believe everything you read; be somewhat skeptical. Be cautious not to be a "Chicken Little." Just because something hits you on the head, do not immediately go running through the chicken yard shouting, "The sky is falling!" First of all, look up to see whether the sky is falling or not.

Though the Kinsey studies of male and female sexual behavior are often quoted and are indeed a classic study, approach these findings with some caution. Kinsey's sample was composed largely of volunteers (many of whom were imprisoned at the time). Perhaps it is only a certain kind of person who will talk about his or her premarital sexual behavior, thus giving a bias to the results. Kinsey asked persons to recall their first sexual experiences, but some of his respondents were near eighty and may not have had very accurate memories. Kinsey also had difficulty with definitions. What he meant by a particular term was not necessarily what many respondents meant. His definition of social class was limited to one variable.

2) Weasel words and shrewdly chosen qualifying words can make a statement technically correct but misleading. It is not a lie, but can imply something that it is not. A woman in a Geritol television commercial says, "After only nine bottles of Geritol, I feel better already." After nine bottles of anything, one would feel different, if for no other reason than because of the passing of time. The ad did not say you would feel better because of Geritol, but it did imply it.

A foot powder ad says, "Brand XYZ foot powder may help reduce foot odors." It does not say the foot powder *will* reduce foot odors, only that it *may* reduce them. It may *not* reduce them also!

3) Watch for quotes out of context. The thief may quote the Bible as saying, "Let him who stole, steal ..." This is solid advice for the thief, if it is taken out of context without completing the sentence—which reads, "Let him who stole, steal *no more.*"

Former President Jimmy Carter's "lusting in his heart" statement in a *Playboy* interview almost lost him the presidential election. This isolated statement was extracted from a very lengthy article of which "lusting in his heart" was only a very small statement.

4) Look carefully at sample sizes. "This bread is better than any other bread tested." How many other breads were tested? Was it one or maybe two? Perhaps the "other" bread was a week old and molded.

An aspirin ad read, "Nine out of ten doctors recommend brand X." How many physicians were in the sample? It could be interpreted as 90 percent of the 550,000 or so physicians in the United States or it could literally refer to a total of ten doctors; and nine of those could possibly work for the company!

A headline several years ago read, "One-third of Johns Hopkins Coeds Marry Professors." One could conclude that a sizable percentage of coeds at this university marry professors. Actually, of the three female students at Johns Hopkins University at that time, one of them did marry a professor.

5) Catchphrases can be "loaded" with connotations for some readers. To suggest that one is gay, has AIDS, and is a member of the Communist party can conjure up all sorts of negatives for many people. For example, some more fundamentally oriented Protestant groups in the United States will not say the Apostle's Creed because of the phrase "holy catholic church." They do not want to say, "I believe in *the* holy catholic church." What they do not know is that "catholic" means "universal," not the Roman Catholic Church!

6) Loaded questions can give very biased results. By phrasing the question in a certain way, one can skew the respondent's answers. For example, to ask a man "Have you stopped beating your wife yet?" produces a no-win response. If the man responds to this question in the affirmative, it implies that he has been beating his wife. If he answers negatively, it could imply that he is still beating his wife.

CONCLUSION: THE RELATIONSHIP BETWEEN THEORY AND RESEARCH

In this chapter we have discussed issues in theory construction. First we explored the three basic components of scientific theories—conceptual schemes, sets of propositions, and contexts for empirical verification. Then we described paradigms as ways of organizing scientific theories. We introduced the social factist and social definitionist paradigms and discussed the four theoretical traditions: structural-functionalist theory, conflict theory, symbolic interactionist theory, and social exchange theory. Finally, we pointed out the value of both inductive and deductive approaches to theory construction and the process of social science research.

Two major questions remain unanswered however: "What is the role of sociological theory in the conduct of social research?" and "How does social research result in sociological theory building?"

To answer these questions we will turn to some of the early but important writings of Talcott Parsons (1938) and Robert K. Merton (1967). Parsons (1938:13–20) listed the four principal functions of theory for social research as follows:

1. Theory can tell us what "social facts" are worthy of social research. There are no facts without theories.
2. Theory can enable us to organize research findings and conclusions.
3. Theory can help us determine gaps in scientific knowledge and provide us with suggestions for further research investigations.
4. Without theory it is impossible to impute causality to the relationships between concepts and sets of interrelated propositions.

To these functions of theory, Merton (1967:151–52) adds three others.

1. Theory can extend empirical generalizations as abstractions of a higher level are formulated.
2. If a theory consists of a set of interrelated propositions, and one derives a new proposition from the theory, then any evidence supporting the deduced proposition will provide substantiation for the propositions from which it was derived.
3. By providing a rationale, theory introduces a ground for prediction which is more secure than mere empirical extrapolation from previously observed trends.

Merton (1967) in his now-famous essay "The Bearing of Empirical Research on Sociological Theory" suggests that social research also fulfills many important functions that help to shape the development of sociological theory. According to Merton (1967:157), research initiates, reformulates, deflects, and clarifies sociological theory.

Empirical research not only tests theoretically derived hypotheses, it originates new hypotheses whenever unexpected observations are made. This serendipitous (accidental discovery) pattern came up earlier when we discussed the role of induction in theory construction.

Research reformulates sociological theory whenever new data exert pressure on the researcher to reconceptualize the variables under consideration. Merton (1967:162) points out that sometimes conceptual schemes do not adequately take all facts into account— they consider some data irrelevant. When new research reveals the importance of these data, the conceptual schemes must be extended and reformulated in order for the theories to become more inclusive.

New methods of empirical research and developments in technology often change the foci of theoretical interests. Today it is possible with the use of a computer and sophisticated statistical techniques to investigate new theoretical issues that were not within the reach of sociologists of an earlier era. For example, new computer simulations make it possible for the researcher to test entire theoretical paradigms while controlling for the influences of many intervening variables. Scientific developments of this type are bringing about new directions in social scientific inquiry.

As research attempts to verify theories, research necessarily helps clarify concepts and the relationships existing between variables. Research thus provides greater clarity and increased specificity for sociological theory—making theories more parsimonious.

The relationship between research and theory, then, is **symbiotic**—research is essential in theory construction, and theory guides research and makes if more fruitful. Both research and theory (discovery and explanation) are vital to the conduct of social scientific inquiry into the sociology of the family.

CHAPTER
REVIEW

- The three basic components of a scientific theory are (1) a conceptual scheme, (2) a set of propositions stating relationships between properties or variables, and (3) a context for verification.
- A scientific theory is a system of interrelated propositions. Every scientific theory must have a context for verification—theories must be testable to be valid.
- Operational definitions convert theoretical concepts into observables by defining theoretical concepts in terms of indicators by which these concepts may be uniformly observed.
- Theoretical paradigms serve as units of consensus, embracing research studies that share general commitments to methodological techniques, research assumptions, and levels of analysis.
- Sociology, like most other scientific disciplines, is a multiparadigm science.
- The social factist paradigm is primarily concerned with group actions and societal structures. From the social factist point of view, society cannot be reduced to a collection of individuals—social phenomena have a reality of their own. Sociological research from this perspective

will study group-related phenomena (social institutions and structures) rather than behaviors of particular individuals.

- Structural-functionalists view society as a social system of interacting parts. Structural-functional theory focuses on the issue of societal maintenance and social equilibrium.
- Conflict theory studies issues related to social change and disequilibrium. Conflict theorists focus on competition, conflict, and dissension resulting from individuals and groups competing over limited societal resources.
- The social definitionist paradigm maintains that the essential feature of society is its subjective character. The social definitionist will emphasize individual behavior over group actions and societal structures.
- From the symbolic interactionist perspective, human beings are autonomous agents whose actions are based on their subjective understanding of society as socially constructed reality.
- Social exchange theory contends that human behavior consists of subjective and interpretative interaction with others that attempts to exchange symbolic and nonsymbolic rewards. Social exchange will always involve reciprocity so that each individual receives something perceived as equivalent to that which is given.
- Induction is the logical process in which generalizations are inferred from specific observations and research investigations.
- Deduction is the process of reasoning from general statements to concrete situations.
- The relationship between research and theory is symbiotic—research is essential in theory construction, and theory guides research and makes it more fruitful.

DISCUSSION QUESTIONS

1. List and describe the three basic components of scientific theories.
2. How are scientific theories verified by empirical research? What is the relationship between theory and research in the social sciences? What is the relationship between induction and deduction in social science research?
3. What are paradigms, and what are their functions for social science research?
4. Compare and contrast the social factist and social definitionist paradigms.
5. Compare and contrast the structural-functional and conflict orientations in family research.
6. Compare and contrast the symbolic interactionist and exchange orientations in family research.

GLOSSARY

conceptual scheme: A system of descriptive and operative concepts that expresses a general idea concerning the relationships between phenomena or offers categories for the classification of phenomena.

deductive system: The process of reasoning from general statements to concrete situations.

dependent variable: The variable whose changes in values the research study attempts to explain or predict. In an analysis of cause and effect, the dependent variable is the effect.

descriptive concepts: Words and concepts that tell us what a theory is about.

dyad: A unit of sociological analysis in which there are only two persons who engage in interaction.

empirical knowledge: Knowledge based on observation, experience, or experimentation.

endogamous: Married to someone with similar social background characteristics. Endogamous marriages are formed when marriage partners are of the same social group.

ethnology: The study and description of culture.

hypothesis: A tentative statement asserting a relationship between concepts. The hypothesis is intended to be tested empirically and either verified or rejected.

induction: Logical process in which empirical generalizations are inferred from specific observations.

norms: Group expectations for what is considered socially appropriate behavior.

observables: Concepts that are immediately susceptible to direct sensory observation.

operational definition: The definition of a theoretical concept in terms of concrete research procedures by which that concept may be uniformly observed.

operative concepts: The variables that make up the propositions of which a theory consists.

paradigm: A unifying concept embracing a set of shared general commitments to methodological techniques, research assumptions, and levels of analysis; a way of organizing bodies of knowledge produced by empirical research.

parsimonious: In an explanation of an empirical relationship or phenomenon, as simple and uncomplicated as possible.

proposition: A statement of relationship between two or more empirical variables.

symbiotic: Characterized by mutual dependence.

theoretical concepts: The concepts that provide the vocabulary for a theory. Theoretical concepts are abstract properties and not immediately verifiable by direct sensory observation.

theory: An explanation of a phenomenon by the use of a deductive system of empirical propositions.

theory inference: Use of empirical evidence for any of the propositions making up a theory to provide empirical support for the entire theory.

variable: A theoretical concept that can take on a variety of concrete values.

SUGGESTED READINGS

Babbie, Earl. 1988. *The Practice of Social Research.* 5th ed. Belmont, Calif.: Wadsworth Publishing Company. *Outstanding treatment of the process of conducting social science research.*

Chafetz, Janet S. 1978. *A Primer on the Construction and Testing of Theories in Sociology.* Itasca, Ill.: F. E. Peacock Publishers, Inc. *A short book dealing with theory construction in sociology that explains and demonstrates the relationship between sociological theory and empirical research.*

Collins, Randall. 1985. *Three Sociological Traditions.* New York: Oxford University Press.

Ritzer, George 1975. *Sociology: A Multiple Paradigm Science.* Boston: Allyn and Bacon.

Two books on sociological theories that will provide more information and analysis on the four theoretical perspectives discussed in this chapter.

PART TWO

Social Change and Families

Historical Perspective on American Families

In the 1960s Bob Dylan wailed, "The times they are a-changing." Historically, the American family has been no exception to Dylan's proclamation. From the seventeenth century to the end of the twentieth century, social historians have observed changes in the form of the family. From the rural colonial family—not only performing the basic functions of reproduction, protection, and socialization of children but serving as a center of economic production, education, religion, and recreation—to the modern urban family with its far more limited functions, the American family has changed with its corresponding social context. Though people in general tend to support cultural inertia (resistance to change), change in itself does not mean that the old was bad and the new good or the reverse. While there were positives and negatives to seventeenth-century family life, there are also pluses and minuses in contemporary families in the United States. This chapter will survey some changing aspects of American families from an historical perspective.

---

*William A. Alcott, *The Young Housekeeper: or, Thoughts on Food and Cookery,* 1838.

SOCIAL AND HISTORICAL ROOTS OF
AMERICAN FAMILIES

The scope of this book does not allow for a thorough discussion of all the native and migrant "roots" embedded in today's American families. It will be helpful, however, to take at least a brief look at life in the New England colonies. In the seventeenth century the settlers of the colonies brought many European traditions to their new land. As one group breaks away from a larger group, however, the few who leave cannot possibly take all the **folkways** (customs) and **mores** (societal rules) with them. Attitudes and behavior are more likely to change as people move and become integrated into a new social environment than if they remain immobile. Thus, as the colonists moved to a new environment, changes from their previous ways of life were bound to occur as they adjusted to new social settings and physical conditions.

Families in the New England Colonies

In the New England colonies during the 1600s, a **village settlement pattern**, or pattern of closely clustered dwellings, was the most common living arrangement. This pattern had been prevalent in Europe and suited the needs of these newcomers to America. A high degree of sociality was possible in this close proximity. As a defense against possible enemies in this new land, a village pattern also gave a sense of security. Furthermore, colonial families found it convenient to live near each other because they soon discovered that in order to survive it was necessary to share resources.

Life in the New England colonies was very difficult for these early Americans. Their medical knowledge and skills were limited, their relationships with the native Americans were not the friendliest, the new climate was often harsh, and having transported relatively few goods from the mother country, their tools and other equipment were limited.

Family life in the colonies was shaped partly by traditions transplanted from Europe and partly by the challenges of an unexplored land. Though life in the beginning was hard, there was plenty of land to be had for these industrious pioneers, land that could be passed on through the male line of descent to future generations. The **patriarchal authority** pattern generally was found among families in the American colonies, since this was the pattern brought over from Europe. That is, the father was the leader and lawgiver in the family.

Not only did the colonial family give a sense of orderliness to individual lives and to a society beset by the uncertainties of pioneer life, the family itself embodied a structure with particular rules and ideals of internal governance. The ideal family was a hierarchy, and the good order of the family depended upon the sovereign authority of the male head (Scott and Wishy 1982:7).

Despite the patriarchal tradition, the legal status of women saw a slight improvement in colonial New England. John Demos (1970:88) notes that a wife in Plymouth was expected to participate freely in family decisions involving land transfers. Decisions involving children being "put out" into foster families were the joint responsibility of both spouses. Wives, as well as husbands, could initiate divorce proceedings. Property rights were about the same for single women as for single men.

Family life was highly prized, and marriage was encouraged. Some communities, for example, imposed a bachelor tax to entice single males to the altar. Hartford, Connecticut, taxed "lone men" twenty shillings a week "for the selfish luxury of solitary living" (Queen and Habenstein 1974:296). According to Arthur Calhoun (1973:67), bachelors were viewed with disapproval and "were almost in the class of suspected criminals." "Ancient maids" of twenty-five were considered by colonists as being "dismal spectacles" (Queen and Habenstein 1974:296). With family life being encouraged and children viewed as an asset to the economy, a favorable attitude toward reproduction prevailed. A man or woman without family ties was "almost unthinkable"; such an anomaly "could not be tolerated," according to Calhoun (1973:67).

Women's Work

Minister Clapp, president of Yale University (1740–66), wrote this about his wife:

She always went through the difficulties of childbearing with remarkable steadfastness, faith, patience, and decency. Indeed she would sometimes say to me that bearing, tending, and burying children was hard work, and that she had done a great deal of it for one of her age (she had six children, whereof she buried four, and died when she was twenty-four), yet would say it was the work she was made for, and what God in his providence had called her to, and she could freely do it all for Him.

Source: James K. Hosmer, cited in Stuart A. Queen and Robert W. Habenstein, *The Family in Various Cultures*, 4th ed. (Philadelphia: J.B. Lippincott Company, 1974), p. 299. Copyright © 1961, 1967, 1974 by Harper & Row, Publishers, Inc. Reprinted by permission of the publisher.

Death held considerable dominion over life in the seventeenth century. Life expectancy at birth was about thirty-five years, while those surviving to the age of twenty-five could expect to live only into their early fifties. Probably slightly over half of all children born survived into adulthood. In the colonies a mother who lived through her childbearing years had, on the average, eight children, though it was probably rare for as many as six of the eight to survive to adulthood (Scott and Wishy, 1982:2). For many colonial women, most of marriage, and thus most of adult life, was spent bearing and raising children.

While romantic love was not absent from colonial New England, its importance was limited by both the struggle for survival and the stern Puritan code (Queen and Habenstein 1974:303–5). In the language of home and church, love meant conjugal love and was defined as "a duty imposed by God on all married couples, and a solemn obligation that resulted directly from the marriage contract" (Morgan 1966:12).

Good Manners for Children

Colonial children would have been familiar with the precepts of "Curtesye" compiled in the nineteenth century by Frederick J. Furnivall. For example:

When your parents come into sight, give them the reverence they are due. Ask for their blessing if they have been out of your presence for a long time. If you dine with your master, let him begin first; don't try to sit in the place of honor, but take the place assigned to you. At table don't pare your nails. If your master speaks to you, take off your cap and stand up.... Don't dip your meat in the common salt-cellar, wipe your spoon clean before putting it down, and take care that it not be stolen. Don't pick the bones clean with your teeth. Don't belch near to another person's face; don't scratch your head at meals; don't spit over the table; or pick your teeth with a knife. Wipe your mouth when you drink. Don't blow your nose on your napkin. Don't fill your mouth too full. Don't blow on your soup or drink, "for if thou be not whole of thy body, thy breath is corruptible." When leaving the table wish good luck to your companions, bow to your master, and withdraw.

Source: Frederick J. Furnivall, ed., *The Babees Book* (1868), cited in Queen and Habenstein 1974:283.

Children in colonial America were to "be seen and not heard." They were taught that to complain about their lot in life was sinful. Needless to say, "kid power" and "children's rights" were not advocated. Discipline was enforced at home and at school. The law required strict obedience and severe penalties for violation (Queen and Habenstein 1974:305–6).

As we indicated earlier, almost everyone in the colonial family was a member of some family group. Today, nonkin groups, other social institutions, and social agencies assist the nuclear family in providing traditional family functions for its members.

Families in the West

Let's look at the family as it existed in another pioneering setting: the American West. A westward movement began in the 1800s as gold and other attractions beckoned some settlers toward the Pacific seaboard, long before occupied by native Americans. These western settlers lived on the land they took over, raised their own food, and made many of their implements—making self-sufficiency an impor-

A long, difficult trek westward showed the determination of American families in the 1800s.

tant value. A strong belief in the positive value of ownership also prevailed. The farm family worked the land, thus functioning as an economic unit. On these early farms, in contrast to today's pattern, absentee farm ownership was not the pattern (Cavan 1969:43–44).

Women were in great demand on the western frontier, and men competed for unmarried women. Thus, as young men and women went West, the seeds of equality were planted: both sexes attempted to survive the harsh conditions of life, and nature made few compensations for gender. (At this same time, in the eastern part of the United States, some women intellectuals were also demanding equality with men as a matter of principle.)

Settlement of the West on individual farms, isolation of the families on farm settlements, and the delay in establishing organized government, churches, and schools placed a heavy responsibility on families. Each family provided its own protection, control of its members, care of the sick, and religious services.

Ruth Cavan (1969:46) notes that this pioneering period made several contributions to the American family. At a time when rural family functions had begun to decrease in the eastern United States with dependence upon factory-made goods, family unity and organization were strengthened, and the scope of family functions was broadened. Self-reliance, taught by pioneer conditions, tended to free younger adults from family ties and responsibilities.

FROM RURAL TO URBAN FAMILIES

In 1790 the first U.S. census revealed that 95 percent of the population was rural; today almost 75 percent of the population lives in urban settings. In view of this dramatic turnaround in demographic distribution over a two hundred-year period, it is important to understand rural and urban societies may differ and what effect these differences can have on the way families function.

Traditional Rural and Urban Differences

An obvious difference between rural and urban settings is that rural populations are overwhelmingly involved in agriculture while urban populations are associated with a variety of highly specialized occupations. **Population density**, or number of people in a given area, also differs in rural and urban settings. With greater concentrations of people in urban areas, informal **social control** (means of keeping order) lose effectiveness; formal means of social control become more important. For example, in a small rural town, gossip serves as an informal social sanction; but gossip is totally ineffective as a social control in a large, impersonal urban setting. Rather than gossip about the family in the 100-unit apartment complex down the street, one simply calls the police if this family is being disruptive. Shunning (failure to recognize the particular individual), practiced so effectively by the Amish, and ridicule (laughing and making fun of the accused), utilized by some Eskimo groups, work very well in these small settings. The more formal, impersonal urban atmosphere, however, requires controls like law enforcement by the police.

The Amish in American Society: Resistance to the Changing Family

While major changes have been occurring in American families, some 15,000 Amish people continue to live in an agrarian, patriarchal, extended, consanguine family style. Being a "peculiar and zealous people," "not of this world," and "nonconforming," the Amish live as most American families lived in the last century.... With large extended families geographically clustered together, their cooperative efforts on the farm result in work as play in that socializing is an important aspect of the work experience....

By allowing Amish children to go no further than eighth grade in Amish schools to acquire the basics of reading, writing and arithmetic, and with little external influence through media (no television or radio and limited access to printed material other than the Bible), this tight "boundary maintenance" keeps the Amish within the Amish community. By "keeping them down on the farm," the possibility of their wanting to move to an urban area is reduced. To marry within the Amish community and to stay on the farm is fulfilling God's will.

Source: Information based on John A. Hostetler, *Amish Society* (Baltimore: The Johns Hopkins Press, 1963).

As families move from rural to urban settings, less of a need exists for large families. Whereas on a farm several children can be an asset (grow your own labor supply), the same size family in a city can be a liability. Thus, the birth rate has traditionally been lower in urban settings. Not only is knowledge about birth control techniques usually increased in an urban situation, contraceptives are likely to be

The Amish continue to live as many American families did in the 19th century. Given their lifestyle, Amish families may be unaffected by some modern changes such as rising gasoline prices.

more available. In today's city pharmacy, condoms and other contraceptives are available on the shelf, not behind the counter.

A higher **sex ratio**, or percentage of males, is found in rural areas, as more men seem to stay on the farm while more females move to the city seeking jobs and new experiences. Urban settings provide women with increased freedoms and opportunities. Rural areas have a higher degree of cultural homogeneity than urban areas. That is, in rural settings families are more likely to have similar occupations, social attitudes, religious backgrounds, political views, and educational levels than in urban areas. Urban families, on the other hand, are likely to be very diverse with regard to social backgrounds and attitudes. Whether or not urban areas function as "melting pots," they are in fact composed of very heterogeneous populations.

Rural and Urban Differences Today

Though differences between rural and urban dwellers are noted above, the gap between "rural" and "urban" is rapidly narrowing in the United States today. With improved communication through mass media (such as television, radio, and newspapers), rural and urban families are not as different from each other as in the past. Indeed, both mass media and better transportation are helping to eliminate many rural-urban differences in social characteristics. With farm mechanization and specialized knowledge of agribusiness management, the family on today's farm is not so closely tied to a traditional rural way of life. For example, modern crop specialization makes it necessary for most farmers to buy many products formerly raised on the all-purpose, self-sufficient family farm. Sophisticated farm machinery has helped foster a trend to fewer, larger farms. And since contemporary farming is big business, it is necessary for farmers to be as well educated and sophisticated as their business counterparts in urban areas.

Just as urban businesses often fail, many contemporary farm families have fallen on hard times. Many traditional family farms are going bankrupt as expenditures exceed income. In some cases, these farms are being taken over by larger corporate bodies. The absentee landlord may drive from the city occasionally to view his or her farm holdings. Some other farm owners today own stock in a farm which they may rarely if ever see—the farms they are a-changing.

FROM EXTENDED TO CONJUGAL FAMILIES

For many years, sociologists have believed that American families have evolved from an emphasis on **extended families**—three or more generations related by blood—to conjugal ties. In the extended kinship pattern, a couple is tied into a network of family and in-laws and is subject to much influence from parents and other relatives. The **conjugal family** (or nuclear family) system permits marriage by personal choice with less parental pressures on selection. As noted by William Goode (1968), industrial expansion and the material goods it brings are closely tied to the development of freedom from old restrictions in family life.

As the United States became more urbanized and moved toward industrialization, the shift from an extended family emphasis to a conjugal system seemed to be natural for the following reasons (Goode 1968:65–66):

1. With freedom of couples to establish their own households independently, they may physically move to wherever the demands of the industrial system call.
2. One with talent can make vertical occupational moves upward without being obligated to everyone in the extended family.
3. Economic decisions are determined without interference by the larger kin network.

4. The young person making decisions about a job is less subject to the traditional thinking of family members.
5. Hiring and promotion are based more on merit and less on nepotism and family ties.
6. Women's talent's are utilized without seeking permission of husbands or fathers.

William Goode (1982:179–80) suggests that industrialization actually weakens the traditional family system. With more people earning their living from jobs, fewer people are dependent on eventually obtaining a share of the family land through inheritance. As efficiency is needed in industry, employers hire competent people with little concern for family background. Since work offers each individual the possibility of making a living, individual workers can become independent of kin. Thus, a change in orientation from the *consanguinal family* (extended family network in an agrarian society) to the conjugal family provides a stronger social base for an industrialized society.

With specialization in the job market today, a career person may have to move hundreds of miles away from the **family of orientation** (birth family) to find a satisfactory job. As a consequence, increased mobility—especially of middle-class American families—has resulted in more dependence upon "fictive kin" or friendship networks. This mobility has allowed, however, for more independence from the family of orientation—a positive step in the eyes of many. Thus, the relationship to the extended family is likely to have fewer face-to-face associations and to become more dependent upon the telephone or the mail for communication. An individual's consanguine family is, therefore, less likely to be physically available to give support or advice. Such a change may be viewed as positive by some and negative by others.

Not everyone is in agreement that the small, nuclear conjugal family resulted from industrialization, however. Sidney Greenfield (1961:322) has argued that the small nuclear family existed in Europe and the United States *before* the industrial revolution and may not simply be a consequence of the urban-industrial revolution. Greenfield's examination of both the comparative and historical evidence indicated that there is no necessary and sufficient causal relationship between the small nuclear family and urbanization and industrialization. In Greenfield's view, any relationship that exists most probably results from the presence of the small family in Northern Europe prior to the industrial revolution.

According to Frank Furstenberg (1966:337), too, changes in American families since industrialization have been exaggerated by some writers. Based on observations of foreign travelers visiting the United States between 1800 and 1850, Furstenberg concluded that the system of mate selection, the marital relationship, and parent-child relations in the preindustrial family all show striking similarities to the family of today.

Family strains commonly attributed to industrialization are evident to observers of the family prior to industrialization (Furstenberg 1966). According to Furstenberg's thesis, strains in the American family resulted from the voluntary choice of mates, abrupt loss of freedom for women at marriage, women's discontent arising from total domesticity, lack of discipline of American children, and the inferior position of women in the society. Some of these tensions may have tended to promote the adaptation to an industrial society. The lack of parental restrictions on American children and the desire of women to improve their position in society and escape the demands of domestic duties may have facilitated the growth of the industrial system. On the other hand, certain strains noted in American families today, such as difficulties with adolescence, old age, and divorce, were not noted in early nineteenth-century families.

Whatever theory you accept as the historical background, it is clear that the characteristic unit today is the conjugal family. Many kinship groups still preserve consanguine ties through occasional reunions (if only at weddings or funerals), mutual aid, frequent contacts, and family pride (a renewed interest in the family's roots). To the average American today, however, "family" refers to the nuclear family, not the extended family.

A FUNCTIONAL PERSPECTIVE ON FAMILIES

Specific Functions of American Families

Some universal family functions have been recognized for a long time. Procreation (having children) has always been an essential ingredient of the family. Granted, having children is not confined to the conventional family situation, but this situation has historically provided the context for birth.

Another family function is status ascriptions. **Ascribed status** refers to the positions or characteristics given to one, as opposed to **achieved status**, which one must earn. Many status ascriptions, such as gender identification, occur at birth. Only in rare instances do people try to alter this ascribed status. Certain physical characteristics, such as skin color, hair texture, and particular physical features, are also ascribed at birth. Making alterations here is often less drastic than a change of sex. Economic class ranking is also

Few Family Functions: The Case of the Ik in Uganda

The Ik of Uganda were relocated by the government prior to World War II in order to use their territory for a national park. As a result, these 2000 nomads had to abandon their hunting and gathering way of life and turn to horticulture—a sedentary way of life for which they had no preparation. This resulted in a mere subsistence level of living with starvation the norm.

The Ik quickly evolved from a very loving, caring family system where mutuality, reciprocity, cooperation and sharing were normal to a survival of the fittest system where children were put out of the house on their own at age three. Self-interest soon became the motivating theme in their daily existence—stealing, treachery and deceit followed. With social disintegration complete, no individual had any concern or consideration for anyone else.

These "loveless people" changed from the epitome of a solid family structure to that of a fractured family. With love being lethal—one could not afford to care for another as food supply and water were so limited—marriage and procreation were rare. Why bother to marry and have children if one literally cannot afford such a relationship? Family sentiment and love were luxuries the Ik could not afford. At the verge of starvation, such luxuries could mean death. Is it not a singularly foolish luxury to die for someone already dead, or weak, or old?

Whereas the Ik have shifted the responsibility from family to the individual, we have shifted from family to the state. Not unlike the Ik, we separate the very young from the very old in homes or day schools and camps. We joke about marital relations and turn health, education and welfare over to the state.

Source: Colin M. Turnbull, *The Mountain People* (New York: Simon and Schuster, 1972).

ascribed at birth—your status is that of your parents, whether poor or rich. Later in life, as an adult, a person achieves class position through his or her own accomplishments.

Family settings also regulate sexual behavior through incest taboos. Although ancient Egyptian royal dynasties allowed brother-sister marriages, and Cleopatra was the product of nearly a dozen generations of "royal incest," no known contemporary society openly approves of incestuous relations. The incest taboo is about as near a universal norm, or expectation, as can be found. However, expectations and actual behavior are sometimes different, and incest as a behavior is not uncommon in the United States.

Having produced children, the family is charged with caring for them. Not only must children be given food, clothing, and shelter; their socialization is important for their survival within a cultural setting. That is, the family must teach the child the dos and don'ts of the culture. When the child behaves "correctly," a pat on the head may reaffirm such behavior. If "incorrect" behavior occurs, punishments may follow. Since humans have a longer maturation process than most animals, their care must extend over several years. With perhaps the exception of Uganda's Ik, who turn their children out at age three to survive on their own, most human cultures prescribe care for children—sometimes even tender loving care.

Since the family is a primary group, it can foster sharing and cooperation within its intimate environment. This ideal of cooperation does not always exist, however, as the family may also be an arena of conflict and the locus of oppression for women.) A division of labor (an assignment of duties) is necessary as families attend to tasks of everyday living. Historically, a division of labor by age and gender has been common. There have been different expectations for different age groups as there have been for males and females. While a small child does not have the responsibilities of an adult, neither is an elderly person supposed to perform as an adolescent. While gender role expectations are rapidly changing, divisions of labor by gender age are still prevalent in the United States today.

Family Functions as Viewed by Three Twentieth-Century Writers

Family functions appear to be dynamic rather than static. Some twentieth-century writers have imagined drastic changes in family functions. In *Brave New World* (1932) Aldous Huxley envisioned test-tube babies. Babies produced in a laboratory would eliminate the need for traditional parenthood. Now that in vitro fertilization and surrogate mothers are not just discussed in novels but are empirical realities, a different light has been thrown on procreation and parenthood.

George Orwell's *1984* (1949) describes procreation occurring for the good of the state rather than from an affectional relationship between two individuals. The year 1984 has come and gone, and Gallup polls are not suggesting that procreation occurs today for the "good of the state."

In B. F. Skinner's utopian vision *Walden Two* (1948), procreation is not reduced to test tubes or to that which benefits the state. Instead, married couples have offspring who are raised in a communal setting with no differential treatment given to a couple's own biological offspring. With the exception of procreation, traditional family functions are taken over by the entire community of Walden.

Changing Functions of American Families

While these writers' visions of the changing functions of the family have not become reality, some changes in the structure of the family have definitely occurred. There is very little evidence that families are any "better" or "worse" than in the past. Yet the belief that families were once more solid and more caring remains strong (Gittins 1986:164). Older persons often comment that "it wasn't like that then" or "in our family we all used to care for each other, not like kids today." Much of this belief probably reflects a tendency for people to select pleasant memories from their past.

One of the biggest changes in U.S. families today is that in one sense people expect more from marriage, childrearing, and sexuality than in the past (Gittins 1986:166). On the one hand, families are

A HAPPY HOME IN OROGRANDE, NEW MEXICO.

A fascination with the "good old days" is exemplified by the title given this photograph. Who is to say whether this family was happy, or whether their descendants are any more or less happy today?

presented as the most fundamental and basic social institution; yet since the nineteenth century love, marriage, and family life have been idealized as a crucial refuge from society and all its ills and injustices. As this family ideology has become stronger, by definition the reality and the ideal have become farther and farther apart. As Christopher Lasch (1977) points out, there is a serious anomaly in family ideology. An institution that is the pillar of society obviously cannot at the same time be a refuge from it.

An obvious change in the U.S. family today is that the number of family members has declined from an average of nearly six in 1790 to under three today. Average family size has declined because of a decreasing number of children being born per family (Figure 4.3). Looking back to the introduction of the factory system in the United States, Amos Hawley (1971:121) observed that the family and kin group were relieved of having to produce a labor force for domestic

Figure 4.3   How American Families are Shrinking (Source: U.S. Census Bureau)

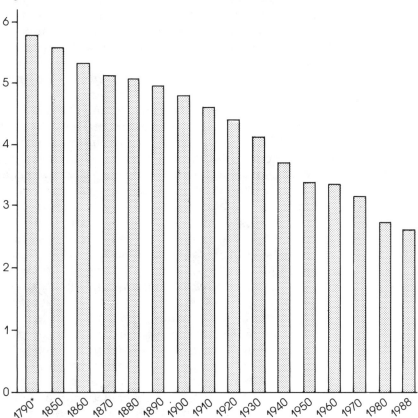

*Figures for 1800–40 unavailable.

industry, thus the childbearing imperative lost its force. Children gradually ceased to represent a valuable resource and became a charge against a wage or salary income, notes Hawley. In addition, more couples today are simply choosing to have fewer children or not to have children at all. With the availability of more sophisticated contraceptives, and with increased occupational opportunities for women resulting in reduced societal pressures to produce children, there is not much social support for the old goal of "getting married and having lots of children."

An aging population also contributes to a declining average family size. Since the U.S. population has shifted from 4 percent over age sixty-five in 1900 to 11 percent today, a greater proportion of American families have no minor children.

Another shift has occurred with the *nature* of family functions. Modification in the importance of the family as an educational, religious, and recreational unit is evident. Formal education today occurs almost entirely in public or private schools, only rarely at home. Religious instruction takes place largely away from the home, in the setting of a church or synagogue. Recreational pursuits, as well, tend to be away from the home, as family members more often seek recreation with their peers. This shift in family functions could be viewed as change either for the "better" or for the "worse," depending on the viewer's perspective.

Amos Hawley (1971) observed that this removal of functions from the household released repercussions in various directions. The number of destinations to be visited by household members multiplied, as well as the number of trips to be made and the amount of traffic on the streets. Setting family members apart for short or long periods during the day exposed them to a wide range of influences, any one of which could have alienating effects. Thus, Hawley argues, some circumstances of industrialization operated to weaken the family's ability to carry out its remaining responsibilities.

With a population shift from rural to urban, as noted earlier, the physical work of the rural family is basically a phenomenon of the past. Today's family uses electrical and computerized technological innovations to do many household chores. Time spent in the kitchen has decreased in many families because of prepared foods, microwave ovens, and the popularity of fast-food restaurants. The domestic task of washing clothes has been simplified by modern appliances; in earlier centuries, doing the laundry entailed drawing water from the well, cutting wood with which to boil the water, making soap to handscrub the clothes, hanging the wash on a line to dry, and finally ironing and folding everything. Such an undertaking as weekly laundry involved members of the family for many hours.

In spite of technological improvements in housework, however, full-time homemakers still work about the same number of hours as

The days of being a generalist—performing a wide variety of functions within the family—are now history. The American family that works as an economic unit is rare today.

they did in 1920 (Vanek 1974). In addition, studies of family time budgets in the 1970s reveal that the typical working woman outside the home still devoted at least thirty hours a week to home duties, although only slight increases have been noted in husbands' involvement in housework when their wives entered the labor force (Ryan 1983:321–22). Though more goods and services used by households are produced outside the home, much time and effort is still needed to produce the standard of living to which most U.S. families aspire. The result is that the hours full-time homemakers devote to housework has not changed much (Blau and Ferber 1986:28–29).

AMERICAN FAMILIES' REACTIONS TO CHANGE

Today sociologists recognize that changes in the American family do not necessarily imply the collapse of the family. This was not the case half a century ago, as illustrated in the writing of the noted sociologist P. A. Sorokin (1937:776):

> *The family as a sacred union of husband and wife, of parents and children will continue to disintegrate . . . . The main sociocultural functions of the family will further decrease until the family becomes a mere overnight parking place mainly for sex relationships.*

Today, however, many analysts feel that with fewer functions, the family may be a more viable unit. To prescribe fewer duties to any institution or individual should free more time and energy for the responsibilities that remain. Clark Vincent (1966:29) maintains that the greatest strength of the family may be its ability to adapt to an ever-changing world rather than to maintain stability and/or equilibrium in its form. Otto Pollak (1967:193–205) argued that the primary function taken away from the family by other institutions was its autonomy in setting its own standards.

Optimism out of Pessimism

Various indicators noted in the media today suggest that Sorokin was correct—that the family of nineteenth-century tradition is disintegrating. However, there are optimistic ways of viewing these indicators (Enoch, Savells, and Dickinson 1976). A high number of marriages ending in divorce suggests marital failure, if marital success is defined as longevity. Yet in the past, death broke up both good and bad marriages in a totally arbitrary way (Gittins 1986:159). The consequence was high rates of widowhood, orphanage, remarriage, and single-parent families. And there were plenty of bad marriages in the past; except for the very wealthy, however, divorce was impractical if not impossible. At least today it is possible to get out of a bad relationship.

Divorce is often cited as a principal cause of children's emotional disturbances and juvenile delinquency, but it can also be the only avenue of release from an intolerable situation (Gittins 1986:161). That divorces occur does not necessarily mean that people are seeking to escape marriage and its responsibilities, nor does it suggest a widespread disenchantment with the marital relationship. The largest percentage of those who divorce will remarry; in fact, many may divorce in order to remarry (Enoch, Savells, and Dickinson 1976). A divorce may not indicate so much a dissatisfaction with *the* marriage relationship as with a *particular* marital relationship.

Today's decreasing birthrate, rather than showing a loss of a family function, may reflect an increased availability of methods of controlling reproduction, a workable method of family planning, or a rationality on the part of married couples formerly not possible. The family may be enhanced through a reduction in the number of children per couple. For example, fewer children in the family allows each child to have a greater share of the family's emotional and financial resources.

There is a natural tendency in all of us to idealize our image of families in preindustrial society. But families of the past were often disrupted just as tragically as families today. As noted earlier, a high percentage of young mothers died in childbirth, and children who survived to adulthood often had to do heavy, health-threatening manual labor. In that environment, an unspoken belief in the survival of the fittest prevailed with ruthless efficiency (Barbeau 1971:31–32). As noted by Ross Eshleman (1985:631), changes that take place and will take place in the family are neither inherently destructive or regrettable, nor inherently constructive or pleasing.

Even though change is constant and often disruptive, it has not lessened the attractiveness of marriage or implied the ultimate deterioration of the institution of the family. During the past hundred years, the marriage rate has been relatively stable (it has remained within the range of 8.5 and 10 per 1,000 population) with only minor adjustments during times of war and economic uncertainty (Eshleman 1985:434). The family today is at a point where it is possible to create relationships not in defiance of society, or in lonely isolation from it, but in coexistence with it (Otto 1970:183).

Growth through Change

One certainty is that functions and values within the family have changed and will continually change as families attempt to survive in an ever-changing world. To refuse all forms of change would guarantee the ultimate demise of the family as a viable social institution.

Since the family is the building block of U.S. society, we frequently believe that all else depends upon its health, and we sometimes equate its vitality with a single normative definition. It is important to remember, however, that the family is enmeshed in the fabric of other social institutions, such as religion, economics, education, and politics. Since social institutions make up a social system, the structure and functions of each institution certainly affect the others. For example, a change in the norms of our society making it more acceptable for women to be employed outside the home has direct implications for the family, the economy, politics, religion, and education.

The family and the larger social system comprise a multitude of variables interacting in a reasonably predictable manner. Alteration of one variable, therefore, may bring about simultaneous change in other variables or even promote resistance to that change (Schulz 1972:11).

History is filled with illustrations of various groups attempting to change the family according to some new vision of what the good life really is. Since many individuals live in families that may not be considered socially "normal," we must remind ourselves that the family we often refer to is a cultural ideal.

The family continues to occupy a strategic position both for its individual members and in the framework of a social system inevitably concerned with the generation of new members who can assume productive social roles. Furthermore, the family remains inevitably linked to the myriad of functions we identity as part of the economic, educational, political, and religious systems in U.S. society. Thus, changes in any of these systems creates the necessity of further adjustments on the part of the family as a social institution.

Perhaps the real strength of American families is found in their flexibility. As Amos Hawley (1971:122) noted, changes in family functions reveal the family to be a highly adaptable institution—no specialized institution could match its flexibility.

CHAPTER REVIEW

- While family life in the New England colonies seemed orderly and stable, it was not the "good old days" sometimes pictured.
- The westward movement contributed to an independent, self-reliant spirit for individuals.
- Informal social controls were more effective in rural America than in today's urbanized society.
- Rural areas have traditionally been characterized as having higher birth rates, a higher sex ratio, and a higher degree of cultural homogeneity.
- Differences between rural and urban families in the United States are rapidly decreasing.
- Conjugal ties tend to be more predominant today than extended family networks.
- A basic family function is status ascription. Ascribed statuses include one's sex, physical characteristics, and class ranking.
- Family functions appear to be dynamic rather than static.
- Though family life in the United States has changed since colonial days, there is little evidence that families today are any "better" or "worse" than then.
- A declining family size and modification in former family functions of education, religion, and recreation reflect a changing American society—a demise of the family is not evident.
- Though technological innovations have eased some aspects of housework, homemakers still work about the same number of hours as they did in 1920.

DISCUSSION QUESTIONS

1. Contrast colonial families with today's families.
2. How did pioneer families moving West in the 1800s differ from colonial New England families?

3. Discuss rural and urban family differences. How have the mass media impacted upon these differences?
4. Why are conjugal families better suited to today's society than extended families?
5. Explain this statement: The nuclear family can be a source of both conflict and cooperation between spouses.
6. Either refute or support this statement: Colonial families were more stable than contemporary American families.
7. Why does a greater proportion of elderly people in our society affect family size?
8. How can the American family continue to survive in an ever-changing society?

GLOSSARY

achieved status: A position that depends to some extent on characteristics over which the individual has some control. For example, through a person's own efforts, he or she can become a college graduate.

ascribed status: A position attached to a person over which he or she has little control (one's sex, for example).

conjugal family: The family in which primary emphasis is placed upon the husband-wife relationship.

consanguinal family: The family in which primary emphasis is placed upon blood relationships between relatives.

extended family: A family that includes more than two generations of family members living together.

family of orientation: The family in which one is socialized as a child— consisting of one's parents and siblings.

folkways: Optional behavior with weak sanctions imposed; e.g. the kinds of foods eaten in a society.

mores: Prescribed behavior based on obligations; stronger sanctions imposed than for folkways.

norms: Group expectations for what is considered socially appropriate.

patriarchal authority: A form of family authority where primary authority and decision making is vested in males.

population density: Number of persons per square mile in a given land area.

sex ratio: The number of males per 100 in a given population.

social control: A means of establishing order.

village settlement pattern: Settlement pattern prevalent in rural areas in most parts of the world; a rural population is clustered together, and not scattered on isolated farms as in the United States.

SUGGESTED READINGS

Calhoun, Arthur W. 1973. *A Social History of the American Family. Vol. 1.* New York: Arno Press. *A vivid picture of life in colonial America. Personal accounts cited in this social history make for especially interesting reading.*

Frey, Sylvia R., and Marian J. Morton. 1986. *New World, New Roles: A Documentary History of Women in Pre-Industrial America.* New York: Greenwood Press. *An account of women in the United States in the seventeenth century; focus on the family, work, religion, and law.*

Otto, Herbert A. 1970. *The Family in Search of a Future.* New York: Appleton-Century-Crofts. *An anthology with suggested alternative lifestyles and family patterns.*

Ryan, Mary P. 1983. *Womanhood in America: From Colonial Times to the Present.* New York: Franklin Watts. *An excellent historical account of women in America.*

Gender Roles and the Family

♦ *What are little girls made of, made of?*
What are little girls made of?
Sugar and spice and everything nice,
That is what little girls are made of.

What are little boys made of, made of?
What are little boys made of?
Snakes and snails and puppy-dogs' tails,
*That is what little boys are made of.**

When a couple announces to the world that they are anticipating a new member of their family, one of the first questions that many Americans ask is "Do you want a boy or a girl?" Many Americans will answer that they hope for a boy—especially for a first child—although overall, families generally prefer a balance of boys and girls rather than all children of the same sex (Williamson 1976).

In the United States there may be no social factor that influences family behavior more than gender. But why is gender so important to American families? Furthermore, when we consider gender-appropriate family behavior, how much is influenced by biological distinctions (physical and hormonal differences) and how much results from differential social conditioning and treatment? Does biology equal destiny in the United States? Does gender merely provide a convenient, arbitrary but necessary order for role differentia-

---

*Mother Goose Nursery Rhyme

tion within the family; or are gender distinctions dysfunctional for the family and for its members? These are some of the questions we will consider in this chapter.

SEX DIFFERENCES—BIOLOGICAL AND SOCIOLOGICAL EXPLANATIONS

Everybody knows that boys and girls differ in many respects. The cause of these **sex differences** is a very interesting issue—is it primarily biological (genetic or innate) or environmental? Obviously both factors affect physical and behavioral differences between males and females, but which is more important, and what is the relative impact of each?

Biological Differences Between Males and Females

Extensive research has provided answers to some, though not all, of these questions. With regard to biological factors, we have discovered the following: Women on the average are shorter, weigh less, and are two-thirds as strong as men; they have higher fat-to-muscle ratios—the average female has 23 percent body fat compared to 15 percent for males (Lowe 1983); they exhale 40 percent less carbon dioxide than men, differ in nitrogen metabolism, have lower metabolic rates, and expel less air after maximum inhalation (Sherman cited by Lott 1987:25); and women have longer life expectancies and lower mortality rates for all ages. However, for each of these differences, the variation within each sex is always greater than the average difference between the sexes. For example, in the 1980s actress Susan Anton was taller and stronger and had less body fat than her then boyfriend Dudley Moore. In actuality, sex (by itself) does not explain much of the variation that exists among human beings.

However, even if the biological differences between the sexes are minimized, some important inherent distinctions remain. From his extensive studies on sex differences, biologist John Money (cited by *Time* 1973:34) has been able to identify only four biological imperatives that differentiate women and men. Only females are able to menstruate, give birth to infants, and breast-feed, while only males are able to impregnate females. These seem to be the bottom-line innate or genetically determined differences between females and males. Yet women and men may choose not to have sexual intercourse, thereby making gestation and lactation unnecessary for women and impregnation impossible for men. Furthermore, menstruation in women is affected by many factors including environmental conditions, exercise, stress, and muscle/fat ratio (Lott 1987:24).

If Men Could Menstruate

What would happen ... if suddenly ... men could menstruate and women could not?

The answer is clear—menstruation would become an enviable, boast-worthy, masculine event.

Men would brag about how long and how much.

Boys would mark the onset of menses, that longed-for proof of manhood, with religious ritual and stag parties....

Military men, right-wing politicians, and religious fundamentalists would cite menstruation ("men-struation") as proof that only men could serve in the Army ("you have to give blood to take blood"), occupy political office ("can women be aggressive without that steadfast cycle governed by the planet Mars?"), be priests and ministers ("how could a woman give her blood for our sins?"), or rabbis ("without the monthly loss of impurities, women remain unclean").

Source: Adapted from Gloria Steinem, "If Men Could Menstruate," *Ms.* (October 1978), p. 110.

These findings have led some behavioral science researchers concerned with sex differences to conclude "that it is the sex assignment at birth—not genetic sex, that is of primary importance in sexual identity" (Lott 1987:18). Michael Lewis (cited by Lott 1987:49), has made this point even more emphatically with the following words:

> *There is no reason to study sex differences at all. What we should be doing instead is studying individual differences in order to determine how behavior is modified by experience.*

Socialization to Gender Roles

If human behavior were determined by the instinctual and biological structure of the organism, as in the case of many other animals, our lives would be free of many of the decisions that consume our time. If we were programmed by our biology, we would not have to be

Advertising that appeals to the stereotypical macho man or sensual woman often misses the mark. From *Cobb Again,* Wild & Woolley, Sydney, Australia.

taught how to act, feel, and think in human ways. In short, our world would be preordered and we would be free to "do what comes naturally."

But such is not the case. Humans must be taught, trained, and/ or educated by society if they are to act appropriately as human beings (as defined by the culture). Sociologists refer to this process of "becoming human" as the socialization process. In the socialization process, individuals take into account the expectations of others as they develop their personal identities and determine the appropriateness of their behavior.

All human societies have differential expectations of behavior based on the sex of the individual. These expectations are called **gender roles,** and they specify right or proper conduct for both males and females. Every culture must socialize its members personally to accept the legitimacy of these roles and act in accordance to them. As one incorporates gender meaning into his or her definition of self (self-concept), his or her behavior conforms to society's expectations.

Males and females must be taught appropriate gender specific roles. As women have joined the workforce, the political arena, and the military, many behaviors have lost their gender specificity.

Bernice Lott (1987:32–33), after reviewing more than a dozen empirical studies concerned with gender differences in the behavior of neonates, concludes that there are "no well-established, reliable sex differences at birth on any measure related to behavior." However, many research investigations (see Rubin, Provenzano, and Lauria 1974; Seavey, Katz, and Zalk 1975; Smith and Lloyd 1978; Haugh, Hoffman, and Cowan 1980; and Sidovowicz and Lunney 1980) have demonstrated that parents, children, and others have different cultural expectations of male and female infants. Parents (especially fathers) perceive daughters to be prettier, smaller, more inattentive, weaker, and softer than sons (Rubin, Provenzano, and Lauria 1974). Furthermore, as parents and others act on these perceptions, they interact with infant daughters and sons in different ways. From the time of birth, boys and girls are expected to act, feel, and *be* different. Should they deviate from their social script and not act according to their appropriate gender, they are sanctioned by being labeled "tomboys" or "sissys."

From a symbolic interactionist perspective, we would expect that as a result of this differential treatment, boys and girls would develop in very different ways. Empirical evidence from studies conducted by Jeanne Block (1976) and by Eleanor Maccoby and Carol Jacklin (1974) clearly demonstrated this to be the case. These two well-known studies, upon which the PBS "Nova" film called *Pinks and Blues* was based, showed that gender differences increase with age as a result of differential socialization. That is, girls and boys are exposed to different life experiences and encounter different consequences of their behavior (Lott 1987:35), and as a result they manifest many gender differences in behavior.

The way in which we are defined by society influences the social roles we acquire. This socialization begins in early childhood with the toys we are given to play with and the behaviors we are encouraged to display.

In her *Women's Lives: Themes and Variations in Gender Learning*, Bernice Lott (1987:35–48) documents the following gender differences between boys and girls as they grow older:

1. *Boys tend to be more independent than girls, while girls are relatively more dependent, passive, and adult-oriented than boys.*
2. *Boys are more physically active and aggressive than girls. They are also more inclined to play outdoors in strenuous play.*
3. *Girls are more attentive and sensitive than boys to other persons' feelings. Boys are less emphatic and other-directed, but more self-promoting and competitive than girls.*
4. *Boys score slightly higher on standardized achievement tests (SAT verbal and mathematical abilities), while girls obtain better grades in school than boys. Yet, girls are more likely than boys to underestimate their achievements and attribute their successes to luck or chance, and their failures to lack of ability.*

Lott attributes the cause of each of the observed differences to differential opportunity and reward structures encountered in the socialization process of males and females. According to Lott (1987:34):

These differences are the result of (a) the situations to which girls and boys are maximally exposed; (b) the meaning and value given to these situations by adults and others; (c) the most probable responses required or demanded by these situations; (d) the opportunities girls and boys are given to practice various behaviors; and (e) the consequences (rewards and punishments) girls and boys experience or receive.

In gender, then, we have an outstanding sociological example of several important sociological concepts: the self-fulfilling prophecy, the "definition of the situation," the looking-glass self-concept, and the labeling theory of deviance. In a self-fulfilling prophecy, expectations bring about the thing expected; so people may act on the basis of false stereotypes, but their behavior can make the stereotypes become true. According to W. I. Thomas' "definition of the situation," if something is defined as real, it will be real in its consequences. In the looking-glass self-concept, a person defines himself or herself through internalizing others' expectations. Finally, labeling theory contends that people do not become deviant until they have been so labeled by authorities. According to this theory, it is society's assumptions that boys and girls inherently act, feel, and *are* different (dubious assumptions at best) that cause empirical differences in the behaviors, feelings, and self-concepts of adult men and women. These empirical differences then naturally lead many people to think that their cause must be biological differences between the sexes.

Having presented the symbolic interactionist argument for the sociological basis for gender differences, I would like to acknowledge some counterevidence for my claim. It has been my wife's and my experience (and the experience of many of our friends) that despite our best efforts to raise our children in an androgynous manner—without stereotypical gender expectations—they became rather traditional regarding gender-appropriate behavior. When our daughter was eight she would wear *only* pink or purple, "played Barbies," and disliked athletic competition, while at eleven our son lived and breathed ice hockey, could not keep grass stains off his knees, and disliked girls.

Some would suggest that either we were poor parents or the sociological explanation is without merit. Actually, a better explanation is that the expectations of peers had a significant influence on our children's behavior (see chapter 12). Furthermore, secondary

What Counts Is Whether You're a Boy or a Girl!

Leroy was the patient and we painted him with iodine so he'd look wounded. I wasn't gonna be no nurse. If I was gonna be something, I was gonna be the doctor and give orders. I told Cheryl I was the new doctor in town. Her face corroded. "You can't be a doctor. Only boys can be doctors. Leroy's got to be the doctor."

"You're full of shit. Leroy's dumber than I am—and being a girl don't matter."

"You'll see," retorts Cheryl. "You think you can do what boys do, but you're going to be a nurse. It doesn't matter about brains, brains don't count. What counts is whether you're a boy or a girl."

I hauled off and belted her one. Course I didn't want to be a doctor. I was going to be president, only I kept it a secret.

Source: Rita Mae Brown, *Rubyfruit Jungle* (New York: Bantam Books, 1973), p. 31.

socialization—socialization occurring outside the family and involving the influences of the media, the school, the church, and other institutional representatives of society—will also have an important impact upon children's understanding of gender roles and personal identity. It does seem that the best-laid plans of mice and men often go awry.

In providing a sociological explanation for gender association, we have emphasized the theoretical insights of the symbolic interactionist paradigm. One could also interpret gender socialization in the light of other theoretical paradigms. For example, a structural-functionalist argument would suggest that gender differences are functional for the maintenance of traditional family norms and values. Positing gender differences based on biological distinctions provides what appears to be an inherent order for relationships between male and female family members. Regardless of the validity of the grounds for making distinctions between the sexes, structural functionalists would argue that clearly defined gender roles provide specific behavioral expectations and promote efficient family functioning while diminishing ambiguity in social relationships.

From a conflict perspective, sex is viewed as one basis on which societies differentiate social status. Each status—or position within a social hierarchy—has different sets of social obligations, rights, responsibilities, and rewards associated with it. Conflict theorists would contend that making gender distinctions between the sexes perpetuates a status system that provides men with more social power and prestige. To the structural functionalists, the conflict theorist would ask the following question: "What group of people benefits from a system that makes distinctions on the basis of biological differences?"

Finally, an exchange theorist might view gender roles as a system of social reciprocity. Both men and women will experience costs and benefits from behavior governed by gender. In traditional role assignments, men were expected to work outside of the home while women were assigned domestic responsibilities. For both sexes there were rewards and obligations associated with this system. The women's movement has suggested, however, that a social system that does not make distinctions on the basis of sex can be more beneficial for all humans—males and females.

In this next section we will consider the effects of gender on employment, marriage relationships, and patterns of family interaction.

WOMEN AND MEN IN THE WORKPLACE

When I was growing up, the most popular television situation comedy shows were "Leave It to Beaver," "Father Knows Best," "Dennis the Menace," and "I Love Lucy." Each of these shows portrayed the "typical" American two-generation nuclear family. With the exception of "I Love Lucy," all of these families lived in middle-class suburbs—and each week we were told that *the* normal American family consisted of a father who worked and a mother who stayed at home with her children, baked chocolate-chip cookies, and was the emotional support for her husband and family.

I could identify with these families because I lived in a Los Angeles suburban community. My father was an insurance agent, played golf with his male friends, and worked on "projects" with his sons. My mother was involved in women's clubs and community activities and always greeted me with cookies and milk when I returned from school. This was the way "normal" family life was supposed to be!

At that time, I knew of only one child who went to day care after school (actually he went to the home of an unemployed elderly woman—there were no day care centers in Sunland, California, in the 1950s and 1960s). Furthermore, I knew of only one friend whose parents were divorced, and I did not know anyone who was raised in a single-parent family. Most of the families in my community were working-class ("blue collar") or lower-middle-class. Today I know that there were families which deviated from the TV models, but back then I thought either that those families did not exist, or that if they did, they certainty were not "normal."

If you looked to television to get a picture of the "typical" contemporary American family around 1990, what would you see? To take a few examples, "Growing Pains," "The Cosby Show," and "Family Ties" depicted three dual-career professional families; in "Kate and Allie" two single-parent families shared an urban apartment; and "Who's The Boss" introduced two unmarried single parents (of the opposite sex and attracted to each other) in a three-generation household where the man is working-class and the woman is a professional. What do these families have in common? Each situation stresses the importance of the parent-child relationship, and all of the women are employed outside of the home!

We can gain two important insights into contemporary family issues by understanding the changes that took place in television shows between the 1950s and the beginning of the 1990s. First, the social structures of American families are diverse—we cannot assume that a single family form exists. Second, family roles for adults are not totally determined by gender differences—mothers and fathers are now both employed, and both assume parental and housekeeping responsibilities. This latter observation leads us to the major focus of this chapter: women and men in the workplace.

As noted by Paul Close and Rosemary Collins (1985), the women's movement of the late twentieth century has had a direct impact upon the relationship between the family, the workplace, and the economy as a whole. Feminist thinking has entailed a reconceptualization and reexamination of many key issues and concerns. For example, according to Herb Goldberg (1976:162), the feminist movement was inspired not by women's oppression but by "the decay and demise of the male." Masculine privilege was "a myth." Barbara Ehrenreich (1983:11–12) notes that in the 1950s and earlier, there was an expectation that men would grow up, marry, and support their wives. By the late 1970s and early 1980s, however, adult manhood was no longer always automatically burdened with the expectation of marriage and breadwinning. Changes in men's roles are usually believed to be derivative of changes among women. Ehrenreich argues, however, that the collapse of the breadwinner ethic had begun well before the revival of feminism.

With a changing attitude toward women in the workplace, the percentage of women working outside the home has increased significantly, especially among married women. Amos Hawley (1971:121) notes that historically, the coming of the factory system to the United States maximized the importance of obtaining a job in order to make a material contribution to the family. In 1950, females accounted for 29 percent of all workers, and married women made up 52 percent of the female labor force. By 1980 the majority of American women

The Mystery of the Closing Pay Gap

According to the new census report, which tracked the job scene from 1979 to 1986, men with 20 years of experience and 10 years at their current job earn an average hourly wage of $12.95. Women with the same experience and seniority earn $8.81, a ratio of 68 cents to every dollar men earn.

However, the differential is significantly less pronounced among younger women. Among workers with less than five years of experience, women made 80 cents for each dollar paid to their male counterparts. The reason? A sharp rise in the proportion of women entering traditionally male-dominated professional, managerial, and technical fields.

Still, according to the Census Bureau, the vast majority of women are likely to be in occupations that pay relatively low wages, which accounts for about 17 percent of the wage differential. Ironically, says the report, the earnings of a person, regardless of sex, will be lowered as the ratio of women in his or her occupation increases. Historically, this has been the case with such workers as teachers, secretaries, and bank tellers.

Not all occupations are affected this way. Supply and demand both have an effect. With lawyers, for example, the demand has not slackened and pay will not decrease. The same goes for computer operators. Carolyn B. Elman, executive director of the 112,000-member American Business Women's Association, says the pay gap is indeed narrowing but predominantly at the middle management level and below. Also, there is a greater male-female pay disparity among professionals than among nonprofessionals. According to Elman, "As more women get into management in nonprofessional fields, they are insisting on pay equity for their employees. But professional women do not discuss their salary, and any time there is secrecy, there can be inequity."

A Labor Department report in 1985 put it more bluntly: "After all measurable variables have been included, there remains a disparity that cannot be readily explained. This variance is attributed to unmeasured factors such as discrimination, personal attitudes, and quality of education."

Source: Robb Deigh, "The Mystery of the Closing Pay Gap," *Insight* (October 19, 1987), p. 44. Reprinted with permission from *Insight* magazine/author—Robb Deigh.

were in the labor force. The majority of two-parent families had two breadwinners (one of whom was female, and the majority of school-age children had working mothers (Ryan 1983:305). In 1986, females were 44.5 percent of employed persons, and married women accounted for 60 percent of women workers (Filene 1986:237 and Bureau of Labor, cited by Rothenberg 1988:69). At present, more than 53 percent of women with children one year old or younger are in the labor force (Trost 1987). Thus, while television shows of the 1950s underestimated women's participation in occupation roles, today far more women are employed than in the 1950s, and for the same reasons that men work—to help support their families, to gain independence, to demonstrate their personal creativity and competence, and to achieve the societal rewards of wealth, power, and prestige.

This changed presence of women in the workplace, however, does not necessarily imply more equality between the sexes, since, as discussed later in this chapter, many wives are still doing most of the domestic work in addition to working outside the home.

Also, while contributing economically to the family, the wife is often locked into a low-paying job, while her husband has superior domestic authority granted by his larger paycheck. Thus, within the American home, there remains an imbalance between male and female, and in the labor force wide margins of inequity separate the sexes (Ryan 1983:323–24).

When we look at women's salaries and financial contributions to family income, we find that a male worker (on average) earns approximately 35 percent more than a female employee (Rothenberg 1988:72). For years women have entered female-dominated occupations (teaching, secretarial, nursing, retail sales, and service jobs), which pay less money than male-dominated careers. However, when we control for occupation, seniority, and number of career interruptions, a gender gap in wages still exists.

While it is difficult to account for all of the differences between male and female salaries, a major cause remains, as mentioned above, job segregation by gender. Eighty percent of all women workers are employed in clerical, sales, service, factory, or plant jobs (National Commission on Working Women 1983). These are generally low-paying jobs. In 1986, women were 4.4 percent of all dentists, 6 percent of all engineers, and 17.6 percent of all physicians (Bureau of Labor, cited by Rothenberg 1988:70).

However, as more women are acquiring advanced education, their numbers are increasing in the higher-paid professional occupations. In 1960, 36 percent of all students enrolled in higher education were women. Twenty years later the majority (52 percent) of all students were women (Filene 1986:238). Table 5.1 provides information on women as a percentage of full-time workers in selected professions for the years of 1979 and 1986. From this information,

TABLE 5.1 Women as a Percentage of Full-time Workers—1979 and 1986.

Occupation	1979	1986
Lawyers	10.4	15.2
Accountants and auditors	34.0	45.0
Managers and administrators	22.1	28.9
Computer programmers	28.0	39.7
Computer System analysts	20.0	30.0
Electrical and electronic engineers	4.0	9.0
Sales representatives	10.1	13.4

Source: Robb Deigh 1987 and U.S. Department of Commerce 1987.

we can see that women have increased their participation in the careers listed. Obviously women still have a long way to go, but present trends are toward **gender parity,** or equality of pay regardless of sex.

Women's participation in the work force is not only the highest in American history, but women are more committed to occupational roles than ever before—they are more likely to work full time; they are less likely to disengage from employment in order to fulfill family responsibilities; and, like men, they are incorporating occupational roles into their definitions of self.

Furthermore, in a trend related to their participation in the work force, women are having fewer children. Historically there has always been an inverse relationship between female labor force participation and birthrates, but in past decades couples were still averse to childlessness and one-child families. However, the present trend is for more women and men to choose to be child-free or to have fewer children later in life (Gerson 1985). These data suggest that the fundamental structure of the relationship between family and work is changing for women and men. With respect to the importance attributed to occupational roles, women and men are becoming more similar.

THE DUAL-CAREER FAMILY

Our concern in this chapter is the effect of increased employment for women upon the family: How do family relationships change when

Egalitarian family structures and increased participation of women in the workplace have changed working relationships in many occupations. This, in turn, affects the family as women put more emphasis on their careers and choose to have children later in life, or not at all.

both parents are employed outside of the home? Raising the question in this way implies that all American families have experienced major changes—and of course this is not true. Among most working-class families, women have been employed outside the home for many generations. Since the primary increase in female labor force participation in recent years has been by middle-class women, we would expect to find most social change to have taken place in middle-class families.

In 1973, Lynda Lytle Holmstrom wrote one of the first books on the **two-career family**—that is, the family where both parents have professional careers. As background to this book, Holmstrom (1973) interviewed twenty dual-career middle-class couples in the greater Boston area. The majority of the book addresses the problems that these couples encountered when they attempted to establish family lifestyles for which there were no clearly defined and sanctioned social models. In the words of Holmstrom (1973:1):

> *Although it appears that the two-career family will become more common in the future, it is now the exception rather than the rule. These couples are therefore "bucking the system," and they have had to face a whole series of barriers which*

assume that only one spouse will work and that, furthermore, it is the husband who will do so.

Many of the students on U.S. college campuses today had parents who were "buckers of the system"—social pioneers of the 1970s. Today, most college students assume that they will have a two-career family and that they will be able to fulfill all of their marital, parental, and occupational role responsibilities. They probably also assume that with hard work and good communication skills, they can have it all—a good marriage, bright children, a nice home, and a respected social position. Is this a realistic expectation?

Before we consider the lifestyle of the two-career family, let's define the term **career.** Careers are occupations that require extensive professional training and education, a high degree of personal commitment to work long hours, and a willingness to compete with fellow workers to progress from lower to higher levels of responsibility and rewards (Mortimer 1979:1). Career employees are typically paid annual salaries (and possibly incentive bonuses), while people who work at "jobs" are paid hourly wages. Career professionals are expected to work sixty or more hours per week. Careers can consume every available hour. To borrow a phrase from popular vocalist James Taylor, careers can "take your soul if you let them." Examples of career occupations include medicine, business management, architecture, educational administration, college or university teaching, law, ministry, and accounting.

In the past, most careers were **two-person careers**—that is, it took two people to meet the demands of a career, even though only one was paid. Two examples of two-person careers are those of the business executive and the minister. The business executive was traditionally expected to entertain clients in his home; actually he brought the client home and his wife did the entertaining. The ministry was another example of a two-person career—the church called the pastor but also received the services (teaching and musical) of his wife. In these careers, single people (and women) were at a great disadvantage and were not as likely to move up the professional ladder of success.

As spouses became less available to be used by employers, expectations of professionals began to change. This happened because women entered the work force and did not have time for their husband's careers, and because when women became professionals, their husbands would not fulfill the traditional spouse's role. Career persons with employed spouses must achieve on their own efforts. This can create stress for the professional and guilt for his or her family members.

Balancing Roles and Responsibilities

One popular image of life in a two-career family is the lifestyle of television's Huxtable family. From the appearance of things, Dr. and Ms. Huxtable's careers place few demands on their time. Even without domestic help, their home is rarely cluttered, dishes are always cleaned and put away, clothes are ready to be worn, and meals are always served on time. For Cliff, Claire, and their five children, all conflicts are resolved within the course of thirty minutes. Furthermore, they never need a babysitter, they spend most of their time interacting with each other in the living room or kitchen, and they seem to have close and supportive friendships in the world outside the family. How are they able to balance all of their occupational, familial, and friendship roles and responsibilities?

The answer to this question is easy. They don't! This is not reality—the Huxtable home has only three walls. The life of the two-career couple with children bears no resemblance to that portrayed on "The Cosby Show." In the real world, two-career couples with children take on time-consuming roles and responsibilities requiring super-human strength and extraordinary commitment. The best of those couples experience tremendous social stress and have doubts about their abilities to survive. Yet they do not find single careers and traditional marriage and family relationships to be satisfying and/or viable alternatives.

Let us consider a fictional case of Jim and Judy Johnson. Jim is a member of a Chicago accounting firm. Judy is principal of a middle school in the Chicago suburb where the family resides. The Johnsons have three children aged eight, five, and three. Jim takes the train into the city each morning at 7:00 and returns home at 5:30 in the evening. Judy must be at work at 8:00 a.m. but drops off her three-year-old son at the day care center at 7:30. The older children take the bus to their school at 8:00 a.m. At 11:30 the kindergartener takes the bus from school to the day care center where her brother is. At 2:30 the oldest child returns home by bus and is supervised by a neighbor, who is a full-time homemaker. Judy picks up her two younger children from the day care center on her way home from work at 5:30.

When Jim returns home, he begins to prepare the evening meal. The family will eat at 6:30. After dinner the children do homework, practice the piano, watch television, and play games (fight) with each other while their parents attend to household chores (do the dishes and a load or two of laundry, vacuum the carpets, and/or repair one of the children's toys). By 9:00 the children are asleep.

Three nights per week Judy has meetings at school or church which start at 7:30 and run two or three hours. On those nights,

Jim cares for the children by himself. On the nights when Judy does not work, Jim and Judy like to sit down, discuss the day's activities, and have a glass of wine. After the ten o'clock news they go to bed.

The weekend provides a needed relief from work and the normal family rush. A typical Saturday morning finds the Johnson family doing household chores. At 10:30 the older two children have piano lessons followed by soccer practice. In the afternoon the Johnsons try to plan an all-family activity. In the evening, Jim and Judy will go out to dinner in the city with friends and possibly take in a play. Meanwhile, the children will be cared for by a high school student.

On Sunday, the Johnsons will attend church and Sunday school. Jim teaches a fifth grade class and Judy is the chairperson of the church council. After church the family will go out to dinner, ideally returning home in time to watch the Chicago Bears beat the Green Bay Packers. The parents spend the rest of Sunday shopping for groceries, doing household chores, and repairing any broken household items.

As long as none of their children becomes ill and as long as neither Jim nor Judy is required to do any work-related travel, the Johnsons are able to survive. On Monday morning, the cycle begins again.

Two-career couples with children, like the Johnsons, must simultaneously juggle six commitments—marriage, children, career, house, friends, and community involvement. The Johnsons live in a world that Cliff and Claire Huxtable know nothing about. This is a world reserved for people with extraordinary energy, extreme dedication, and the resiliency to cope with high stress. Welcome to the real world of the two-career family.

Family: Both Cause of and Cure for Stress

A new and more complex view of the powerful effects of stress on the nation's families has emerged from a gathering of interdisciplinary scholars at the Conference on Social Stress Research. The researchers offered new insights on the family's paradoxical role in both causing and relieving stress, and underscored the importance of the family in social scientists' attempts to understand how stress affects individuals.

There were two traditions represented at the conference. One views the family as a haven from stress in the external world, especially the world of work. The other perspective sees the family itself as a source of stress. According to Leonard I. Pearlin, professor of medical sociology at University of California at San Francisco, "the family has the capacity not only to foul us up but also to throw us a life preserver." The conference examined in greater detail just how these two forces interact.

In categorizing the causes of family stress, Dr. Pearlin claims that some sources are primary—conditions generated within the family. Among many kinds of primary stress, Pearlin cited "scheduled life events," eventual changes rooted in the life cycle such as marriage, childbirth, or the aging or death of parents or spouses. Examples of other primary sources of stress include "role overload," as when homemakers feel their talents are underused. Also stressful is "role captivity," as when homemakers prefer to have other employment, or when those with outside employment wish they were homemakers.

Pearlin claims that researchers are developing a more sophisticated understanding of the family as a source of "secondary" stress. Emotions such as anxiety, anger, and depression can be brought from the workplace into the household and displaced on family members, tainting the relationships between worker, spouse, and children.

Illustrating the complexity of such interactions, Dr. Pearlin cited the case in which a spouse deliberately tries not to bring problems home from work. The other spouse notices the change in mood, is perplexed by the air of mystery, and wonders, "Did I do something to make my spouse feel bad?"

Other research at the conference pointed to "male-biased assumptions" about stress, as Grace Baruch termed them. "Stress is seen as an ailment that can be caught at work and not at home," said Dr. Baruch, program director of the Wellesley College Center for Research on Women. "The home has been seen as a sanctuary and a haven, while work has been viewed as a high-stress environment."

However, according to Dr. Baruch, the family is also a stressful environment. Increasingly for men and women, work can buffer family stress—especially enjoyable work. Dr. Baruch mentioned the "Thank God it's Monday syndrome" and quoted a colleague as saying, "A job is to a woman as a wife is to a man—the ultimate stress buffer."

Source: Adapted from Glenn Collins, "Family: Both Cause of and Cure for Stress," *The New York Times* (June 9, 1986), p. Y15. Copyright © 1986 by The New York Times Company. Reprinted by permission.

Strategies for Successful Family Survival

Since the publication of the early foundational works on the two-career family by Rhona and Robert Rapoport (1971) and Lynda Lytle Holmstrom (1973), four strategies have emerged for coping with the role overload and stress inherent in dual-career families. These strategies are role sharing, role cycling, role substitutes, and role disengagement.

In **role sharing** the couple rationally organizes and shares family role activities. In the case of the Johnsons, for example, Judy chauffeurs the children to and from day care, and Jim cooks the evening meal. Some couples divide role responsibilities on the basis of interests and talents, while others use a more traditional gender-based assignment.

The Johnson case oversimplifies this problem, however, because there is always more to be done than any two professional people can possibly accomplish in the hours before and after work. At one point my wife and I tried to implement this strategy in a rational and systematic manner. First we wrote every household task on an index card. Then we divided the cards into stacks based on the amount of time required to complete each task and how often the task had to be performed. Finally we took turns selecting cards from each pile until all the cards were gone. We tried this division of labor until we

Role sharing redefines traditional gender-specific behaviors within the home. Men may help out with cleaning or cooking; women may handle the household finances or maintenance. Many couples have found role sharing enjoyable, as it frees them to do the things they like and do well.

realized that a task needs to be done many times, but the person responsible is unavailable to perform his or her duty. Furthermore, over time new tasks must be added to the list of responsibilities, and occasionally the amount of time required for tasks changes with lifestyle changes. For example, there is more laundry to do when the size of the family increases, and moving from an apartment to a home requires more household maintenance.

A second strategy for handling role overload is **role cycling.** Role cycling is a modification on role sharing where responsibilities are reassigned in a more flexible manner. If a person experiences extra pressure at work, he or she is released from responsibilities at home and the spouse or other family members must taken on additional tasks. Jeylan Mortimer (1979:12) suggests that couples arrange their multiple roles in such a way that the peak demands of work and family do not occur simultaneously.

The problem with role cycling is similar to that of Murphy's Law—peak demands always occur simultaneously! Furthermore, since for most people their normal responsibilities are more than they can manage, how can they possibly take on additional work? It is this lack of flexibility that makes illness and work-related travel crisis events for two-career families.

The third strategy is **role substitution,** which involves hiring others to perform many of the functions traditionally fulfilled by husbands or wives. Examples of subcontracted services include day care or babysitting, laundry services, auto repair, house cleaning and painting, restaurant meals, convenience foods, and gardening services. The advantage of the role-substitution strategy is that it deals directly with the problem of role overload; and it is practical, because most dual-career families have enough money to make these services affordable. However, services of these types are often hard to secure. Many times, too, when families hire others to do what they believe to be their responsibility, they feel guilty (this is especially true of childcare). Another problem with hiring the services of others is that the costs of these services can make one of the careers only marginally beneficial.

The final strategy for successful family stress management is **role disengagement.** In this strategy the husband and wife attempt to lessen the role demands of both career and family. This may mean they will have fewer or no children; or they may live in a smaller house (requiring less maintenance) or in a townhouse or condominium where maintenance is provided. Two-career couples can also scale down professional activities, restrict work-related travel, become less competitive, and be satisfied with their present career status (possibly even turn down a promotion). In some careers, it is possible to become less than a full-time employee.

In attempting to balance family and work responsibilities, two-career couples generally have to employ one or more of these four strategies if they are to survive role overload and stress. They may also find it necessary to receive assistance from friends and family members.

As the reading below demonstrates, however, in the contemporary American family it is still the superwoman who manages the home.

Cooking and Cleaning Is Still Women's Work

Women may be knocking down the traditional divisions of labor on the job, but not at home. Most domestic duties remain women's work, even in households where both husband and wife work, says a recent Conference Board study of 5,000 families nationwide.

In 78 percent of the two-income families surveyed, the man of the house rarely cleans it and is even less likely to do the laundry, the report shows. In the kitchen, fewer than 30 percent of all men wash the dishes frequently and only 25 percent cook on a regular basis.

Male attitudes toward housework do not seem to be changing. Overall, the survey found men in their 20s and 30s only slightly more likely to help out around the house than older men.

Women, on the other hand, are performing traditionally male chores. Among the working wives surveyed, 48 percent regularly take out the garbage and 34 percent prepare the tax returns. However, the term "handyman" is still accurate. The study shows that fewer than 20 percent of all women do minor home repairs.

Source: Susan Dillingham in *Insight* (July 13, 1987), p. 44. Reprinted with permission from *Insight* magazine/author—Susan Dillingham.

Table 5.2, constructed from data provided by Joyce Beckett and Audrey Smith (1981), makes the point more graphically.

DAY CARE: A FAMILY CRISIS

According to Judy Goldsmith (cited by Hewlett 1986), the president of the National Organization for Women from 1982 to 1985, the top priorities for future agenda of the women's movement should be prenatal care, maternity benefits, job-protected parental leave, and high-

TABLE 5.2 Weekly Hours Worked in Tasks by Wife's Employment Status

	Wife not employed	*Wife employed*
Wife's hours of housework	35.1	25.0
Husband's hours of housework	2.4	4.5
Wife's hours of child care	17.7	9.8
Husband's hours of child care	4.1	5.3
Combined hours for wife	42.8	34.8
Combined hours for husband	6.5	9.8

Source: Joyce O. Beckett and Audrey D. Smith, "Work and Family Roles: Egalitarian Marriage in Black and White Families," *Social Service Review* 55 (June 1981), p. 321, table 3. Reprinted by permission of the University of Chicago Press.

quality child care. These issues are critical at this time because a majority of women are combining paid employment with parental responsibilities. This is creating a crisis in the United States: Over half of babies under one year of age have mothers in the workplace at a time when federal funds for day care assistance have been cut by 25 percent since 1980 (Hewlett 1986).

Day care is *the* crucial issue for working parents. Three major problems face parents related to the care of their children during work—cost, availability, and quality. The federal government is doing little to deal with these problems.

The actual cost for acceptable day care in the United States is between $75 and $100 per week per child. At this rate, parents working fifty weeks per year could spend as much as $10,000 on day care expenses for two children. A person working for $6.00 per hour would earn $10,500 for fifty weeks of work before taxes and work-related expenses.

If this were not bad enough, even when parents can afford child care, there is a tremendous shortage—and the quality of what is available is often poor. Waiting lists for quality centers are so long that some parents submit applications even before conception. There are no federal standards to protect the safety and well-being of children in day care. The government has not sought to provide incentives for providers and/or employers to establish more day care services throughout the country. Since President Nixon's veto of child-care legislation in 1971, there has been no federal action to increase the supply of day care, despite the fact that in 1990 approximately ten million children aged five or less need care outside of the home.

At the present time the only thing that the federal government is doing to assist parents is providing a tax credit for child and dependent care. The maximum amount of this credit is $1,400 for lower-income families (with two or more children and $4,800 of child care expenses) and $720 for higher-income families (with the same requirements for expenses and number of children).

Furthermore, the United States is the only modern industrialized country that does not guarantee a woman a leave of absence after she has given birth. *Time* (1987:60) lists the following parental benefits for other developed nations: (1) In Sweden both parents are guaranteed a one-year leave of absence after childbirth, and the mother can receive 90 percent of her income for the first six months. (2) In France mothers receive sixteen weeks of maternity leave and 84 percent of their salaries. (3) In Israel mothers are entitled to twelve weeks of paid leave and forty additional unpaid weeks. (4) In the Soviet Union women receive four months of fully paid maternity leave and 25 percent of salary for up to eight more months.

The reluctance of the U.S. government to become involved in assisting working parents reflects American ambivalence regarding the combination of motherhood with occupational roles. Many people feel that federal involvement in this area will encourage mothers to leave their young children. Some federal officials have even claimed that government-sponsored day care can lead to an Orwellian *1984*-style nightmare (*Time* 1987:56).

cathy®
by Cathy Guisewite

America is one of the least progressive of the developed countries in dealing with day care and maternity benefits for workers. (CATHY COPYRIGHT 1986 UNIVERSAL PRESS SYNDICATE. Reprinted with permission. All rights reserved.)

As a result of the U.S. government's unwillingness to guarantee a woman's employment after maternity and/or to require that employers provide some financial benefits for mothers of newborns, 53 percent of American mothers return to work within the first year of their child's life. Yet in a recent survey of 1,014 adult Americans (*Time* 1987:59), it was reported that the majority (over 50 percent) of men and women felt that businesses should offer day care for their employees and that the government should do more to provide day care nationally. Fifty-seven percent of these same respondents felt the present American day care situation is bad for children. Former Secretary of Labor William Brock laid the blame on industry, commenting that "we still act as though workers have no families. Labor and management haven't faced that adequately, or at all" (*Time* 1987:59).

In spite of the grim picture we are providing, there are some reasons for optimism. A *Wall Street Journal* article by Cathy Trost (1987) discussed ten major corporations that are providing child-related benefits for workers and are improving the working environment for parents. These employers believe that it is in the best interest of business to provide day care and maternity benefits for workers because these benefits reduce absenteeism and worker turnover. According to the *Time* (1987:60) survey, "Parents lose an average of eight days a year from work because of child-care problems and nearly 40 percent consider quitting."

The reading below describes what Merck and Company (manufacturer of pharmaceuticals) is doing for its employees.

Merck Wins Points with Responsiveness

Merck and Company repeatedly shows up on lists of good places for working women and parents. After studying employee attitudes regarding conflicts in working and parental roles, Merck has made many changes to improve the working conditions for women and parents.

The company offers both men and women unpaid parental leave of up to 18 months for preparation for childbirth and for care after the birth or adoption of a child. Seven years ago, Merck invested $100,000 to help establish a child-care center near its headquarters in New Jersey. Now, it is helping to build a new site to house the center and has provided support to a child-care center near one of its plants. Merck has also begun an awareness-training program for senior management, designed to help them better understand employees' family related needs, and provides workshops on family matters for all of its employees.

Other employee benefits provided by Merck include flexible hours, spouse-employment assistance and, particularly for those returning from maternity leave, limited part-time work and work-at-home options. A company study on productivity found that as a result of flexible work schedules, absenteeism and tardiness was decreased.

CONCLUSION

In considering gender roles within the family, we have emphasized the importance of social factors in creating differences between boys and girls, and men and women. Social expectations of family roles are also influenced by gender considerations. Yet gender expectations for men and women are changing, and this is affecting the relationships between family and the workplace.

In this chapter we have discussed television series as reflections of American images of the family. We have observed that while the parent-child relationship continues to be emphasized, current TV shows portray parents as having both working and family responsibilities and provide many structural models of the family. Yet I find it interesting that through the magic of syndication, my children have the opportunity to view the shows that were current when I was being raised—"Father Knows Best," "I Love Lucy," "Leave It to Beaver," and "Dennis the Menace." This fact provides us with further evidence of the plurality of American perspectives on gender roles and family structures.

As contemporary families attempt to cope with family- and work-related responsibilities, they will need to develop support structures for the lifestyles they choose to adopt. Extended family members and close friends (fictive kin) are valuable resources for men and women who will experience their families as both cause and cure for social stress.

CHAPTER
REVIEW

- Even though there are no well-established, reliable sex differences at birth on any measure related to behavior, research has demonstrated that parents, children, and others have different cultural expectations of male and female infants. Therefore, many researchers have concluded that it is the sex assignment at birth—and the consequent rearing and life histories of individuals—not genetic sex, which is of primary importance in sexual identity.

- In physical characteristics, the variation within each sex is always greater than the average difference between the sexes.
- The only four biological imperatives that differentiate women and men are menstruation, gestation, lactation, and impregnation. Only females are able to menstruate, give birth to infants, and breast-feed, while only males are able to impregnate females.
- In recent years women have greatly increased their participation in the labor force. Furthermore, at the present time, 53 percent of women with children one year old or younger are in the labor force.
- Today most women are employed, and for the same reasons that men choose to work—in order to help support their families, gain independence, demonstrate their personal creativity and competence, and achieve the societal rewards of wealth, power, and prestige.
- On the average, males earn approximately 30 percent more than female employees. Even if we control for occupation, seniority, and number of career interruptions, a gender gap in wages still exists.
- There is an inverse relationship between female labor force participation and birthrates. Currently, there is a trend for couples to have fewer or no children as a method of managing the responsibilities of career and family.
- Two-career couples with children must simultaneously juggle six commitments—marriage, children, career, house, friends, and community involvement. Surviving in a two-career family requires extraordinary energy, extreme dedication, and the ability to live with high stress.
- Dual-career couples may utilize any or all of four strategies to cope with role overload and stress—role sharing, role cycling, role substitution, and role disengagement.
- Three major problems face parents related to the care of their children during work—cost, availability, and quality. The federal government is doing little to deal with these problems.
- The United States is the only modern industrialized country not guaranteeing a woman a leave of absence after she has given birth. The reluctance of the U.S. government to become involved in assisting working parents reflects American ambivalence regarding the combination of motherhood with occupational roles.

DISCUSSION QUESTIONS

1. Why do you think most American couples prefer their first child to be male?
2. What four factors distinguish males from females on biological grounds? What does the following statement mean? "The variation within each sex is always greater than the average difference between the sexes."

3. Discuss the following as they relate to gender socialization: "looking-glass self-concept," "self-fulfilling prophecy," "labeling theory," and "the definition of the situation."
4. Interpret gender differences from one of the following theoretical perspectives: structural functional theory, exchange theory, or conflict theory.
5. If you wished to maximize the differences between two children (one a boy and the other a girl), what would you do?
6. Should the United States try to equalize pay for men and women? What might be done to bring this about? What are the benefits of perpetuating the gender gap in wages?
7. If you were to marry in the future, would you wish to have a two-career family? Why or why not?
8. How would you deal with the stress and role overload of the two-career family lifestyle?
9. Why are so many American married women working? Why are there so many working mothers? Should the government encourage or discourage this trend?
10. Why would couples decide to be childless? Have you ever considered this option? What would be the advantages and disadvantages of childlessness?
11. Is it possible to have it all—family, career, house, friends, and community involvement? If not, what compromises would you make regarding these goals?
12. How involved are American men in the tasks of child care and housework? Do you expect that men will change their behavior around the house?
13. What should the government and industry do (if anything) to help solve the day care crisis in America?

GLOSSARY

career: Occupation that requires extensive professional training and education, a high degree of personal commitment to work long hours, and a willingness to compete with fellow workers to progress from lower to higher levels of responsibility and rewards.

gender roles: Differential social expectations of behavior determined by the sex of the individual.

role cycling: Husbands and wives have a flexible assignment of responsibilities within the home—the one with the least pressing career demands performs more household tasks. As career demands change, roles are reassigned.

role disengagement: Couples attempt to lessen role demands made by both career and family. Having no children or fewer children is an example of role disengagement.

role sharing: Couples divide household and child care responsibilities in an equitable manner.

role substitution: Couples hire others to perform many of the tasks normally performed by family members. Day care and house cleaning are two examples of role substitution.

sex differences: Differences between males and females caused by biological or genetic factors.

two-career family: A family where both the husband and wife have professional occupations.

two-person career: A career that takes two people to meet the demands of the occupation. The ministry is one traditional example of a two-person career.

SUGGESTED READINGS

Filene, Peter G. 1986. *Him/Her/Self: Sex Roles in Modern America*. Baltimore: Johns Hopkins University Press.

Lott, Bernice. 1987. *Women's Lives: Themes and Variations in Gender Learning*. Monterey, Calif.: Brooks/Cole Publishing Company.
Two excellent books dealing with men's and women's roles in contemporary society. Distinctions are made between sex differences and gender roles.

Gerson, Kathleen. 1985. *Hard Choices*. Berkeley: University of California Press. *This book is concerned with the role conflicts created by commitments to occupational and family roles.*

Kimball, Gayle. 1983. *The 50-50 Marriage*. Boston: Beacon Press. *A qualitative study of 150 traditional and egalitarian couples dealing with issues of employment, child care, housework, romance, sexuality, and family values.*

Rossi, Alice S., 1984. "Gender and Parenthood." *American Sociological Review* 49 (February); 1–19. *This article reviews gender differences in parenting as reflected in recent research on solo fathering and mothering, nontraditional family arrangements, and egalitarian marriages that show significant paternal involvement in childrearing. It also assesses the adequacy of current social explanations of gender differences in parenting.*

Subcultural Variations: Ethnicity and Families

◆ *Variety's the very spice of life,*
*That gives it all its flavour.**

While the United States is sometimes referred to as a "melting pot" nation where numerous **ethnic groups** (groups with different cultural heritages) have come together and assimilated, the fact of the matter is that the "melting" is far from complete. The ethnic identity of numerous groups today differs from that of their forebears, but present groups still retain elements of the old merged with new influences from their experiences in the United States. One of the exciting aspects of American family life is the high degree of diversity found in it. In addition to cultural heritage, racial background and religion are important in distinguishing distinct subgroups in American society. If variety is "the very spice of life," American families have contributed much spice to the American way of life.

What is of significance for an ethnic group is that the people with a particular ethnic identification think of themselves as sharing special bonds of history, culture, and kinship with others. For example, several million Americans are descendants of persons who migrated here from Sweden. Some like Swedish food, others do not. Some are Lutherans, others are not. It is the sentiment of shared culture binding these families into solidarity that is of importance (Hechter 1974).

The many ethnic families in the United States today can often be found clustered in pockets in cities and small communities across

---

*William Cowper, *The Task*, ii, 606 (1784).

the country. Ethnic communities provide individuals with congenial associates, help organize experience by personalizing an increasingly impersonal world, and provide opportunities for social mobility and success within an ethnic context (Greeley 1969:30). Families often maintain their ethnicity through preservation of the native language, religious institutions, and cultural traditions brought over from the "old country." These ethnic customs are of value to families who are interested in learning about and continuing their "roots."

This chapter addresses diversity in American families based on national, cultural, religious, and racial identification. These differences are embedded in ethnic groups. Identification with, and membership in, an ethnic group has far-reaching effects on both groups and individuals. Participation in an ethnic group offers many people access to opportunities in life, feelings of well-being, and influence over the futures of their children (Mindel and Habenstein 1976).

This chapter will not attempt to discuss all the ethnic groups represented among American families today; the range is too vast. Instead, we'll focus on a few groups to give an idea of the **cultural heterogeneity,** or diversity, of contemporary American families. The groups we have chosen come from different geographical regions of the world and from a rather wide spectrum of distinguishable groups. These groups also make up some of the largest ethnic populations found in the United States today. Many Americans, while they may trace descent to foreign nations such as Germany and England, do not retain much of an Old World cultural heritage. It is difficult to distinguish their lifestyles from others. In contrast, the ethnic groups we will investigate continue to express their ethnicity through family relationships. These groups include black American families, Jewish American families, Mexican American families, Italian American families, Chinese American families, and Japanese American families.

BLACK AMERICAN FAMILIES

Over two decades ago, Senator Daniel P. Moynihan (1965) issued a government document, based on the 1960 census, which concluded that the black family in the United States was falling apart and failing to prepare black children to make their way in the world. Moynihan's report was refuted by social scientists (Billingsley 1968:199—201); over the succeeding years the report has also been misinterpreted many times. Nevertheless, Moynihan's study reached a wide audience and certainly gave the black family in the United States a negative image.

From what we know of the original African families from which many black Americans came, they were the epitome of family sta-

This father's efforts to improve his sons' performance at the track show pride and a belief in hard work—values his sons will hold long after the track meet.

bility, displaying caring, reciprocity, solidarity, and sharing. Large kinship groups were concerned with the success of marriages and took a vested interest in family relationships. Males maintained a dominant position within these families, and the family system was characterized by orderliness and continuity (Scanzoni 1971:5).

Centuries of slavery, however, had an impact on family life among American blacks. Southern slave laws allowed for husbands/fathers to be sold away from their families, but mothers could not be separated from their children. Thus, it was often difficult for black men to establish, maintain, and protect family ties. Though slavery is officially over, black people have never been compensated economically, politically, socially, or psychologically for two centuries of bondage (Billingsley 1968:69–71). For thousands of blacks, emancipation meant the freedom to die of starvation and illness. Emancipation had some advantages for black families, however: Family members could not be sold away from their families and marriages were legalized and recorded.

Contemporary studies of American families (Hill 1972; Gary 1983) report that many blacks have a strong work achievement and religious orientation, believe firmly in the institution of the family, and find their greatest source of life satisfaction in family life. However, as Robert Staples (1978:13) suggests, as with white families, no single type of black family can be used as a model of all black families in existence in the United States today. And when we look at black families and marriages, we are likely to focus primarily on lower-class families rather than on black families as a whole, since there is a strong relationship between poverty and the specific patterns of family structure that are notable in this ethnic group.

Social Class

As we shall discuss further in Chapter 7, social class variations in American families contribute significantly to cultural heterogeneity. Charles Willie (1985:271) compares black and white families in the United States by social class. Willie notes that black and white middle-class families are similarly affluent and contribute service to the community and society. Their patterns of consumption of goods and services are almost identical. They differ, however, in their goals, aspirations, and interactions with family members.

Willie (1985:274) notes that probably the greatest difference between black and white families in the middle class is the role of the wife and mother. All the women in middle-class black families in his study are in the labor force. Their income is essential in maintaining their families' style of living. Like their white middle-class counterparts, black middle-class women have renounced matriarchal authority within the family and invited their husbands to share more fully in child care and household management.

How to sacrifice in behalf of others is the common wisdom of working-class blacks and whites (Willie 1985:276–78). Parents in both groups labor long to earn sufficient income to provide adequately for their families. Their goal is for their children to have a life easier than their own. Black and white working-class parents have similar educations and aspirations for the education of their children, and they perform similar work. Black and white working-class families are very much alike in their structure and in their lack of community participation. Willie reported that most working-class blacks believe that they have to work twice as hard to make it "in a white world." Overall, however, Willie concludes that black and white working-class families have more similarities than differences.

In comparing black and white poor families, Willie (1985:279–81) found both similarities and differences in lifestyles. They both suffer much. Poor whites emphasize the value of the group and the responsibility of the individual to the collectivity; poor blacks emphasize the value of the individual and the responsibility of the collectivity for the individual. Educational attainment in the two groups is similar, the majority not having completed high school. While the black poor blame their poverty on an unjust society, the white poor blame their situation on personal inadequacy and bad luck. The two groups also differ in their attitudes about life. Poor whites experience despair of things ever changing and a sense of resignation, while poor blacks have hope for a better life and a sense of resistance and even rebellion.

As discussed in Chapter 3, exchange theory argues that people will continue to do what they have found rewarding in the past and will discontinue behaviors perceived to be too costly. Almost half of black Americans are not married or living in traditional **nuclear family** units. Robert Staples (1985:1005) argues that this situation predominates among poor blacks and results in part from the perceived outcome of marriage, a perception derived from knowledge of past rewards and costs. Among many blacks alternative arrangements are preferred risks.

Carol Stack (1974:117) observed that the lack of employment opportunities for the urban poor and the unlikeliness of a livable guaranteed minimum income make it very difficult for urban low-income blacks to form lasting conjugal units. Furthermore, even if a man and woman set up temporary housekeeping arrangements, they continue to maintain strong social ties with their kin. Kin regard any marriage both as a risk to the woman and her children and as a threat to the durability of the kin groups. The emphasis on the extended family among blacks, then, creates a situation where relationships with kin are more stable than conjugal relationships. (The opposite tends to be true of white families.) From an exchange theory perspective, therefore, the "rewards" for poor blacks are greater in consanguine relationships than in conjugal ties. Thus, as Staples noted, blacks are less likely to live in traditional nuclear family relationships.

Female-headed Families

A striking change in the black family during the past three decades has been the increase in the number of female-headed households. Jacqueline Jones (1985:305–6) states that the percentage of black households headed by a woman grew from 18 percent in 1950 to 28 percent in 1970 to 40 percent in 1980. Comparable figures for white households were 9, 11, and 15 percent.

Limited educational and career options, weighed against the appeal of bearing a child, have helped bring about this increase in female-headed households. A welfare system (Aid to Families of Dependent Children, or AFDC) that formerly required men to be absent from the home is another reason for a high number of female-headed households. (AFDC requirements no longer, however, penalize households with husbands present.) Black women realize that even meager welfare payments may be more reliable than a man who cannot get gainful employment, and this fact makes it difficult for an unemployed black man to compete with a woman's kin for authority and for control over her children (Staples 1985:1009; Stack 1974:118). Therefore, the extended kin network plays an important role in many black families, giving support to female-headed households.

These factors explain the 1985 finding (U.S. Bureau of the Census) that, as shown by numerous demographic and economic indicators, poverty has been both ghettoized and feminized. Thirty-one percent of blacks (67 percent of them in female-headed families) fall below the poverty line, while only 11 percent of whites are poor. Fifty-five percent of all black babies are born to unmarried women, many of them teenagers. According to Jacqueline Jones (1985:277), many of these single women are in effect wedded to a mean-spirited provider, the welfare bureaucracy, and they chafe under the dependency enforced by this "supersexist marriage." Yet though more black babies than white babies are born to unmarried mothers, the proportion is declining for black women, while it is increasing for white women.

Marriage

There seem to be too few black males to go around in the marriage arena. Robert Staples (1985:1007) suggests that, since there are more black males than females at birth, the apparent shortage of black males over the age of fourteen may result from a higher infant mortality rate and a significantly greater mortality rate caused by homicide, accidents, suicide, and drug overdose among very young blacks. The "supply problem" may also be a problem of quality rather than quantity. Black women may select a mate partly on the basis of gainful and regular employment, but middle-class black males marry to a disproportionate extent outside their ethnic group, thus contributing to the shortage of marriageable black males.

A greater proportion of black marriages than white end in divorce, and black women who divorce are less likely than their white counterparts to remarry. Andrew Cherlin (1981) observes that a number of social characteristics contribute to this high divorce rate. Blacks have a higher rate of urbanization, an earlier age at marriage, an earlier age for giving birth, a higher education and income level for the wife, and a lower income status for the husband.

Changes in Black Families

As cited earlier, the Moynihan report of 1965 presented a pessimistic view of the black family. Robert Staples (1985:1011) comments that social scientists continue to view the deterioration of the black family as the problem when, in reality, the reason for the negative outlook for the black family is the structural conditions that prevent the fulfillment of black family ideals.

In addition, Carol Stack (1974:122–23) writes that many single-parent female-headed households have been noted among low-income blacks but that these statistics do not accurately reveal patterns of domestic organization. Households have shifting membership but on the average maintain a steady state of three generations of kin: males and females beyond childbearing age, a middle generation of mothers raising their own children or children of close kin, and the children. Such an **extended family** helps provide stability for low-income black families; such a kin support is typically lacking in white middle-class families today.

Marriages Between Races Have Doubled Since 1968

The number of interracial marriages in the United States has doubled in the years since the Supreme Court ruling that invalidated laws against such unions. Marriages between people of different races totaled 18,853 in 1980, or about 1.9 percent of all marriages in the United States, according to the National Center for Health Statistics. Although that is still a very small share of all weddings, it is more than twice the 0.7 percent recorded in 1968, the year after the Supreme Court threw out state laws against miscegenation. At the time about twenty states had such laws. The most common interracial marriages involve white brides and black grooms. They accounted for about 0.5 percent of all marriages in 1980, up from 0.2 percent in 1968.

White brides with Asian or other nonwhite grooms, excluding blacks, accounted for 0.4 percent of marriages in 1980, about the same as white grooms with Asian or other nonwhite brides, excluding blacks. Both those shares were doubled from 1968. Black brides with white grooms totaled 0.2 percent of marriages in 1980, also twice the share of 1968. The number of blacks marrying nonwhites outside their race was too small to be evaluated statistically in either year.

Interracial marriages were more likely to be second or subsequent marriages than were marriages of partners of the same race. Brides and grooms marrying interracially were older than their counterparts marrying within their race.

Source: Adapted from Randolph E. Schmid in *Lexington Herald-Leader* (Lexington, KY. July 8, 1984) p. A13.

Though there are many similarities between middle-class black and white families in the United States, as noted on the previous page, the "melting pot" phenomenon does not seem to include many intermarriages between the two groups. While the reading points out that marriages between racial groups have increased in recent years, overall, an insignificant number of individuals marry outside their racial group.

Large numbers of blacks, especially middle-class blacks, seem to be taking on values of the majority culture. Robert Frumkin (1954) found that a change in black family organization was taking place in the direction of "white norms and ideals." For example, George Dickinson (1975), in a longitudinal study of black and white adolescents over a decade, concluded that blacks' dating behavior was changing in the direction of whites' behavior. Thus, while frustrations may result for some black families, "the winds of change" will "continue to blow" (Powell 1973:46–47) for all American families.

JEWISH AMERICAN FAMILIES

Jewish families came to America from many countries. The majority of Jews in America are descended from those who emigrated from Russia, Poland, and other Eastern European countries in the last two decades of the nineteenth century and the first two decades of the twentieth century (Rischin 1987:15–19). Though most late-nineteenth-century Eastern European Jews were orthodox in religious practice, others were attracted to different forms.

Jewish Traits Brought to America

In Eastern Europe in the late 1800s, narrowing economic opportunity in the countryside and government decrees were forcing Jews from small towns into the larger urban centers, where the factory bell determined the pace of work. As a result of this migration, over half of all Eastern European Jews lived in urban areas by 1898 (Weinberg 1988:53). Thus, the traditional world of many Jews was beginning to give way before the forces of modernization. Despite the agitation and differences in background, however, a sense of a shared heritage, religion, and culture bound together the Jews of Eastern Europe. Gentile neighbors perceived Jews as different and sometimes discriminated against them, which often intensified their sense of solidarity.

In traditional Jewish society before the late nineteenth century marriage was seen as too important to be left to the young (Weinberg 1988:23). A man or a woman was considered incomplete without a spouse and children, and marriage was an essential arrangement involving mutual duties and obligations whose main purpose was raising a family. Betrothals were arranged by parents, usually with the assistance of a marriage broker, with romantic love playing no role in the process.

In the late nineteenth and early twentieth centuries, women were central to the Jewish family's emotional and economic well-being (Weinberg 1988:19—44). The mother performed the traditional female roles of keeping a family together (caring for children, cleaning, sewing, and tending to the religious atmosphere of the home); often, too, she might contribute to the family's living by working outside the home, if her husband was a scholar or made little money at his trade. The mother often made the important decisions in the family, although children were encouraged to view their father as the head of the family. From a young age, Jewish daughters were expected to take on serious responsibilities within the home and sometimes in the workplace. Education was valued highly in Jewish culture, and many women had absorbed a reverence for the written word. Middle-class women, while they rarely worked for others, frequently played an active role in their husbands' businesses. This somewhat differentiated Jewish women at that time from most European women, who had little secular life outside their families.

Living in America

Once Jewish immigrant families had arrived in America and made initial adjustments to new living and working conditions, the next important step was to become Americanized. The internal values and traditions of the Jews were almost tailor-made for success in the American economy. Jewish families coming to America brought with them strong family ties, a familiarity with urban conditions, commercial and industrial skills, and a tradition of women working outside the home.

Jews from Eastern Europe were very successful in the U.S. economy. Mark Hutter (1988:115) notes several possible explanations for this success. First, though Jews experienced considerable discrimination, the Jews were not treated as a separate caste group as blacks were and for the most part, therefore, could pursue whatever economic activities they chose. Second, they came to America with exceptionally strong backgrounds in skilled trades and entrepreneurial activity and were able to establish themselves rather quickly in America's expanding economy. Third, they took advantage of the educational opportunities offered in urban centers. Finally, job opportunities in chosen occupations awaited them upon graduation from high school and college.

Adjustments to America were not easy, however. Many a Jewish married woman had no desire to become Americanized and made the effort only because of a husband's insistence or a child's embarrassment at her foreign ways (Weinberg 1988:106–15). Most women eventually came to terms with the changes they found in America, however. Some Jewish men felt trapped by their inability to support their families and thus abused, divorced, or deserted their wives. The requirements of orthodox religion created major tensions between parents and children anxious to be "real Americans."

The high emphasis placed on the value of the family has been a major trait of the Jews in the United States. American Jews are the most successful of American major ethnic groups with regard to family planning and birth spacing (Farber, Mindel, and Lazerwitz 1976:359). Family size has been reduced drastically since the turn of the century. Reduction in the Jewish birthrate derives not only from effective use of contraceptives but also from American Jews' tendency to marry later in life then their European ancestors.

Family stability is evidenced by Jewish divorce rates. In comparing divorce rates by religious affiliation, data from seven U.S. national surveys (Glenn and Supancic 1984) revealed that marital dissolution is lower for Jews than for Catholics, who in turn have moderately lower rates than Protestants. The higher rates are for persons with no religion.

Solidarity seems to have been a mark of Jewish families throughout history. Jack Balswick (1966:167) reported a greater cohesiveness on the part of Jewish families than in other families. A decline in extended-family households has occurred in recent years, however, as families have moved to the suburbs and to the South and the Southwest (Farber, Mindel and Lazerwitz 1976:366).

As Jewish families moved to the suburbs after World War II, the wife, because of her increased duties and responsibilities within the family, became the modern matriarch of Jewish suburbia. Accordingly, the father began to lose his traditional priestly status in the family (Farber, Mindel, and Lazerwitz 1976:368).

Of the approximately 100,000 American Jews who marry each year, a third marry non-Jews (Volsky 1985). The Reform Jewish movement has sought to encourage conversion of Gentile spouses to Judaism, a move that has been criticized by Orthodox and Conserv-

The bat mitzvah (bar mitzvah for boys) is a traditional rite of passage celebrated in Jewish families as the child moves toward adulthood.

ative leaders as creating confusion about who is a Jew. It is estimated that the number of conversions to Judaism is more than 10,000 annually. Conversion in interfaith marriages is important because the children tend to be reared as Jews and the family identifies itself as Jewish. In marriages where the non-Jew does not convert, the children are less likely to gravitate to the Jewish faith, and the family is less likely to maintain Jewish traditions.

In a study of 309 people married to Jews (Volsky 1985), converts report that their parents accept their Jewish spouses more readily than their Jewish in-laws accept them, even though the in-laws urged them to convert. Most converts find it easy to fit into Jewish circles. Most also believe that people born Jews neither fully understand the feelings of converts nor accept them without reservation into the Jewish fold.

Jews seem proud of their history. A survey of 900 Soviet Jewish refugees in fourteen cities in the United States (Simon 1985:31–32) showed that 90 percent would prefer being Jewish, if they had the choice. Reasons cited for this response were: "proud of their Jewish heritage," admiration for Jewish ethics and values, and the belief that Jews contributed a great deal to world cultures and knowledge. Just as the family is pivotal in Jewish tradition, being Jewish is often a source of strength and cohesiveness in Jewish American families.

MEXICAN AMERICAN FAMILIES

The culture of Mexican Americans goes back to Spain; they are both Spanish and Indian in ancestry. Almost nine million persons of Mexican origin or descent live in the United States today, making them the second-largest minority group in the country (Leslie and Korman 1985:281).

Mexicans were living in the area that is now California, Arizona, New Mexico, and Texas when these states were incorporated into the Union. Thus, rather than becoming a part of the United States through immigration, the first Mexican Americans joined through annexation. But although this southwestern geographical region had settlements of Mexican families long before the Americans arrived, most Mexican Americans came into the United States in the twentieth century (Corwin 1973:571). And today Mexican Americans are one of the fastest-growing ethnic groups in the United States population.

Nineteenth-Century Family Patterns

Joan Moore (1976) observed that in the nineteenth century rather different social patterns existed among Mexican American families in different regions. In Texas, for example, cattle ranching dominated the economy for many years; but when land ownership, rather than cattle, became the key to prosperity and power, the Mexicans became a depressed class working for the Anglos.

In New Mexico the situation was different. With relatively few Anglos, Spanish-speaking ranchers both dominated the economy and controlled the legislature. Intermarriage between Mexican and Anglo families occurred frequently, and relative harmony existed.

The population of Spanish-speaking residents in what is now Arizona was controlled by the Anglos in the middle of the nineteenth century, as the Anglos operated the mines and used the Mexicans to work them. Discrimination against the Mexican workers was more drastic than in Texas or New Mexico.

Being more geographically isolated in California, wealthy and powerful Mexican families dominated the central and southern part of the state. The discovery of gold, however, changed the situation significantly, as Anglo and Mexican miners arrived in large numbers. The elite culture of the wealthy families clashed with the aggressive ways of the miners, and the Anglo miners made no distinctions in their hatred between working-class Mexican miners and wealthy Mexican landowners.

Twentieth-Century Family Patterns

As this brief background survey might suggest, Mexican American family patterns today vary widely from one geographical area to another (Leslie and Korman 1985:283). Families in California tend to be more completely assimilated than are families in Texas. The more rural the Texas environment, the more traditional is the family system. And in Colorado and New Mexico, some old-family Mexican Americans show virtually no tendencies toward assimilation.

Many Mexican immigrants have found work as outdoor manual laborers. Growing up as a child in northeastern Texas, I remember large truckloads of Mexican American families traveling through the state picking cotton and then going to the North to work other fields there. Whether the temperature was over a hundred degrees in the shade or torrential downpours of rain were occurring, these trucks with uncovered beds rolled along with Mexican American families jammed into them like sardines in a can. At that time no laws existed to protect these migrant families from the inhumane conditions in which they were transported.

For Mexican American families who are migratory farm workers, educational opportunities for children are often less than desirable. Tracking the children's academic progress is not very reliable in many states, and the families' temporary residence in communities makes it difficult to place students in appropriate courses.

The extended family is a strong tradition among Mexican Americans. Close relationships go beyond the nuclear family to include aunts, uncles, grandparents, cousins, and in-laws. In this extended family, members sustain each other in attaining goals that might otherwise be very difficult to achieve (Alvirez and Bean 1976:277–78). Mutual obligations strengthen the relationship of the entire extended family both as a symbol of cohesiveness and because the members need each other, notes Ruth Horowitz (1983:56) in her study of an inner-city Mexican American community in Chicago. She observes that the exchange of economic and personal services is frequently necessary, since these families rarely turn to outside agencies like public welfare or public employment. Among the Mexican Americans in Horowitz's study, such outside help is regarded as a failure of a family's solidarity and as a sign of diminished social worth.

Early in life children are assigned responsibilities necessary for the welfare of the family. Since children are expected to get along with each other, with the older taking care of the younger and brothers protecting the sisters, there is probably less sibling rivalry in these homes than in Anglo homes (Alvirez and Bean 1976:279). The sibling relationships that develop are often more important than parent-child relationships—a very different pattern from that in Anglo

Traditionally, strong ties exist among siblings in Mexican American families, often more so than between parents and children.

homes. Older people tend to receive more respect from youth and children than is generally characteristic in Anglo homes. The majority of Mexican Americans live in families with both parents present.

Ruth Horowitz (1983) concludes that a strong network of intergenerational ties fosters traditional gender-role relationships in the family—male domination, motherhood, daughters' virginity, and respect of older people. These symbols of family life provide order and stability for everyday social interactions in the context of a highly industrialized and educated urban community.

In adapting to new situations and opportunities, however, the internal structure of the Mexican American family has changed. As the Mexican American family becomes subjected to many different social forces and situations, with some families clinging to the old rural ways and others acquiring new urban ways, it is certain that it will become increasingly difficult to speak of "the" Mexican American family.

ITALIAN AMERICAN FAMILIES

The first major wave of Italian immigrants to arrive in the United States came from northern Italy in the 1870s. In the early 1900s over five million Italians came, the majority from southern Italy. These southern Italians were largely of the peasant class of farmers and day laborers, possessed a willingness to work, and were basically illiterate and unskilled (Femminella and Quadagno 1976:64, 70).

Family Life in Italy

In Italy, each member of the nuclear family had his or her own special functions or responsibilities (Nelli 1983:132). Italian families were patriarchal in that the father was the head of the family, held the highest status, and was responsible for making a living. The typical father was highly authoritarian and a strict disciplinarian, customarily using verbal and physical punishment to control the children. In many families, the father's control was based on fear inculcated in the family members; positive reinforcement tended to be doled out sparingly.

The mother, on the other hand, was the center of the family and had a strong voice in important family decisions (Nelli 1983:132–33). She had primary responsibility for raising the children and mediating between them and the father. She ruled the house, though only at the direction of her husband. The wife usually enjoyed the respect and admiration of all family members. Typically, as the parents aged and the father's authority declined, the prestige of the mother increased.

Italian parents expected respect and obedience from children, who assumed responsibilities at an early age. When the children were ready for marriage, they were expected to accept a mate chosen by the parents. Romantic love played little if any part in the selection of a mate—marriage represented the union of two families as well as of two individuals (Nelli 1983:134). Yet the major social unit remained the nuclear family. Since a person derived his or her personal identity from the family, and family membership was essential in terms of defining each individual's place in society, the most shameful condition was to be without a family. Work was highly regarded and showed that one had become a man or woman—a contributing family member (Giambino 1974:31, 80).

Family Life in the United States

Italian immigrants recreated their village life in the United States as much as possible, a practice that often resulted in a distrust of strangers. Since they were highly **endogamous** and married within the Italian group, assimilation into the American society was slow (Gans 1962:35). Religion was not a strong competitor for the loyalty of these Italian immigrants, though most were Catholics in affiliation.

Italian American families experienced problems similar to those of other emigrants when the children expressed their acquired American expectations and attempted to transmit them in the family situation, while parents attempted to reinforce the patterns of the Old world (Nelli 1983:136–37). The father no longer inspired awe. He was more likely to be loved than feared, since the children had gained a degree of independence undreamed of in Italy. As the children learned English, family roles began to alter. The children—not the parents—better understood the world in which they lived. Children thus gained a voice in family affairs.

In her research on Italian American families, Colleen Johnson (1985:183) concluded that Italian American parents differed significantly from non-Italians interviewed. With their teenage children, they were more likely to extend a higher level of nurturance, to use stricter discipline techniques, and to delay or discourage independence from family. These parents in turn tended to satisfy the needs of their elderly parents.

Work, not education, was for the average Italian more than a basic necessity—it was also the major source of respect (Johnson 1985:35). If a choice had to be made between a mother or a child working, family goals dictated that it be the child, since the mother played a far more central role in the maintenance of family integrity. Schools were not necessarily rejected, work simply had more meaning. Early generations of Italian Americans put much of their energy into labor union activities. Though traditionally Italian women had not worked much outside the home, many first- and second-generation Italian American women found that work was necessary for family survival in the United States (Femminella and Quadagno 1976:71).

Though the Roman Catholic church influences the divorce rate and fertility among Italian families, stability is suggested by Italian Americans' low divorce rates. As for family size, impoverished Italian immigrant women had exceptionally large families, but their second-generation daughters and subsequent generations have reversed this pattern. Richard Giambino (1974:163–64) explains this intergenerational difference in fertility by suggesting that large families resulted from the fact that traditional Italian couples did not use birth control; Giambino also points out that several children were an asset to a family in southern Italy.

As the years went by, Italian Americans began to place a higher value on education. Second-generation Italian families began to adjust to American ways, though not at the expense of repudiating all parental ties. The extended family took on a greater importance than it had with first-generation Italians. By the 1940s, the second-generation Italian family had oriented itself "increasingly toward an American way of life" (Nelli 1983:150).

CHINESE AMERICAN FAMILIES

In the nineteenth century many Chinese came to the United States as contract laborers and worked in gangs under the supervision of a fellow countryman, as they were unfamiliar with the language and culture of the United States. Chinese laborers worked hard in agriculture, railroad building, and other taxing physical labor; they played a significant role in extending railroads to the western United States. In addition, they worked cheaply and lived frugally—virtues that made the Chinese feared and hated as competitors by white workers (Sowell 1981:136).

The institution of family among the Chinese has traditionally been held in high esteem. An old Chinese saying that a man should marry a spouse whose front door faces his own indicates the traditional emphasis on **homogamy,** or marrying one's own kind (Huang 1976:128). But although it is leveling off today, an imbalance of the sexes existed for decades among Chinese Americans (twenty-seven males for every woman in 1890). This imbalance resulted from the fact that initially only Chinese males came to the United States; to compound the problem, the Chinese Exclusion Act of 1882 curtailed Chinese immigration to this country. Thus, a people historically dedicated to the family had only limited opportunities to have families in the United States.

The Chinese generally disapprove of divorce, which has traditionally been viewed as a great shame and tragedy. Consequently, the divorce rate is relatively low in Chinese American families. Younger generations born in the United States, however, may not be as conservative in their views as their foreign-born parents (Huang 1976:133).

Chinese children are raised among adults in the extended family and are seldom left at home with baby-sitters. Chinese child-rearing customs stress control of aggression, resulting in a passive-oriented people. Parents and grandparents encourage children not to defend themselves but to give in during a quarrel (Huang 1976:134).

Chinese Americans value education highly. Parents consider education to be one of the most important symbols of success and to be a channel for upward social mobility (Huang 1976:137). According to Olga Lang (1968:337), college education has been the most potent medium of westernization of the Chinese family. While Chinese Americans as a group are prosperous and well educated today, Chinatowns remain pockets of poverty. Overall, however, Chinese Americans have overcome tough odds in integrating into American society both occupationally and residentially, while at the same time retaining their own ethnic ways.

JAPANESE AMERICAN FAMILIES

The family system of traditional Japan was a strong, stable, extended one. Unlike other migrants, Japanese coming to the United States were mostly middle-class people with some formal education and experience in the ownership and management of land (Vogel 1963). Despite early experiences of discrimination, by the 1970s Japanese American families were considered one of America's most "successful" ethnic groups (Hutter 1988:127). This success was due in part to the compatibility of American and Japanese values. Traditionally, the Japanese value diligence, commitment to long-term goals, respect for authority and parental wishes, politeness, keeping up appearances, social sensitivity, and suppression of desires and emotions.

Emigration from Japan to the United States began in the late nineteenth century. Employers initially welcomed Japanese to work as agricultural laborers and in other strenuous laboring jobs. The Japanese worked hard for low pay and without complaining. Their virtues of thrift and industry eventually turned some Americans against them. In addition, the early Japanese family in the United States faced many difficulties—the stresses of adaptation to a new land, crowded and inferior housing, poverty, and little expectation of immediate social change (Kitano 1969:64).

The placing of Japanese in "relocation camps" for their "protection" after the bombing of Pearl Harbor displayed some of the hatred and jealousy held by some Americans toward the Japanese. Economic factors continued to operate in prejudice against the Japanese in the period of their "relocation" from the West Coast during World War II. Gradually, however, from 1943 on, residents of the relocation centers were allowed to leave, to attend college, to accept jobs, and to enter the armed services. After the war, 80 percent of Japanese American families returned to the West Coast (Simpson and Yinger 1965:93–94). Many families had been split when older sons and daughters left the centers and the first-generation parents and younger children remained behind. Within two years after the centers were closed, however, Japanese Americans again made substantial progress toward making a stable place for themselves on the West Coast.

In the traditional Japanese family interaction was based on clearly prescribed roles, duties, and responsibilities, rather than on Western-style sentiments (Kitano 1969:66). Marriage, for example, was generally arranged for the couple, not based on romantic love. In the rearing of children, the more typical American ideal of maintaining social control through love and affection was secondary to an appeal to duty and obligation. This more impersonal type of interaction may have helped the Japanese to fit into social structures such as bureaucracies with less difficulty than many other Americans. In an urbanized and industrialized society where efficiency is sought, an impersonal orientation would be an asset toward adjustment.

One goal in the socialization of Japanese children is to establish a dependency on the family and to reinforce the mutual responsibility and reciprocity accompanying dependent relationships. An ultimate weapon used by Japanese parents to encourage children to behave is the threat of banishment from the family circle. This traditional push for dependency, when contrasted with the stress on independence for children in the United States, is often a source of conflict in Japanese American families (Kitano and Kikumura 1976:52). Socialization into the Japanese culture also cultivates the art of deflection and the avoidance of direct confrontation.

Current dating and marriage patterns suggest a high proportion of **out-group** (outside of individuals' own group) interaction. Before the 1960s, however, Japanese American marriages were primarily within the ethnic group (Kitano and Kikumura 1976:51). The extended family remains especially important for young families. As the children grow older, they tend to break away from the family (as is true in most groups in the United States), but family unity continues to be reaffirmed during holidays and anniversaries.

A survey of Japanese American families today by Harry Kitano and Akemi Kikumura (1976:57–59) notes an intact family structure with low divorce rates. Many stereotypical qualities often attributed

Solidarity is characteristic of Japanese American families.

to the Japanese seem to have some validity: quietness, conformity, loyalty, diligence, maximum effort, good citizenship, high academic achievement, and group orientation. As with other ethnic families discussed above, however, there is no one Japanese American culture. Japanese families in the United States differed from each other to begin with, and their stay in the United States has been one of many influences leading to further change.

THE SPICE OF LIFE

As this overview of families in six ethnic groups indicates, American families certainly represent "the very spice of life," if that is what variety is all about. Indeed, many subcultural variations of families constitute the U.S. population. Though all of these ethnic groups maintain varying degrees of cultural identity, they "blend" enough to exist in a rather cooperative manner in a large heterogeneous society.

Initially, the ethnic family of the mid- and late-nineteenth-century United States represented a transplanted, adaptive, primary social unit engaged in the business of conserving and rebuilding ethnic culture and, through its distinctive socialization process, of creating new generations in the image of the old. In the ethnic family's typical form are found the patterning of structural characteristics, the operation of distinctive principles of organization, and a set of discernible functions (Mindel and Habenstein 1976:415). Families and kin tend to generate ethnic neighborhoods, which become known as collective refuges and, along with kinship ties, attract fellow immigrants.

Each of the ethnic family types described in this chapter has its distinctive social biography. Some common threads, however, run throughout these six ethnic groups (Mindel and Habenstein 1976:413–28). Ethnic families in America are no longer transplanted social entities but have become integral to a distinctive type of **pluralist,** or many-cultured, society whose internal differences are more likely to be homegrown than imported. The modern ethnic family remains to a considerable extent place-centered. Extended family organization continues to remain important both as a backup system of social support and as a resource for services, sponsorship, and financial assistance.

Many of the above-cited groups have managed to survive in spite of the ways they were initially treated. Though adjustments to this new land were difficult for most, they managed to adapt to a new environment and yet maintain some of the "old country" within their family structure. With a common language being acquired by most and with monogamy being the prescribed marriage rule, this subcultural mix of American families makes for an interesting "brew."

When we compare and contrast cultures everywhere, the similarities between groups seem to be greater than the differences. Among American ethnic families, too, there are many overlapping traits. Still, differences exist; and distinctive ethnic traits contribute to the uniquely pluralistic society that is the United States today.

CHAPTER REVIEW

- Families in a particular ethnic group think of themselves as sharing special bonds of history, culture, and kinship with others.
- Black Americans believe firmly in the institution of the family and find their greatest source of satisfaction in family life, according to contemporary studies of American families.
- Female-headed black households have grown extremely rapidly since 1950.
- Interracial marriages have doubled since the Supreme Court abolished state laws against miscegenation in 1967, but interracial marriages still make up only approximately 2 percent of all marriages in the United States.
- Family solidarity has historically been a mark of Jewish families.
- Rather than migrating to the United States like other ethnic groups, most Mexican American families became U.S. citizens through annexation. Mexican Americans are currently one of the fastest-growing ethnic groups in the United States.
- Assimilation into the American society was slow for Italian families, in part because they reestablished their village life in the United States and somewhat isolated themselves.
- Chinese American families have overcome tough odds in integrating into American society occupationally and residentially while retaining their own ethnic ways.
- Japanese families migrating to the United States beginning in the late nineteenth century were mostly middle-class and had some formal education and experience in the ownership and management of land.
- Many ethnic families have managed to survive in spite of the ways they were initially treated in the United States.

DISCUSSION QUESTIONS

1. Discuss why the "melting pot" has not fully occurred in the United States.
2. Why is there no such thing as "the" black American family?
3. How are different types of black American families similar to other family groups discussed here?

4. Why have Jewish American families been so economically successful in the United States?
5. Discuss some of the strengths of Mexican American families.
6. Discuss family stability among Italian American families.
7. List some of the obstacles Chinese American families had to overcome to survive in the United States.
8. How are Japanese American families like and unlike other American families?

GLOSSARY

cultural heterogeneity: Differences in cultural traits such as religion, educational status, political views, and socioeconomic status.

endogamous: Married to someone with similar social background characteristics. Endogamous marriages are formed when marriage partners are of the same social group (socioeconomic class, for example).

ethnic group: A group distinguished by customs, characteristics, common history, and language.

extended family: A family that includes more than two generations of family members living together.

homogamy: Marriage of persons having similar background characteristics.

out-group: A social group with which individuals do not identify and toward which they feel a sense of competition.

pluralist: Including many different groups with varying racial, cultural, and religious heritages.

SUGGESTED READINGS

Daniels, Roger, and Harry H. L. Kitano. 1970. *American Racism.* Englewood Cliffs, N.J.: Prentice-Hall. *An account of ethnic crises in the United States through an exploration of the nature of prejudice.*

Kephart, William H. 1982. *Extraordinary Groups.* 2d ed. New York: St. Martin's Press. *An interesting account of seven "extraordinary" groups, some of which are not well known in the United States.*

Jones, Jacqueline. 1985. *Labor of Love, Labor of Sorrow: Black Women, Work, and the Family from Slavery to the Present.* New York: Basic Books. *A well-written book describing the work and family life of women whose foremothers were brought to this country in chains as slaves.*

Mindel, Charles H., Robert W. Habenstein, and Roosevelt Wright, Jr. 1988. *Ethnic Families in America.* 3d ed. New York: Elsevier. *An excellent anthology describing ethnic families in the United States.*

Weinberg, Sydney Stahl. 1988. *The World of Our Mothers: The Lives of Jewish Immigrant Women.* Chapel Hill, N.C.: The University of North Carolina Press. *A most interesting book about Jewish women coming to the United States.*

Social Class and Families

◆ *All animals are equal, but some animals are more equal than others.* *

While raising chickens as a small child, I often observed that the chickens pecked on each other. Some seemed to be pecked quite frequently, others only occasionally, and a few rarely if ever. One poor old hen seemed to be pecked by all the other chickens, to the point where she had no feathers in the top of her head. A "pecking order" seemed to exist within this flock of chickens. As a boy of six or seven, I was not aware that both zoologists and social scientists studied pecking orders. Indeed, these scholars suggest that pecking orders are common not only throughout the animal kingdom but in human societies.

When visiting a primate center in Madison, Wisconsin, several years ago, I learned that when a new monkey was placed in the compound, the other monkeys would test it to determine where it would stand in relation to them. Some monkeys rather quickly acquire "henchmen" to be their bodyguards and help them to establish a higher "status position" within the compound. In a similar fashion, a new prisoner must also establish his or her place within a prison

---

*George Orwell, *Animal Farm*

community. Sometimes, in fact, survival may require that the new inmate identify with a certain group. And in normal patterns of social living as well, we are aware of the fact that newcomers must establish a place within the school, job, and/or community. A newcomer is rarely accepted outright but must slowly work his or her way into various groups, social situations, and status positions.

One's place within the hierarchy of any social system must be acquired one way or another. As noted in chapter 4, a person's social class initially depends on the status position of his or her parents. Through the late 1960s, most analysts considered the family to be the basic unit within stratification systems, and most studies assumed that the social standing of the male head of the household determined the social standing of the family. Women determined their own social status only when they were not part of a family. Until recently, few questioned these assumptions; however, this "status-borrowing" model is not the only possibility (Jackman and Jackman 1983:140). With more women entering the labor force, this model has come under increasing attack. When both adults are in the labor market, a sharing of statuses seems appropriate.

Valerie Oppenheimer (1982:255–65) examined the relationship between status and women's socioeconomic role in the family. Neoclassical economics has relatively well-developed theories regarding the effect of wives' potential economic contribution on their actual work behavior. But the emphasis has been primarily on the wife's potential wage, rather than on more sociological factors such as the effect of the wife's potential occupational status on her decision to work. If income and status were perfectly correlated, then the potential status impact of wives' working could be ignored. However, this is not the case.

Oppenheimer argues that the family's desires for status maintenance or enhancement produce pressures on the wife to work. The same status considerations influence how serious and long-term her work commitment will be, if she does work, as well as her occupational level. For reasons of status maintenance, status *compatibility* among family members is important, although status *equality* is not as essential. In terms of the wife's socioeconomic role, this means that she is more likely to work if her potential job status—and its economic rewards—would serve to enhance the family's socioeconomic status. If her relative dollar contribution to the family were to be negligible and her job status much below that of her husband's, however, she would be less likely to work because her working would provide little net socioeconomic advantage to her or her family.

This chapter will discuss social inequality, how social class is determined, family profiles of various social classes, and social mobility.

In every society there are people who are favored and admired, and there are others who are avoided and looked down on. Two of the more common ways in which individuals are distinguished from each other, for example, are by age and by gender. Societies recognize differences between young and old people and between males and females. Accordingly, people are treated differently—some are favored and others are discriminated against—solely on the basis of their age and sex.

The Universality of Status Distinctions

Even children seem to distinguish (at a very early age) differences between various "categories" of people. Children acquire this sensitivity through simple observation of others' behavior and through contact with various media. The television show "Sesame Street" (though some feminists have criticized it because most of the characters are not female) is in general an exception to our society's social differentiation based on distinctions between individuals and groups of people. The "people in our neighborhood" are all basically treated the same. No matter what social attribute of individuals are being considered—gender, age, race, or occupation—they are all "people in the neighborhood." No lines of demarcation are drawn because of who one is. Social equality seems to prevail on Sesame Street.

Obviously, Sesame Street is not the real world. Sesame Street represents an **egalitarian society:** a society where, generally speaking, no individual or group has more access to resources, power, or prestige than any other. Egalitarian-like societies are sometimes found among hunting and gathering peoples. While gender, age, and individual differences do occur among hunters and gatherers, one may be a better hunter than another, yet everyone can become a good hunter. But today there are few hunting and gathering societies in the world. Therefore, while the idea of an egalitarian society exists in theory, it is rare to find one in reality.

Indeed, there is no known society today that is truly "classless" or unstratified. Values placed on the elderly, on physical characteristics, and on personality traits, for example, vary from society to society. However, shared perceptions of status variation among individuals, social positions, or groups are fairly universal in contemporary American society.

A Functionalist Approach to Social Inequality

As noted by Lloyd Warner (1949) in his study of social class, when societies are complex and have large populations, they always possess some form of status system which, by its own values, places people in higher or lower positions. From a functionalist perspective, this probably happens because the society coordinates the efforts of all its members into common enterprises in an effort to preserve the group. According to Warner, those who occupy "coordinating" positions acquire power and prestige because their actions partly control the behavior of the individuals who look to them for direction. And Warner argues that the family helps maintain the class system within the United States, since American children are always born into their families' position. Thus, social class, though often an object of our disapproval, continues to exist in our complex social world.

Social inequality can be viewed as the uneven distribution of privileges, material rewards, opportunities, power, and prestige among individuals or groups. When social inequality becomes part of the social structure and is transmitted from one generation to the next, **social stratification** exists. As to why societies tend to be stratified, functionalists argue that stratification must have some useful social function. (Compare the various "functions" of the family noted in Chapter 4.) Functionalists contend that all societies need to place and motivate individuals in social positions. In general, positions conveying the best rewards, and therefore usually having the highest

Miscegenation (marriage between a man and woman of different races) can be a source of unnecessary and unwelcome conflict for some individuals in the United States. For the conflict theorist, however, tension and competition are normal within a society.

rank, are those with the greatest importance for the society and those requiring the greatest training or talent. Thus, a society which values physicians more than schoolteachers will give higher status and rewards to the physicians. The classical functionalist position is that this unequal distribution of social rewards is functional for the society as a whole because the ablest individuals are drawn to the most demanding roles (Davis and Moore 1945:244).

The functionalist approach has been heavily criticized in recent years because stratification systems do not work as neatly in real life. Rewards are not always associated with importance. A person with inherited wealth or someone fortunate in the stock market may be highly rewarded, but the individual may have limited value for the society itself. A functionalist view tends to support the status quo since it argues that the existing system is necessary. Because this approach suggests that stratification is based on functional criteria, it overlooks the existence of stratification by other factors such as race and gender.

A Conflict Approach to Social Inequality

Conflict theorists, too, have proposed explanations for social stratification. Conflict theorists oppose the functionalist view, which suggests that the system is basically in a state of equilibrium. Supporters of conflict theory regard tension and competition as an important factor in a society. Thus, for example, when labor reaches a point of tension with management that cannot be resolved, a strike by labor is often a step toward better rewards for laborers. This tension between groups is inevitable and can have a leveling influence between the "haves" and "have nots" in a society.

THE EFFECTS OF SOCIAL STRATIFICATION

Stratification studies in the United States have shown that social class affects many aspects of family life (Enos and Sultan 1977). Lower-class families are sick more often than are others. Diet and living conditions are closely related to health, and the upper classes have better access to more sanitary housing and can have more balanced and nutritious food. Members of lower-class families do not live as long as those in the upper classes. The birth rate is higher for lower classes than upper classes. Women more often head lower-class families. Social class affects everything from the success of marriage to the recreation families engage in, their sleeping arrangements, the meaning attached to sexual behavior, and even the procedures followed in sexual intercourse (Eshleman, 1985:250–51).

Middle-class women discipline their children differently than do working-class mothers; the former will punish boys and girls alike for the same misbehavior while the latter often have different standards for sons and daughters. Middle-class mothers will also judge the "bad" child's intention, whereas working-class women are more concerned with the effects of the child's action (Tischler, Whitten, and Hunter 1986:293). Rates of juvenile delinquency tend to be lower among children of the upper classes. Furthermore, a connection exists between social class and types of mental illness suffered (Hollingshead and Redlich 1958).

People in the higher social classes tend to score higher on standardized tests. In a study for the Carnegie Council on Children, Richard de Lone (1978) correlated test scores of 647,031 students who took the Scholastic Aptitude Test (SAT) with the economic status of the students' families. As is shown in Table 7.1, the higher the students' family income, the higher the probability that he or she will score higher on the SAT.

Middle-class adolescents are more likely than lower-class adolescents to engage in petting, but the latter are more likely to engage in sexual intercourse. The age at marriage is higher for men and women in the upper classes, and they travel greater distances, on

TABLE 7.1 Relation of SAT Scores to Family Income

Students' scores	Students' mean family incomes
750–800	$24,124
700–750	21,980
650–700	21,292
600–650	20,330
550–600	19,481
500–550	18,824
450–500	18,122
400–450	17,387
350–400	16,182
300–350	14,355
250–300	11,428
200–250	8,369

Source: Richard de Lone, *Small Futures* (New York: Harcourt Brace Jovanovich, 1978), p. 102. Copyright ©1979 by Carnegie Corporation of New York, reprinted by permission of Harcourt Brace Jovanovich, Inc.

the average, to obtain spouses. Better-educated women are more likely than the less educated to experience orgasm in sexual intercourse. (Goode 1966:583).

The above examples point out that social class in the United States has very real and immediate consequences for individuals and families. Probably no other single variable affects our lives as much as does social class membership. A look at the literature on the causes of juvenile delinquency reveals that not everyone has an equal opportunity to acquire the same "goodies" in life. With the tremendous impact of mass media on American families, the adolescent in the working-class family and the adolescent in the upper-class family may see the same ads on television. While the upper-class child's family has the economic means to purchase some of these items, the child from the working-class family may have no legitimate way to acquire the particular product seen on television. An alternative illegitimate means, however, sometimes seems like a way to achieve the same goal. Therefore, while of course not all working-class adolescents turn to crime, it does become an option for some young people in a world where the doors of legitimate means do not always seem to be open to them.

DETERMINING SOCIAL CLASS

While William Domhoff (1983:6) notes that most individuals have some concept of the idea of social class, Robert Hodge and Donald Treiman (1968) argue that clear, agreed-upon perceptions of social class categories are unlikely to develop in the United States. Families are not likely to categorize themselves or others clearly according to "class." Evidence of this lack of preciseness concerning social class was presented by Richard Curtis and Elton Jackson (1977:85). They asked people in Indianapolis questions related to social class differences. The results suggested that consensus about social class was incomplete and partial and existed only on a very general level. About one-third of the respondents replied that they did not know about social class differences in their community, and often the term "social class" was unfamiliar to them. This kind of result is probably not unique to Indianapolis.

Thus, social class perceptions in the United States are not well defined; and in this country the lines of demarcation between social classes are also blurred. How can we measure class status? Let's look at some classical socioeconomic perspectives.

Karl Marx

The writings of Karl Marx and Friedrich Engels (1848) in the mid–nineteenth century defined class in terms of access to the means of production. Marx viewed a social class as any aggregate of persons who perform the same function in the organization of production. The two classes, according to Marx, are the **bourgeoisie** (owners of the means of production) and the **proletariat** (the workers). Marx predicted that as the capitalist system evolved, the proletariat would eventually become fed up with their exploitation by the bourgeoisie and the unequal distribution of wealth and would revolt, leading to the successful overthrow of the bourgeoisie. The result would be a classless society. Marx believed that work is the basic form of self-realization for individuals. The idea that individuals under capitalism would revolt was based on an assumption of what prompts people to be satisfied or dissatisfied with their work (Bendix and Lipset 1966:7–10).

Rayna Rapp (1982:170–71), applying a modern perspective to Marx, defines "social class" as a shorthand for a process, not a thing. She notes that the process is the one by which different social groups' access to the means of production are inherited and reproduced under capitalism. As Marx developed the concept, the process of capital accumulation generates and constantly deepens distinctions between two categories of people. People then are labeled blue collar or white collar. Rapp says that what are actually accumulating over time are changing categories of proletarians. Class formation and class composition are always in flux—it is relationships that accumulate.

Max Weber

Max Weber (1946), a well-known social scientist of the late nineteenth and early twentieth century, thought that Marx's strictly economic view was too simple. In Weber's view, classes, status groups, and parties are phenomena of the distribution of power within a community. "Class" to Weber refers to any group of people with similar "life chances" determined by their economic position in society. "Property" and "lack of property" are the basic categories of all class situations. Class situations are differentiated according to the kind of property that can bring returns and according to the kind of services that can be offered in the market. Those who have no property, but who offer services, are differentiated as much according to their kinds of services as according to the way in which they make use of these services.

Weber defines social status as a hierarchical position within the social structure of a group. Status is not completely the consequence of property relations, but can be the source of property relations. Therefore, a person can enjoy status (or prestige) without having large accumulations of property. Weber says that the genuine place of "classes" is within the economic order and the place of "status groups" is within the social order, while "parties" live in a house of "power." The action of parties is oriented toward influencing a communal action no matter what its content may be. Power is the ability to manipulate others with or without their approval. Thus, for Weber, limiting social class to the economic realm does not tell the entire story.

Measures of Social Class

Whether one prefers to discuss a two-class system or systems with three, five, six, or even twelve categories of class, what are some contemporary ways of determining social class?

Sociologists have not reached agreement upon the criteria essential for determining social class. For example, if only income is used, a skilled laborer often makes more money than a schoolteacher. If income were the single criterion, the skilled worker would have a higher social class position than many teachers or members of the clergy who have much more formal education. Likewise, drug dealers or "godfathers" in the criminal world would have a higher status rating than most legitimately employed persons. With this problem in mind, let's consider three different approaches developed by sociologists to measure social class.

The *objective approach* to the measurement of social stratification establishes one or more observable criteria by which persons and families will be evaluated. These criteria may include such factors as occupation, source of income, years of formal education, housing type, and area of residence. The *reputational approach* determines social class according to the opinions of other persons concerning the community members being studied. In this way the researcher gains an understanding of how persons in the community rank each other. Researchers employing the *subjective approach* ask the persons being studied to place themselves in one of several categories, such as lower, middle, or upper social class. A major problem with this method, however, is that the overwhelming majority of persons will place themselves in the middle category.

Determining social class is not an easy task. Social scientists often rely on the objective approach, though they also employ the reputational and subjective approaches. In cases where the reputational approach is feasible to use, determining social class with both the reputational and the objective approaches is a good way to help verify the class structure.

UPPER, MIDDLE, AND WORKING-CLASS FAMILIES

As noted earlier, the number of social classes assigned to various communities in the United States has been as few as two, more often three, and sometimes as many as five, six, or more. When classifying the entire country, social scientists most often designate three levels—upper, middle, and working class (which may include upper lower and lower lower "poor"). John Walton (1986:111) divided the class structure into three levels, using source of income as a shorthand for designating specific positions (Table 7.2).

Walton (1986:113) notes that the most dramatic change in the labor market over the last few generations has been an increase in the number of wage earners and a decline in the number of independent professionals, farm and small business owners, and trades people. The number of family members employed in industrial settings (traditional blue-collar workers) has also declined with automation and the transfer of production to workers in other countries.

While the corporate rich and the technical and skilled middle-class worker have been the beneficiaries of these changes, the industrial working class has been the principal victim. The market power once held by industrial workers—by virtue of their necessary skills and union representation—has been severely eroded.

TABLE 7.2 Contemporary Class Structure in the United States

Upper Classes		2%
Property owners		
Corporate and business owners, large employers		
Financiers		
Middle Classes		52%
Executives, managers, technocrats (top and middle levels)	12%	
Small-business owners and employers	6%	
Self-employed business and professionals	7%	
Employed professional, skilled crafts	10%	
Supervisors, foremen	17%	
Working Classes		46%
Industrial workers	16%	
Trades and construction	12%	
Clerks, attendants, office, and service workers	14%	
Manual and agricultural labor	4%	

Source: Compiled by John Walton, *Sociological and Critical Inquiry,* (Chicago: Dorsey Press, 1986), p. 112. Taken from Erik O. Wright, "The American Class Structure," *American Sociological Review* 47 (December, 1982); pp. 709–926 and the U.S. Census of Population, 1980.

With these trends as background, let's look at family life in the upper, middle, and working classes.

Upper Class

A small percentage of the United States population, as noted in Table 7.2, is categorized as being in the upper stratum, yet this group controls much of U.S. production. But as is often said by social scientists, we know little about the very wealthy families because they do not answer our questionnaires; they fund them rather than answer them!

G. William Domhoff (1983:24), a sociologist who has done extensive research on the upper class, suggests that members of the upper class receive a distinctive education from infancy through young adulthood—beginning in private schools and ending with matriculation at one of a small number of heavily endowed private universities such as Harvard, Yale, Princeton, or Stanford. Such a separate educational system supports the distinctiveness of the mentality and lifestyle of the upper class. Such a start in life inevitably tends to make "some animals . . . more equal than others."

Upper-class membership gives members an edge in the economic world from preschool through college and throughout life. Members of the upper-class tend to have greater opportunities for networking within their fields and travel in elite social circles that may also enhance their status.

Upper-class families tend to be **endogamous;** that is, children are encouraged to marry someone of their own social class. According to Domhoff (1983:34), the original purpose of the debutante season for upper-class families was to introduce "highly sheltered young women" to eligible marriage partners. Families in the upper class tend to be concerned with who they are rather than what they do. People have access to one another through their control of neighborhoods, schools, universities, clubs, churches, and ritual events (Rapp 1982:182). They are ancestor-oriented and conscious of the boundaries which separate the "best" families from others.

While social activities play an important role in the lives of upper-class families, the most frequent preoccupations of men of the upper class are business and finance (see Table 7.2). Most members of the upper class are, and have traditionally been, hardworking people— even those who are the most wealthy. Typically, finance, business, and law are the occupations of upper-class males (Domhoff 1983:37–38). The upper-class women tend to be people of both power and domesticity—playing decision-making roles in various cultural and civic organizations while fulfilling essential roles at home (Ostrander 1984).

Since upper-class families are at the top of the social hierarchy, they do not aspire to be upwardly mobile—they are "already there." Having achieved their position through inheritance, hard work, or a stroke of luck, these families represent a small proportion of the total population and do not typically rub shoulders with members of other social strata. The sons and daughters of the Gold Coasts (Chicago), the Main Lines (Philadelphia), and the Park Avenues (New York) of America are more likely to receive recognition for their efforts than the children of the slums. The distance these privileged young people travel to achieve success is shorter than the long hard pull necessary for ambitious children of the less fortunate middle class, and certainly less difficult than for children of working-class parents (Warner 1949).

Distinctions are sometimes made between the upper-upper-class families and the lower-upper class. The former have "old money" (inherited wealth) while the latter have "new money" (money they have acquired themselves). A person with "old money" will have several generations of grandparents with money, possibly also with high political positions, and will have lived in the same community for many decades. The family of Joseph Kennedy, for example, represents new money in that Joseph himself acquired the wealth and passed it on to his children, John, Robert, Ted, and the others. Upper-class families in general place more emphasis than middle-class families on relationships with members of the larger kin group. For the upper-upper class it is important to keep in close contact with the extended family.

Family sociologist Ruth S. Cavan (1969:101) once caricatured the upper-class family this way:

> In almost every home on the wall in a prominent position is the family tree, appropriately framed. Many families have a crest, which is also framed, and which is used on stationery, rings, and so forth. The Social Register, a book containing only the names of people who are considered upper-upper class, is used as the telephone directory. Very seldom does anyone in the family find it necessary to use the regular telephone directory. Outsiders are made to see that they are not wanted. Money has nothing to do with getting into the Social Register. The criterion used is the family background. If the family dates back for many generations, if the members belong to exclusive clubs . . . the family is considered upper class.

We now turn our attention to the middle class, which constitutes a large segment of the U.S. population.

Middle Class

The term "middle class" historically referred to the Marxian definition of the petty bourgeoisie: people who owned small amounts of productive resources and had control over their working conditions in ways that proletarians did not (Rapp 1982:180). We now use the term to refer to a different sector—employees in corporate management, government and organizational bureaucrats, and professionals.

As Table 7.2 shows, people in the middle class tend to work in service occupations with other people. Whereas most working-class occupations focus on the manipulation of objects, most middle-class occupations focus on the manipulation of ideas and symbols that require creativity (Leslie and Korman 1985:239). Middle-class individuals generally work for a salary or fee, while members of the working class are usually paid an hourly wage. The middle class are usually characterized as being very ambitious status seekers. They have long-range goals, making plans for the future rather than taking one day at a time—as is sometimes true of the working class.

A desire of many middle-class parents is for their children to have a better life than they have experienced. Consequently, they emphasize education as the means for upward social mobility. Middle-class parents often endeavor to instill particular values in their children, including responsibility, respect for property, good manners, constructive activity, status achievement, and refraining from physical violence.

Unlike the upper class, who tend to stay in the same geographic area for generations, the middle class are geographically mobile, often moving to take better jobs in other parts of the country. With higher geographical mobility, middle-class families establish fewer geographic roots. This causes middle-class families to place more emphasis on the conjugal unit, even though they also value ties with extended kin—especially close kin. Lifestyles of middle-class families vary considerably, but they are usually characterized by the possession of a common set of material goods—what some call the "standard American package" of a home in suburbia, two cars in the garage, a white picket fence, and crabgrass in the yard.

Middle-class families have a stable resource base that allows for some amount of luxury and discretionary spending. When exceptional economic resources are needed, nonfamilial institutions usually are available. Rayna Rapp (1982:181–82) presents the following "hunches" about middle-class kinship patterns: (1) Kinship probably shifts from the **lateral** (that is, from indirect line of descent—mother's brother or father's brother) toward the **lineal** (that is, direct line of descent—grandparent to parent to son or daughter); and (2) friendship rather than kinship is likely to be the nexus within which the middle class invests its psychic and "familial" energies.

While middle-class families may be becoming more committed philosophically to equality of the sexes as more women work outside the home, in general middle-class husbands do not tend to participate more in housework and child care. In her study of middle-class and working-class families, Lillian Rubin (1976:99) suggests that middle-class men are more secure and have more status and prestige than working-class men, and that these factors enable the middle-class male to assume a less overtly authoritarian role within the family. For him, there are other places and other situations where his authority and power are tested and accorded legitimacy. Therefore a more egalitarian family ideology is possible. For the working-class male, however, the family is often the only place where he can exercise power and demand obedience to his authority. Thus, according to Rubin, there is less opportunity for an egalitarian family ideology to emerge in a working-class family.

Working Class

The most salient characteristic of organization in the working class is dependency on hourly wages (Rapp 1982:171). Stable working-class families participate in production, reproduction, and consumption by sending out their labor power in exchange for wages. How much labor power needs to be sent out is determined by the cost of maintaining the household, the earning power of individual members, and individuals' availability to work outside the home.

The work done in families primarily by women is not simply about babies. Yet since housework is wageless, it keeps its workers dependent on others for access to commodities bought with wages. And when women work outside the home, their primary definition as houseworker contributes to their working in the lowest-paid sectors of the labor market.

Since working-class families are usually nuclear, marriage is supposed to be "for love" and not "for money" (Rapp 1982:173). The distinction between love and money corresponds to the distinction between private family life in the home and work life outside the home. The two are experienced as opposites. One must work for the sake of the family, and having a family is the "payoff" for leading a good life. Founding a family, not work, is what people do for personal gratification and for autonomy.

A distinctive feature of working-class families is that the great majority have limited choices about the kinds of work available to them. Their "choices" are often the "leftovers" in the job market. People do seek self-esteem and personal affirmation in their work; the working classes resemble the middle classes in coming hopefully to their jobs. However, given the way in which production and con-

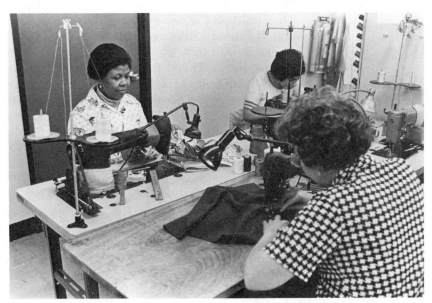

Job opportunities for working-class family members often involve skilled positions. Pride and personal satisfaction in one's work can be found throughout the job market.

sumption are organized in advanced capitalist societies, members of the working class often experience exploitation in struggling to work at jobs that may be less than meaningful (Walton 1986:105–6).

Working-class people often have jobs that require less skill than middle-class jobs, that have less room for independent judgment, and that leave them with little freedom or autonomy. Lillian Rubin (1976:158) claims that working-class jobs offer few intrinsic rewards and little status. But in analyzing the meaning of work related to personal images of self, J. A. Walter (1979:29) claims that people do their utmost to persuade themselves that their work is meaningful in one way or another. Furthermore, most people are on the whole satisfied with their work and claim not to be alienated.

Working-class families typically hold to the traditional notions of gender in marital roles. A high degree of gender segregation exists within the family. The husband's world revolves around the provider role, while the wife has primary responsibility for the home and children in addition to working outside the home. According to Gerald Leslie and Sheila Korman (1985:238–39), sex segregation of this type tends to be accompanied by a lack of communication between the spouses. Unlike middle-class couples, who highly value partner companionship, working-class couples are less likely to rely on each other for friendship and companionship. Wives have a tendency to maintain close ties with relatives, and husbands to continue premarital peer group associations (Berger 1960).

In a study of the value system of working-class families, Herbert Hyman (1966:488–90) says that working-class people place less emphasis than middle-class people on upward social mobility and the importance of achieving intermediate goals such as attending college. Working-class families are more keenly aware of the lack of an opportunity structure that would lead to long-term success. Their value system presumably arises out of a realistic appraisal of their life experience and therefore prepares the individual for a lower status position. With considerable formal education required for many types of higher status positions, and because working-class values do not support educational aspirations, upward social mobility is very difficult. The problems facing the working class are even more striking when contrasted with the "start" given upper-class children.

It might seem reasonable to expect that higher education would be more available today because colleges are basing financial aid more upon need, and that a goal of educational attainment would certainly be within reach of working-class children who possessed the motivation. However, Leslie and Korman (1985:240) observe that unlike middle-class parents, who stress educational achievement for their children and sacrifice to ensure it, working-class parents expect their children only to fulfill the minimum state legal educational requirements. Since people tend to perform at perceived levels of others' expectations, low expectations are likely to produce low performance. It is difficult for any of us to achieve something that is not encouraged by significant others.

Herbert Hyman (1966:496) notes that subtle factors may discourage persons in the lower strata from desiring changes. While they may really have aspirations for accomplishment of a particular goal, they often accommodate themselves to lesser opportunities and reduce their aspirations in order to guard against failure and the experience of frustration.

Unemployment has also influenced the functioning of the working-class family. The realization that unemployment is a permanent fixture of our society has brought into question such traditions as the Protestant work ethic, the separation between work and leisure, the identification of work with paid employment, and the image of work as a major means of acquiring self-worth and full adult status.

Lillian Rubin (1976:38) observes that a child born into middle-class families can have dreams that are relatively unfettered by constraints. Early in life he or she becomes aware of future possibilities and begins planning (backed by family resources) for the future. Role models with prestigious occupations are readily available for a middle-class youngster. Such a child is encouraged to test the limits of his or her ability—to reach for the stars.

A very different situation exists for the working-class child who is born into a family where daily survival may be problematic—where he or she sees only a frantic scramble to meet daily needs and to pay tomorrow's rent or past-due bills. It may be very difficult if not impossible to see beyond the present situation. Of what can working-class children dream in such circumstances? As the reading here suggests, some individuals have little time to think of educational achievement.

When Are You Poor and Needy?

Depending on which approach one uses, it is possible to document that anywhere from 14 to 45 million Americans are living in poverty. Despite what the public believes, the "poverty index" was not originally intended to certify that any individual or family was "in need."

The poverty index has become less and less meaningful over the years. Its continued use and misuse, however, has given it somewhat of a sacred character. Few who cite it know how it is calculated and [most] choose to assume it is a fair measure for determining the number of poor in the country.

The poverty index was first used in 1965 and designated the official statistic for documenting the poor in 1969. It was calculated in the following way. It estimated the national average dollar-cost of a frugal but adequate diet. Food costs were then multiplied by three to estimate how much total cash income was needed to cover food and other necessities—based on a 1955 study showing that food accounted for an average of one-third of basic budgets for U.S families of three or more people. Regional differences in cost of living were not taken into account. Food typically accounts for a considerably smaller proportion of family expenses now than it did in 1955.

Source: Adapted from Joseph M. Dukert, "Who Is Poor? Who Is Truly Needy?," *Public Welfare* 41 (Winter 1983), pp. 17–22. Used by permission of American Public Welfare Association. Copyright 1983.

An elderly black couple picked tomatoes and other vegetables for over sixty years as migratory laborers traveling up and down the west coast of the United States. Now they pick up cans along the highway in Florida near their dilapidated two-room shack and eat a chicken neck and rice each evening for dinner. They supplement their monthly Social Security check of $235 with the cans they pick up for which they receive thirty-five cents per pound.

Now all those tomatoes and other vegetables they picked are gone. You and I ate them. Is it right that now all we give them are our empty cans?

Source: Charles Osgood, reporting on the CBS Evening News with Dan Rather, June 24, 1988.

It probably matters little to poor families what arbitrary definition of poverty is set by a government agency. What is important is the experience of the families who live these lives. The deprivation is real to them—real when children know their parents are having trouble paying the rent, when they do not have shoes that fit, when the telephone is disconnected, when the repossessors come to take an appliance away. The fact that the wages are not enough colors every dimension of life and contributes to a world over which parents and children have little control (Rubin, 1976:30).

This powerlessness has a profound impact on family life in the working class, because—what happens during the day and on the job—affects what happens at home at night (Rubin 1976:164). Working-class men in their mid-thirties are generally at the top of their truncated career ladders. They can anticipate increased earnings only insofar as union negotiations are successful or in routine cost-of-living adjustments. Certainly, the unequal distribution Marx described exists in the United States. However social classes may be divided up, some families have more control over their lives than others.

SOCIAL MOBILITY

Social mobility from one stratum to another is possible in a social class structure. Social mobility refers to the ability or tendency of an individual or social object to move from any one social position to another. According to P. A. Sorokin (1964), there are two types of social mobility. **Horizontal social mobility** refers to the transition of an individual (or social object) from one social group to another on the same level. A person moving from one family to another by divorce and remarriage or the transition of a social object like a job or occupation within the same social stratum are examples of horizontal social mobility. **Vertical social mobility** refers to the transition of an individual (or social object) from one social stratum to another. Vertical mobility involves social climbing and social sinking—one can ascend or descend. For example, a person may move up or down in social class by occupational attainment—or through marriage, although most marry horizontally (within their class stratum).

Let's look a little more closely at the various avenues of vertical social mobility. Certainly many people move up the social ladder through promotions on the job or by changing jobs. These *occupational moves* are usually available if an individual performs well on the job and gives it his or her best shot. *Family inheritance* is another way to move upward. However, we don't recommend that you sit around waiting for an inheritance, as this is not a likely avenue for most people.

Additional formal *education* can usually enhance a person's chances for obtaining a higher position in society. Not only is the education itself of importance, but the contacts made during college may someday be of benefit. The person sitting next to you in class or living near you in the dormitory may in the future achieve a significant social position through politics or accumulated wealth. Influential people have positions to fill through appointment, and you could find yourself climbing up the social ladder with the help of your college friends.

Many move up the ladder through the *political process.* Who would be familiar with the names of Richard Nixon, Lyndon Johnson, Jimmy Carter, Gerald Ford, Ronald Reagan, or George Bush were it not for politics? (Perhaps some would have known President

Not only does a college education enhance students' opportunities in the job market, but former classmates from college may often assist each other in moving up the social ladder.

Reagan through his movie career.) Females, more than males, improve their social class position through *marriage*. In other words, if a female marries outside her social class, she is more likely to "marry up" than are males. (Social mobility of this type may create problems for newlyweds in dealing with in-laws, other kin, and friends.)

Religion provides another means for vertical social mobility. In the past many children of immigrants obtained an education and social prestige by becoming priests or other members of the clergy. Among today's television preachers, most have come from working-class backgrounds. But religious denominations tend to be rather homogeneous with regard to status, so denominational switching is common among the upwardly mobile.

To possess *special talents* in areas such as singing, acting, or playing professional sports is certainly a quick way to move up the social ladder. Most of us do not have these special talents, however. Besides, if the majority had special abilities in sports or could make musical sounds that were pleasing to large numbers of people, these individuals would not be "special." It is a supply and demand situation. If the talent supply were great, the rewards of talent would not be so great.

To move upward from one class to another may cause major adjustments for the individual. It is difficult to cross social class lines, because different norms and behavior exist at different social levels. The movie *The Unsinkable Molly Brown* and the television show "Beverly Hillbillies" presented situations where individuals jumped from working-class to upper-class status almost overnight. They did not have time to develop the social graces required of the upper class and were therefore embarrassingly uneasy (especially Molly Brown and her husband) in the presence of middle- and upper-class individuals.

Upward mobility also creates difficulties in relationships with nuclear and extended families. For a person from the working class, to become middle-class and experience middle-class patterns often means changing daily experience. This may mean that an individual finds less and less in common with his or her relatives—they may feel that "all this education and social status has gone to his head." Compounding this experience of social distance between relatives is the geographical distance often required with upward mobility.

As this chapter has pointed out, social class is not easily determined, yet social class has a significant impact upon how families are viewed and how they behave. Whether you are a rooster in a flock of chickens or a child in a human family, the "pecking order" will be an important aspect of your daily routine. While your initial "ranking" in the larger society is linked to your family of orientation, your eventual social class position depends to a great degree on what happens after you "leave the nest." Inequality runs rampant among American families. While some animals may seem more equal than others, vertical social mobility gives everyone an opportunity to change his or her social class position no matter what the initial family background of the person.

CHAPTER REVIEW

- An individual's social class status is initially determined by his or her family of orientation. This type of status is referred to as ascribed status.
- Status compatibility for the family is an important factor in husbands and wives working. The wife is more likely to work if her potential job status serves to improve the family's socioeconomic status.
- Egalitarian societies do not exist in reality. To name just two factors, age and gender contribute to social differentiation in societies all over the world.
- Social stratification exists in virtually every society. Functionalist theory argues that social stratification is positive and necessary and produces a balance in social systems. Conflict theory, on the other hand, regards tension and competition to be an important factor in a society.
- Social class affects many aspects of daily life, including health, longevity, birth rates, discipline of children, standardized test results, and premarital sexual relations.
- Karl Marx discussed two classes, the proletariat and the bourgeoisie, whose conflict would result in a classless system.
- Max Weber suggested that power in a community is distributed through economic classes, status groups, and parties.

- Social class is measured by the objective approach (specific criteria), the reputational approach (opinions of others), and the subjective approach (self-rating self). The objective approach is the one used most often by social scientists.
- Upper-class families constitute a small percentage of the U.S. population. They are well-educated, endogamous, and often occupied in business and finance. They have limited upward mobility since they are at the top.
- Middle-class families are very conscious of vertical social mobility, constitute a large segment of the population, generally work for a salary or fee, and are geographically mobile.
- Like middle-class families, the working class makes up a large percentage of the population, but working-class people have somewhat limited choices of jobs—often requiring less skill than middle-class jobs. Gender segregation exists to a large extent within working-class families.
- Two types of social mobility are vertical and horizontal. Vertical mobility refers to movement up and down the social ladder, and horizontal mobility refers to movement from one group to another on the same level.

DISCUSSION QUESTIONS

1. How does social class affect American family lifestyles?
2. Why do you think a "classless" society never developed as Marx had predicted?
3. Briefly describe three methods sociologists use to measure social stratification.
4. How are working-class families different from middle-class families?
5. Discuss various means of achieving upward vertical social mobility.
6. Briefly describe how you imagine a utopia, with no class distinctions, might affect family relations.
7. Do you feel that it is possible to achieve the American dream—where each person has an equal opportunity of reaching the top? Does each person have an equal opportunity? Why or why not?

GLOSSARY

bourgeoisie: The "haves." Owners of the means of production, such as in a factory.

egalitarian society: Society in which individuals and groups have equal access to resources, power, and prestige.

endogamous: Marrying within one's own socioeconomic status, religion, ethnicity, or whatever grouping is prescribed.

horizontal social mobility: Movement within the same social stratum.

lateral kinship: Indirect line of descent. For example, an aunt or uncle-kin relationship goes through one's father or mother.

lineal kinship: Direct line of descent. From parent to child to grandchild, etc.

proletariat: The "have nots." The workers, for example, in factories.

social inequality: The uneven distribution of privileges, resources, opportunities, power, prestige, and influence among individuals or groups.

social stratification: A ranking or status in groups.

vertical social mobility: Movement up or down from one social stratum to another.

SUGGESTED READINGS

Bendix, Reinhard, and Seymour M. Lipset. 1966. *Class, Status, and Power: Social Stratification in Comparative Perspective.* New York: Free Press. *A collection of articles on social inequality.*

Domhoff, G. William. 1983. *Who Rules America Now? A View for the 80s.* Englewood Cliffs, N.J.: Prentice-Hall. *An updating of his earlier book on the power elite families in the United States.*

Rubin, Lillian B. 1976. *Worlds of Pain: Life in the Working-Class Family.* New York: Basic Books. *An intensive study of twenty-five middle-class and fifty working-class families in the United States.*

PART THREE

The Institution of Marriage

Mate Selection

◆ The farmer takes a wife
The farmer takes a wife
Hi ho the dairy-o
The farmer takes a wife

When I was a child of four, like most American children of my age, I learned to sing "The Farmer in the Dell." As much as I disliked girls at that age, I never questioned the fact that someday I would marry and raise children. I assumed that normal people married. Every adult that I knew had followed in the footsteps of the farmer and married. I figured that getting married was one of those rules that adults had to follow. Yet I always wondered how this great event would happen to me.

When I was an eighth grader, my motivation for getting married began to change. Rather than "having to get married"—an extrinsic motivation for marrying—I had convinced myself (with the help of a classmate named Susan Ogletree) that someday I might want to marry—a more intrinsic reason for marrying. However, for me a new question began to emerge—"How would I choose my partner, and how would I know when I had found *the* right person?" My parents and other adults didn't help me answer this question. Their reply was always, "You'll know when it happens!"

The goal of this chapter is to help you understand the mate selection process in the United States within its social context. We'll emphasize largely historical and cross-cultural perspectives.

RULES OF EXOGAMY AND ENDOGAMY IN MATE SELECTION

One rule that everyone knows is that you cannot marry "just anyone." Even young children know that some individuals are more desirable than others. Very young boys, for instance, often want to grow up and marry their mothers. These same children expect that nobody will ever want to marry their sisters. So it is with some mixed feelings that they discover that their future mate must be selected among individuals who are not members of their family.

This norm, or rule, of mate selection—requiring an individual to marry outside a specific group of which he or she is a member—is called **exogamy.** Exogamous groups can include members of one's kinship group (e.g., the extended family or clan), social group (e.g., very close friends or peers—sometimes called fictive kin), and social category (e.g., persons of the same gender). Every society in the world designates classes of individuals who are not eligible as marriage partners. Rules of exogamy require that individuals marry persons who differ from themselves. The most common of all rules of exogamy is the universal prohibition against incest in the nuclear family.

Gerald Leslie and Sheila Korman (1985:48) point out that while all societies forbid cross-sex relationships within the nuclear family, and while these taboos usually extend to other members of kin groups, societies differ regarding which kin member they will define as an acceptable or unacceptable sexual partner. Furthermore, in certain societies incest taboos may not include rather close blood relatives (e.g., cousins), but sexual relationships with more distant kin may be strictly forbidden (e.g., in-laws). According to Leslie and Korman (1985:48), "those groups who are prohibited tend to be those the system of descent defines as closely related."

Like all other rules of exogamy, the incest prohibition is learned during the process of socialization and is enforced by the group internalizing this norm. This process is so effective that the incidence of incest within the nuclear family is less than two cases per one million U.S. citizens (Leslie and Korman 1985:49). Furthermore, adult siblings are unlikely to experience sexual arousal even when living in close proximity and observing each other in partial undress.

Rules of **endogamy** are just the opposite of rules of exogamy. Endogamous norms require that marriage partners be of the same social group and share similar social background experiences. The mate selection process tends to produce **homogamous marriages,** which are supported by rules of endogamy and achieved against some rules of exogamy (e.g., incest rules). Homogamy is greatest when society has few rules of exogamy. In the United States endogamous

Despite the saying that opposites attract, most couples share similar social backgrounds regarding race, ethnicity, religion, education, and social class.

norms are operative in the following areas: socioeconomic status, race and ethnicity, religious preference, age, and place of residence.

DOWER AND DOWRY SYSTEMS IN MATE SELECTION

In Chapter 3 we discussed theoretical paradigms and frameworks employed in sociology. As you will recall, paradigms define what should be studied, what questions should be asked, how they should be asked, and what rules should be followed in interpreting the answers obtained.

One of the theoretical frameworks described was *social exchange theory*. Human behavior, from this perspective, involves reciprocity; individuals both give and receive symbolic and nonsymbolic rewards in their interaction with others. Furthermore, individuals will only continue to participate in social situations as long as they perceive that they derive *perceived* benefits from their participation.

Many sociologists and anthropologists apply social exchange theory in attempting to explain mate selection behavior. They contend that fundamentally the process of mate selection functions like a market system—where individuals and families barter with symbolic and nonsymbolic rewards (e.g., money, property, beauty, status, esteem, love) in the process of arranging a marriage.

For the social exchange theorist, three important questions concerning mate selection must be addressed from a market system perspective.

1. What does each potential marital partner bring to the relationship, and how does society evaluate the relative worth of the respective contributions of each individual?
2. In what way can the party bringing the most to the relationship be compensated so as to achieve relative equality and promote reciprocity in the relationship?
3. Over the course of the relationship, how can the marriage continue to promote an equitable social exchange where partners are adequately rewarded for their investment in the relationship?

Individuals bring to a marriage many personal attributes and assets that make them desirable as potential mates. Consider Maria Shriver as a marriage partner. Her father, Robert Sargent Shriver, Jr., was the brother-in-law of President John F. Kennedy, the first director of the Peace Corps, and the Democratic party's nominee for vice-president in 1972. Her mother, Eunice Kennedy Shriver, was the daughter of Joseph and Rose Kennedy and sister of John, Robert, and Edward Kennedy. Mrs. Shriver was the founder of Special Olympics and recipient of four honorary doctorate degrees (one from Princeton University); she has served in many high-level governmental, political, and civic positions. Maria graduated from Georgetown University with a major in American studies and then pursued a career in broadcast journalism. She served as news producer and reporter for a number of local news programs, was a national reporter for "PM Magazine," and became the anchor for the CBS morning news and NBC Sunday morning news programs. In addition to her personal wealth and access to tremendous family wealth, she is a beautiful woman, extremely articulate, and very bright. What more could any American contribute as personal attributes than beauty, wealth, power, prestige, and intellect? (Ah, but "can she bake a cherry pie?") From a marketing perspective, Maria Shriver could acquire a highly desirable mate. And, in fact Maria Shriver did not marry just anyone. On April 26, 1986, she married Arnold Schwarzenegger—three-time Mr. Universe, movie star, author, and international celebrity.

In all societies, including U.S. society, that is the way most marriage partners come together—people of relatively equal value (as evaluated by their respective kin) come together. In most cultures

The Partners Must Invest an Equal Share

Hopeless, you say? I'm not the sort of fool
That likes his ladies difficult and cool.
Men who are awkward, shy, and peasantish
May pine for heartless beauties, if they wish,
Grovel before them, bear their cruelties,
Woo them with tears and sighs and bended knees,
And hope by dogged faithfulness to gain
What their poor merits never could obtain.
For men like me, however, it makes no sense
To love on trust, and foot the whole expense.
Whatever any lady's merits be,
I think, thank God, that I'm as choice as she;
That if my heart is kind enough to burn
For her, she owes me something in return;
And if in any proper love affair
The partners must invest an equal share.

Source: Jean Baptiste Poquelin de Molière, *The Misanthrope,* translated into English by Richard Wilbur (New York: Harcourt Brace Jovanovich, Publishers, 1955), p. 80.

the marriage partners themselves are not the primary marriage negotiation agents. Some societies rely on matchmakers or go-betweens (e.g., Yenta in the play *Fiddler on the Roof*), while in other societies mate selection is either arranged or controlled by elder family members—usually males, but with influence from older, high-status females in the kinship group. Cultures where marriages are arranged by third-party agents or kin members tend to practice unilineal kinship reckoning and patrilocal or matrilocal residence; often, composite family structures predominate. Consequently, these cultures view mate selection not as an individual taking a spouse (like the farmer in the dell), but primarily as the family acquiring a new member.

The colonial period of American history has many examples of fathers (or masters) arranging marriages for their children. In 1640, Emanual Downing (cited by Queen and Habenstein 1961:277) wrote in his diary that he wanted his son, James, to marry a niece of Mr. Endicott. Endicott claimed "that he had made a 'verie good match' for his niece, getting her married to a young man with an estate of 400 or 500 pounds."

However, the more common pattern in the American colonies was for adult children to decide to marry and then ask their fathers for permission. According to Queen and Habenstein (1961:277), "A young man was required by the laws of several colonies to secure the consent of his prospective father-in-law before beginning the courtship, and this was not always easy to obtain. Aside from personal likes and dislikes, fathers of eligible maidens looked into young men's economic status. The young men in turn looked out for their own interests and bargained for dowries."

The play *Fiddler on the Roof* tells the story of a Jewish father and the marriages of his three daughters, a story that parallels the history of mate selection in the United States. Tevye arranges a mate for his first daughter, but she does not approve of the man selected and asks her father for permission to marry another man. The second daughter finds her husband on her own and *tells* her parents of her intention, receiving permission under duress. The third daughter selects a Russian soldier as her mate, experiences opposition by her parents, and marries the man against the wishes of her family.

Condemned to Choose

In India some years ago, David and Vera Mace held a discussion with a group of ten girls concerning mate selection. After the Maces described how young people in the West are free to meet each other and have dates, how a boy and a girl fall in love, and how, after a period of going together, they become engaged and get married, the following conversation took place.

"Wouldn't you like to be free to choose your own marriage partners, like the young people in the West?"

"Oh, no!" several voices replied in chorus.

Taken aback, we searched their faces. "Why not?"

"For one thing," said one of them, "doesn't it put the girl in a very humiliating position?"

"Humiliating? In what way?"

"Well, doesn't it mean that she has to try to look pretty, and call attention to herself, and attract a boy, to be sure she'll get married?"

"Well, perhaps so."

"And if she doesn't want to do that, or if she feels it's undignified, wouldn't that mean she mightn't get a husband?"

"Yes, that's possible."

"So a girl who is shy and doesn't push herself forward might not be able to get married. Does that happen?"

"Sometimes it does."

"Well, surely that's humiliating. It makes getting married a sort of competition in which the girls are fighting each other for the boys. And it encourages a girl to pretend she's better than she really is. She can't relax and be herself. She has to make a good impression to get a boy, and then she has to go on making a good impression to get him to marry her."

Before we could think of an answer to this unexpected line of argument, another girl broke in.

"In our system, you see," she explained, "we girls don't have to worry at all. We know we'll get married. When we are old enough, our parents will find a suitable boy, and everything will be arranged. We don't have to go into competition with each other."

"Besides," said a third girl, "how would we be able to judge the character of a boy we met and got friendly with? We are young and inexperienced. Our parents are older and wiser, and they aren't as easily deceived as we would be. I'd far rather have my parents choose for me. It's so important that the man I marry should be the right one. I could so easily make a mistake if I had to find him for myself."

Source: David and Vera Mace, *Marriage East and West* (New York: Doubleday, 1960), pp. 144–45. Copyright © 1959, 1960 by David and Vera Mace. Reprinted by permission of Doubleday, a division of Bantam, Doubleday, Dell Publishing Group, Inc.

In the United States today individuals are relatively free to choose their mates without the influence of other family members. (Of course this is not absolutely true in practice, because parents, grandparents, siblings, and other kin do voice their evaluations of a potential spouse—even when such opinions are not solicited.) Consequently, most American young couples do not ask their parents for permission to marry; rather, they tell their parents of their intentions. When my wife and I had decided to marry, however, I visited my prospective father-in-law to ask for his permission to marry his daughter. After I asked the question, I thought to myself "Why am I doing this?" I think that he was as dumbfounded as I with my strange behavior. I suppose that I had watched too many late movies and the idea had been placed in my head by a culture that had existed thirty years earlier.

In the market structure of mate selection—whether self-arranged or controlled by members of the kinship group—a fair amount of negotiation and haggling always takes place. In the United States a female who comes from a low-status family but is well educated and attractive is more likely to marry a male with higher socioeconomic status than her own. Conversely, a college drop-out female with parents of higher status may be more likely to marry an individual of lower social status.

Other cultures equalize the value of potential spouses with dower and dowry systems. A **dower** (bride's price) or **dowry** (groom's price) is an exchange of money, goods, or services associated with the marriage arrangements. The following are examples of dower and dowry systems:

1. Patrilineal family structures such as the Japanese and Chinese have a bride's price associated with marriage arrangements.
2. Matrilineal and matrilocal Hopi provide a groom's price to his family.
3. Societies that practice patrilocal residence, including many of the tribal groups of New Guinea, compensate the family of the bride for the loss of her services.
4. Polygynous groups, such as the Baganda of Uganda and the Bahaya of Bukoba, require that the groom and his family give gifts to the family of the bride.

The functions of the dower and dowry system are to compensate the parents and kin members for the past expenses of raising the child and for the loss of future services of the child who will now become a member of another family. On occasion a dower or dowry system also rewards the new spouse for services performed for his or her "new family." Finally, dower and dowry systems become a form of marriage insurance—because the extended family of the spouse, having received a bride's or groom's price, puts pressure on the spouse to become a good marriage partner. Should the marriage not be successful, the family must return the payment. However, if it is judged that the other spouse or his or her family is at fault, the innocent spouse may return to the family of orientation without any obligation of repayment. For this reason there is real pressure on both parties involved to make the marriage successful. For this among other reasons, almost all cultures of the world have lower divorce rates than those found in the United States.

Dower and dowry systems give rise to many forms of exchanges other than money. Some cultures, such as the Chinese on the island of Taiwan, practice the custom of exchanging relatives. A *simpua*, or "little bride," is a female child adopted at a very young age and raised to become the future wife for one's son. Many times Chinese families will trade daughters—thus solving the mate selection issue without involving any bride's price for either family.

Simpua—"The Little Bride"

As soon as a daughter is old enough to be useful in the house or in the fields, she is also old enough to marry and leave the family (at no small expense to her parents) to give her labor and her sons to another family. The general village (Peihotien, Taiwan) attitude is summed up in the words of an old lady who told me why she disposed of her daughters: "Why should I want so many daughters? It is useless to raise your own daughters. I'd just have to give them away when they were grown. So when someone asked for them as infants, I gave them away. Think of all the rice I saved."

Faced with a luxury in which he did not want to indulge, Lim Han-ci took the same course. His daughter was given to another family as a simpua ("little bride,") to be raised as a wife for one of their sons. As Lim Han-ci's wife had milk to nurse a child, the family then adopted a girl from a third family to raise as wife for their own son, Lim Hue-lieng. The family thus ridded themselves of a "useless" daughter and acquired a girl, Lim A-pou, who could marry their son and perpetuate their line of descent. In giving away their own daughter they saved themselves the expense of raising her and providing her dowry; in adopting another child in her place they avoided paying an extravagant bride price for an adult daughter-in-law. Marriages involving a "little bride" do not have the prestige of those that bring a daughter-in-law into the home as a young adult, but they are recognized by local custom throughout northern Taiwan and were common among poor peasant families at the time (of my visit). Nearly half of the village men of Lim Han-ci's generation married in this fashion. The early and prolonged association of husband and wife often affects their later marital relationship, but this is not considered adequate reason for foregoing the advantages of such a marriage. The desires of the parents and the needs of the family take precedence over the personal interest of the children.

Source: Margery Wolf, *The House of Lim* (New York: Appleton-Century-Crofts, 1968), p. 40.

Another form of exchange is the "gift of labor" provided to the family that is about to lose a family member. In chapter 2 we mentioned this custom in our discussion of matri-patrilocal residence. In matri-patrilocal residence the groom lives with and works for the family of the bride until he has met the requirements of the bride's price. After he has fulfilled his obligations, he and his new spouse return to his family, where they will establish their permanent residence.

Finally, many dower and dowry systems include exchanges in kind in lieu of money or currency. Such exchanges may include animals (e.g., water buffalo for the Toda or goats or cows for the Bahaya), jewelry or shells, land or property, or wife transfer.

High Cost of Wives

The high cost of wives is arousing many modern Africans. Government price controls have been suggested to curb inflated prices. Many want to abolish the auction-like atmosphere surrounding marriage arrangements.

The bride price is hallowed tribal custom which demands a down payment from prospective husbands and additional installments in exchange for permission from the bride's family to marry. In Nigeria the fee is usually cash, payable before the marriage. Kenya custom sometimes permits payment in goods such as livestock, lumber, and bicycles. The dowry in Kenya can be equivalent to five years of the groom's income.

A Nigerian schoolteacher commented: "Even when the price is reasonable it takes away the money a man needs to set up a home, unless of course he is just adding a new wife to an old household."

Africa remains a masculine stronghold. Male offspring are pampered while small girls are set toiling in the fields or put out as petty traders as soon as they can count. Often the only important occasion a girl's family has to make her subject of celebration is upon arrangement of a profitable marriage. Losing a daughter, they may gain a herd of goats.

Source: Kenneth L. Whiting, *Kalamazoo Gazette* (December 5, 1965).

This discussion of the market system of mate selection may seem to suggest that family members in cultures with dower or dowry systems are involved in the process of purchasing spouses for their children. But this is not the case, because the participants do not think of these activities as bargaining for a spouse but rather as an attempt to create a favorable marriage for the benefit of the individuals involved and their extended families. Furthermore, no matter which direction the wealth flows (in the dower or dowry system), there will always be a counterexchange required of the family that receives the greatest wealth. Over time these countergifts will generally be equal to the gifts received. These patterns of gift giving become another means by which families are able to demonstrate symbolically the status of the kinship unit to the larger society.

Wedding Extravaganzas in Japan

Japanese bridal couples used to have a reception for their relatives at the groom's house after a sacred ceremony at a shrine. But now most weddings are held at hotels and wedding halls, and they are getting showier all the time. Advertisements describe the happiness of getting married as though happiness were proportional to the degree of extravagant display.

In fact, the Japanese wedding is like a bride-and-groom fashion show, and the bridal couple look surprisingly like the magazine photos of noted entertainers. The similarity is deliberate. Young women want to stage the biggest ceremony of their lifetime after the fashion of the publicized wedding ceremonies of film and television personalities. Gorgeous wedding ceremonies, once a luxury of the rich and famous, are now within the reach or ordinary young people. This mirrors, above all, improved financial conditions in Japan.

According to the 1984 bank survey, the average total cost of getting married, including the cost of the wedding and of setting up housekeeping is 6.79 million yen for the 600,000 couples who marry in formal ceremonies each year. (At an exchange rate of 250 yen per U.S. dollar, the cost comes to *$26,400.*) Of this amount, the bride pays 3 million yen and the groom, 3.6 million yen, which is equivalent to his average annual income.

In most cases, it is the prospective groom who chooses the wedding site and the bride determines the format of the ceremony itself. They seem to have no realistic budget in mind when they show up at the wedding center. But after all, they mostly count on their parents to pay the expenses, and the families take the lead rather than the couple themselves.

According to Onishi Toshiyuki, president of the center, the wedding industry is supported by women. For the *kyoiku mama* (a mother overzealous about her children's upbringing and education), a child's marriage is her last momentous undertaking. The wedding becomes a grand ceremony blending the daughter's dreams and the mother's vanity and parental authority.

Source: Kamata Satoshi, *Japan Quarterly* 32, no. 2, pp. 168–70. Published by Asahi Shimbun.

Do Americans follow dower or dowry systems? Do families in the United States give gifts as a form of bride's or groom's price? Your first impulse may be to answer "no"—however, consider wedding traditions in America and the patterns of gift giving associated with them. At the wedding ceremony, when guests are seated, they are asked, "Are you a friend of the bride or groom?" Wedding showers are typically given by families of both bride and groom. Many times gifts are on prominent display at the wedding reception, and occasionally newspaper articles describing the wedding list the wedding gifts of the parents of the bride and groom. Furthermore, socially sanctioned traditions specify which family is expected to pay for the various parts of the wedding. By tradition, the groom and/or his family pay for the rehearsal dinner, the bridal bouquet, the mothers' corsages, the engagement and wedding rings, the honeymoon trip, the honorarium for the clergy, and the bride's gift; the bride and/or her family pay for the reception, the flowers at the wedding, the photographer, the groom's wedding ring, the food at the reception, and the groom's gift.

As you can see, getting married in the United States is not cheap! According to CBS News (1988), the average cost of a wedding in the United States is $13,000. Here as in other cultures, weddings provide an opportunity for families to demonstrate symbolically to the larger society their place in the social stratification system.

"WHAT'S LOVE GOT TO DO WITH IT?"

You may be starting to wonder where love comes into mate selection. Few Americans today are particularly conscious of, say, rules of exogamy or symbolic exchanges when they choose their mates. Indeed, in my own life, the norms and patterns described in the preceding sections seem unrelated to the warm fuzzy experience I remembered from when I was a participant in the mate selection process. I got married because I was in love. I could not have cared less that my wife's parents had an educational background similar to that of my own parents. And I have no recall of any bartering related to the expenses of getting married. I did not view the engagement ring as a form of the bride's price. I just wanted to spend the rest of my life with this person whom I respected, cared about, confided in, and found physically attractive.

What is the role of love in the mate selection process? Especially in recent times, most Americans are at a loss for words to explain their marital choice except in terms of "love." Indeed, the most commonly stated reason for selecting a mate is "love" (Rubin 1973). But "love" may actually mean anything from economic security to sex.

cathy® by Cathy Guisewite

There are many reasons for marrying, and these reasons are different at every stage in the life cycle. (CATHY COPYRIGHT 1988 UNIVERSAL PRESS SYNDICATE. Reprinted with permission. All rights reserved.)

In a recent survey of couples in the United States (Safran 1985), the following reasons cited for marrying add up to a good definition of love: "ability to laugh and have fun together" (75 percent), "strong sexual/physical attraction" (63 percent), "ability to share thoughts and feelings" (59 percent), "the many things we have in common" (51 percent), and "desire for emotional security" (46 percent). "Love" can mean different things to different people, and the kind of love one person feels for another changes over the course of the life cycle.

In 1954 Robert Winch, Thomas Ktsanes, and Virginia Ktsanes attempted to provide an explanation for the role of love in the mate selection process with their theory of complementary needs. This theory, as explained in more detail in chapter 3, contends that individuals seek their mates among a "limited pool of eligibles" which has been created by society's endogamous norms. That is to say, each of us tends to select a mate among people who have similar social backgrounds (race, religion, social class, and age). According to this theory, the final selection of the mate is based on complementary psychological needs and personality profiles—that is, a dovetailing of strengths and weaknesses that will provide need gratification for the one choosing. For example, a dominating and outgoing individual may prefer a spouse who is submissive and receptive.

This **theory of complementary needs** is predicated upon many of the assumptions found in exchange theory. Personal need gratification (which for Winch and his associates is highly associated with the feeling of being in love) is the reward that one seeks in the mate selection process. Eugene Mathes and Cheryl Moore (1985:321) summarize this complementarity theory of romantic love:

> *One explanation of why people experience the twentieth-century, Western phenomenon of falling in love is the concept*

of complementarity. One falls in love with someone who is different from oneself yet promises benefits that he or she cannot attain alone or with someone similar. The prototype of complementarity is found in heterosexuality. An individual does not fall in love with someone who is similar to himself or herself, that is, someone of the same sex. Instead, he or she falls in love with someone who is different, someone of the opposite sex. Thereby, the pleasure of sexual intercourse and procreation, pleasures that the individual could not achieve alone or with someone of the same sex, are made possible.

Extensive research by Winch and many other researchers has attempted to verify this theory, but with limited success (see White

---

Mate Selection and Marital Happiness: The Day After

He married her because, among other things, her hair looked so beautiful. ** He divorced her because she spent so much time fixing her hair.

She married him because his muscles rippled so when he swam. ** She divorced him because he spent more time in the bedroom doing sitting-up exercises than anything else.

He married her because she was such an adept conversationalist, never at a loss for a word. ** He divorced her because she never got off the telephone.

She married him because he had a robust masculine appetite and appreciated her cooking. ** She divorced him because he never wanted to take her out to eat.

He married her because she was so "vivacious." ** He divorced her because she was too restless.

She married him because he was a "real sport." ** She divorced him because he refused to give up the sporting life.

He married her because their families shared a common background. ** He divorced her because her family kept interfering in their affairs.

She married him because he was so courteous and attentive in all the little things that matter to a woman. ** She divorced him because he was so punctilious about little things, and so oblivious to important things.

Source: Sidney J. Harris, *Detroit Free Press*, November 21, 1966, p. 15-A. By permission of King Features Syndicate, Inc.

---

and Hatcher 1984; Solomon 1986; Thelen, Fishbein, and Tatten 1985; Lewak, Wakefield, and Briggs 1985; and Mathes and Moore 1985). In fact, most contemporary research studies conducted on married partners in community settings have provided empirical support for the alternate point of view—that mate selection is based upon similarity rather than dissimilarity of personalities of marriage partners. These studies have concluded that marriage partners tend to be more alike than different (see Tharp 1963; Thelen, Fishbein, and Tatten 1985; and Eysenck and Wakefield 1981). Furthermore, at least four empirical studies (Blazer 1963; Katz, Glucksberg, and Krauss 1960; Meyer and Pepper 1977; and Murstein and Beck 1972) have demonstrated that marital adjustment is positively associated with similarity of needs and not at all with complementarity. This finding has led Stephen White and Chris Hatcher (1984:16) to speculate as follows on need complementarity:

> It is the very characteristics partners find appealing about each other, leading to their attraction, that eventually become the focus, if not the cause, of major conflicts. In the case of a controlled, rational man, and his dependent and fun-loving wife, each is attracted in the other to qualities felt lacking in the self. As time progresses, however, the woman views the man as distant and unfeeling, while he sees her as irrational and needy.

Zahava Solomon (1986) has attempted to integrate mate selection models which stress either **homogeneity** (similarity) or **complementarity** (dissimilarity) with Bernard Murstein's (1971) Stimulus–Value–Response model. Murstein's theory postulates that mate selection results from a bargaining process in which self-acceptance or perceived self-worth is a key negotiable asset. In studying forty-eight couples from Israel who had applied for marriage licenses, Solomon (1986) discovered the following:

1. People tended to select partners who showed a self-acceptance similar to their own level.
2. Individuals possessing a high level of self-worth tended to choose partners whom they perceived as similar to themselves; individuals possessing a low level of self-acceptance tended to choose partners whom they perceived as different from themselves.
3. People with low self-acceptance tended to settle for partners who differed from their concept of ideal partners, but people with high self-acceptance chose mates who fulfilled their concept of ideal partners.

Solomon's (1986) findings relative to self-acceptance and perceived self-worth provide some empirical evidence that may help reconcile mate selection theories focusing on homogeneity or complementary needs of partners. According to Solomon (1986:5), "if level of self-acceptance plays a role in mate selection, given that there is a relationship between self-acceptance and ideal mate, then it follows that the ideal mate image will be relevant to mate selection by individuals with a high level of self-acceptance. In the case of those with low self-acceptance, however, who seemingly have settled for something less than their desirable mate, ideal image would not be implicated in the process of mate selection."

Whether we adopt the homogeneity or the complementarity theory of love, in most cultures of the world, love, as a factor in free mate selection, is very threatening to social order. Love tends to minimize the responsibilities that individuals feel toward their extended families. Love also tends to undermine the stratification system and parental authority.

Why Do Men Get Married?

Men don't want to get married. At least so American popular culture would have us believe. Movies, the comic pages, and our jokes tell us that men yearn to stay free as long as possible; men get married only when they've been trapped by feminine wiles and become adjusted to settling down. In old western films, the eastern schoolmarm weans the cowboy hero from his devotion to his horse with difficulty; their marriage is a microcosm of the taming of the west itself. We tend to believe that marriage is designed by women for women, and is consequently better for women than for the men who naturally avoid it.

Yet in real life men *want* to get married. As they talk about their own marriages, men rarely claim they were pursued or caught by their wife. Instead, many say they were consciously looking for a marriage partner at the time they met her. Some men even believe they wanted to get married more than their wife did, and recall having to talk her into the marriage.

Why do most men find marriage attractive? The reasons become clear when men speak about what their marriage means to them. Most husbands emphasize the importance of the companionship, intimacy, and emotional support they get from their marriage. And they value the security and safety of a home life where they can be themselves and find acceptance. Men with more traditional ideas about family life also say they like their role as "head of the family," the everyday support services that their wife provides, and even just the idea of being a "family man" itself; men with less traditional ideas say they also value talking to, learning from, and being challenged by their wife. Some men find satisfaction in building the kind of solid family life they missed as a child. Others find that being "tied down" actually helps them grow out of the rather chaotic emotional life they led as a bachelor.

We might conclude, then, that men get married because they sense that marriage will be *good* for them. And it is. Studies indicate that married men are happier, healthier, more emotionally stable, and live longer than single men. Men in both more and less traditional marriages find the companionship and intimacy in marriage something they don't usually experience with male friends, and the personal security and acceptance something they don't necessarily get from their work. And men in more traditional marriages enjoy the privileges, services, and image their married status provides, while men in less traditional families particularly enjoy the give and take of a more egalitarian relationship with a less traditional woman.

Perhaps the puzzle isn't so much why men get married. It's why our cultural myths continue to portray marriage as an institution which any normal man would want to avoid.

Source: Dr. Bruce Nordstrom, Department of Sociology, Saint Olaf College, Northfield, Minnesota.

Yet in Western societies, persons who get married for reasons other than love are highly suspect. Why is this so? The answer to this question may lie in the American family structure. Any society that (like U.S. society) highly values the isolated nuclear family of orientation and emphasizes individualism and privatism requires a strong motivating factor to encourage individuals to establish their own family of procreation. Referring to love, Christian and Jewish wedding ceremonies often recite Genesis 2:24, which says, "Therefore shall a man leave his father and his mother, and shall cleave unto his wife: and they shall be one flesh." Whenever individuals develop strong emotional attachments to institutions, only more powerful sentiments will enable them to change these primary commitments. Again, from an exchange perspective, only the power of conjugal love can overcome the loyalty and commitment that children feel for their parents. Fortunately, under most situations, the parents and their children both long for the day when these primary commitments will become redirected.

As we think about the socialization process that encourages Americans to value love above all things, we should not be surprised that "it's so easy to fall in love." Think about the many love songs we hear on the radio every day. It is easy to get the impression that "love is all there is."

William Goode (1964:39) summarizes the main connections between love and the other social structures in the United States this way:

1. The family unit is relatively independent of the larger kinship group so that husband and wife are free to love each other without serious competition from their kin.
2. The parent-child relationship is so strong that falling in love provides the motivation necessary to free the younger person from this attachment in order to enter the independent status of spouse.
3. In contemporary American society, adolescents have great personal freedom and autonomy providing them with the opportunity to meet many potential mates, thus increasing the likelihood that they will fall in love.
4. In the twentieth century, love has become the mechanism for filling the gap left by the decline of arranged marriages.

From a cross-cultural perspective, we find that as family structures in other cultures evolve to approximate those found in the industrialized West, love becomes an important factor in mate selection. Furthermore, as family structures become characterized by neolocality, monogamy, the importance of conjugal relationships, and the two-generation family, the mate selection process provides individuals with greater freedom and independence in their choice of spouse.

DATING: MATE SELECTION AND A WHOLE LOT MORE

As discussed earlier, self-arranged marriages have not always been the norm for American couples. Colonial society viewed marriages as contracts between persons that served the function of bringing order to daily family living. Couples might come together through matrimonial advertisements, third-party go-betweens, or everyday social relationships between members of the opposite sex. But whatever the means, no one expected courtship to drag out over a long period, and the law required couples to obtain permission from the bride's father *before* initiating courtship.

As a cultural custom, dating did not become normative in the United States until after World War I. Three social changes in the 1920s led to the custom of social dating—increased rural-urban migration, the more and more widespread personal ownership of automobiles, and the growing popularity of coeducational colleges. Each of these trends helped provide freedom and opportunity for young men and women to engage in leisure-time activities before marriage (Leslie and Korman 1985:336).

Today, Americans tend to think that dating is a necessary prerequisite to mate selection. Yet most people date for many reasons other than mate selection. Consider your reaction to this situation:

A woman asks a man if she may provide dinner for him after work. He responds, "To what do I owe this good fortune?" And she replies, "I have decided it is time I get married and I thought you would be a good prospect."

Clearly, acquiring a spouse may only be a latent social function of dating. Most people (under usual circumstances) would consider marriage a very remote, if not unlikely, outcome of social dating. Rarely, if ever, would a person turn down an invitation to go out on a date by saying, "Thank you for asking, but I must decline your invitation because, while I find you a nice person and good friend, I don't think that we should get married."

So what are the reasons for dating? In addition to mate selection, most family sociologists identify four social functions of dating: recreation, socialization, confirmation of social self, and status acquisition. Under most circumstances people will say that they date for companionship or to "have a good time." Dating is viewed by participants as being an end in itself—*recreation*. I remember a time when I had just broken up with my girlfriend and went to a movie with a group of male friends. Looking down my row and seeing my ex-girlfriend with her roommates, I realized that even though I was engaging in the same objective behavior (attending the theater), it was a less enjoyable experience in this nondating situation. Most daters will agree that even with all its potential for causing pain— rejection, exploitation, and embarrassment—social dating is an enjoyable recreational experience.

Dating also provides people with the *opportunity to be socialized*—to learn the norms, roles, and values related to heterosexual relationships. Observing other male-female couples (even one's parents) cannot substitute for the opportunity to test one's own skill in these situations. Within the social context of a dating relationship, a person can learn a lot about gender roles, physical intimacy, and interacting with members of the opposite sex—even when dating a less than enjoyable partner. More dating experiences tend to help us become more relaxed and comfortable in these situations.

Closely related to the socialization function of dating is the *opportunity to gain insight into one's self-identity.* Sociologists who adhere to a symbolic interactionist perspective would point out that dating provides participants with the quintessence of what Charles H. Cooley (1922) called the "looking-glass" self-concept. From the interactionist perspective, the self is a product of social interaction— we come to understand who we are as we reflect our "image of self" off of others. Cooley (1922) claims that this happens in three steps: (1) We imagine how others are *viewing* us; (2) we imagine how others are *judging* us; and (3) we respond with feelings of pride or of mortification.

As two people become involved in a dating relationship (especially in the first few dates), each of them is conscious that he or she is attempting to convey to the other "an idealized image of self." Sociologists claim that dating requires a significant amount of "impression management." Daters are very aware that their "self" is extremely vulnerable or "on the line" in dating situations. Consequently, dating provides the opportunity both for confirmation of self and for self-doubt. Typically, people continue to date those who bring out the best in them while dropping those who make them feel uncomfortable. In this process relationships emerge that can facilitate positive self-development.

The final function of dating is *status achievement.* Dating among single individuals is generally a positively evaluated activity. That is, the more one dates, the more likely one's status is to rise in one's social group. Furthermore, someone who dates persons rated as "highly desirable" by the social group is likely to gain vertical status mobility.

In 1937, Willard Waller published a study of college students and described a "rating and dating complex" where men and women were classified according to their desirability as dating partners. Factors affecting favorable evaluations included membership in a fraternity or sorority, attractive physical appearance, dressing well, owning a nice car, good manners, and being a good dancer. A student tended to gain status or social position on campus by being able to date those people considered highly desirable dating partners.

Of great sociological interest in this research was Waller's analysis of the "principle of least interest." Waller discovered that when dating partners were of unequal "dating status," the partner of greater status had less to gain from the dating relationship. Furthermore, the person with the least interest in continuing the relationship was

cathy®

by Cathy Guisewite

The dating partner who is the most vulnerable to exploitation is the one who cares most about the relationship. (CATHY COPYRIGHT 1988 UNIVERSAL PRESS SYNDICATE. Reprinted with permission. All rights reserved.)

most able to control the relationship and exploit the other dating partner.

The "principle of least interest" is especially important because it provides us with an insight into the relationship between commitment and exploitation. For example, a young man who feels that he is being exploited may accuse his dating partner of "using" him. Should the partner wish to continue the relationship (even for personal gain), she will try to convince the man (and herself) that she is committed to the relationship and that the accusation is false. This type of confrontation leads either to increased commitment on the part of the "least interested partner" or to a breakup of the dating relationship.

COHABITATION

In 1966, Margaret Mead, a famous anthropologist from Columbia University, wrote a highly controversial article for *Redbook* magazine entitled "Marriage in Two Steps." In this article she advocated a renovation of American marriages through the creation of two separate types of marriages. In the first type, which she called *individual marriage*, a couple would live together in a committed relationship for as long as they wished. The relationship would be based on mutual attraction and affection rather than on economic ties. Neither partner would be ultimately responsible for economic support, nor would alimony be paid if the marriage ended. The purpose of the individual marriage would be to give the couple a chance to know each other intimately within the context of a publicly validated marriage of uncertain duration. Couples in this type of marriage would not be permitted to have children.

Parental marriage, the second type of marriage, would have its own license, ceremony, and expanded set of responsibilities and commitments. Always preceded by an individual marriage, a parental marriage would require that the couple be financially able to support children. This kind of marriage would involve obligations to extended family members and to children born to, or adopted by, the couple. Consequently, compared to the first type of marriage, parental marriage would be harder to contract and to dissolve.

The major point of Mead's "Marriage in Two Steps" message is that two types of relationships exist in contemporary marriages—a deeply personal intimate relationship between the couple and a set of multigenerational and interpersonal family relationships. Most heterosexual single people experience a need to build intimate relationships with persons of the opposite sex before they are ready to make commitments that include other family members. Yet couples desire for their pair bonding a kind of social support that tradition-

Cohabitating couples may live together more for convenience than for emotional and affectional reasons, although most prefer to live with people they enjoy.

ally has been accorded only to "incipient families"—people intending to create families of procreation. Mead's two-step marriage system was an attempt to deal with this situation.

While marriage laws in the United States never incorporated Margaret Mead's proposal, in the 1970s and 1980s cohabitation among single adults of the opposite sex became widely practiced. The United States Bureau of the Census tracked this increase in cohabiting couples. They refer to these persons as POSSLQs (pronounced possel-kews)—which is an acronym for Persons of the Opposite Sex Sharing Living Quarters. In 1970 the census recorded 523,000 households in this category, while in 1984 this number had risen to 1,988,000, an increase of 280 percent in fourteen years (U.S. Bureau of the Census 1984). The majority of these householders (61 percent) were between the ages of twenty-five and forty-four. However, 22 percent were under twenty-five and 6 percent were older than sixty-four. Most POSSLQs (69 percent) did not have any children present, and almost half (48 percent) of cohabitors had never been married.

Cohabitation is an important issue related to mate selection because it raises the following question: Is cohabitation an alternative to marriage or an alternate form of courtship? The answer: Cohabitation is both, because there are many types of cohabiting relationships. Eleanor Macklin (1978) delineated the following five basic types of cohabiting relationships:

1. *Temporary or casual relationships for convenience:* People cohabiting for this reason do so because they find their relationship convenient and/or financially mutually beneficial. The relationship in the television show "Three's Company" was of this type.
2. *Affectionate dating or "going together":* This is an extension of a dating situation involving greater personal intimacy. People cohabiting for this reason do so because they find their relationship pleasurable.
3. *Trial marriage:* This type of cohabitation is similar to the second, but with the intention to marry. It is assumed that cohabitation of this type is short-lived, to be ended by either marriage or separation.
4. *Temporary alternative to marriage:* This type of relationship is very similar to a trial marriage, but marriage is more likely to take place in the distant future. Couples typically want to get married but do not find their present situation conducive. College students who are financially dependent upon their parents or persons waiting for a final divorce decree are two examples of couples who find themselves in this situation.

Divorce Rate High Among Swedes Who Lived Together Before Marriage

Couples who lived together before marrying have nearly an 80 percent higher divorce rate than those who did not, and seem to have less regard for the institution, according to a study of Swedish women by the National Bureau of Economic Research.

"We are not saying in any way that cohabiting causes higher divorce rates," said Neil Bennett, sociologist at Yale University and one of the study's authors. "What we are saying is that it appears that people who cohabit premaritally are less committed to the institution and are more inclined to divorce than people who do not live together."

The study was based on a 1981 survey of 4,996 Swedish women. The respondents were 10 to 44 years old and had lived with their spouses for one month to 10 years before marriage. Swedes were chosen because they tend to precede United States social trends by 10 to 15 years. A higher proportion of Swedes cohabit before marriage, but the practice is increasing in the United States. An estimated 2 million American couples live together unwed, or about 4 percent of couples. In Sweden, 12 percent of couples are unmarried.

Statistics on women were used because no such data were kept on men, although the findings apply to both sexes. The marriage dissolution rates of women who cohabit premaritally with their future spouse are, on average, nearly 80 percent higher than the rates of those who do not.

Source: Associated Press, *Minneapolis Star and Tribune* (December 7, 1987), p. 2A.

5. *Permanent alternative to marriage:* This is a living situation caused by the fact that the couple either rejects the institution of marriage or is prevented from marrying for some reason. Many older persons cohabit rather than marry because if they remarry they will lose some of their Social Security benefits.

While we can see that the practice of cohabitation is becoming increasingly more popular in the United States, there is still much social science research needed to provide an understanding of this complex phenomenon. At present we do know that couples cohabit for many different reasons—some as a path to marriage and others as an alternative to it.

- The mate selection process tends to produce homogamous marriages, which are supported by rules of endogamy and achieved against some rules of exogamy (e.g., incest rules).
- In the United States endogamous norms are operative in the following areas: social class, race and ethnicity, religious preference, age, and place of residence.
- Fundamentally, mate selection functions like a market system where individuals and families barter with symbolic and nonsymbolic rewards. Through this process, people of relatively equal value (as evaluated by their respective cultures) find and marry each other.
- In the United States individuals are relatively free to choose mates with only limited interference from parents, grandparents, siblings, and other kin. In many other cultures, members of the larger kinship group control mate selection.
- Most cultures equalize the value of potential spouses with dower and dowry systems.
- Winch's theory of complementary needs is predicated upon many of the assumptions found in exchange theory. Personal need gratification is the reward that each person seeks in the mate selection process.
- Extensive research has attempted to verify this theory with limited success. Most contemporary studies conducted on married partners in community settings have provided support for the alternate point of view—mate selection is based upon similarity of partners rather than dissimilarity with respect to personality makeup. Furthermore, marital adjustment is positively associated with need similarity, and not with complementarity.
- For most cultures of the world, love, as a factor in free mate selection, is very threatening to social order. Love tends to minimize responsibility toward extended families, and to undermine the stratification system and parental authority.
- Any society that highly values the isolated nuclear family of orientation and that emphasizes individualism and privatism requires strong motivating factors to encourage individuals to establish their own family of procreation. We find that as family structures in other cultures evolve to approximate those found in the industrialized West, love becomes an important factor in mate selection.
- Even though dating did not become normative in the United States until after World War I, Americans today tend to think that dating is a necessary prerequisite to mate selection. In addition to mate selection, most family sociologists identify four social functions of dating: recreation, socialization, confirmation of social self, and status acquisition.
- Cohabitation can be thought of as both an alternative form of mate selection and an alternative to marriage.

1. What is meant by homogamy? How are homogamous norms related to endogamy and exogamy?
2. Describe the range of variation on the continuum from arranged marriage to free choice of mate. What are the functions of arranged marriage? What selection criteria are important in arranged marriage? What factors constrain choice of spouse in the United States?
3. What is the central idea of exchange theories of mate selection? How does exchange theory operate in dating relationships? How do bargaining and exchange differ?
4. Think about dating and mate selection in the United States as a game. What are the objectives for men and women? What rules govern the game? Who enforces the rules? What sanctions are applied if the rules are broken?
5. Explain Waller's "principle of least interest." What empirical evidence can you think of to support this idea?
6. Explain the theory of complementary needs. What does research show? Do you think further development of the theory is needed?
7. How is cohabiting both an alternative to marriage and an alternative to traditional mate selection and dating?
8. How does nonmarital cohabitation affect subsequent marital adjustment? How would you expect it to affect traditional gender roles?
9. What functional values does nonmarital cohabitation have for college students and for the elderly?

GLOSSARY

complementarity: Property of a relationship where the partners have dissimilar personality needs and attributes.

dower: A bride's price or an exchange of money, goods, or services given to the family of the bride to compensate her family for their past expenses and their future loss of her services.

dowry: A groom's price or an exchange of money, goods, or services given to the family of the groom to compensate his family for their past expenses and their future loss of his services.

exogamy: The norm requiring an individual to marry outside a specific group of which he or she is a member.

endogamy: The norm requiring marriage within one's own socioeconomic status, religion, ethnicity, or whatever grouping is prescribed.

heterogamy: Marriage of persons having dissimilar characteristics.

homogeneity: Property of a relationship where the partners have similar personality needs and attributes.

homogamous marriage: Marriage of persons having similar background characteristics.

theory of complementary needs: Robert Winch's theory that individuals will seek their mates within an endogamous pool of eligibles using maximum psychological need gratification as the final criteria for selection.

SUGGESTED READINGS

Macklin, Eleanor. 1978. "Nonmarital Heterosexual Cohabitation." *Marriage and Family Review* 1 (March/April): 463–72. *An interesting study of cohabiting couples in the United States.*

Queen, Stuart A., Robert W. Habenstein, and Jill S. Quadagno. 1985. *The Family in Various Cultures.* 5th ed. New York: Harper and Row, Publishers. *This book describes courtship in many different cultures, subcultures, and historical periods. It provides an interesting comparative approach.*

White, Stephen G., and Chris Hatcher. 1984. "Couple Complementarity and Similarity: A Review of the Literature." *The American Journal of Family Therapy* 12, no. 1: 15–25. *An excellent review of the literature on Robert Winch's theory of complementary needs.*

Issues in Human Sexuality

♦ *Sex is one of the nine reasons for reincarnation. . . . The other eight are unimportant.**

Why is human sexuality included in a book on the family? The importance of sexual relationships, both within a marital setting and outside of marriage, has historically played a significant role in societies around the world. Powerful social norms, which vary from society to society, control what is okay and what is taboo regarding sexual behaviors.

While some societies allow—even encourage—sexual relations outside of marriage, others frown on such behavior and impose sanctions to discourage the activity. In the United States, for example, society has traditionally approved of sexual relations between married individuals and disapproved of sexual activity outside of marriage. In most, if not all, societies, norms are established and enforced to forbid consanguine sexual relations. The incest taboo is about as close as one can come to a universal norm.

How do husbands' and wives' perceptions of sexuality differ? They typically differ in the circumstances leading to sexual arousal, in some of the criteria that determine sexual attractiveness, and in the occurrence of sexual jealousy. Men are more likely than women to be aroused by the visual stimulus of a member of the opposite sex. Females are aroused primarily by tactual rather than by visual stimulation. Both sexes tend to perceive good health, especially as evidenced in skin condition, as attractive. Attractiveness of both sexes

*Henry Miller in *Big Sur and the Oranges of Hieronymus*

diminishes in old age, but before old age female attractiveness declines much more rapidly than male attractiveness. Sexual jealousy is a more nearly universal aspect of male than of female psychology (Symons 1985:145–47).

Many Americans think of the "sexual revolution" of the 1960s and 1970s as a response to a sexual marketplace that had dominated and marginalized women. But this "revolution" is probably better understood as an evolution in middle-class women's sexuality. Men changed their sexual behavior very little in the decades from the fifties to the eighties. They "fooled around," got married, and had affairs, just as their fathers had done before them. American women, on the other hand, moved from a pattern of virginity before marriage and monogamy thereafter to a pattern that much more resembles men's. Between the mid-sixties and the mid-seventies, the number of women reporting premarital sexual experience went from a small minority to a sizable majority. The proportion of married women reporting active premarital or extramarital sex lives is now close to half in some estimates. The importance of female virginity is rapidly disappearing in many circles (Ehrenreich et al. 1986:1–2).

Middle-class women not only were having more sex, and with a greater variety of partners, they were also having sex on their own

Although gender equality has yet to be achieved, a more egalitarian society exists today, in part because of the "sexual revolution" and the women's movement.

terms and enjoying it as enthusiastically as men. As recently as the 1950s, Americans acknowledged nonorgasmic responses by females as their greatest sexual dysfunction. Some estimates were that over half of American women were completely nonorgasmic. Yet a 1975 survey found that 81 percent of the 100,000 respondents were orgasmic "all or most of the time" (Ehrenreich et al. 1986:2).

The roots of the women's sexual revolution lie in a set of circumstances rising from the late 1950s and early 1960s. The private dissatisfaction of many middle-class women centered on marital sex. Improvements in birth control in the sixties, especially the introduction of the pill in 1962, gave women a sense of freedom and flexibility that the more cumbersome methods had never done. Legal abortion also became a powerful factor in women's sexual liberation in the 1970s and 1980s. New career opportunities were opening up for women. With a proliferation of jobs for women, young single women crowded into the major cities and began to enlarge the gap between girlhood and marriage, filling it with careers, romances, and casual sexual relationships. Even very young women were finding a space of their own between childhood and womanhood. These new "spaces" incubated the women's sexual revolution (Ehrenreich et al. 1986:6, 196–97).

During the "sexual revolution" of the 1960s, I was teaching marriage and the family. I remember receiving a brochure advertising a book about some one-hundred-plus ways to have sexual intercourse! By using your imagination, you might think of a dozen or more ways, but over a hundred? The gamut of possibilities must have run from hanging from a light fixture by one arm to standing on the floor on one toe. It was educational looking at the brochure and wondering how anyone ever came up with that many ways to do anything, let alone have sex.

Source: Author.

From a feminist perspective, the sexual revolution challenged the old definition of sex as a merely physical act (Ehrenreich et al. 1986:193). Many women reject such a version of sex as narrow, male-centered, and unsatisfying. They feel that such a form of sex imitates rape and is obsessive, repetitive, and symbolically tied to the work of reproduction. Feminists advocate a broader, more playful notion of sex, one more compatible with women's broader erotic possibilities and more respectful of women's needs.

The reader of books on human sexuality should be alert to the many "cookbook approaches" to the sexual scene, epitomized by the title of Alex Comfort's early 1970s bestseller *The Joy of Sex: A Gourmet Guide to Love Making.* Many of today's sex manuals pay only lip service to the communicative and emotional aspects of intercourse, stressing instead its sensuous side—the "body-centered" attitudes that used to be regarded as typically male-oriented (Hunt 1983:225).

This chapter will explore issues in human sexuality that have been affected by the changes of the past three decades and the "sexual revolution." The feminist movement has contributed significantly to these changes, and has helped bring about a freedom for females not previously experienced in the United States. In the following discussion on human sexuality we'll discuss sex education, birth control, same-sex relationships, extramarital sexual relationships, sexually transmitted diseases, and sexual dysfunctions.

SEX EDUCATION

Should sex education be taught in a school setting, or should the family be responsible for educating children about human sexuality? A 1985 Louis Harris poll showed that 85 percent of the American public supported sex education in the classroom; yet nationwide, only 10 percent of school districts offered any sex or contraceptive education program (Perlez 1986). Sex education seems, however, to be more popular in cities with populations over 100,000. An Urban Institute study in January 1982 found that 85 percent of students in cities with over 100,000 population received some form of sex education in school (Johnson 1986).

Traditionally, sex education has not been offered in U.S. schools, and students have turned to other sources for information. Studies of sex education going back to the 1940s suggest that peers, written materials, and parents were the major sources of socialization regarding sexual behavior (Dickinson 1978).

A study (Dickinson 1978) of over four hundred high school students in a rural east Texas community found that *actual* and *preferred* sources of sex information differed significantly. The *actual* sources of sex information for these adolescents (in descending order of importance) were friends, then books and pamphlets, and finally mothers (for the females). The *preferred* source for these adolescents, however, was parents, while friends and written materials were a very distant second choice. Since in real life peers serve as a major source of sex information, many parents and educators feel that these peers should be exposed to accurate sex information through a medium such as the school.

The need for sex education was brought home to me several years ago, when I shared an office with another sociologist who was

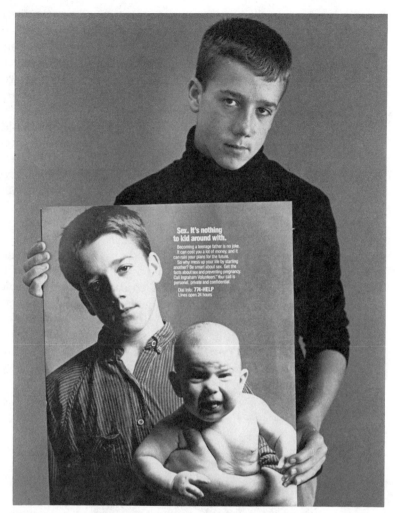

Sex education in American schools remains a controversial topic, yet today more schools are offering sex education than in the recent past. With the alarming rate of teenage pregnancy, there is a growing awareness of both parents' and teachers' responsibilities for giving children the facts. Teenagers themselves are helping in this effort, many of them sharing hard-learned lessons.

also a counselor. Early one winter morning on that Pennsylvania college campus, a freshman came to see my colleague. She was crying and obviously very upset. When he asked what the trouble was, she responded in quavering tones that she was pregnant. He then asked her how long she had been pregnant, and she said, "Since last night!"

I excused myself at this point and started out of the room to give the student some privacy. As I was slipping quietly out the door, I heard my office-partner ask how she knew she was pregnant so soon after the event. She responded, again through a shower of tears, "Because he kissed me!" This was an eighteen-year-old college freshman. Though this may be an unusual case, it highlights the need for accurate sex education starting at an early age.

The question of what topics sex education should cover is fraught with controversy. The sex education curriculum put in place in 1984 in the New York City school system tackles subjects once considered taboo, such as premarital intercourse and contraception (Johnson 1986). On the elementary level, under that curriculum, kindergarteners learn that "living things begin as eggs" and that "family members love each other in a variety of ways." Upper-grade classes give students information about sexually transmitted diseases, their effect on fertility and pregnancy, and single-parent families.

Some state legislatures are still wrestling with the issue of sex education courses and the content of such courses in the public schools. *Time*'s prediction a generation ago (Time Essay 1967) missed the mark in saying that "since sex education in the schools has moved forward at startling speed, experts estimate that two years from now, 70 percent of the nation's schools will have broad, thorough sex-education programs." While we have come a long way regarding sex education in the schools, we still have a long way to go.

What to teach in sex education and in which grade to begin are sources of disagreement in many U.S. schools. One thing, however, is clear—students need the facts and need them now.

Some Say Sex Education Should Begin at Birth

Preschoolers are definitely sexual beings, and curious ones at that. A child's sexual explorations can either put parents into a panic or give them a chance to explain sex before the child hears about it from confused schoolmates.

In the context of AIDS prevention, U.S. Surgeon General C. Everett Koop recently suggested that sex education should begin in the third grade. But more basic birds-and-bees briefings should begin as early as age two, say sex educators. The "big talk" at adolescence is an outdated, clumsy, and belated approach to sex education and should be replaced by continual communication that begins when children learn the names of their body parts.

Children are not only better informed when they get this early start but are also more likely to feel comfortable talking to parents about sex when they become teenagers. Parents concerned about child molestation should consider that failure to educate children about sexuality keeps them not innocent but exploitable.

The questions and behavior of preschoolers offer parents "teachable moments" to explain sex, but parents need not wait to be asked. For example, a pregnant relative might spark discussion about where babies come from. A three-year-old masturbating in the living room also offers parents an opportunity to explain which activities are appropriate in public and which are best done in private. It is not necessary to wait until your child asks about sex.

Before the subject comes up, parents should think about what kind of messages they want to impart. Negative attitudes tend to stay in terms of later feelings of guilt and anxiety surrounding sexuality, so it is important that parents give positive messages.

Preschoolers are most curious about birth, bodies, and babies. They want to know such things as where they came from and how they got there, and they want to know why boys have penises and girls do not. Straightforward answers are the best response, although parents are often unsure just how much information a preschooler can grasp. If they get bored, you are probably giving too much detail. Give information as the child asks questions. Do not overload him or her with too much at a time. Answers should be clear and specific since children are literal thinkers. Building self-esteem about the goodness of sex and putting children in charge of their bodies are vital steps in a sexual maturation that begins earlier than most parents realize.

Source: Adapted from an article in *The News and Courier* (Charleston, S.C., January 4, 1987).

BIRTH CONTROL ISSUES

Couples practice **birth control** (voluntary control of childbearing) to limit family size, to space the arrival of children, and to enjoy a freer and more harmonious sexual relationship within marriage. When you think about it, a couple's ability—or inability—to regulate the number and spacing of their children practically defines what the family's life will be like. The family's daily routine and their entire pattern of behavior will be affected by the size of the family. Chapters 11 and 12 discuss the impact of having or not having children.

All human groups consciously attempt to regulate their fertility. Birth control has been practiced since primitive times in all cultures. In the United States almost all fertile married couples practice birth control in some form. As Alan Guttmacher observes in *The Complete Book of Birth Control* (1963:7), in the earlier half of the twentieth century the more fortunate people practiced birth control, and the less fortunate did not. But a radical change has occurred in the past seventy-five years, and today families of all social classes, religions, and ethnic backgrounds practice birth control with varying degrees of success.

Social Control and Sexual Intercourse Sexual intercourse and the reproduction of human beings, however, are subjected to a high degree of social control. And since sex is surrounded by a multitude of taboos and sanctions, contraceptive practices are also a social issue. In her discussion of abortion and the "decision not to contracept," Kristin Luker (1975:42–51) presents four themes occurring within the social and cultural meanings of contraception: (1) Contraception means acknowledging intercourse; (2) contraception means planning intercourse; (3) continuing contraception over time means that socially a woman is sexually available; and (4) contraception means that sexual activity is intentional and cannot be spontaneous.

The increased use of birth control practices is to a great degree a result of changes in attitudes toward sex. As we've mentioned, not too many years ago, sexual satisfaction was popularly thought to be a masculine monopoly and sex something to be endured by women. Today, however, both males and females feel that they can—and should—seek sexual satisfaction.

The "Burden" of Birth Control In her book *Taking Chances* (1975:124–27) Kristen Luker emphasizes the burdensome and inequitable side of women's responsibility for contraception. She asserts that the domination of the contraceptive field by the pill is the result of a "deliberate" clinical and research decision in the late 1950s to shift emphasis to "female-oriented methods" whose use would be removed from sexual intercourse. Luker notes that before the pill, virtually all contraceptives were intercourse-related, and she suggests that they involved at least some degree of shared responsibility by men. The shift to "female methods," such as the pill, the intrauterine device (IUD), and abortion, worked primarily to reinforce the patriarchal ideology of women's exclusive responsibility for reproduction.

Rosalind Petchesky in *Abortion and Woman's Choice* (1984:172) argues that Luker's feminist analysis of the pill's advent and its impact romanticizes the past. Luker's perspective ignores the fact that some methods used "prior to the pill" were not "intercourse-related," such as illegal abortion or sterilization, and that even those that were (the condom, the "rhythm method," or withdrawal) may have been used *effectively* only when women asserted their own sense of need.

Petchesky (1984:172–73) contends that the "male" or "female" responsibility involved in a fertility control method is not a question intrinsic to its technology or form but is determined by the social relations of its use. Luker's argument disregards women's desire and need for control, even if control means assuming *all* the risks. Luker's position ignores the feminist understanding that pregnancy involves an irreducible biological dimension; the experience, and therefore the responsibility, cannot totally be transferred.

The rise of birth control developed side by side with broad changes in sexual attitudes, values, and practices. The concept that "sex is sin" began to wane early in the 1900s (Guttmacher 1963:12–13). In earlier centuries, in Christian and Jewish culture, the belief was that men and women's whole physical being was tainted by sin and that only the soul could be pure. Sexual activity was viewed as the key mechanism by which "original sin" was transmitted from generation to generation. Such beliefs formed an important part of the "Victorian morality" of the nineteenth century. But with the development of social and medical sciences, new knowledge about sexual needs emerged. Also, many theologians concluded that sex could be seen as a stabilizing, elevating force in marriage. And contraception itself, by helping remove the fear of pregnancy, has made sexual relationships more enjoyable.

The Use of Birth Control How frequently are birth control measures used by American couples? Approximately thirty years ago, the extent of contraceptive practice among American families was documented in a study (Freedman et al. 1959) known as the "GAF Study" (Growth of American Families). In this nationwide sample of more than 2,700 married white women of childbearing age, extensive interviews revealed that a majority of the couples had taken some steps to prevent or postpone pregnancy. While the effects of religious beliefs on birth control practice were significant, seventy percent of Roman Catholic wives reported using birth control. Ninety-five percent of all Jewish couples reported practicing birth control, and 84 percent of Protestant couples were using birth control measures.

The GAF Study also reported that education and family income had more influence than religion on the practice of birth control. Among wives not going beyond grade school, 66 percent had practiced birth control; among high school graduates, 83 percent used contraceptives; and the percentage rose to 88 percent for college graduates. A positive correlation was also evident between family income and proportion of families practicing birth control: as income level goes up, the practice of birth control increases.

BIRTH CONTROL MEASURES

Family planning was popularized after World War II by established organizations like the Planned Parenthood Federation of America. The idea was that the planned spacing of children would strengthen the nuclear family and thus increase social stability. According to Thomas Shapiro (1985:9), however, the concept of family planning primarily addresses the needs of heterosexual, monogamous married couples. Family planning centers introduce couples to various technologies that help them space their children and limit the number of children they have. Table 9.1 summarizes information on selected methods of birth control.

Condoms

Condoms, rubber sheaths named after an eighteenth-century physician and made for men to use, appeared to be losing favor in the 1960s and 1970s because of the popularity of birth-control pills, diaphragms, and other devices made for women to use (Hyde 1982:149). These women's products appeared to be more convenient or were not felt to interfere as much with sexual pleasure (Berger 1987). The condom, however, has the advantage of being the only contraceptive method now available for men except sterilization. It is also relatively inexpensive, readily available without prescription, and fairly easy to use; and it is one of the few contraceptive devices providing some protection against sexually transmitted diseases **(STDs).** The disadvantages of the condom include the inconvenience of having to put it on during sexual activity and the potential that it may tear or come off. Some form of spermicide is necessary for condoms to be fully effective in preventing pregnancy and in preventing many sexually transmitted diseases.

TABLE 9.1 Selected Birth Control Methods

Method	Advantages	Disadvantages
Abortion	Removes the embryo/fetus, thus is effective	Any procedure such as this could involve physical and emotional suffering for the mother; expensive
Birth control pills	Highly effective; not used at time of coitus; improved regularity of menstrual cycles	Side effects like nausea; must be taken regularly; requires prescription
Condom	Easy to use; some protection from sexually transmitted diseases (STDs)	Interferes with coitus; less effective than the pill
Diaphragm with cream or jelly	No side effects; inexpensive	Aesthetic objections
Intrauterine device (IUD)	Questionable	In some users, anemia, cramping, spotting, backaches; 20 percent expel IUD in first year; serious health concerns; some IUDs no longer sold because of problems
Rhythm (calendar method)	No cost; accepted by Roman Catholic church	Requires high motivation, prolonged abstinence, self-control; unreliable
Sterilization	Permanent and highly effective	Permanent; psychological complications may occur; involves some risk; expensive
Vaginal foam	Easy to use, widely available	Messy
Vaginal sponge (with spermicide)	May improve vaginal lubrication; some protection against STDs	May produce vaginal odor and itching; may be torn or shredded in attempt to remove
Withdrawal	No cost	Requires high motivation and self-control; often ineffective

Source: Adapted in part from Janet Shibley Hyde, *Understanding Human Sexuality*, 2d edition (New York: McGraw-Hill, 1982), p. 168. Material used by permission.

Given the rational concern over STDs (AIDS, herpes, and a wide range of venereal diseases), the condom regained much popularity and became an issue in the media during the late 1980s. The pendulum started to swing with growing public awareness of AIDS. Marketing strategies for condoms are increasingly being directed toward women (Gross 1987). Condoms are now on sale in many drugstores right next to feminine hygiene products, and some new condom products are packaged to appeal to women—in pastel-colored boxes, often featuring photographs of couples. Previously viewed as a taboo topic on television commercials and in magazines, condoms are advertised in publications like *Ms.*, the *Ladies' Home Journal*, *Bride's*, *American Baby*, *Newsweek*, *U.S. News & World Report*, the *New York Times*, and *U.S.A. Today*.

Television has opened up more on the issue of advertising contraceptives (Arar 1987). In 1985, an American College of Obstetricians and Gynecologists was accepted by the three networks, but a public service announcement to promote a pamphlet on birth control only after the sentence "Unintended pregnancies have greater risks than any of today's contraceptives" was changed to "There are many ways to prevent an unintended pregnancy."

In mid-January of 1987 (Berger 1987) KRON-TV of San Francisco began to air condom commercials, saying it would donate profits to AIDS research; about this same time, KCOP-TV in Los Angeles approved condom ads to be run on their station. KRON's fifteen-second commercial depicted a box of Trojan condoms. An announcer's voice told of the Surgeon General's statements endorsing con-

---

Colleges Condone Condoms: Valentine's Day 1987

Valentine's Day 1987 may be remembered for condoms, not Cupids, on campuses where groups gave out the birth-control devices to educate students about contraception and help safeguard them against AIDS. A brandy snifter filled with candy and almost 600 packages of condoms was the centerpiece for "Love Carefully Day" at Greenfield Community College in Massachusetts. The highlight of the day's activities was a speech entitled "AIDS: Don't Die of Ignorance." People must begin to understand that AIDS is a homosexual disease *and* a heterosexual disease.

In Minneapolis, the University of Minnesota's main campus celebrated National Condom Week by sponsoring speakers and movies on AIDS issues, with activities beginning on Valentine's Day. Condoms are also being distributed in campus rest rooms.

The women's center at the University of Wisconsin at Madison sponsored Contraceptive Awareness Week for the second year by making 200 joint packages of contraceptive sponges and condoms available to students in the union each day. Each package was accompanied by a poem: "Roses are red, violets are blue. We have a great way to say, I care about you."

Source: Adapted from Note Book, *The Chronicle of Higher Education* (Washington, D.C., February 18, 1987), p. 27.

doms and added: "This is a box of Trojans. Use it in good health. Trojan. For all the right reasons."

The year 1987 saw condoms distributed in new ways. After preaching a sermon on moral responsibilities regarding sexual issues, for example, one minister reportedly had the ushers hand out condoms during a church service. Activist groups, trying to diminish the spread of AIDS, handed out condoms to students on their spring breaks on the Florida beaches. As a result of concern over AIDS and other STDs, Columbia, Princeton, and Rutgers Universities broadened their efforts to distribute condoms and inform students about their use (Berger 1987). The reading on condoms suggests that other college campuses are busily making condoms available to their students.

Sterilization

Sterilization is a surgical procedure whereby an individual is made permanently sterile (unable to reproduce). Sterilization is a rather emotion-laden topic for the following reasons: (1) It conjures up images of government-imposed programs of involuntary sterilization for groups such as the mentally retarded and criminals; (2) some people confuse male sterilization with castration (though the two are quite different!); and (3) sterilization means the end of a woman's or a man's capacity to reproduce (Hyde 1982:154). Despite these emotional issues, both male and female sterilization have become increasingly popular as methods of birth control in the United States, and an estimated 7 million adult Americans are now sterilized (Hyde 1982:155).

The male sterilization operation is called *vasectomy* (named for the vas deferens, the tube that carries the sperm, which is tied or cut). The procedure requires about twenty minutes and is done under local anesthesia. The physician makes a small incision on each side of the upper part of the scrotum, then separates the vas from the surrounding tissues, ties it off, and cuts it. This procedure makes it impossible for sperm to move beyond the cut in the vas, thus the semen ejaculated contains no sperm.

Female sterilization has historically been more complicated and commonly performed under general anesthesia. The procedure involves blocking the fallopian tubes in some way to prevent the sperm and egg from meeting. *Tubal ligation* is the most common method of female sterilization. The surgeon makes an incision in the abdomen or at the end of the vagina, cuts out a small section of each fallopian tube, and ties it off at the incision. A newer procedure, which can be done on an outpatient basis, is the *endoscopy*. The physician inserts a small tube, with lights and a mirror, through the abdomen, the vagina, or the uterus to locate the fallopian tubes and cauterize (burn) them with a small instrument. This more recent procedure makes female sterilization operations no more difficult or involved than vasectomies.

The majority of women seeking sterilization are married at the time of being sterilized (87 percent), and the most common ages are around thirty to thirty-four (Petchesky 1984:178–79). Many married women arrange to have their tubes tied when they go to the hospital to deliver their last child, for the convenience of taking care of everything at once. An important part of the history of sterilization, however, is the incidence of coercive sterilization and sterilization abuse among mainly poor and minority women in the United States. Sterilization programs today still tend to have subtle population control objectives aimed at particular groups—the "poor."

Abortion

Twelve times between 1972 and 1986, the National Opinion Research Center of the University of Chicago **(NORC)** asked Americans their views on legalized abortion (Sussman 1986). Though the percentages which follow seem consistent over time, abortion is an issue that causes much conflict within individuals. Over the period reported by NORC the results basically stayed the same: About 40 percent of respondents indicated that they supported abortion on demand, 10 percent opposed abortion under any circumstances, and 50 percent believed that abortion should be legal under certain circumstances. More than 80 percent believed abortion should be legal if "there is a strong chance of serious defect in the baby" or "if a woman becomes pregnant as a result of rape," and 90 percent favored it "if the woman's health is seriously endangered." By contrast, almost 60 percent said abortion should not be legal if a woman "is married and does not want any more children," and more than half were opposed in the instance of a single woman who is pregnant but "does not want to marry the man." The public was evenly divided in the case of a family that is poor "and cannot afford any more children."

The term **abortion** refers to the ending of a pregnancy and the expulsion of the contents of the uterus. Abortion may be spontaneous (in which case it is generally called "miscarriage"), or it may be induced by human intervention. It is the induced abortions that are the subject of controversy. From the early 1900s to 1973, abortion was generally illegal throughout the United States. For the most part, therapeutic abortions were legal only when the woman's life was threatened by the pregnancy (Rodman, Lewis, and Griffith 1984:117). Illegal abortions occurred by the thousands for those who could afford them, but the poor had no financial means for an abortion. Between 1966 and 1972, thirteen states did reform their abor-

Although abortion was legalized in 1973 in the United States, it has remained a most controversial issue. The recent Supreme Court case, *Webster* v. *Reproductive Health Services of Missouri,* has resurrected all the emotional intensity and political protest of *Roe* v. *Wade.*

tion laws to permit therapeutic abortions on the following grounds: preserving the woman's health, fetal deformity, and pregnancy due to rape or incest. Although abortion remains controversial, its legal and constitutional status was strongly affected by the U.S. Supreme Court's Roe versus Wade decision of 1973, which made abortion legal throughout the United States—a woman's right to have an abortion was granted constitutional protection, and abortion became increasingly available.

Legalization of abortion prompted the rapid emergence of a new health care delivery system—free-standing abortion clinics (Cates 1986:315). And experience gained in the delivery of abortion services at free-standing clinics led to an expansion of other services at these facilities. Today, in addition to abortion, many clinics are providing infertility investigations, male and female sterilization procedures, family planning and contraceptive counseling, and routine outpatient gynecologic care.

The availability of legal abortion had a profound impact on women's health in the 1970s and 1980s (Cates 1986:318). Fifteen hundred women were estimated (Tietze 1984) to be saved from pregnancy-related deaths between 1973 and 1983 because of legal abortions. Legal abortion allowed pregnant women to make safer choices, physicians to develop better surgical techniques, and free-standing clinics to emerge as important health care providers. The fact that rising numbers of abortions and increased contraceptive use are related trends contradicts the widely held impression that many women are substituting abortion for contraception. Among sexually active teenagers, a high proportion use some method of contraception, and seven out of ten teenage girls become regular contraceptive users after a first pregnancy (Petchesky 1984:190).

In the United States the majority of women seeking abortion are under twenty-five and unmarried and have no children (Petchesky 1984:179). Two theories exist as to why women have unwanted pregnancies. First, unwanted pregnancies exist because women lack the contraceptive expertise to prevent them. Second, women have the contraceptive skills to prevent pregnancies but experience psychological resistance to using them.

Kristin Luker (1975:78–111) suggests a third theory, characterizing unwanted pregnancy as "contraceptive risk-taking" behavior that results from conscious decision making. This theory assumes that individuals perceive options, assign values to these various options, choose one option over another, and then act to implement that choice in behavioral terms. Luker argues that women who do not want to become pregnant but who do not use previously demonstrated contraceptive skills have engaged in a "rational" decision-making process.

SAME-SEX RELATIONSHIPS

You may wonder why a discussion of same-sex or **homosexual** relationships is included in a book on family relationships. The answer is, as pointed out in previous discussions in this book, that family patterns in the United States and throughout the world are highly diverse. And homosexual-oriented family patterns, while far less prevalent than opposite-sex or **heterosexual**-oriented patterns in the United States, are the preferred lifestyles of many adults today.

Why Same-Sex Relationships? Why some individuals prefer same-sex family relationships and others seek opposite-sex arrangements is a difficult question. There are probably as many theories attempting to explain homosexuality as there are pages in this chapter. There is one certainty regarding homosexuality—almost every homosexual was born to a heterosexual couple. The evidence of heredity, hormonal imbalance, and interactional patterns of parents is very sparse and lacking credibility (Gordon and Snyder 1986:73).

Gay Couples Persons unfamiliar with gay male relationships often tend to "heterosexualize" them; that is, they tend to envision one partner as masculine and the other as engaging in complementary feminine activities. The one thing the literature most clearly shows about intimate gay relationships, however, is that they seldom

Contrary to popular belief, few homosexual couples, male or female, engage in stereotypical "butch/femme" role playing within their relationships.

approximate this version of traditional husband and wife roles (Harry 1983:217). Although a few gays may organize their relationships in a "butch/femme" manner, research strongly indicates that gay relationships are more likely to be patterned after a "best friends/roommates" model than after a heterosexual sex role model. The butch/femme hypothesis has also been applied to lesbian couples, but such role playing is also relatively rare among gay females.

Data indicate (Harry 1983:219) that there is a wider range of age differences among gay partners than among heterosexual couples. The median age difference between gay male partners is 4.9 years, while the median age difference between heterosexual partners is approximately 2 years. The literature also shows that many gay male relationships are considerably less sexually exclusive than heterosexual ones or lesbian relationships (Harry 1983:222).

Since some gays have been heterosexually married, many gay men are fathers. The large majority of these fathers, however, do not retain custody of the children at the time of divorce—the courts have traditionally preferred to give custody to the mother. Gay men may also become fathers by becoming foster fathers or through single-parent adoptions.

Lesbian Couples **Lesbian** partners, or female homosexuals, are more likely to live together than are gay male partners. Approximately 75 percent of lesbian couples live together, compared with slightly more than 50 percent of all gay male couples (Harry 1983:225). Lesbians tend to meet their partners through lesbian friendship networks, with the period of courtship lasting from one to nine months (Tanner 1978:66–71). On the other hand, the courtship period for gay men is truncated and is often preceded by sexual relations. Thus, while sexual relationships among lesbians usually arise out of a developing affectional relationship, among gay men affection frequently develops out of a sexual relationship. Similarly, among heterosexual males and females, evidence exists that women often develop emotional attachment first, then sexual attraction, while men are often attracted sexually before becoming emotionally involved.

Regarding the durability of gay relationships (Harry 1983:227), it seems that more lesbians than gay men go from one exclusive relationship to another, a sort of "serial monogamy." Most gay men do not live in monogamous relationships, and more gay men than lesbians are promiscuous, whereas lesbians are more likely to be in exclusive relationships. Any comparison between the two groups, however, should be made with many reservations. Studies of lesbian couples, more than for gay male couples, have focused largely on samples of persons in their twenties and thirties; thus, the duration of lesbian relationships in general may be greater than these studies seem to indicate.

Lesbian households are considerably more likely to include children than are gay male households, largely because a higher percentage of lesbians have been heterosexually married (Harry 1983:229). Like gay fathers, lesbian mothers often advise their children to be cautious about describing their home life to others. To date, no court has recognized marriages between same-sex couples, although there have been a number of attempts by gay and lesbian couples to obtain legal marriages.

EXTRAMARITAL SEXUAL RELATIONSHIPS

Approximately 70 percent of American adults disapprove of extramarital sex (Weis 1983:203). It is difficult to say how many Americans are sexually unfaithful to their spouses, but a 1983 *Psychology Today* poll reported that between one-third and one-half of married people have affairs. Most extramarital sexual relations appear to be secretive and are likely to be short-term.

Of the various forms of consensual extramarital sex, [the one receiving the most attention] is "swinging" or mate sharing. Some 2 percent of the American population has been estimated to participate in swinging (Hunt 1974). Swinging couples share sexual interaction with others in a social context, defined by the participants as recreational play. Married couples "swing" together. For either spouse alone to form an extramarital sexual relationship, however, is a violation of swinging's implicit norms. In relation to the population as a whole, swingers tend to be less religious, overwhelmingly middle-class, predominantly white, and otherwise "normal," with the exception of their swinging behavior (Weis 1983:204).

In a comparison of swinging and nonswinging couples, Brian Gilmartin (1978) found that the swingers have less-rewarding relationships with their parents, interact more frequently with their friends, are less attached to agents of social control like the church, gain heterosexual experiences at a younger age and with more partners, have sexual relations more frequently, marry younger, and are more likely to have been divorced in a previous marriage. Husbands tend to initiate swinging behavior, and wives usually initially respond negatively to the suggestion (Weis 1983:204–5).

Quite different from swinging, where husbands and wives share in the behavior, are "open marriages," where couples mutually agree to allow each other to have openly acknowledged, independent sexual relationships with other partners (Macklin 1980). These couples reported such problems as jealousy, loneliness, complex negotiations, lack of social support, and conflict over free time. Benefits cited from sexually open marriages were increased self-esteem and increased awareness of self and others. After having had extramarital affairs, most spouses were unwilling to return to a more traditional monogamous sexual relationship (Weis 1983:205).

SEXUALLY TRANSMITTED DISEASES

An increased emphasis on sexually transmitted diseases (STDs) through the media in the 1980s made many people think twice about engaging in sexual relations with several partners. The "sexual revolution" of experimentation may be slowing down as the 1990s begin. Engaging in extramarital sexual relationships can be hazardous to an individual's health, and should that person become a parent, some STDs could become a family problem.

Genital Herpes

Between five and twenty million Americans are believed to suffer from **genital herpes,** which produces painful, fluid-filled blisters on the genitals (Laskin 1982). Since genital herpes is caused by a virus, there is at present no cure, thus a person has it for life. Some herpes victims have mild bouts and view the disease as no more than an inconvenience, while others are in almost constant pain. Nearly all, however, must endure an emotional crisis so distinct in its assault on their sense of worth that psychologists speak of a "herpes syndrome." Herpes victims feel tainted, fearful no one will ever want to love them. Newborn babies can pick up the virus in the birth canal, with devastating results.

Herpes viruses have been around since ancient times, causing cold sores on the lips as well as blisters on the sex organs. Health officials say, however, that genital herpes became a growing problem only during the mid-1970s, after sexual codes had loosened in American society (Laskin 1982). Since then, the disease has spread at an ever-increasing rate. The average herpes sufferer gets four or five outbreaks of the highly contagious blisters a year. The blisters heal by themselves as the virus retreats from the skin via nerve pathways to a nerve cluster at the base of the spine, where it lies dormant until the next outbreak.

Herpes sufferers usually transmit the infection during an outbreak of the blisters. Thus, the best way to avoid passing on herpes is to abstain from sex from the moment a recurrence appears until the lesions are entirely healed. The most agonizing questions raised by herpes involve telling others about it. Most Herpes Resource Center officials believe that a prospective sex partner should be told, but they disagree on where and how to tell (Laskin 1982).

AIDS (Acquired Immune Deficiency Syndrome)

First diagnosed in the United States in 1981, **AIDS** (Acquired Immune Deficiency Syndrome) cripples the body's immune system and opens the way for so-called opportunistic infections. AIDS is spread primarily through sexual intercourse, through infected drug needles, and from mothers to their unborn children. (Before the disease was widely recognized, some AIDS cases were also caused by transfusions of contaminated blood.) Both daunting and deadly, in the United States AIDS has largely infected male homosexuals and intravenous drug users, but about 4 percent of the cases have been attributed to heterosexual sex, primarily male to female (Berger 1987:16). It is estimated that by 1990 the leading cause of death for American males between the ages of twenty-two and sixty-five will be AIDS.

Though the AIDS virus is transmitted by semen, blood, or blood products, it is present in but not transmitted by tears and saliva. Why? No one knows. Many rumors have developed and spread about the AIDS susceptibility of persons not in the high-risk groups. According to information from the Communicable Disease Center, AIDS is not spread by casual contact. You cannot acquire AIDS by sitting next to a person with AIDS, swimming at a public pool, eating with your infected friends, or sharing a bathroom with your infected roommate.

In a 1986 study of heterosexuals infected with the AIDS virus (through blood transfusions or through sexual partners), only 17 percent of their subsequent sexual partners acquired the virus ("More Questions than Answers," *Post-Courier*). Another unexpected statistic emerging from the study was a higher rate of infection in those who reported fewer sexual contacts over a shorter period of time than in those with more sexual activity over a longer period of time. Perhaps some people are better able to transmit the virus than others, or some people are better able to pick it up. At this writing, we have much to learn about the AIDS virus.

Symptoms of AIDS may appear as early as a few months after exposure but may not appear for many years, or not at all. The signs and symptoms of established AIDS are those of the secondary "opportunistic infections." While many of the following symptoms of AIDS are common among college students, and not specific only to

Condoms and Use as AIDS Barrier

The AIDS virus has been documented to spread only through direct exchanges of blood and through anal and vaginal intercourse with those who carry the virus, according to many research studies. Some scientists suspect that the AIDS virus can spread in oral sex.

Scientists warn against deep kissing involving extensive exchanges of saliva with people known to be infected with the virus. Many experts said they believed that the virus has spread most readily during anal intercourse because it often involves breaks in rectal tissues, thus allowing easier entry of the virus to the blood stream. But there is much uncertainty about the exact way the virus passes from person to person during sex. One study has suggested that the virus may be able to directly infect cells in the colon.

Laboratory studies have shown that the AIDS virus cannot pass through a condom. However, condoms sometimes break or can be improperly used. Experts suggest that condoms must be used throughout the sexual act to provide maximum protection.

Condoms are not foolproof. In one study, the virus was transmitted from one sexual partner to another in two separate instances even though the couples said they had used condoms over the extended study period.

Source: Joseph Berger, *The New York Times* (February 12, 1987), p. 16.

AIDS, it is important to have them checked out by a physician: (1) excessive tiredness for no apparent reason; (2) periodic or regular fevers, shaking, chills, or night sweats; (3) weight loss of more than ten pounds in two months that is not related to diet or increased activity; (4) unexplained swollen glands (usually in the armpits, neck, or groin) for more than two weeks; (5) pink to purple, flat or raised blotches or bumps, usually painless, beneath the skin or on the mucous membranes (mouth, nose, eyelids, or rectum); (6) persistent unexplained sore throat, white spots in the mouth, or heavy cough; (7) persistent diarrhea of unknown cause; (8) easy bruising; (9) unexplained bleeding from any orifice; and (10) blurred vision or persistent, severe headaches. There have also been reports that many AIDS sufferers develop dementia (madness) at some point, but figures on AIDS dementia are still uncertain. The greatest risk with AIDS is that the individual will get Kaposi's sarcoma—a formerly rare type of cancer that is always fatal.

Even with all the research being directed to the problem of AIDS, much more needs to be learned. Research labs are wrenching the virus apart, testing it piecemeal, probing its chemical requirements, its makeup, its action in the test tube and in laboratory animals. From the small cadre of original investigators back in 1981, the number of researchers has burgeoned ("More Questions Than Answers," *Post-Courier,* 1987).

In some workplaces, a person with a "sexual disorder" like AIDS might be discriminated against. In March of 1987, however, the U.S. Supreme Court held that victims of some contagious diseases are covered by the same law that protects handicapped workers from on-the-job bias (Press 1987:33). This decision reversed an earlier view of the U.S. Justice Department, which told AIDS victims in the summer of 1986 that if a boss feared their contagious diseases, federal antidiscrimination law offered them no more help than medical science. While important, the Supreme Court decision has limitations. The law does not guarantee a job for a worker too sick to fulfill his or her duties. And the court specifically left open one important question: Does the antidiscrimination statute protect AIDS carriers who do not suffer any symptoms?

AIDS may well become a deeply divisive social and political issue— but it is first and foremost a crisis in public health, an epidemic that may be out of control (Morganthau 1986:34). AIDS differs from other epidemic diseases in two respects: (1) As far as is known, it is fatal in every case; and (2) it utterly disables the human immune system, which is the bedrock on which medical and public health strategies have always been built. As with many other epidemic diseases, however, poor families, particularly in large urban ghettos, may be hardest hit by the current AIDS crisis.

AIDS has been a central health issue in the 1980s and 1990s. The disease has become a social, political, and economic issue.

Gonorrhea

Historical records indicate that gonorrhea ("the clap," "the drip") is the oldest of sexual diseases (Hyde 1982:487). It is now once again at epidemic proportions, and of all communicable diseases is second only to the common cold in prevalence. Most cases result from genital intercourse. In the male, the gonococcus bacterium invades the urethra and produces inflammation of the urethra. Initially a thin, clear mucous discharge seeps out of the opening at the tip of the penis and becomes thick and creamy within a day or so. A burning sensation results during urination, and the urine may contain pus or blood. When such symptoms occur, the male should seek medical treatment.

About 80 percent of women infected with gonorrhea have no symptoms during the early stages of the disease (Hyde 1982:488). Therefore, many women have no way of knowing that they are infected unless they are told by a male partner—either the partner they get the disease from, or a partner they transmit it to later. The gonorrheal infection in the woman invades the cervix, discharging pus, but the discharge is so slight that it may not be noticed. The inflammation may spread to the urethra, causing burning pain during urination. The effective treatment for gonorrhea is a large dose of penicillin administered by a shot in the buttocks.

Chlamydia

An inflammation of the male's urethra that is not caused by a gonorrhea infection is known as NGU (nongonococcal urethritis), and the *Chlamydia* parasite is the cause in about half the cases (Hyde 1982:495). NGU has recently become one of the major sexually transmitted diseases and is particularly prevalent in higher socioeconomic groups and among university students. Main symptoms of chlamydia are a thin, usually clear discharge and mild discomfort on urination, somewhat similar to gonorrhea. Since chlamydia is not caused by bacteria, it does not respond to penicillin, but it can be treated with tetracycline or erythromycin.

Syphilis

Whatever the precise origin of syphilis, its naming seems to have been a good example of "it wasn't my fault" (Hyde 1982:491). The French called it "the Naples disease." In Naples it was called "the French disease," and in England it was called "the Spanish disease." As one person correctly noted, however, it is really "the disease of him who has it." The name was coined by an Italian physician who in 1530 wrote a poem about a shepherd boy named Syphilis who was afflicted with the disease as punishment for violating the will of the sun god (Hyde 1982:491). The poem was widely read, and the name stuck.

The parasite that causes syphilis typically enters through the mucous membranes of the genitals as a result of intercourse with an infected person. A major initial symptom of syphilis is a round, ulcerlike genital lesion with a hard, raised edge, resembling a crater. Though it looks terrible, the lesion is painless; it appears about three to four weeks after intercourse with the infected person.

A frightening aspect of syphilis is that the lesion goes away by itself within one to five weeks after it appears, but the disease has not gone away. It has only gone underground. The disease organisms go into the bloodstream and circulate throughout the body. One to six months after the original appearance of the lesion, a body rash develops. The rash, too, goes away in two to six weeks, lulling the person into believing that the disease has disappeared. The disease may stay in this latent stage for years, only to develop into cardiovascular late syphilis, which can lead to death, or to neurosyphilis,

As an undergraduate biology major taking a course in parasitology, I remember studying *Treponema pallidum,* the parasitic carrier of syphilis. The professor noted that ninety-nine and ninety-nine hundredths percent of the time the disease is spread through sexual intercourse. He said it is *very remotely possible* to acquire the little parasite through a hair brush or from a toilet seat (assuming a break in one's skin) but not to blame it on the barber or the toilet seat if one is diagnosed as having syphilis!

Source: Author.

which is usually fatal (Hyde 1982:491–93). At the very earliest suspicion of syphilis, the individual should seek a blood test and, if positive, be treated, usually with penicillin, in order to eradicate the disease.

Most states require blood tests for persons applying for a marriage license to ensure that they are free of venereal disease. A few states, however, allow the license to be issued even if syphilis is discovered, since the couple is informed of the situation.

SEXUAL DYSFUNCTIONS

Though many couples experience problems in sexual adjustment at one time or another in marriage, chronic problems with sex, or **sexual dysfunctions,** probably affect only a minority of couples. Just as the frequency of intercourse usually declines throughout the married years, for most couples other sexual aspects of marriage change over time. Therefore, a couple must seek additional outlets for sexual expression as they move from the honeymoon to the retirement years.

A sexual dysfunction (malfunction) is any one of various disturbances or impairments of sexual functioning (Hyde 1982:448) such as inability to get an erection in the male or inability to have an orgasm in the female. William Masters and Virginia Johnson (1970:342) estimated that as many as 50 percent of all couples have some sort of sexual dysfunctioning on the part of the husband, the wife, or both spouses. This was an estimate, however; an exact number is virtually impossible to obtain since many persons with sexual dysfunctions do not seek help unless the problem is chronic.

Impotence in Males A sexual dysfunction found in males is impotence (erectile dysfunction) or the inability to have an erection or to maintain one. Probably there are few men who in their lives have not experienced difficulty with erection at some time. Anxiety or a loss of self-esteem may cause many males to experience impotence. A psychological cause of impotence may be anger toward a spouse who has come to seem dull or unattractive, resulting in sex being viewed as a chore rather than a pleasure (Leslie and Korman 1985:446).

Premature Ejaculation in Males   A second sexual dysfunction of males is premature ejaculation (that is, ejaculation too soon). The definition of "premature" orgasm varies. Some writers have suggested that normally ejaculation should not occur less than thirty to ninety seconds after the penis has been inserted into the vagina. Masters and Johnson (1970), however, define prematurity as the inability to satisfy the woman 50 percent of the time in intercourse, regardless of the time required. This dysfunction is probably the most common complaint among both men and their partners and tends to be tied to psychological rather than physical experiences. The quick ejaculation may result from first sexual experiences involving masturbation. The fear of "being caught" or "doing something wrong" may place an emphasis on speed. Or the male may ejaculate quickly out of a lack of awareness of the partner's need for prolonged intercourse. Also, a man's ability to sustain lengthy intercourse may diminish with age.

Retarded Ejaculation in Males   A third sexual dysfunction of males is retarded ejaculation, where the man is unable to ejaculate even though he has a solid erection and has had more than adequate stimulation. This problem is not very common among males. Masters and Johnson (1970) found only 17 cases of this dysfunction in 510 couples treated. They speculate that retarded ejaculation may be a way for a man to hold back on his wife or to express anger over a situation or to wield power in an unhappy marriage.

Sexual Dysfunctions in Females   One of the sexual dysfunctions found in women is orgasmic dysfunction (inability to have an orgasm). Helen Kaplan (1974:380) estimates that only about 8 to 10 percent of sexually active women never experience orgasm. Others experience orgasm in some situations and not in others. A woman who has been taught that sex is shameful may not be responsive in marriage because she feels guilt about her sexual feelings. Another type of dysfunction, vaginismus (a spastic contraction of the outer third of the vagina), can produce a problem for couples. This dysfunction in women is usually associated with a prior history of pain involving sexuality, such as rape or incest. Dyspareunia (painful intercourse) is another problem experienced by some women. This can be caused by either physical or psychological factors.

Reducing Sexual Dysfunctions   Three general categories of "causes" of sexual dysfunctions are organic causes, drugs, and psychological causes (Hyde 1982:454–64). About 10 to 20 percent of cases of sexual dysfunction result directly from organic or physical factors. Some drugs may have side effects causing sexual dysfunctions. For example, drugs used in treating peptic ulcers and some allergy drugs may decrease erection capacity in men. Psychological sources of sexual dysfunction can be broken down into two groups: immediate causes (anxieties such as fear of failure, the constructing of barriers to the experience of erotic pleasure, failure to communicate with one's partner, and negative thoughts) and prior learning and experience.

While many therapy programs are available to treat sexual dysfunctions, Janet Hyde (1982:481–82) offers some practical advice or "preventive medicine" to head off these problems: (1) Communicate with your partner; talk to him or her while having sex, or use nonverbal communication such as placing your hand on top of your partner's and moving it where you want it; (2) do not feel as if you are putting on a sexual performance that you constantly need to evaluate; (3) do not set up goals of sexual performance, since goals may result in failure, and failure produces dysfunctions; just relax and enjoy yourself; (4) be choosy about the situations in which you have sex; and (5) "failures" will occur; do not let them ruin the relationship.

As this chapter has indicated, sexual relationships can enhance couple interaction, but negative effects of sexual relations may also result. Some can be harmful to one's family and one's health, others can be detrimental to one's self esteem, and some can put at risk one's acceptance by society at large. Sexual relations, however, can also be a very powerful bonding force within a marriage. Sexual issues discussed in this chapter will likely evoke many different reactions from readers. While there is much to be said for Alex Comfort's "joy of sex" approach, the reader should be mindful of precautions noted in the latter sections of this chapter. Follow the practical advice of Janet Hyde, but do not hesitate to seek medical advice, if needed. Though required by only a few states, a complete physical exam prior to marriage would not be a bad idea. Preventive medicine is often easier to apply than seeking a cure after the fact. In view of the prevalence of STDs today, such prevention could be an asset to you, your spouse, and children. In the end, your entire nuclear family could benefit.

CHAPTER REVIEW

- Sexual relationships have historically played a major role both within and outside of marriage. The "sexual revolution" of the 1960s and 1970s had an impact on sex roles within and outside of marriage.
- While sex education in the schools has traditionally been very controversial in the United States, nonetheless, sex education—beginning in the elementary grades—is increasing.

- As a contraceptive technique, condoms have been around since the eighteenth century. Birth control practices have increased in the United States partly because of attitude changes. The majority of U.S. couples use some method of birth control today.
- With the spread of AIDS in the United States, the advertising of condoms in the media is becoming more acceptable. Some college health services distribute condoms to students.
- Sterilization is becoming more popular as a birth control measure in the United States. Though some risks are involved with vasectomies and tubal ligations, sterilization is an almost certain way to prevent pregnancy.
- Abortion remains one of the more controversial issues of human sexuality in the United States. Since 1973, the availability of legal abortion has had a profound impact on women's health.
- Lesbians tend to practice "serial monogamy" more than gay men and are more likely to include children in the relationship.
- While extramarital sex is disapproved of by the majority of American adults, one-third to one-half of married people are reported to engage in extramarital sexual relationships.
- Acquired immune deficiency syndrome (AIDS) has presented a crisis in public health, an epidemic that may be out of control. Sexually transmitted diseases (STDs) have been discussed more in recent years in the media, thus making people more alert to the dangers of STDs.
- Sexual dysfunctions affect some marriages in the United States today. Sexual dysfunctions found in males include impotence, premature ejaculation, and retarded ejaculation. Sexual dysfunctions in females include orgasmic dysfunction, vaginismus, and dyspareunia.

DISCUSSION QUESTIONS

1. What were major sex information sources for you as a child growing up? Were your *actual* sources the same as your *preferred* sources?
2. Sex education in U.S. schools is controversial. Present arguments for sex education in the schools—elementary and secondary—and suggest arguments against sex education.
3. "Birth control methods should be advertised on television and in the print media." Refute or support this statement.
4. Why did condom sales increase significantly in the late 1980s?
5. Same-sex relationships are generally viewed negatively in the United States. Why do you think this is?
6. How are the physical, emotional, and social effects of herpes similar to those of AIDS? How do they differ?
7. Define sexual dysfunctions. List at least three types for both males and females.

GLOSSARY

abortion: The ending of a pregnancy and the expulsion of the contents of the uterus, whether spontaneous (miscarriage) or induced by human intervention.

AIDS: Acquired immune deficiency syndrome, which cripples the body's immune system.

birth control: The more or less voluntary planning and actions taken by individuals to regulate the number and spacing of children.

genital herpes: A sexually transmitted viral disease characterized by painful bumps on the genitals.

heterosexual: A person who is sexually attracted to, or engages in sexual activity with, members of the opposite gender.

homosexual: A person who is sexually attracted to, or engages in sexual activity with, members of the same gender.

lesbian: A female homosexual.

NORC: National Opinion Research Center in Ann Arbor, Michigan.

sexual dysfunction: A problem with sexual response.

STD: Sexually transmitted disease.

SUGGESTED READINGS

Aries, Philippe, and Andre Bejin, eds. 1985. *Western Sexuality: Practice and Precept in Past and Present Times.* New York: Basil Blackwell. *An anthology resulting from a seminar in France covering such topics as homosexuality in ancient Rome, Saint Paul and the flesh, sex in married life in the early Middle Ages, and extramarital unions.*

Beach, Frank A. 1977. *Human Sexuality in Four Perspectives.* Baltimore: The Johns Hopkins University Press. *An anthology using four perspectives on human sexuality: developmental, sociological, physiological, and evolutionary.*

Belcastro, Philip A. 1986. *The Birth Control Book.* Boston: Jones and Bartlett Publishers. *A brief description of birth control methods with advantages and disadvantages of each highlighted.*

Butler, J. Douglas, and David F. Walbert. 1986. *Abortion, Medicine, and the Law.* 3d ed. New York: Facts on File Publications. *In-depth coverage of the legal, historical, political, ethical, religious, sociological, and medical aspects of abortion.*

Gordon, Sol, and Craig W. Snyder. 1986. *Personal Issues in Human Sexuality.* Boston: Allyn and Bacon. *A practical approach to understanding sexuality and sex-related issues.*

Hyde, Janet S. 1982. *Understanding Human Sexuality.* 2d ed. New York: McGraw-Hill. *A well-written, thorough review of research on human sexuality.*

Luker, Kristin. 1975. *Taking Chances: Abortion and the Decision Not to Contracept.* Berkeley: University of California Press. *A sociological understanding of the meaning of contraceptive use, problem pregnancy, and abortion.*

Petchesky, Rosalind P. 1984. *Abortion and Woman's Choice: The State, Sexuality, and Reproductive Freedom.* New York: Longman. *Feminist ideas about reproductive rights, including such topics as fertility control in theory and history, abortion practice in the 1970s, and sexual politics of the 1980s.*

Marriage and Marital Issues

◆ *A good marriage, if such there be,*
rejects the company and conditions of love.
*It tries to reproduce those of friendship.**

*Marriage is the cure of love, and friendship the cure of marriage.*** *

Polls uniformly show that Americans place a high value on marriage and the family. A nationwide 1981 Gallup poll revealed that in a list of nineteen social values, "good family life" was rated as more important by more respondents (over 80 percent) than any other value (Gallup Report No. 198, p. 4). Thus, whatever particular family form these respondents may have had in mind, some kind of family life does seem to be of significance in this survey.

In the past, marriage has been a resilient institution. It has a remarkable survival power under changing conditions. Like any other social institution, marriage has a life of its own and makes its own contribution to society. It therefore influences, as well as reflects, the rest of society (Davis 1985:20–21).

Marriage is never static, and couples who stay together for many years pass through many stages of the marital life cycle. First they are newlyweds, next often young parents of young children, then older parents of adolescents, then "empty nesters" when the children leave, and finally senior citizens (Porat and Carr 1987:51–52). Each

---

*Michel Eyquem de Montaigne, *Essays* III:5
**Philip Dormer Stanhope (1694–1773)

stage in the cycle overlaps with the preceding one and the one to come. A couple may not even notice the gradual changes as one stage fades into the next. Yet each stage brings unique conflicts and chal-

---

The Seven Levels of Marriage

According to Cynthia Smith, young couples getting married can expect to go through seven "levels" or stages, which may last for varying periods, may overlap to some extent, and sometimes can occur concurrently. Smith's research on the levels of marriage began soon after her husband died, just before their thirty-fifth wedding anniversary. Data were gathered through interviews. About 90 percent of the respondents stated that their spouse was their best friend. Smith's book is geared primarily toward those rearing a family, in fact a traditional family where the husband has the career and the wife raises the children. The book also does not address problems or levels in second or subsequent marriages. The seven levels of marriage are:

1. *Entry.* The relationship is still "you and me," my family and your family. It is a time of judgment and adjusting to new roles.
2. *Acceptance.* This is a time of shared experiences, of thinking as a team and developing the trust to be best friends.
3. *Deciding on parenthood.* It is a bigger issue today than it was in previous generations, when parenthood almost always followed marriage.
4. *Family.* Living with—and paying for—babies and growing children can cause confusion, jealousy, and strife.
5. *Rebirth* (hers) and *reconciliation* (his). This is the time of the mid-life crisis. The kids are old enough so that she can start a new life, and he is trying to accept the limitations of his career quest.
6. *Humdrum.* He may be using Grecian Formula, and she may be considering a face lift. Either or both may be having affairs.
7. *Freedom.* The kids are gone. There can be vacations just for the two of them. If a couple has made it this far, this can be the glorious finale. There can also be problems—adult children returning home and illness.

Source: Cynthia Smith, *The Seven Levels of Marriage: Expectations vs Reality* (New York: Ivy Books, 1988).

---

lenges and must be handled differently. The challenge of marriage was apparently too much for Solomon Grundy; note what happens on Thursday, the day after marriage:

> *Solomon Grundy,*
> *Born on a Monday,*
> *Christened on Tuesday,*
> *Married on Wednesday,*
> *Took ill on Thursday,*
> *Worse on Friday,*
> *Died on Saturday,*
> *Buried on Sunday.*
> *This is the end*
> *Of Solomon Grundy.*

While seeing a spouse through "sickness and health" is an important aspect of the relationship, marriage involves many other aspects. The decision to get married, while influenced by sexual attraction and ideas of love and romance, also means entering into an economic relationship or contract of mutual benefit. It can also be seen as an important status passage for both men and women (Gittins 1986:85–86). It confers adult status. It represents an important change from being someone's dependent child to becoming someone else's spouse.

Marriage is, then, not only an evolving relationship but an institution that plays many social roles. In this chapter we'll look at the following topics: changing views on marriage, love and marriage, communication in marriage, marital satisfaction, and commuter marriages. This chapter is by no means an exhaustive treatise on the U.S. marital system; instead, it addresses some issues and trends that are central to marriage today.

CHANGING VIEWS ON MARRIAGE

In the 1950s, most Americans assumed that marriage would last forever (Porat and Carr 1987:2). Roles of husband and wife were clearly defined, and stability went hand in hand with marriage. The golden wedding anniversary symbolized the ideal goal; a successful marriage was one where the man and woman stayed together until one of them died.

In the 1960s, however, the postwar baby boomers came of age, and many were somewhat rebellious against the status quo. The sixties were a time of various social movements directed at bringing about change in the society. This era of women moving into the labor market in large numbers was a time of restlessness and freedom marches. For some, marriage became a relationship where each partner was free to do "his or her own thing." In the 1970s, an emphasis for some was on experimentation, freedom, "**open marriage**" (mutual tolerance of extramarital sex), and multiple options (Porat and Carr 1987:2–3). For others, marriage was no longer "till death us do part" but "till the going gets tough" or "till we get bored." **Serial monogamy** (a series of marriages) became more acceptable—no longer the "golden anniversary" goal.

Today, people are again reviewing their values and taking a hard look at marriage (Porat and Carr 1987:3–8). Since the experiments of the sixties and seventies did not work for many, many couples are striving to build relationships that embody more conventional values of the past—loyalty, trust, commitment, and permanence. Couples are deliberately choosing marriage as a lifestyle, knowing that it is riskier and more challenging today than in the past. A good marriage is a relationship in which two people respect and like each other, become friends, and agree on mutual values and goals. They learn that crises are an important element within marriage—a crisis may be an opportunity for growth. They are willing

---

Marriage in America: Why Marry?

There are some 50 million married couples in the nation. Survey after survey shows that a good marriage ranks at the top of most people's sources of satisfaction—above wealth, fame, and status, above good health and good jobs, above other friendships and relationships. Again and again, happily married couples and marriage professionals acknowledge marriage as an end in itself. What is it then that marriage offers?

Sharing and commitment, commitment and sharing are two ideas which run like a drumbeat throughout strong marriages, researchers say. As social historians explain—and as happily married couples confirm—the marriage tradition is tightly interwoven with the expectations and values of a larger society. As one person notes, "If you're working very hard together to attain something, it's very hard to fall apart, or to grow away from one another. I'm sure you have to work at cohabiting, too. But maybe you don't work quite so hard if you don't feel a commitment to making this liaison work out."

Source: Rushworth M. Kidder, *The Christian Science Monitor* (December 2, 1985), pp. 34–5.

to work together for a successful relationship that combines quality and stability.

The reading on page 228 suggests the importance of cooperation and commitment in making a marriage a satisfactory experience for both wife and husband most of the time. The concepts of sharing, reciprocity, and mutuality suggest an element of love in a relationship. "Love" in marriage is a two-way street. One must be willing to go 75 percent of the way in marriage in order for the relationship to work. With an attitude of willingness to go more than halfway in marriage, head-on collisions on this two-way street are more likely to be avoided.

LOVE AND MARRIAGE

Especially in the West, we are socialized from the earliest years to fall in love and to believe that romantic love is an appropriate basis for a marriage (Tavuchis and Goode 1975:8–9). Children are asked whom they love and learn to encourage and invite such feelings in themselves as well as others.

Throughout most of the twentieth century, romantic love has been considered an important aspect of the American dating and marriage scene. In the 1970s, however, feminist writers alerted us to an important effect of the concept of romantic love on women in our society. They argued that the romantic love idea in our culture constitutes one of the main forces keeping women tied into traditional gender roles and in a subordinate position to men. Because women are tied by bonds of love and dependence to their husbands, they have fitted into the traditional gender division of labor without much protest (Firestone 1970). Thus, feminists stated, this "romantic love" idea has been a hindrance to women's achieving equality in our society.

Nearly all societies and ages except our own have made distinctions between love within and love outside marriage (Aries 1985). In some traditions, not romantic love but constraint and bashfulness precede marriage, as illustrated by Rebecca's behavior in the Bible (Genesis 24, 63–67). She had left her parents to meet Isaac. When she saw him, "she took her veil and covered herself." She was thus apparelled when "Isaac conducted her into the tent and took her as his wife." The wife-to-be had to remain veiled up to her wedding night, and until then had to be more concealed from her future husband than from other men.

Such a custom of staying away from one's future husband lends itself to substitutions. In another biblical example, Jacob had chosen Rachel for his wife. Rachel's father, Laban, however, wanted to marry off his elder daughter Leah first, so he slipped her into the bridal bed instead of Rachel, and Jacob never noticed until the next morning.

Heterosexual love has not always been held in the highest esteem. To some among the ancient Greeks, "true love" was between members of the same sex. Marriage was significant for the purpose of procreation, but as the Greeks saw it, the absence of any common interests between men and women made it difficult for marriage to become a partnership and personal companionship. In the unromantic conditions prevailing in Greece in the fourth and fifth centuries B.C., a fatherly interest in the care, education, and well-being of a young and dutiful wife was as much as could be expected, since a woman was debarred from acquiring a fully developed mind and personality of her own (James 1965:228).

In the first centuries of our era, before the spread of Christianity, the moral philosophy taught by the Stoics saw procreation as the object and justification of marriage. The Christians took over Stoic ethics to the extent that the distinction between dutiful love in marriage and **passionate love** (unrestrained romantic and physical love) outside it became no longer the description of a custom but part of a moral code. This distinction is clear in a text by Seneca on marriage (*Contra Jovinium* I, 49), quoted by Saint Jerome (Aries 1985:134):

> *Any love for another's wife is scandalous [so much for adultery]; so is too much love for one's own wife [too much love simply means love without restraint, the passion lovers feel outside marriage]. A prudent man should love his wife with discretion, and so control his desire and not be led into copulation. Nothing is more impure than to love one's wife as if she were a mistress. . . . Men should appear before their wives not as lovers but as husbands.*

If a man is inclined to have a married mistress on the side, however, Ovid (in *The Art of Love* and *The Loves*, cited in Tavuchis and Goode 1975:11–12) suggests how a married mistress should behave at a party:

> *. . . get there before him, and when he reclines, you beside him,*
> *Modestly on the couch, give my foot just a touch,*
> *Watch me for every nod, for every facial expression,*
> *Catch my signs and return them, never saying a word.*
> *I can talk with my eyebrows and spell out words with my fingers,*
> *I can make you a sign, dipping my finger in wine.*

When you think of the tumbles we've had in the hay
  together,
Touch your cheek with your hand; then I will understand.
If you're a little bit cross with the way I may be behaving,
Let your finger-tip rest light on the lobe of an ear.
If, on the other hand, what I am saying should please you,
Darling, keep turning your ring; symbol enough that will be.
. . . Let him drink all he wants; keep urging him, only don't
  kiss him.
Keep on filling his glass, secretly, if you can.
Once he passes out cold, perhaps we can figure out
  something—
Time and circumstance maybe will give us a chance.

While not encouraging a mistress on the side, Saint Paul (an advocate of virginity) accepted the institution of marriage and extolled the perfect union of man and wife (Aries 1985). He exhorted husband and wife to "become one flesh," meaning not merely sexual penetration, but also mutual trust, fondness for each other, and identification of one with another. Such love does not come suddenly like love at first sight, nor does it have to exist prior to marriage but can grow within the marriage.

A good historical example of this kind of married love is provided by the French philosopher Claude-Henri Saint-Simon at the end of the seventeenth century. Having made no secret of the fact that he chose his wife for purely material reasons without any pretense of sentiment, he had become over time so devoted to his wife, who died before him, that in his will Saint-Simon asked that their two coffins be chained together so that they could be united in death as they had been in life. Philippe Aries (1985) notes, however, that such revelations were rare, as men preferred not to speak of the love they found in marriage, except in wills where such testimony became more frequent.

After the eighteenth century, society began to reconcile the two traditionally opposed kinds of love (Aries 1985). The West gradually adopted an ideal of marriage wherein husband and wife would love each other (or appear to anyway) like real lovers. Extramarital erotics found their way into the marriage bed, expelling traditional prudishness in favor of real feeling. There was now one kind of love, powerfully eroticized, and the earlier concept of conjugal love was abolished or thought of as an awkward relic standing in the way of the triumph of passion (Aries 1985).

The recent increased divorce rate, resulting in serial marriages, may represent a kind of reaction against that fusion of conjugal and passionate love—a return to the earlier dualism. Many would argue that passionate love has a feverish beginning, a flowering, and then an end. Passionate love does not last; marriages based on it do not last either (Aries 1985). Therefore, divorce should not be regarded as a means of retrieving a mistake, but as the normal write-off of a feeling which cannot and should not be expected to last.

Despite this ebb and flow of attitudes, love has long played a part in marriage, and love tends to contribute toward the survival of marriage. The above reading makes some practical suggestions to help love last beyond the feverish passionate beginning of the first year of marriage.

As noted earlier, the institution of marriage has had remarkable survival power under changing conditions. If couples choosing marriage as a lifestyle today strive to make marriage a lifetime contract, long-term love may make a comeback. As the years go by, couples will perhaps love each other because they have loved each other for a long time. We may begin to see a revival of the kind of lifelong devotion that has lately seemed to be a thing of the past.

Helping Love Survive the First Year of Marriage

Newlyweds rarely want to face the fact that the first year of marriage poses the greatest danger to their survival as a couple. According to family therapists Thomas and Marcia Lasswell, most of the serious differences leading to a breakup occur in the first year of marriage; one out of four first-time marriages ends in divorce within two years after the wedding.

How can love best be helped to survive the high-risk first year of marriage? Counseling couples *before* marriage has been increasingly prescribed as preventive medicine for this epidemic of early divorce. According to marital therapist Neville Vines, the major issues bedeviling the first year of marriage fall into the following categories.

Sexual disappointment. The person with little or no previous sexual experience often idealizes marital sex, expecting peaks of passion found only in paperback romances. Couples who have been intimate before marriage, however, must now put sex in the perspective of their total relationship.

Difficulty in gaining emotional freedom from your family. In-laws may not create as many problems as do buried messages from our own families. Couples do not realize that conflicts over money, displaying affection, or men's and women's roles are essentially replays of their parents' values. Once they see this, they can stop blaming each other and decide how they want to manage their own lives.

Coping with change. For some couples, the intense emotional and physical closeness of marriage is a frightening change from their previous independence. One partner may feel overwhelmed and pull away. When this happens, the other may feel abandoned. A couple who before marriage wanted only to be together now cannot understand what happened to them. Couples need to develop the flexibility to accommodate change rather than fight it.

Handling anger. Husbands and wives are usually so fixated on *what* they are arguing about that they do not realize the problem often is the *way* they argue. As a result, some young couples see any conflict as a threat to their marriage and thus shun arguments altogether. Rather than express their anger openly, they either hold it back or let it out in ways such as sulking, nagging or refusing sex, perhaps more damaging than a productive fight.

Three factors help love survive the first year of marriage. First, the couple should be able to tell each other how they feel. Second, they should be able to do that at the moment they are feeling it, rather than nurturing a grievance. Third, they should be able to say what each needs from the other, when they need it. By openly declaring their feelings and needs, they will have a solid base for the years ahead.

Source: Adapted from Norman Lobsenz, *Parade* (May 26, 1985), p. 14. Reprinted with permission from Parade, Copyright © 1985.

COMMUNICATION IN MARRIAGE

A marriage may succeed not so much because the partners avoid problems as because they are able to deal with the problems they encounter. And every marriage benefits from the spouses' ability to communicate in ways that are open, comfortable, and reassuring. Being able to compromise on the "tremendous trifles" of life—the small, yet large, issues—such as whether or not to raise the bedroom window at night or how much to raise it should also prove helpful in marital relations. Being able to understand and communicate with each other is essential for a durable marriage. Communication is one key to overall **marital adjustment**—that is, relative agreement on issues perceived to be important, sharing of tasks, and demonstration of affection.

The importance of communication as a factor contributing to marital success has long been noted by social scientists. In a study (Navran 1967:183) of "happy and unhappy couples" marital adjustment was found to be positively correlated with the capacity to communicate. A study (Karlsson 1951) of Swedish marriages at the middle of the century suggested that an important prerequisite for marital adjustment is that the partners' expectations be revealed to each other. The communication of intentions was also found to be positively related to marital satisfaction—knowing how a spouse thinks most of the time helps to give one a feeling of security. The Swedish study also found that communication of love and respect is associated with marital satisfaction. One in a dissatisfied marital relationship might be more prone to misinterpret the other's nonverbal signals, thus adding to the possibility of marital conflict. Thus, open channels of communication in marriage assist in the transition from passionate, romantic love to a long-term love relationship.

In discussing family communication, Kathleen Galvin and Bernard Brommel (1982:86) note that family members experience special moments of closeness in which they feel good about themselves, the other family members, and their connectedness to each other. For some individuals such moments are an everyday occurrence, yet in others they are rare. A desire for marital or family closeness may be stymied by inadequate communication. Such intimacy requires

SALLY FORTH   **BY GREG HOWARD**

Good communication contributes to martial satisfaction. Communication involves both giving information and actively receiving (listening). (Sally Forth reprinted by permission of North American Syndicate.)

effort and risk-taking behavior, but it provides rewards for those choosing to develop such closeness in their relationships. As suggested by the reading here, however, too many married couples' communication channels may have interference from other channels.

Turn Off the TV and Turn Up Marital Communication

Too many couples are turning on the television set instead of each other. This can have disastrous effects on a marriage. Some couples watch the screen rather than face their emotional, sexual or financial troubles. "TV watching is an easy, inexpensive, passive habit that can work as a substitute for intimacy," notes psychiatrist Pierre Mornell. He further suggests that if you are watching more than an hour or two per night, it is a signal you could be more tuned into television than to each other.

Couples do not have to interact when watching television. It is like going to sleep early to get away from each other. A gradual withdrawal from the TV habit rather than getting rid of it cold turkey is likely to prevent a seizure on the part of the husband or wife. Watching television should be the exception, not the rule.

Some tips for cutting down on television watching are suggested below:

1. Remove the television from the dining room and bedroom—prime areas of interaction between spouses.
2. If a "televisionless" meal is too drastic, set aside one or two TV-less meals a week.
3. Sit next to your spouse on the couch when watching TV.
4. Only turn on a program because it interests you, not just because it is there.

Source: Adapted from an article in *The News and Courier* (Charleston, S.C., June 29, 1986), p. 14-E. Associated Press.

With less television, observers of the marital scene have suggested, married couples may be tuned in to each other more often, perhaps share more with each other and become better friends. Most couples, happy or not, say they are quick to share good news with each other. According to a recent survey (Safran 1985) of couples in the United States, however, the happily married also share the bad news, turning to each other when they feel sad or depressed. In the long run, better communication channels between married couples should enhance love's chances of surviving in marriage.

MARITAL SATISFACTION

Marital adjustment and satisfaction are highly personal, and a person's satisfaction with other aspects of life are likely to affect his or her satisfaction with marriage. Certainly marital satisfaction is not static, and most couples experience minor fluctuations in the amount of satisfaction they feel in their marital relationships. Low income is associated with less marital satisfaction. Children can be sources of disagreement as well as sources of great pleasure. Sexual adjustment is associated with overall marital adjustment (Smart and Smart 1980:214–15).

While every marriage has its challenges, contentment in marriage seems widely evident today, at least as reported by two surveys. In 1982 a National Opinion Research Corporation poll concluded that couples of various degrees of marital duration seemed happy in their marriages. Ninety-six percent of respondents surveyed described their marriage as happy (Davis 1985:15). In the same year, 79 percent of 5,000 readers of *Better Homes and Gardens* said their expectations of happiness in marriage were being fulfilled. Eighty-one percent said if they had it to do over again, they would choose the same marital partner (Hastings and Hastings 1984:285–89).

Longevity and Marital Satisfaction

Longevity seems to make a positive contribution to marital satisfaction. Unless marriage is ended by divorce, increased years in life expectancy contribute to marriages lasting longer than in the past. Also, a couple staying married for a lifetime have many more years on their own without children in the home. For couples staying together for a lifetime, marriage in the mid-nineteenth century lasted thirty-four years on the average until the death of a spouse, and at least one child under eighteen was in the family for about thirty-two of those years. By contrast, today's marriage for couples remaining together for a lifetime lasts nearly fifty years, and husband and wife are in each other's company without the responsibility of schoolchildren for about twenty-eight of those years (Bane 1976).

A recent survey of married couples in the United States (Safran 1985) found that the longer people were married the more they felt strongly that they could rely on each other in times of trouble. Time also brings a growing tolerance. Couples said that a marriage works when you work at it and when you have an understanding that marriage has its ups and downs.

What about physical attractiveness in marriage today? According to a recent study, physical attractiveness remains important in marital sexuality, and the relationship between attractiveness and sex appeal is stronger for men than for women (Margolin and White 1987). If men place more emphasis on their partner's attractiveness, then we should expect to find that response to a spouse's aging was independent of one's own aging. Instead, the results of the study suggest a more complex exchange model. Men in the survey seem to be saying, "Grow old along with me, but do not age as rapidly." Since physical appearance is more important to men, a double standard of aging seems to exist, with men attaching more importance than women to the changing balance of physical assets. This male emphasis on physical attractiveness is evidenced by the widespread phenomenon of middle-aged husbands leaving their wives and children for younger second wives.

Regarding children's leaving home, studies reveal that both men and women enjoy greater individual and marital happiness in their postparental years than in the parental stages (Glenn 1975). Since the parental stages of the family life cycle tend to be the most difficult, satisfaction and **marital happiness** (emotional response to satisfaction) often increase once the children have left. The couple can then devote time to themselves and each other. With retirement, as will be noted in chapter 13, most individuals feel good about their lives and are pleased that they retired when they did.

Marital Conflict

No matter how satisfactory a marriage seems to be, conflict is inevitable in marriage.

Some conflict theorists assert that marital relationships reflect and reinforce gender inequalities (Degler 1980). Examples that support such an assertion are: (1) Until the past few years, a husband could rape his wife and not be charged; (2) in traditional marriage vows the bride is "given away" to the groom; and (3) the woman has traditionally taken the surname of the husband after marriage. Conflict theory helps to explain the extent of violence in families, where care and cooperation are supposed to exist—something not easily explained by functionalist theory.

Good communication skills do not prevent conflict. Actually a conflict, followed by a confrontation, can produce positive results

(Porat and Carr 1987:121): Feelings are expressed; each person can let the other know his or her feelings; each can gain new knowledge about the other; a level of renewed intimacy may be reached; and a workable compromise may be found. Not only is it important to permit differences, but one should strive to actually rejoice in them. A relationship grows when two people enjoy each other's differences and celebrate each other's uniqueness.

One study (Madden and Janoff-Bulman 1981) reported causes of marital conflict in the order of frequency noted below:

1. Spending money
2. Relations with relatives
3. Children (rules and discipline)
4. Division of housework and child care
5. Communication, honesty (especially concerning negative feelings)
6. Location of residence, whether to move
7. Own or spouse's nonsexual attachment to another person
8. Husband's occupational choice, husband's income
9. Choice of recreation or vacation
10. Whether or not to have children
11. Socializing (amount and type)
12. Amount of time spent together
13. Physical illness creating tension
14. Power and control over family decisions in general
15. Methods of doing chores

Frieda Porat and Jacquelyn Carr (1987:127–28) discuss three different kinds of conflict. *Content conflict* is a confrontation based on message accuracy over a fact, inference, or definition, such as over something read in the paper or heard on television. Content conflicts are relatively easy to resolve, as facts can be verified, inferences tested, and definitions clarified. These conflicts are generally more logical than emotional. *Value conflict* occurs when people differ in their views of life, such as over religion or politics. Values cannot be verified and are based mainly on belief systems. It is often easier to acknowledge the difference and agree to disagree over the issues. *Ego conflict* involves endangering one's personal image. Judgmental statements about a person threaten his or her self-concept and self-esteem and are difficult to resolve. A judgmental statement about someone's appearance (clothing or hairstyle), for example, is often remembered for a long time and is not easily forgiven—if the comment was unfavorable.

Studies Say Sex Loses Appeal for Many Young Marrieds

"It started on the honeymoon," he said. "Sex for the two years we had been together before the wedding was terrific. But suddenly, I stopped wanting her in the same way. At the end of just a year of marriage, we were sleeping together just once every three or four weeks. My wife likes sex, and she started complaining. She wanted to know what was wrong. I couldn't tell her. I didn't know."

A young woman remembers that sex with her husband was fine throughout their courtship and honeymoon. But when they returned home, she began to feel that sex with him was repulsive. She started rejecting him, preferring to masturbate secretly when she was alone.

What is happening to the sex lives of these couples? Something that affects up to 75 percent of newlyweds, according to recent studies—lack of sexual desire. Some call it "the honeymoon effect," but whether it occurs during the first, third or twelfth month of marriage, the result is the same.

Sex, frequent and enjoyable during courtship, falls off dramatically after the vows have been taken. In fact, the frequency of sexual intercourse drops by an average of fifty percent during the first year of marriage, says sociologist William James. This applies to couples who have had sex while dating, as opposed to those who have lived together before marriage. According to Pepper Schwartz and Philip Blumstein in their recent survey of American couples, however, unmarried cohabiting couples can also experience a fizzling of passion.

Surveys show that the happiest couples are those who place a high value on sex. Of course there are many happy couples who get by with little sex, and in some cases without any. These are relationships in which neither partner thinks sex is very important. In most cases, however, when one partner turns off, the other stays turned on. The partner still wanting sex almost inevitably feels rejected, hurt and confused.

Sometimes the stress of a new marriage, or of the wedding itself, is to blame for a lagging sex drive. Planning a wedding can be exhausting and sometimes exasperating. After the honeymoon, there is bound to be a period of adjustment as the partners settle into their new life.

Source: Adapted from Tracey Harden, *Lexington Herald-Leader* (Lexington, Ky., March 31, 1985), p. F7. © 1985 New York News Inc. Reprinted with permission.

Although communication channels in marriage are not always open, conflicts resulting from such problems sometimes may have a positive outcome. Resolving a problem by reaching a mutually agreeable compromise requires a willingness to give a little, but may ultimately strengthen the relationship.

Sexual problems in marriage may be the cause or the result of marital conflict. The reading on page 239 demonstrates, however, that sex may lose its appeal to many young marrieds.

As noted earlier, marital relationships are not static and tend to change with the passing of time. Nevertheless, married people report the highest life satisfaction, followed by the never-married, and then by the widowed and divorced. French sociologist Emile Durkheim's finding that the suicide rate is lower for the married than for singles, widowed, or divorced says something positive for the institution of marriage. Though it may have its ups and downs, marriage continues to be popular in the United States—something "satisfactory" must be occurring with marriage.

COMMUTER MARRIAGES

Till death or till career relocation? The latter has produced increasing geographical separation of married couples in recent years. As of 1983, only five states had laws stating that a married person could establish his or her own domicile (Winfield 1985:1); thus the law has not traditionally sanctioned married couples living apart. But in the 1970s, career-committed women began refusing to leave their work when their husbands transferred to new locations. And today still more women are committed to careers, rather than merely jobs (Vrazo 1985). Modern-day commuter marriage is a "female-determined" arrangement that rarely existed when wives routinely sacrificed their own career desires for those of their husbands.

Commuter marriage in the strictest sense refers to the marital status of employed spouses who spend at least three nights per week in separate residences but are still married and intend to remain so (Gerstel and Gross 1984:1–2). The separation is a result of commitment by both husband and wife to careers in different geographic locations. Representing only a small percentage of U.S. families, these couples choose to live apart and preserve their families while meeting career goals. Maintaining ties between husband, wife, and offspring and striving for success in the work world keep these commuters in the mainstream of American values.

Other kinds of regular separation because of one spouse's job include certain military personnel (such as Navy submarine crews), construction workers, politicians, professional athletes, entertainers, traveling salespeople, and business executives. In these cases,

---

Military Wives in College

Twenty-seven military wives, primarily Navy, enrolled in two southeastern coastal undergraduate institutions in the United States and separated from their spouses for weeks and months at a time, participated in a study about how their husbands' departure affects their school performance. Being a military wife and being separated provided an opportunity to devote more time to academic work. On the other hand, the most frequently noted hardships experienced during separation included loneliness, loss of companion, loss of the handyman, and boredom. For many military wives, the adjustment upon return of the husband after three to six months at sea was more difficult than the departure, since they had "settled into" a pattern without having to deal with another individual.

Perhaps for some military spouses, going to school may actually be a way of "coping" with the husband's departure. By "burying" oneself in academic work, not only is one enhancing her career, but she does not have to constantly worry about her husband's potentially dangerous situation.

Source: F. Carson Mencken, Louisiana State University; unpublished manuscript, College of Charleston, Charleston, S.C., spring 1986.

however, it is usually only one spouse's occupation that occasions the separation, the separation is involuntary, and often a separate home is not established (Gerstel and Gross 1984:6–7).

Commuter marriage may be thought of as a further expression of the individuating trend that began to disperse family members centuries ago—that is, the trend from large multigenerational extended families to small nuclear families, and from group-oriented values to emphasis on individual achievement. Thus, commuter marriage is not just another alternative in a pluralistic potpourri, but an embodiment of the tensions between the economy and the family in contemporary society (Gerstel and Gross 1984:13–14).

Though commuter marriage may be an adaptation to the disjunction between the single-residence nuclear family and the modern economy, just how well does it fulfill the needs of individuals, couples, and families? Talcott Parsons (1965) argues that the nuclear family goes with industrial society's need for geographic mobility, but he also defines certain "irreducible functions" of a family, such as emotional support and adequate socialization of children, and says that a shared residence is necessary if the family is to fulfill these functions. Parsons insists that the daily face-to-face interaction of family members in the shared home makes these specialized family functions possible.

For both spouses to find suitable jobs in their fields, commuter marriages are often necessary in dual-career families. Although a physical strain, absence might actually "make the heart grow fonder."

Couples Meet in the Middle to Have Careers

In decades hence, when a history of the American social revolution of the 1970s and 1980s is written, there no doubt will be a list of casualties—all the working couples who split up over their diverging careers and the spouses who surrendered their careers, and a bit of themselves, to keep their marriages intact. But there will be a list of survivors and heroes, too, and that list should include the couples whose marriages flourished despite their diverging careers. For some, that may demand the sacrifices of a commuter marriage. But for others with jobs in separate cities, the secret to wedded bliss may lie in living midway between the two cities, in what some have called "accordion" marriages.

True, there are sacrifices. The alarm clock often rings before sunrise, husband and wife brush their teeth side by side over the same sink, one hops into the running shower after the other has just hopped out, they kiss goodbye over the morning coffee and then face a long commute to work. He, for example, may be driving to Philadelphia, and she may be headed for the train to midtown Manhattan. But at the end of the day they head toward home— and each other.

Source: David O'Reilly, Knight-Ridder Services, *Lexington Herald-Leader* (Lexington, Ky., June 30, 1985), p. G-1.

If Parsons's argument is correct, a change in the nature of the family would be expected when its members reside in separate households. Recent research, however, suggests that geographic distance does not destroy individuals' relationships or their ability to help each other in practical ways (Gerstel and Gross 1984:14–15). Industrial societies provide technology that allows dispersed family members to survive, such as long-distance communication via telephone, getting together quickly by means of air travel, and exchanging financial aid across distances.

Spouses separated from each other can also turn for support to other sources, such as clubs and organizations, fellow employees, and neighbors. On the other hand, if the geographical distance between workplaces is not too great, a couple can meet at home in the middle, after commuting in opposite directions during the day.

Relationships in commuter marriages may actually be enhanced by separation for periods of time. Naomi Gerstel and Harriet Gross (1984:17) suggest that in traditional family structures strains may occur as members engage in daily interactions over long periods of time. The nuclear family may even prevent couples from achieving satisfaction and intimacy. The marital **dyad** (two persons in a relationship) may embody a form of social control that imposes unnecessary and excessive constraints on each spouse. One may ask, then, not only what couples lose by living apart but what positive outcomes result for commuters as a result of their separations. Absence may "make the heart grow fonder."

In summary, for a marriage to survive, the elements of love (including care, reciprocity, and sharing) and clear communication channels seem to be essential ingredients. Marital conflict is inevitable when two persons live together, and marital satisfaction fluctuates throughout the life cycle. National surveys suggest, however, that the majority of couples in the United States achieve marital happiness. Whether husband and wife live together or in a commuter marriage, the marital system in the United States is dynamic and maintains its remarkable survival power under changing societal conditions.

CHAPTER REVIEW

- A high value is placed on marriage and the family in the United States, according to opinion surveys.
- Marriage is not only an economic relationship, it can be an important status passage for both men and women.
- Couples today choose marriage as a lifestyle, knowing that couples must work together to make the relationship succeed.
- To the ancient Greeks, true love was homosexual love. In later centuries a duality of love existed—married love versus passionate love outside of marriage.
- After the eighteenth century, the Western world adopted an ideal of marriage requiring husband and wife at least to pretend to love each other.
- The first year of marriage is a crucial year in the overall survival of a marriage.
- A marital relationship is enhanced through open, comfortable, and reassuring communication.
- National opinion polls have shown that the majority of married people are happy in their marriages.
- Marital happiness and satisfaction often increase *after* the children have left home.
- Marital conflict is inevitable, but it can be constructive. A marital relationship grows when two people enjoy each other's differences and celebrate each other's uniqueness.
- Married persons report the highest life satisfaction, followed by the never-married, and then by the widowed and divorced.

- Commuter marriages have resulted in geographical separation for some dual-career couples today.

DISCUSSION QUESTIONS

1. Why do you think couples marry today?
2. How would you describe love in marriage for American couples today?
3. What factors would you expect to cause American men and women to postpone marriage today?
4. Discuss the pros and cons of a commuter marriage.
5. Why does sex lose its appeal for many newlyweds?
6. Give examples to support this statement: "Effective communication is positively associated with marital success."

GLOSSARY

commuter marriage: Marriage where employed spouses spend at least three nights per week in separate residences, choosing this arrangement to meet career goals but intending to remain married.

dyad: Two persons in a relationship.

marital adjustment: A wife and husband's relative agreement on issues perceived to be important, sharing tasks, and showing affection.

marital happiness: An individual's emotional response to satisfaction in marriage.

open marriage: Marriage where the husband and wife agree that either or both may have extramarital relationships, and it is okay.

passionate love: Love that is erotic, romantic, and usually short-lived.

serial monogamy: Marrying one person, then divorcing and marrying another, etc.

SUGGESTED READINGS

Davis, Kingsley, ed. 1985. *Contemporary Marriage: Comparative Perspectives on a Changing Institution.* New York: Russell Sage Foundation. *An anthology on the meaning and significance of marriage in contemporary society, including such topics as the revolution in marital behavior, the limits of variation in marital patterns, comparative studies of marital change, law and the revolution of sex roles, and calculation and emotion in marriage.*

Galvin, Kathleen M., and Bernard J. Brummel, 1982. *Family Communication: Cohesion and Change,* Glenview, Ill.: Scott, Foresman and Company. *An examination of the family from a communication perspective.*

Gerstel, Naomi, and Harriet Gross. 1984. *Commuter Marriage: A Study of Work and Family.* New York: The Guilford Press. *An excellent discussion of the pros and cons of commuter marriages.*

James, E. O. 1965. *Marriage Customs Through the Ages.* New York: Collier Books. *Anthropological and historical background of marriage, including discussions of the Christian and civil background and the practical, moral, and philosophic issues of marriage.*

Murstein, Bernard I. 1976. *Who Will Marry Whom? Theories and Research in Marital Choice.* New York: Springer Publishing Company. *A good source for the theoretical and research-minded student of the system of marriage.*

PART FOUR

The Institution of Family

The Parenting Years

◆ *Frustrated teenager to parent who is trying to help with homework: "But Latin has changed a lot since you were in high school."*

For many individuals, marriage is followed by having children. The choice of a mate and the decision to marry tend to be relatively voluntary decisions within the constraints of timing and income. On the other hand, parenthood may not be a voluntary act, if it is an unanticipated effect of sexual intercourse which is recreative (not procreative) in intent (Rossi 1968:30). Our language reflects this distinction: One "decides" to get married—a purposeful action—but one "becomes" a parent (Aldous 1978:158).

Today, however, far more than in previous times, parenthood can be a choice rather than an inevitable event. Previous generations have not been so free to choose. The option to delay parenthood or to remain childless has become a realistic and viable alternative for many contemporary couples.

The dictionary defines a parent as a person who has produced an offspring or has legally become a father or mother through the adoption process. But "parenting" means far more than just being a parent in dictionary terms. G. S. Morrison (1978:23) defined parenting as "the process of developing and utilizing the knowledge and skills appropriate to planning for, creating, giving birth to, rearing, and/or providing care for offspring." J. B. Brooks (1981) notes that parenting is a process that includes nourishing, protecting, and guiding the child through the course of development. Parenting is, then, a continuous series of interactions between parent and child, in a process that changes both (Hamner and Turner 1985:2).

In this chapter we will discuss various issues related to parenting: the question of why individuals have children and become parents; the feminist perspective on motherhood; the socialization into parental roles—how one "learns" to be a parent; the couple's adjustment to a "third party" called baby; the question of how many children to have; and the primary socialization of children.

HAVING CHILDREN: WHY BOTHER?

Why do people decide to have children? Given the economic costs involved in raising children, one can scarcely make the argument that it is financially expedient to have children just to get income tax deductions. Consider the real costs of having children. According to the reading here, raising a child in the 1990s can be an expensive proposition.

Crib to College

The cost of raising one child in constant 1986 dollars for a two-parent, two-child household is presented below. The father is employed full time, the mother is employed part time, and the child attends public school in a suburban area.

Food (at home)	$17,900
Food (away from home)	4,500
Shelter	9,000
Fuel and utilities	4,700
Household goods	10,200
Clothing	7,200
Transportation (to activities and lessons)	24,900
Health	5,800
Recreation	9,500
Personal care (haircuts, etc.)	5,600
College costs (4 years private institution)	40,000*
TOTAL	more than $135,000

*Estimate: The College Board

Source: Taken from "Three's a Crowd," *Newsweek* (September 1, 1986), p. 71. © 1986 Newsweek, Inc. All rights reserved. Reprinted by permission. Source of data was the Urban Institute. Private college costs are rising at the rate of 7 percent per year.

Costs of having children are relatively high in the child's first year of life, decrease until age five, then rise through age twenty-two. The largest factors in the increase with age are food at home, transportation, and education. As the number of children in a family rises, total costs rise although the per-child cost falls. Costs of children rise with family income, although the percentage of income spent on children falls. Thus, when we compare lower- and higher-income families, low-income families spend less on their children, but these costs take a larger bite out of total income (Olson 1983:56).

The decision to have a child, then, rather than saving money, causes a substantial loss of future affluence. As discussed in Chapter 8, Margaret Mead (1966) highlighted the importance of parents' demonstrating their economic ability to support a child prior to having one when she suggested marriage in two steps. Mead simply wanted the family to think through the consequences of having children and be as sure as possible that parenting was something that they could afford. The costs of raising children include not only the expenses incurred in feeding, clothing, housing, and educating them but the time parents devote to child rearing (Blau and Ferber 1986:119–20). That so many young couples still decide to have children attests to the nonmonetary benefits they expect to derive from their progeny. In purely monetary terms, couples would be much better off putting their money in a savings plan for their old age (Olson 1983:58).

Other "costs" of having children are the loss of personal freedom and flexibility and the associated gain in responsibility (Polit-O'Hara and Berman 1984:24–28). Those with no children, as well as parents of children, also frequently mention children's interference with marital communication and intimacy as a "cost."

Despite all these costs of having children, people continue to produce offspring. Improvements in contraceptives and knowledge and availability of contraceptives have made it possible for couples to plan more effectively for having children. Most couples desire children and have them early in marriage. Nearly one out of every two couples produces a child within the first two years of marriage, and at least 90 percent of all couples produce at least one child eventually (Pebley 1981:171–75). However, not all couples choose to have children, as the reading on page 252 indicates.

In general, people feel that the rewards of having children are deeply personal and nontangible (Polit-O'Hara and Berman 1984:35). With shifts from an agrarian to an industrial society (as discussed in Chapter 4), children are no longer viewed as an economic commodity, a labor force for the farm or the family business. Nor are children viewed today as affirming the father's masculinity or the mother's femininity. Rarely nowadays do people feel the need to have

More Married Couples Choosing to Remain Childless

An increasing number of married couples are looking over their lifestyle and choosing not to have children. Child-free marriages no longer carry the stigma of failure or neurotic unfulfillment. As many as 25 percent of young women now in their twenties will remain childless.

Marriage counselors and therapists agree that the key to making a decision about childbearing lies in asking the right questions and answering them honestly. These include:

Do I have the energy for a job and a child?

Am I ready to give up the freedom to do what I want to do, when I want to do it?

Do I know how much money it takes to raise a child, and am I willing to make the necessary financial sacrifices?

Can I deal with noise and confusion and 24-hour-a-day responsibility?

If I were angry or upset, would I take it out on a child?

Do I want a child to prove I'm a woman—or a man—or to show how grown-up I am?

Child-free couples are primarily urban middle class. A recent study found that couples who chose childlessness were those experiencing rewards in their careers. Experts are unanimous in urging couples to actively make a decision, rather than drift into childlessness the way 1950s couples drifted into having children.

Couples must sort out the differences between having a child and being parents. Some couples, once they start thinking about raising children, are not that interested in it. These are probably the people who will be happier not having them. A couple must explore the parenting decision together to make sure that each clearly understands the other's anxieties and concerns and that each knows exactly what the other means by "sharing child care."

Source: Adapted from Associated Press, *The News and Courier* (Charleston, S.C., December 7, 1986), p. 10-F.

children to pass on the family name. Children are valued more in our society just for themselves.

When parents are asked what they value about having children, the most commonly mentioned response is that they are a source of love, affection, and familial enrichment (Bulatao 1981). To put it another way, having children around can be stimulating and fun.

Parenting is full of responsibility, but it yields many rewards as well. Whether reading a book together or walking on the beach, parents tend to discover life anew "through the eyes of a child."

Other frequently mentioned values are that children are their own reward (it is a source of great satisfaction to watch a child grow and develop) and that children are an important source of companionship of a different nature than is possible with same-aged friends (Polit-O'Hara and Berman 1984:19–20). Lois Hoffman and Jean Manis (1979) noted additional reasons why children are desired. Particularly for females, parenthood establishes a person as a mature, stable, and acceptable member of the community; a need for social identity is satisfied. Having children is an expansion of the self—an attainment of "immortality." Individuals have children for any number of reasons. The point is that people "bother" to have children because they want them.

FEMINISTS' THINKING ON MOTHERHOOD

Although low birthrates, high rates of female labor force participation, and associated trends surfaced dramatically only recently, they have been developing for many decades (Gerson 1985:217–18). Except during the post–World War II period, women's movement out of the home has been steadily gaining momentum since at least the turn of the century. Women's changing commitments stem from underlying structural changes that are widespread and tend to reinforce each other over time. These structural changes, such as increased marital instability, pressures for greater female workplace opportunities, and a heightened need for women's earnings, have rearranged the options many women face.

In the late 1960s and early 1970s feminists raised questions about mothering. They argued for safe, legal abortions and contraception, criticized the health-care system, and advocated maternity and paternity benefits and leaves. These arguments centered on the strong belief that women's lives should not be totally constrained by child care or childbearing. These feminists argued that women should be free to choose not to bear children, should be able to continue their other work if mothers, and should have available to them good day care. Shulamith Firestone in the *Dialectic of Sex* (1970) argued that the reproductive difference between the sexes (women bear the children) leads to a sexual division of labor that is at the heart of all women's oppression by men, class, and race. Women must be freed from this biology. Firestone suggests the solution to be a technology that eliminates biological reproduction united to anyone's procreative body.

More recent feminist writing on motherhood has focused more on the experience of mothering. Who should parent and how should the parenting be done? (Chodorow and Contratto 1982:54). Some feminist writing on motherhood assumes an all-powerful mother who is totally responsible for how her children turn out and is, therefore, blamed for everything from her daughter's limitations to the crisis of human existence. In this view, mother and child are an isolated **dyad,** or two-person interacting group; thus women's all-powerful mothering shapes the child's entire psychological, social, and political experience (Dinnerstein 1976:253).

Another theme in recent feminist writing on motherhood links motherhood to violence and death. Being a mother is a matter of life and death. And over the millennia of human existence, motherhood has been associated with maternal death, children's deaths, the blood of childbirth, spontaneous abortions, stillbirths, the inability to conceive, childbirth as an experience of death, obstetric torture techniques, unmothered monsters, child murder, and incest (Chodorow and Contratto 1982:60–61).

Cultural understandings of mothering have a long history, but the roots of present-day parenting ideology lie in the nineteenth century. At a time when lives were being affected by the frenzied growth of developing industrial capitalism, mothers were seen as having total control and unlimited power in the creation of their children. This cultural ideology blames mothers for any failings in their children and idealizes possible maternal perfection. More recently, as women have entered the paid labor force, and as some have chosen not to become mothers, mothers have been blamed more for "maternal deprivation" than for "maternal overprotection." Nancy Chodorow and Susan Contratto (1982:63–71) argue that feminists need to move beyond these extremist assumptions and fantasies since they have led to the cultural oppression of women in the interest of a child whose needs are also fantasized.

Despite the rise of women's nondomestic aspirations, gender inequality at the workplace remains deeply entrenched in American society—and this fact is part of a vicious cycle. Inequality at the workplace inhibits equality in the division of parenting responsibilities; inequality in parenting, in turn, inhibits occupational and economic equality (Gerson 1985:224).

Kathleen Gerson (1985:225–26) argues that effective social policy must address sexual inequality on both fronts. Equality at work would reduce income disparity between males and females, would lessen the devaluation of women's work, and might ultimately draw more men into female-dominated jobs. If jobs became more sexually integrated and the disparity between male and female earnings narrowed, women and men would find it more economically rational to share equally in parenting.

During recent years, support for women working outside the home has increased dramatically among both sexes. A majority of both sexes, however, still support sex segregation in the labor market and a sexual division of labor at home (Quarm 1984:206). The backlash against more equal roles for men and women has already begun—under attack in the late 1980s were affirmative action, reproduction rights, government-supported day care, and even maternal–child health programs. As long as men do not participate in childrearing on an equal or nearly equal basis, women and children will continue to receive a smaller share of society's rewards.

To reduce the barriers working parents face, Kathleen Gerson (1985:226) recommends two types of social policies. First, legislation requiring employers to offer paid parental leave to both men and women on request would increase the options open to dual-earner households. Similarly, the development of a wide range of child-care services and facilities would assist parents in better integrating their work and family lives.

SOCIALIZATION IN PARENTAL ROLES

As we noted above, parenthood is a major role assumed by a large percentage of individuals. Major social roles typically require a long period of socialization and anticipatory training. But parenthood, unlike other major social roles, is not always anticipated and, because of social norms and institutions, certainly is not reversible (Rossi 1968). If a marriage does not work out, divorce is a solution. A person may also leave an unsatisfactory job and get another one. But once a child is born, there is little possibility of undoing the commitment to parenthood—except for placing the child up for adoption (Hamner and Turner 1985:21).

As the persons primarily responsible for child rearing, mothers and fathers should have sufficient knowledge and skill to fulfill the roles of coordinators of family and work life, cultivators of school and community relationships, caregivers, teachers, and spouses (who ever thought that parenthood would be easy?). While today's parents have many tasks to organize and manage, they may not have a clear conception of the job of parenthood or of their identity as parents. Nonetheless, societal expectations for perfection may be great (Cataldo 1987:51).

Parent Education

Parent education in the modern era had its beginning early in the nineteenth century. At that time publications on child rearing began to appear, and organizations emphasizing education and support for parents began to form. The major impetus for parent education in the twentieth century came during two periods—the 1920s and 1960s. The National Council of Parent Education and the American Home Economics Association were formed in the 1920s. Also, nursery schools and child study centers at colleges and universities were established at that time. In the 1960s the Economic Opportunity Act was passed, and the War on Poverty was launched. According to Tommie Hamner and Pauline Turner (1985:29), the rapidly changing and complex technological society of the 1980s and 1990s necessitates continual support for parents. In their book on parenting, Hamner and Turner (1985:23–24) summarize the reasons why parent education is needed in our society:

1. A large percentage of the total population are, or will become, parents.
2. Education for parenthood does not appear to be provided in the home, nor is it stressed in most educational systems.
3. Insufficient guidelines for successful parenthood create confusion and anxiety for parents.
4. Effective parenting is critical for all aspects of the child's development.
5. Being a parent is not easy.

6. Parents want and need help.
7. There is a need for greater involvement of fathers in child rearing.
8. There are many myths about parenthood that need to be dispelled.

A most important characteristic of the family is that much that is learned within the family carries over to other institutions and social relationships in the larger society. If a child is brought up in a family where love and care are constantly displayed, the probability is great that that individual will reveal such traits outside the family. On the other hand, if the child's parents show hatred and lack of love and concern, odds are that the individual will display these same qualities to others in society. Certainly the latter individual is not the preferred type, and any social setting where there are too many of these persons is an undesirable place to live. Thus, being a parent should not be treated lightly.

Strategies for Child Rearing

Because many parents seek help in rearing their children, several strategies for child rearing have been developed to assist parents in being more effective in their roles. Some of the more popular contemporary strategies for parenting (Hamner and Turner 1985:84–100) include (1) Parent Effectiveness Training **(P.E.T.),** developed in 1962 and based on a theory of human relationships believed to be applicable to all relationships between people; (2) Transactional Analysis (TA), established originally in 1961, a therapeutic technique to encourage parents to develop their adult states so that children can have an appropriate model for developing their own adult ego states; (3) behavior modification, established by B. F. Skinner in the 1950s, which emphasizes changing a child's behavior through the use of reinforcements (rewards and punishments); and (4) the humanistic approach of Haim Ginott, who in 1965 advocated improved communication between parents and children and emphasized the importance of parents' listening to and understanding the feelings of the child.

To step into parenthood without any preparation and, therefore, to rely on "on-the-job training" is not unlike sex education on the honeymoon or death education on the death bed. Because of the tremendous importance of effective parenting, anticipatory socialization into parental roles is beneficial to the child, the parents, and society.

From Dyad to Triad

As Jessie Bernard notes in *The Future of Motherhood* (1974), women become mothers regardless of how much training they have in other areas and how little they have in mothering. Many are entering the role completely unprepared and must resort to "on-the-job training." And the transition from dyad to **triad**—from couple to three-person group—is sudden.

How do new parents react to their changed roles and responsibilities? Despite the fact that some psychological changes occur during the transition to parenthood, the bulk of the data suggests that parents are only moderately bothered by the addition of children and that a majority of parents derive positive feelings from parenthood (Roopnarine and Miller 1985).

Parenting infants, toddlers, and preschool children is a rewarding but challenging task. During the first years of life, a child evolves from a helpless infant who can do little but make a few sounds and keep someone busy changing diapers, to a toddler stumbling around getting into everything, to a preschool child with more questions than a Philadelphia lawyer and a boundless supply of energy. At this stage, parents are the most influential people in the life of the child, and lasting impressions are made on the child's mind and personality.

Not only does a parent assume the parental function rather abruptly, but his or her role changes from that of caregiver to protector to nurturer in a remarkably short time (Hamner and Turner 1985:55). The reciprocal interaction established between parents and

Calvin and Hobbes   by Bill Watterson

Parents survive the "terrible two's" and soon find themselves confronted with striving-to-be-independent teenagers. Through it all, parental influence is central, and many teenagers eventually grudgingly admit the value of their parents' rules and boundaries. (CALVIN AND HOBBES COPYRIGHT 1988 UNIVERSAL PRESS SYNDICATE. Reprinted with permission. All rights reserved.)

children remains fairly consistent throughout the parenting years, as parents and children continually respond to each other's needs and behaviors. Parents themselves undergo developmental changes similar in importance to those of their children.

PRIMARY SOCIALIZATION OF CHILDREN

Oscar Ritchie and Marvin Koller (1964:160) describe the family setting as the "nursery of **socialization.**" That is, besides providing care and protection, the family furnishes the child with initial and basic instruction regarding attitudes, values, norms, and skills. The family ideally offers models to be emulated, aspirations to be pursued, and security when the child is threatened.

Initial and Basic Instruction

As noted by social psychologist Charles H. Cooley (1915:23–24) at the early part of this century, the family fits most of his criteria of a **primary group.** That is, it comes close to involving the whole personalities of its participants, not merely fragments of personalities; it is close-knit and personal and involves face-to-face relationships over long periods of time. A spontaneous, unrehearsed, relaxed informality exists in family relationships. A family member is likely to express himself or herself freely, sometimes to the point of brutal frankness, with little fear of major retaliation. The socialization processes inside family units are often unconsciously conducted.

And the family of orientation is primary not only in the sense of which Cooley speaks; it is primary in that it is the first group to which a child belongs. As the initial contact group during the formative years, the family plays a most significant role in the **socialization** of the child. The family is the initial builder of personality attributes.

Oscar Ritchie and Marvin Koller (1964:78) do suggest caution in describing the primacy of the family institution in child socialization. They note it would be an error to assume that the family has the total responsibility in child rearing and that other groupings are inconsequential. Though the family is fundamental to personality formation, it is only one of a series of primary and secondary groups affecting socialization.

Most children enter a family unit which is already ongoing, with a history, a heritage, a name, and a reputation. Family members are intimately identified with the newborn, and their experiences and those of their children become mutually meaningful (Ritchie and Koller 1964:82). If the child is developing in an "acceptable" way, he or she is patted on the head and given encouragement; if the direction of behavior is away from acceptability, he or she is discouraged from repeating such action.

Along with acquiring a growing awareness of self, within the family a child discovers the existence of others. Many people will come and go in his or her life, but the parents tend to remain longer and reappear more often in the growing child's world. While other kinship ties will become known as the child moves from infancy, such relationships seldom reach the intensity associated with the parent-child bond. Parents alone observe the child's metamorphosis from a helpless bundle of life to an adult with a place in the world (Ritchie and Koller 1964:141).

Parents have a great impact on their children not only by their words but by their actions. The models they present, consciously or unconsciously, often help shape what their children will become. Since young children have yet to acquire skill in dealing with abstractions, they are very impressed by the living models around them. They may imitate some actions and reject others. Models may be positive, or they may be negative (Ritchie and Koller 1964:156). Certainly, many a parent has been embarrassed by his or her young child imitating the parent's behavior in public—often a mannerism the parent was not aware the child was internalizing. Thus, it is important that the parent be careful what he or she says or does in the family—it may come back to haunt the parent.

Disciplining Children

One of the major concerns of parents with young children is how much or how little to discipline them. In socializing a child, parents strive to develop the child so that he or she will be accepted into the society. The child is reprimanded if he or she gets out of line with the parents' understanding of society's norms and values.

If and when a parent deems it advisable to administer punishment for a given act, the punishment should meet several conditions (Hamner and Turner 1985:45). First, the punishment should immediately follow the act. Second, punishment needs to be both deserved and understood. Finally, punishment needs to be related to the act. If the parent remains calm and focuses on the child's behavior rather

An important aspect of child socialization is discipline. The child is taught to behave in a manner acceptable to society. Discipline may involve everything from respect for parents to kindness and sharing when playing with siblings or friends.

than on the child himself or herself, the child does not suffer damaged self-respect in the process of learning acceptable behavior (Hamner and Turner, 1985:45).

It is important for parents to remember to be as objective as possible and to refrain from venting their own anger at the child's expense. Too often, discipline, especially physical punishment like spanking or other forms of **corporal punishment,** serves as a release of parental frustrations but does not help the child learn appropriate behavior. In utilizing corporal punishment, the parent is modeling aggressive, angry behavior for the child and is, in essence, telling the child that hitting another person when one is angry is okay or that violence is an appropriate method of settling disputes.

Parents' self-esteem is partly dependent on the behavior of their children. If the child acts up in public, the parents' presentation of themselves as good and adequate parents is threatened. In these situations, some parents resort to "disciplining" a child in public by hitting or smacking him or her. Until such parents' self-esteem becomes less dependent on the behavior of their children, they may continue to use corporal punishment. But the humiliation of being hit in public probably rarely does anyone any good and can certainly have negative consequences.

Swedish laws prohibit public corporal punishment, and in 1979 the Swedish Parliament, by a vote of 259 to 6, adopted legislation stating, "A child may not be subjected to physical punishment or other injurious or humiliating treatment" (Vinocur 1980). This law includes parents and guardians in the home. In the United States, corporal punishment is allowed in the schools in forty-three states (Satchell 1985:4). According to Michael Satchell (1985:4),

> *Thousands of pupils from kindergarten through the 12th grade are spanked every school day, sometimes for such trivial offenses as forgetting supplies, making small academic errors, being late, not finishing their lunches or talking too loudly on the school bus.*

We allow corporal punishment not only in public in the United States, but in private as well. As you reflect on your own childhood, how constructive was the physical punishment you received? Was it simply an adult venting frustration? Too often, an innocent third party—be it a child or the pet cat—is the victim of misdirected violence. The day at the office did not go well; the parent comes home in a bad mood, and, being unable to release his or her frustrations with the boss, at the slightest provocation hits the child or kicks the pussy cat halfway across the room (rather than hug or pet it as is often the case). The cat or the child stands (or lies, depending on the blow) in bewilderment as to what in the world is going on. Just how often, if ever, is corporal punishment necessary? The answer, most experts now agree, is never. There is no crime a young child can commit that is most effectively corrected by a parental beating. When you pause to consider, a parent deliberately hurting a child is merely a bully. And as with all parental examples, the bullying lesson sinks in. Certainly, it has been pointed out in the child abuse literature (see Chapter 16) that those adults who abuse children almost without exception were abused as children.

> You're not leaving this table until you clean your plate. We're only doing this because we love you. I can't wait until you grow up and have children of your own. If your friends all jump off a bridge, does that mean you will too? Knock it off, or I'll turn this car around right now. How do you know you don't like it, you haven't even tasted it. I said no, and I mean no. You're not leaving this house looking like that. I don't want to have to spank you, but I will. No, you'll spoil your dinner. I do and I do and I do for you kids, and this is the thanks I get. I'm going to say this once and only once. Just wait 'til your father gets home. If you don't stop crying, I'm going to give you something to cry about. Because your father and I say so, that's why. If I ever hear you use that word around here again, I'm going to wash your mouth out with soap. Some day you're going to thank me for this. I love you.
>
> Source: Anonymous.

WHEN IS ENOUGH ENOUGH?

Once a family has one child, the question is when—or whether—to make the family trio into a quartet. Life is filled with choices, and whether to have one or more children is one of those decisions every American family makes (unless, of course, accidents occur).

Family size ideals have begun to favor smaller families worldwide. The two-child family has become the most popular for young couples in the United States as well as in other countries. A 1980 Gallup poll in twenty-two countries asked people to indicate ideal rather than expected family size (Gallup 1981). In the United States 55 percent responded that two children are ideal. Except in smaller nonindustrialized countries with primarily agricultural economies, there was a general, worldwide consensus that two children constitute a perfect family size.

Only 2 percent of Americans, by contrast, believe that one child is ideal (Polit-O'Hara and Berman 1984:29–30). Reasons noted for having more than one child are sibling companionship and the belief (right or wrong) that an only child is developmentally handicapped because of the absence of siblings.

On the other hand, parents with only one child point out that an only child enjoys numerous advantages: financial advantages, increased parental attention, increased opportunities to be involved in the parents' activities and planning, better parent-child relations, and the absence of sibling conflict. Indeed, some research evidence suggests an only child may be particularly independent, mature, and assertive (Polit-O'Hara and Berman 1984:30–31, 67).

A curious tendency exists for children in small families to do better in school, score higher on IQ tests, and compile higher college entrance exam scores than children from larger families. Several theories have been offered to explain this tendency (Polit-O'Hara and Berman 1984:44–46). First, the prenatal environment changes in successive births. Second, statistics show that parents with high IQ test scores have fewer children than those with lower scores. (This second "explanation" could well be a function of social class position and related to income and social milieu rather than intelligence.) Third, in larger families there are fewer resources for special courses, trips, and other activities conducive to their intellectual growth. Last, parents with few children have more time to devote to each child, thereby fostering intellectual advances.

In addition to doing better on tests of intelligence, other advantages experienced by children from small families (Polit-O'Hara and Berman 1984:66) are that they go farther in school and show more motivation to achieve. As a group they tend to be better developed physically and less likely to get in serious trouble with police authorities than those from larger families.

One must keep in mind, however, that even though children in small families seem to have the best opportunities when growing up, research results cannot be generalized to all families. There are bright, healthy, happy, accomplished children in large families and unhappy, dull, and unhealthy children in small families.

Many factors contribute to a child's development; many of these are beyond a parent's control, but in the United States today, family size is not. With few exceptions, parents can actually make some conscious choices about whether to have one, two, or more children.

When is enough enough? The number of children a couple decides to have can have a major impact on their lives (Polit-O'Hara and Berman, 1984:73–93). As noted earlier, children reduce family income. On the other hand, children appear to have an inhibiting effect on divorce. Parenthood itself has more substantial effects on husbands and wives than does the number of children as such. Thus, it is up to the couple to clarify what they want as a couple. Information on demographic trends and data on pros and cons of small families can only help each couple choose the best way to achieve the most suitable lifestyle for their family.

Charles H. Cooley was correct many decades ago when he described the family as a primary group—it is the nursery in which one first learns to cope with the world. Serving as keeper of the "nursery of socialization" is an awesome responsibility. Each person should give careful consideration to the question of whether or not to become a parent. Disciplining of children should be treated seriously and not done haphazardly. Parent education would likely enhance the effectiveness of most of us parents. Society needs to assess the roles of mother *and* father in parenting to address the issue of sexual equality. Whether to have one child, two, or more is not a decision to be taken lightly. Despite the undeniable importance and seriousness of the job of parenting, however, many parents would testify that it's the most exciting job they've ever had.

CHAPTER REVIEW

- One "decides" to marry, but one "becomes" a parent. Parenting today is becoming more of a choice for many couples.
- The economic costs of having children are high, although personal rewards are also great. It appears that some couples are choosing not to have children today.
- In the 1960s and 1970s feminists argued for safe, available abortions and birth control and advocated maternity and paternity benefits and leaves. Support for women working outside the home has increased dramatically among both sexes.
- Effective social policy must address sexual inequality at the workplace and in parenting.
- Sufficient knowledge and skills for parenting are needed in our society. Several current strategies for parenting are available today.
- The parental role is assumed rather abruptly, and the role changes quickly throughout the life cycle.
- The family, which fits C. H. Cooley's definition of a primary group, also plays an initial and most important role in the socialization of the growing child.
- "Disciplining" a child is a major concern of parents and should not be taken lightly. Parents need to refrain from venting their own anger at the child's expense.
- The "ideal" number of children is two, yet many Americans feel there are advantages to having only one child. The number of children a couple decides to have can have a major impact on their lives.

DISCUSSION QUESTIONS

1. Discuss the different kinds of "costs" of having children.
2. What issues on motherhood have been raised by feminists?
3. Cite several advantages of having children.
4. When did modern parent education begin? Why do you think parent education had its beginning at that time?
5. State reasons as to why parent education is needed.
6. Is parenthood really a crisis in a couple's life? Why or why not?
7. Do you approve of corporal punishment for children? Explain why or why not, with examples.
8. What are some advantages of limiting yourself to two children?
9. Discuss the advantages and disadvantages of having only one child.

GLOSSARY

corporal punishment: Punishment inflicted directly on the body.

dyad: Two persons in a relationship.

P.E.T.: Parent Effectiveness Training, a strategy for parenting that emphasizes parents' helping children become responsible by creating an atmosphere of acceptance, respect, and consideration.

primary group: A small group of persons interacting in a personal, face-to-face, and close-knit group.

socialization: The process by which one acquires the way of life of his or her society so as to become an acceptable member of that society.

triad: A group of three persons.

SUGGESTED READINGS

Arnold L. Eugene. 1985. *Parents, Children and Changes.* Lexington, Mass.: Lexington Books. *An anthology with ideas about nurturing and nourishing children.*

Davis, Kingsley, Mikhail S. Bernstam, and Rita Ricardo-Campbell. 1987. *Below Replacement Fertility in Industrial Societies: Causes, Consequences, Policies.* Cambridge: Cambridge University Press. *An anthology about economics and fertility.*

Hamner, Tommie J., and Pauline H. Turner. 1985. *Parenting in Contemporary Society.* Englewood Cliffs, N.J.: Prentice-Hall. *An excellent, very thorough book on concepts, challenges and changes in parenting, contemporary variations on parenting, and support systems for parents.*

Hanson, Shirley M. H., and Frederick W. Bozett. 1985. *Dimensions of Fatherhood.* Beverly Hills, Calif.: Sage Publications. *An anthology presenting roles of fatherhood throughout the life cycle and variations of fatherhood.*

Polit-O'Hara, Denise, and Judith Berman. 1984. *Just the Right Size: A Guide to Family-Size Planning.* New York: Praeger Publishers. *A well-written guide to aid in decisions about how many, if any, children a couple should have.*

The Middle Years

◆ *When I was seventeen I heard*
From each censorious tongue,
"I'd not do that if I were you;
You see you're rather young.

Now that I number forty years,
I'm quite as often told
Of this or that I shouldn't do
Because I'm quite too old.

O carping world! If there's an age
Where youth and manhood keep
An equal poise, alas! I must
*Have passed it in my sleep.**

We now turn our attention to the stage of life referred to as "the middle years." While there appears to be no agreement among social scientists as to the exact beginning of middle age, most seem to suggest that this period of life starts between ages forty and forty-five. The U.S. Census Bureau defines middle age as being ages forty-five to sixty-four. Vera in the Broadway play *Mame*, on the other hand, describes middle age as being "somewhere between forty and death." An English dermatologist early in the twentieth century noted that middle life actually falls for most, not at fifty, but nearly twenty years earlier (MacKenna 1933). A century is a nice round figure, however, so we divide it by two and make fifty the halfway house in life. Middle-aged women have been defined (Brown and Kerns 1985:2)

---

*To Critics by Walter Learned

as "women who have adult offspring and who are not yet frail or dependent."

While the exact date of onset of middle age is ambiguous, there are certainly ways of defining the middle years other than by chronological age. Situations characteristic of this period include such major events as relationships with adolescent children, children's leaving home, the peaking of the family's economic situation, the consideration of retirement from work, the arrival of grandchildren, the beginnings of chronic illness, and the responsibility for elderly parents.

As middle-aged men and women realize "they ain't what they used to be" when it comes to getting around, this realization may come as a shock. When I realized, at age forty-five, that my fourteen-year-old son could finally outsprint me at the end of our daily jog, I concluded that Daniel was getting stronger rather than that I was beginning to lose it. In reality, I knew all along that it was a combination of both factors!

The proportion of Americans reaching mid-life is on the rise. This group constituted only about 20 percent of the total population in 1979 but are expected to account for 25 percent by 2010 (U.S. Bureau of the Census 1981:1–3). At age forty-five, men can expect to live another twenty-nine years; women can expect an additional thirty-five years of life. Ninety percent of middle-aged persons currently live in families, and the vast majority live with their spouses. Incomes of middle-aged persons are at or near their lifetime peak, yet even for year-round full-time workers, women's incomes are still only 56 percent of men's incomes—a discrepancy found throughout the life cycle.

While middle age may be presented as a period when men achieve a level of self-actualization not possible in younger adulthood, and while it is a period characterized by security, reduced external pressures, and the maturity to enjoy that which life has to offer, it may also be viewed as a crisis. The realization that one's life expectancy is on the short side—that one's grandparents, and perhaps parents, are dead and the middle-aged group is "next in line" to die—creates a high death anxiety for persons at mid-life. Some have referred to the feelings brought on by this situation as the "mid-life crisis." Indeed, William A. Nolen entitled his book about males at mid-life *Crisis Time!* (1984). It can be very frustrating to the middle-aged person to realize that his or her life is over half gone when there is still much he or she would like to accomplish.

In the middle years of a family, the parents-versus-peers issue can become significant in the lives of adolescents. Parents, children, and the children's peers become intertwined in a network of relationships that may be characterized as cooperative, competitive, or in conflict. The next section will address the issue of parents and peers; it will be followed by sections on the launching phase of the family, grandparenting, and marital quality in later life.

PARENTS AND PEERS

Secondary Socialization

While primary socialization takes place within the family, secondary socialization occurs to a large extent within the school. As a formal socialization agency, the school is designed to teach the cognitive skills needed to get along in society, while the family supposedly specialized in the child's social and emotional development. But contacts with teachers and peers at school also affect social development, just as family conversation and family interests affect cognitive development. Teachers are concerned with a child's internalizing moral values, acquiring social skills, and learning self-control. Ideas gained from school associates affect a child's reception of parental rules and discipline. By the same token, interactions within the family affect a child's school career (Aldous 1978:250).

High school students spend an average of seven or eight hours per day in school, and potentially many additional hours in extracurricular activities before and after school. Most people, because they desire to be accepted by others and to be popular with their peers, are inevitably shaped by their peers and associates. Consequently, high school may very well have a powerful influence in shaping adolescents' concepts of what they are and what they want to become.

Ideally, family and school socialization should complement each other. School authorities seek the cooperation of parents both in encouraging a child's learning and in motivating a child to conform to school rules and regulations. Parents, on the other hand, may seek assistance from the school in socializing their child.

High school may be viewed as a way station toward the larger world into which teenagers are moving. The school can provide more access to, and can exercise more authority over, the peer group. Also, high school officials and faculty are freer than parents to view adolescents objectively—teachers are not as emotionally involved with teenagers as are their parents. And high school teachers also have less reason than parents to feel personally responsible for an adolescent's behavior or state of mind (Jersild, Brook, and Brook 1978:466).

High school years have a tremendous impact on determining the teenager's self concept. Peer influences sometimes clash with parental ideas as to how the adolescent should behave.

The secondary socialization of the high school years can have a significant impact on the adolescent. In the process of becoming an adult, the adolescent is gaining independence, beginning to drive a car, testing gender roles while going out on dates, joining the world of work on a part-time basis, shaping his or her future by performance in the academic setting, and often acquiring lifelong friends. In this transitional stage of life a boy or girl is accountable not just to parents but to peers, school officials, and others—which makes it difficult to please all parties involved. The adolescent is expected to "act like an adult," yet he or she may still be treated as "just a kid." With such role conflicts, perhaps it is a miracle that any of us survive the adolescent years and come out even halfway sane.

Situational Adjustment

One mechanism in the adolescent's secondary socialization into high school and eventually into adulthood is referred to by Howard Becker (1964:44–46) as **"situational adjustment."** Moving in and out of new social situations necessitates that an individual be able to assess accurately what is required of him or her and be able to meet these expectations. Successful adaptation of this type causes the individual to become the kind of person the situation demands. In other words, the person is molded or acquires a sense of self by learning what is expected of him or her and then doing it. Thus, the peer group with which an adolescent associates plays an important role in the secondary socialization process leading to adult status.

Becker (1964:46–48) further notes that situational adjustment is often not an individual process but a collective one—**cohorts,** or groups of same-aged people, undergoing an institution's socializing effects are socialized as a unit. Situational adjustment may have a collective character even where people are not processed in groups (such as vocational or college preparation tracks or in special programs like athletics, choir, or band). A boy or girl may enter the high school alone—for example, as a transfer student in the middle of the year—but join a larger group already there. The larger group is more than willing to "tell it like it is" and will clearly signal what a student should do to be accepted. Much of the change in any one individual is a function of the interpretive response made by the entire group to the problems it faces. Since group consensus tends to have the character of "what everyone knows to be true," the individual being socialized leans toward the group's view of the world. Therefore, the collective character of the socialization process has a profound effect upon individuals within the group.

The process of situational adjustment accounts for changes people undergo, but people also exhibit some consistency as they move from situation to situation. Becker (1964:49–51) uses the term "commitment" to refer to an individual's consistency in a sequence of varied situations. A variety of "commitments" constrain each of us to follow a consistent pattern of behavior in many areas of life. For example, one's moral values may hold fairly solid throughout the life cycle, even as one adjusts to new situations.

Thus, as the adolescent moves toward adulthood, the primary socialization of the formative years within the family is not canceled out by secondary socialization experienced in the high school. Rather, the peer socialization of the high school years presents the adolescent with additional alternatives that sometimes complement, at other times contradict, the primary socialization experienced within the family. As the adolescent grows up, many ideas from many sources are fed into his or her personal "computer." It is up to the individual to sort out these data as he or she is socialized into the world at large.

Parents "versus" Peers

As children mature into adolescents, they spend more time with their peers—their age-mates—and less time with their parents. Over two decades ago a growing body of research concluded that peers are at least as effective as parents in influencing the behavior of the adolescent child (Bronfenbrenner 1970:232). Yet young people continue to identify strongly with their parents on most occasions. As noted by Eastwood Atwater (1983:166), the relative degrees of influence of peers and parents depend on several factors. The age of the adolescent is important, as evidenced by the changing patterns of parent and peer influence with increasing age. The amount of influence by parents or peers also depends on the type of choices being made—parents are more influential over occupational aspirations, peers more instrumental in decisions relating to clothing or recreational choices. However, it should be remembered that adolescents differ greatly among themselves.

According to a study by Hans Sebald (1986), between the mid-1960s and the mid-1980s changes occurred in the orientation of adolescents toward parents and peers. Sebald studied various social issues during the 1960s, '70s, and '80s in an attempt to determine which concerns and/or problems were peer-oriented and which were patient-oriented. Sebald concluded that teenagers were more conservative (with a high parent orientation) in the early 1960s; that they were strongly influenced by the counterculture youth movements of the mid-1970s, resulting in an all-time low parent orientation and an all-time high peer orientation; and that they assumed an intermediate stance during the quieter late 1970s and early 1980s. The increase of peer orientation between the 1960s and 1970s, and its decline thereafter, forms a marked **curvilinearity,** or curve, and indicates the recovery of some parental influence. This ties in with society's general trend away from the "me generation" and somewhat of a tendency back to more traditional values and an increased interest in "roots."

Parents as Friends

Although adolescence is a time that tries the souls of most parents, it can also be very satisfying when things are going moderately well. Parents often discover a new creature unfolding before their eyes, yet this new person retains fond and familiar traits of an earlier day. As observed by Jersild, Brook, and Brook (1978:317), it is fascinating just to watch a child grow with all the many rapid changes occurring.

Psychologists use two central terms to describe adolescent-parent interaction: *emancipation* and *conformity*. Emancipation—freedom—refers to the belief that in order to establish their own individuality, adolescents must free themselves from the parental bond. Conformity refers to the parents' roles as mediators between the family and society—parents try to instill standards and values to help maintain society, and many teenagers do internalize these standards and values. Not everyone thinks of society as something to preserve as is, however, or as something that young people should perceive as benevolent. From this perspective, society is filled with problems, and parents must use their experience as well as their material and mental resources to guide their adolescent children in new directions. For parents to desert these adolescents would be irresponsible; however, to seek to duplicate existing social patterns in their children would be equally **dysfunctional,** or counterproductive (Youniss and Smollar 1985:92–93).

Most adolescents love their parents, seek and welcome their advice, and hold their standards in esteem. At the same time, they may be critical of their parents (Rogers 1981:228–29). Teenagers may question their parents' competence for decision making simply because they belong to an older generation. Youth may also view parents as symbols of their own dependency, which fosters their own feelings of a lack of personal autonomy. As long as teenagers live with their parents, too, their personal prestige is tied partially to that of their parents. At the same time, wider contact with other adults leads them to make comparisons, which may cause them to be critical of their parents' faults, resulting in less of an overidealization of parents.

Yet a decade ago (Phillips 1979:4), there seemed to be much agreement between adolescents and their parents on many issues. With the exception of the use of marijuana and alcohol, 63 to 85 percent of the youth in a large national study agreed with parental attitudes toward religion, drugs (other than marijuana), education, and career goals for modern women. Fifty-eight percent agreed with their parents about racial issues and conservation of resources.

Critical evaluations of the relationships between parents and adolescents usually tend to be exaggerated. Youth and their parents are more likely than not to have a friendly view of each other. Not only are parents undisturbed by their children's predictable rebellion, youth do not live up to the stereotype that they should reject family values and behavioral standards. Each seems to admire the other, as far as ideological and base values are concerned.

On the other hand, youth may try to shape their parents' behavior, just as parents seek to modify their children's behavior (Rogers 1981:229). Adolescence is a period when individuation of the self occurs; the young person becomes increasingly self-reliant and insists upon making up his or her own mind. This leads to independence and confidence in personal decision making. By asserting his or her developing ability to speak out without constant support, the adolescent is signaling parents that past communication directives no longer fit the situation (Galvin and Brommel 1982:221).

In studies conducted over a four-year period with over one thousand adolescents, James Youniss and Jacqueline Smollar

(1985:89–90) concluded that adolescents, in general, continue to perceive their fathers as they did when they were children. They still seek their fathers' approval and believe fathers have important insights concerning the society that they are about to enter. According to these studies, fathers seem to have narrow views of their sons and daughters, thinking of them as potential adults and caring most about those activities that will prepare them for the adult roles they are about to assume. Fathers, therefore, tend to share only a small part of adolescents' current interests. Thus, fathers and adolescents do not get to know each other as individual personalities but understand each other in instrumental ways through social roles.

Mothers, no less than fathers, hold adolescents to performance standards that refer ultimately to impending adulthood. Mothers, like fathers, seem to want their adolescent children to meet their expectations and become the kind of adults of which they can be proud. Mothers, however, communicate their desires in a different style. They maintain regular contact with their offspring, and this interaction is not focused solely on their children's future. Mothers tend to engage themselves in the adolescent interests of their children. While they may act as advisors and disciplinarians, in their daily involvement with the lives of their adolescents they do not solely take on the role of authority, but serve as confidants who share experiences. Thus, mutuality enters into the relationships of mothers and adolescent children (Youniss and Smollar 1985:90–91).

Youniss and Smollar (1985:159) conclude that parents are not friends, and friends are not parents. The respective structures of the two relationships require distinctive accommodations to be made by the adolescent. Hence, the relationships with parents and peers contribute different, but equally valuable, experiences necessary for the task of adolescent development.

THE LAUNCHING PHASE OF THE FAMILY

There comes a time, usually in the parents' middle years, when their children complete their secondary school commitment and prepare to leave the **family of orientation** (the family that raised them) for the "real world." Some young people will go to college, others will join the military, and others will enter the job market full time. Although recent data (Glick and Lin 1986) suggest that adult children are staying at home for longer periods than in the past, most will depart during the parents' middle years to make their own lives. This section discusses the "launching" phase of the family life cycle.

Encouraging children to explore skills such as cooking gives them a feeling of importance and well-being. Working together at such tasks helps build strong relationships between parents and children.

According to *Webster's Dictionary*, one meaning of the word "launch" is "to start a person on some course or career." We often think of launching in connection with our national space program, which periodically launches a rocket or shuttle into outer space. Launching children outside the spatial dimensions of the home can be compared to NASA's launchings. Much that the adolescent will encounter out there may be unexpected, though he or she has been trained (socialized) for this venture. The adolescent must be prepared to steer his or her course in a direction approved by society. This launch will not be easy and no doubt will be filled with trials and tribulations. Decisions will sometimes have to be made without "ground control" giving advice—requiring the launchee to rely on manual control at times. The family of orientation only hopes that their child is prepared for this launch and all that is to come thereafter.

As the launch approaches, the adolescent's days of dependence on the family of orientation are quickly slipping away. Perhaps the feeling of this transition is best summed up by Charlie Brown of *Peanuts*. When Lucy asks him what he thinks security is, he responds, "Security is sleeping in the back seat of a car when you're a little kid and you've been somewhere with your mom and dad and it's night. You don't have to worry about anything. Your mom and dad are in the front seat and they're doing all the worrying. They take care of everything." Lucy smiles and says, "That's real neat." Then Charlie Brown, who never seems to know when to stop, gets a serious look on his face and raises a finger and says, "But it doesn't last. Suddenly you're grown up and it can never be that way again. Suddenly it's all over and you'll never get to sleep in the back seat again."

There is a kind of loss that goes with growing up (Hughs 1987). It comes with the recognition that we no longer have someone in the front seat taking care of us, serving as a buffer between us and the world. Overnight, it seems we are the people in the front seat who have to decide which way to turn and which motel will be the best without being too expensive, and where we should eat supper. Those days of sleeping in the security of the back seat when the rain and windshield wipers made us fall asleep are gone. But then part of growing up is moving up to the front seat.

While the time of the young leaving the nest comes sooner or later throughout the animal kingdom, it comes "later" for humans, since our maturation process is longer than for other animals. And the length of maturation in humans means that parents have time to anticipate their children's acquiring adult status. With time to anticipate, parents can prepare both themselves and their children for this launching phase. By gradually letting go of their control of adolescent children, parents can help to assure a smooth transition and a closeness after the break (Aldous 1978:264). The reading here describes some of the emotional experiences occurring over the family's life cycle, including the launching phase of the middle years.

Intense Emotional Experiences within the Family

Certainly it is within the family that some of the most intense emotional experiences of a lifetime occur, and the adolescent's leaving the family is one of these experiences. Literally from the cradle to the grave (the womb to the tomb), these intense emotional experiences affect the family. When the baby was born, it was such an experience. Who else but the closest of kin remember the events surrounding the birth itself? Soon this "seven-pound bundle of joy" can be seen walking down the road to catch the bus on the first day of kindergarten—carrying a little bag with supplies and food. A tear may fall on the cheek of the parent(s) as junior disappears down the road. Before one knows it, the child has graduated from high school and the extended family attends this event. Again, a tear may swell in the eye of the parent(s) as "the baby" receives a diploma—an experience of significance to the immediate family.

Having made it through high school, our "little one" may then decide to enter into the halls of higher education. Again, for the parent(s) this can be, and often is, an emotional experience as an awareness of the passing of time is confronted—to say nothing of the financial challenge ahead with a child in college.

If success continues to follow, and graduation finally comes after four (or perhaps five) years of college, surviving family members gather for this event. When the hordes of students receiving a certain degree are asked to stand by the appropriate dean, the family strains to spot their graduate. With all graduates having on the same costumes—usually a very colorful black with matching hat—the graduate may be difficult to pick out of the crowd. Nonetheless, the graduating family member is supposed to be somewhere in that homogeneous-looking group. This can be an emotional experience for the family, since it is another important event in the life of their child—perhaps emotional because they really never thought graduation would come for this "not exactly Phi Beta Kappa" kid of theirs.

If the college graduate follows a fairly typical pattern, he or she will soon be at the marriage altar. This intense emotional experience within the family again brings out the kin. As the groom steps forward with his best man nearby (for both moral and physical support, in the event that he may hyperventilate and faint), the long-awaited audience stares at this figure. Typically, he is not from the hometown where the wedding is occurring, so he is really being sized up. After what seems like an eternity for the groom (no norm in our society tells him exactly how to stand, what to do with his hands, whether to look up toward heaven for divine guidance, look down at his feet like he is praying, or stare back at the audience), the bride comes down the aisle, preceded by her attendants. All eyes abandon the groom and turn their heads to catch a glimpse at the attractive bride with her "wow, what a gorgeous dress." Her father (or some significant male figure) usually brings her down the aisle and "giveth her away" (this probably says something about the status of women in our society). It is of interest to note that the groom is not given away by anyone. He walks down the aisle on his own two feet—Mr. Independent.

Again, for the parent(s) the marriage of their offspring can be an intense emotional experience—emotional because they thought it was such a remote event and would never happen to their child, or perhaps because it brings closure to a period in the life cycle of their family. A few months after the wedding, this cycle may begin all over again with the birth of a child into this family of procreation. And somewhere in the future, the truly intense emotional experience of death will occur within the family.

As the child moves toward independence during the preparation for the launching phase, however, it is not always easy for the parents to relinquish their authority (Farrell and Rosenberg 1981:154). Parents are ambivalent about having their children cease to depend upon them. The ambivalence may lead to vacillation and overreaction by both parents and children.

For example, as the adolescent child wrestles with the problem of finding a place in the larger society, he or she may act as a "boundary tester" of the family culture (Farrell and Rosenberg 1981:151). Although the teenager may feel like a marginal person trying to find a place in the world, he or she is still a member of the family group. And as new identities are tried, the adolescent is likely to become more or less deviant in relation to family values. In adapting to the high school environment, the adolescent takes on and brings home values, ideas, dress patterns, and hair styles not accepted in the culture of the nuclear family. At the same time, as parents observe their children openly consider alternative lifestyles, they tend to gain a deeper appreciation of and commitment to their own values. Rather than being a sign of family disorganization, then, a limited amount of teenage deviance can serve positive group functions. Conflict over behavioral standards can bring members of the family out of the ruts of routine conversation and into communication with each other.

According to Michael Farrell and Stanley Rosenberg (1981: 154–55), launching-phase parents continue to regard the family as a sanctuary but express greater acceptance of the idea that their children must now involve themselves in the outside world. Rather than fighting against the children's demands for autonomy, they may begin to complain that the children are "too clingy." At this point in their lives, parents often view their children's accomplishments or adjustment to their newly acquired adult status as a kind of summation or index of their own success in parenting.

Having interviewed 200 men between the ages of twenty-five and thirty and 300 men between the ages of thirty-eight and forty-eight (as well as some selected spouses), Farrell and Rosenberg (1981:156–57) concluded that during the launching phase many fathers displayed sadness and semipointless puttering, while mothers typically seemed ready and eager to begin a new phase of their lives with enhanced freedom and possible marital closeness. Numerous other studies seem to support this observation. Marjorie Lowenthal and David Chiriboga (1972:13) discovered that for mothers in the launching stage, children continue to be a source of pride and interest but are no longer associated with the burdens of socialization and physical care. Bernice Neugarten (1970:83) noted in a study of middle-aged women that the loss of child-care roles—even when there is no compensatory gain in community, occupational, marital, or kin roles—does not necessarily lead to unhappiness. L. K. George (1980) observed that the hypothesized stress accompanying the launching of the last child is not substantiated in the literature and that for women the empty-nest transition is probably the most expected of all the changes and role transitions common in middle life. Finally, N. D. Glenn (1975) noted that greater marital happiness is reported by postparental women than by women in the same age range who are still in the parental role.

Interaction between most parents and children is markedly different at this point; it begins to take on a quality of adult-to-adult interchange. Parents tend to identify much more directly with their children in this phase as they remember themselves as young adults and relive earlier choices and struggles they encountered.

According to studies cited by James Youniss and Jacqueline Smollar (1985:77–78), with separation resulting from the launching phase, a large proportion of young adults still maintain definite connections with their parents. They feel respect for and are respected by their parents. They still express a definite desire to please their parents, to meet the expectations that parents have for them, and to seek their parents' approval. Many newly independent young people keep parents informed about their lives, consulting their parents as advisors on personal matters. In general, young men and women

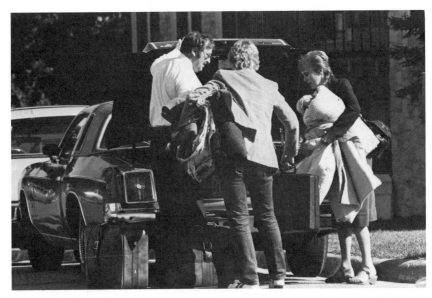

The relatively dependent adolescent must become more independent when leaving home for college. Parental support and approval helps make the transition easier.

have a sense of being members of a family, of having obligations to the family, and of feeling an attachment to their parents.

For mothers, the launching phase involves more than just the absence of the children from the nest. According to research by Ken Smith and Phyllis Moen (1988:507), if the empty-nest transition is anticipated with a high degree of certainty and if any change is to occur for women, they may increase their attachment to work, since they tend to view this stage as a period of increased freedom. Women who are already in the labor market have apparently invested in both home and market skills, thus their perceived gains from home production are likely to diminish while the incentives for work outside the home continue.

It is difficult to predict the chronological relationship between the empty-nest transition and changes in employment activity for the woman who has been working at home, note Smith and Moen (1988:505–7). While this woman may be willing to supply more time to the labor force, the demand for her particular set of skills in the labor market may be minimal. Until recent years, young women were apt to terminate their schooling earlier than men because of marriage and parenthood. In a related pattern, women tend to delay entry into continuous full-time employment as child-rearing and home production responsibilities increase following marriage. Thus, middle-aged women of the 1990s may move into the empty-nest period "undoing" or reversing those events which originally defined their movement into adulthood.

Smith and Moen (1988:521–22) also point out that women enjoy the greatest middle-years economic benefits when the only family transition they experience is the empty nest. Married women with children present in the home enjoy better economic outcomes in mid-life if they experience the empty nest transition while keeping their marriages intact. Single parents who launch their last child from home do not experience these same economic benefits.

As life goes on after the launch, it is not uncommon for the middle years to be times of grandparenting. The baby of yesterday becomes the mother or father of tomorrow. Let's turn now to grandparenting in the middle years.

GRANDPARENTING

Grandparenthood is increasingly becoming a middle-age phenomenon. And many middle-aged couples and singles take satisfaction in being with and doing things for their young grandchildren—as they did with their own children earlier—but without the responsibilities and authority of the parental role.

Grandparents are in a unique position in the family network: They are not the parents of the younger generation, but they do have a vested interest in the development of the grandchild. Since family values and themes are continued by each generation, grandparents have a generational stake in their grandchildren (Troll 1980).

If recent Wisconsin legislation regarding the financial responsibilities of grandparents is adopted by other states, grandparents' "stake" in grandchildren may become even greater. The Wisconsin law holds parents financially responsible if their children under the age of eighteen have babies. Under this measure, a welfare agency could take either pair of grandparents to court to make them pay for the expenses of raising the baby. The law is intended to reduce teenage pregnancy by increasing discussion between parents and teenagers on sex (*New York Times* 1985).

Eighty percent of grandmothers studied by E. M. Timberlake (1980) valued their intergenerational relationship because it provided a continuity of parental roles and gave them opportunities to demonstrate creativity, accomplishment, competence, and a reconfirmation of their own identity. Timberlake (1980) found that the ninety grandmothers who had frequent contact with their grandchildren felt strong support for their social identity.

Just what is the meaning of being a grandparent? H. Q. Kivnick (1982) addressed this question and identified the following various meanings of grandparenthood: (1) Being a grandparent can be a salient feature of aging; (2) grandparents are viewed as elders with eufunctions (positive consequences) accompanying that role; (3) grandparenthood creates a feeling of one's immortality; and (4) older persons can relive life through grandparenting.

Being a grandparent seems to be in vogue in the United States, as 70 percent of older people have grandchildren (Atchley 1977:301). As of the late 1980s, the average age of first grandparenthood was in the forties (but this age varied widely among individuals as well as among groups), and relatively few people have young grandchildren after age sixty-five. The time when the grandchildren are small seems to be the most satisfying for the grandparents. As the grandchildren grow older, the grandparent role becomes rather limited for older people; ideological differences between three generations, a strong peer orientation of adolescents, and geographical mobility of families leave limited room for interaction with older persons. Therefore, grandparents must work at being valued—this is an achieved role based on the personal qualities of the grandparent and not automatically ascribed to all grandparents (Troll 1971).

What do grandchildren think of grandparents? One study of 178 young adult grandchildren (Hartshorne and Manaster 1982) found that they were satisfied with their relationships with the older generation. They viewed grandparents as important and felt they

Grandparents of young children can have all the fun times of parenthood without the day-to-day frustrations and responsibilities.

were important to their grandparents. A study of the attitudes of children between the ages of four and twelve (Kahana and Kahana 1970) also concluded that grandchildren favorably viewed grandparents and valued their relationships with them. The reasons for this positive assessment varied by age, however, as the youngest were spoiled or indulged by grandparents, the children in the middle shared fun or pleasurable activities, and the children in the oldest age group appreciated the distance in years from their grandparents.

MARITAL QUALITY IN LATER LIFE

A restlessness within the marital relationship seems fairly common among couples in their forties. **Cross-sectional studies** (studies undertaken at a particular point in time) as well as longitudinal studies have reported that marital satisfaction declines as couples approach middle age, reaching its lowest point when adolescent children leave the nest (Pineo 1961; Rollins and Feldman 1970). Michael Farrell and Stanley Rosenberg in *Men at Midlife* (1981) note that middle age represents the doldrums of marriage in our culture. They also note, however, that all is not lost, since after the children are gone the relationship seems actually to recover and marital satisfaction tests reveal scores approaching those of the early stages of marriage.

The Land the Old Ones Keep

Snow is on the head of him who plows
The steep New England acre green with May;
No quicksilver boy drives home the cows,
It is a man who brings them, old and gray.
The women tending flowers in November,
The keeper of the house, lonely and old;
This northerly New England is an ember
Burning low and graying towards the cold.

No young voices fill the twelve-roomed house,
No sons put the stones back in the wall;
The only quick things here are mind and mouse,
All seasons are the quiet one, the Fall.

There are more dead than living in these small
Villages below the Northern lights,
The chimneys smoke but an hour or so in all,
Windows grow dark early all the nights.

It is a sadness that was always so;
Always New England places knew the doom
Of having to see the hosts of children go,
Of having a house to keep with too much room.

This is a cradle for the richer places,
This is the land the old ones keep and tend;
They sweep their rooms, and hope still turns their faces
Towards Spring and children at the south road's bend.

Source: Robert T. Tristram Coffin, *Collected Poems* (New York: Macmillan, 1948). Reprinted with permission of Macmillan Publishing Company. Copyright 1952 by Robert P. Tristram Coffin, renewed 1980 by Richard N. Coffin, Mary Alice Westcott and Robert P. T. Coffin, Jr.

Beginning with the early forties, some individuals begin to give serious thought to marital problems that they previously ignored or gave only mild attention. One party in the marriage may come to recognize that the marriage was flawed from the beginning. Without a strong emotional attachment, the marriage may have occurred for any number of reasons. The relationship may never have jelled, and with time the situation may have worsened. The couple may have

Middle-Age Dating

I'm dialing a phone number, and when I've touched five digits, I suddenly hang up. For two or three minutes I sit on my bed, my lips moving occasionally, as if I were an actor going over a part. Then I pick up the phone, hesitate, start to put it down again. Instead, I quickly touch seven tones. A woman answers.

I'm a nervous man in his 50s, calling a woman also in her 50s to ask her to dinner. It will be a blind date. It will be my second blind date this month. Dear God, how I dread it.

Middle-age dating is now a common thing in America. It wasn't always. You started dating in adolescence, and you continued until you got married. Ten years, maybe 20, that was the dating period. Sometimes an older man who lost his wife set out to replace her. If he dated, though, it wasn't apparent. He remarried, usually some nice widow he'd known for years. Dignified. Inconspicuous.

But now that half of us get divorced sooner or later, and some of us manage to do it twice, or even more, there is no end to this dating. It can recur at intervals throughout one's life. I am not finding that it gets any easier.

We older daters (the very word is ludicrous when applied to anyone over 40) do have certain advantages. We've picked up a lot of assurance since those far-off teen-age years, and generally a good income, too. We know how to keep a conversation going; we handle restaurant checks with an easy smile. We are not usually timid about phone calls. But consider some of the problems. Consider them in two categories: when we take younger women out, and when we date our contemporaries.

I, at least, often do take younger women out. (And it's not all one way; I know at least four middle-age women who take out younger men.) I do it because they have long shining hair and good figures. I have other reasons, too. Not only is some sleek divorcee of 38 likely to be better looking than women of my own age, she's also likely to be more adaptable. She's got youthful verve. If she has children, they're apt to be small and cuddly. It's a lot more fun to be reading aloud to a 6-year-old than it is to be taking on a faintly paternal relationship with a couple of scornful college students.

But take out such a woman, as I did all of last year, and you let yourself in for endless playacting and for a surprising amount of humiliation.

The playacting has to do with energy. She has more. We're visiting a museum. After an hour and a half, I'm ready to go, or at least to sit down to rest for five minutes. She's a really nice person; she would gladly do either. But I don't always want to tell her I'm tired; it's so ... middle-aged. Ditto with naps on Sunday afternoons, which, in recent years, I've come not just to love but pretty much to depend on. She enjoyed taking them with me. But what if we're in the country on a winter weekend, and she'd like to go cross-country skiing before it gets dark at 4:30? So would I, only I want to nap first, which will make it a mighty short ski. I go napless.

As for the humiliation, it has nothing to do with being taken for father and daughter. It has to do with remorseless physical processes. The lens of the human eye, for example, gets steadily less flexible as one ages. I can no longer read a road map without snatching my glasses off, and if the print is really fine, I just about can't read it at all. I begin to see, looming ahead, the horrible prospect of the magnifying glass. The idea of using one in front of her appeals to me about as much as suddenly going bald.

So why not take out women my own age? They'll want to leave museums at just the right time, understand perfectly that one needs a little nap on Sunday, probably have a magnifying glass handy in their purses. Well, I am indeed taking them out, and I mean to continue—but don't think there aren't problems.

The biggest is how to get started. Those first dates are hard. They're not hard to arrange—half my friends know someone I should call. What's hard is the actual evening. There is not going to be that instant and spontaneous attraction that leads to second and third dates when you're young. For the young, sexual attraction serves as a kind of handy glue, keeping a couple together until other and more durable bonds take hold. Shared memories, shared thoughts, perhaps, eventually, shared children.

A little of that glue is still available to people in their 50s (and even older, I hear). In rare cases, quite a lot. More typically, though, a man and woman in their 50s spend the first date making allow-ances for its absence. They're thinking that if they should come to love each other, her wrinkles or his potbelly would be no barrier. But how do you get from first meeting to love, to what was once called being stuck on someone—with so little glue?

One way is to share some memories before you start. That's why so many people, when they get divorced or widowed, look around to see who they knew in high school that might also be coming back on the market.

Another is to try a different brand of glue. Wealth and fame have served older men quite well for centuries—usually, I grant, to cement relationships with younger women rather than with their contemporaries. They have also served wealthy and famous women. "A duchess is never more than 30 years old to a snob," Stendhal once wrote. But these artificial glues, though handy for some pur-

stayed married for the sake of the children or in response to family pressures. Daniel Levinson (1978:256) suggests that suddenly one partner in the marriage may see the spouse as a person and understand the nature of their relationship for the first time. In stepping back and looking into the marriage, that partner may become acutely dissatisfied. It is easy to blame all kinds of shortcomings on the spouse, if the marriage seems to be coming apart. Sometimes other possibilities begin to look more appealing.

This desire for a change may simply be a yearning for something different—a spouse may be tired of the old and looking for something new. The husband may convince himself that his wife is overly controlling or smothering him. He may find another woman who seems to be more understanding (Levinson 1978:256–57). On the other hand, the wife may be the one who starts reappraising the marriage; she may seek to expand her own horizons and begin new ventures outside the home. But starting over in one's forties or fifties is no picnic, as the reading on dating points out.

In surveying the literature on marital phases, Farrell and Rosenberg (1981:121–25) report that the distribution of power in the marital relationship changes with various stages of the marriage. In the early stage, the power relationship tends to be close to egalitarian, with the husband having slight dominance over the wife. With the arrival of children, the wife loses ground and reaches her low point in influence over major decisions. As the children approach

Since most individuals date during adolescence and young adulthood, to begin dating again at age forty or fifty can be awkward and intimidating.

adolescence, however, she begins to gain more power. Advancing into middle age, the wife is perceived as the force to be reckoned with in the family. The husband, on the other hand, is seen as a "passive, contemplative background figure." This changing distribution of power in the home generally places strain on the husband-wife relationship, especially in the sense that the husband resents the dwindling of his power.

After reviewing available literature dating back to the 1950s on marital adjustment during the middle years, Gerald Leslie and Sheila Korman (1985:487) conclude that in most relationships romance is closely linked to novelty. A consistent pattern exists wherein marital adjustment declines steadily from almost the beginning of marriage to at least the stage where children are grown and leave home. On the other hand, these researchers note that in almost all of the studies a significant proportion of marriages continued to be characterized by closeness, affection, and effective communication. Some even improve in communication and empathy as the years pass.

The middle years, though defined in various ways, have their ups and downs. If children are in the family, the family enters the parent-versus-peers stage, where uncertainty is mixed with good times. During the launching phase of the family, adolescents leave school and begin breaking away from the family of orientation and mingling in the real world of adulthood. With husband and wife now back as a "couple" again, though with less vigor than twenty years earlier, they move into a new period in their relationship. This new period in a marriage can be an especially trying time, or it can produce some of the best of times.

Quiz Answers Questions about Marriage

West Lafayette, Indiana (AP). Why do couples marry? What keeps them together? What makes them happy? Clifford Swensen, professor of psychological sciences at Purdue University, has spent much of his professional life researching these questions. For the answers to this true-false quiz he draws from his own studies and the research of others:

1. The more alike they become, the happier and more satisfied two people become with their relationship.

   True. When couples "speak the same language," it reduces the potential for conflict and disagreement—there's less to argue about.

2. The longer two people are married, the more they confide their feelings to their spouse.

   False. Even though long-married couples feel comfortable and happy together, there is less of an inclination to "rock the boat" or expose feelings that might lead to controversy. Hence the hesitation to self-disclose.

3. Opposites may attract, but the longer they stay married, the less these differences hold.

   True. When two people first meet, there is often an attraction for opposite traits—that is, we tend to need to complement our own qualities with those which we lack. But the longer a couple stays together, the more they tend to become similar, with their differences becoming less dramatic.

4. A couple's happiest years may vary from one country to another.

True. In a study conducted by Swensen in this country, most respondents said the post-retirement years were the happiest in their marriage—probably due to fewer problems. But the same study conducted in Norway found that couples were happiest during child-rearing years.

5. The more differences in a couple—such as race, religion or ethnic background—the higher the rate of conflict in the relationship.

True. Couples from different backgrounds spend a lot of time "translating"—they just don't speak the same language. Unlike other couples, who can resolve basic issues early in their marriages, these couples are faced with constantly surfacing issues. As a result of cultural differences, they may have opposing ideas on how to raise the children, deal with the in-laws and even how to treat the grandchildren.

6. In general, people tend to be attracted to people with the same level of emotional development or ego development.

True. People tend to marry individuals much like themselves even in emotional development. It's extremely rare to see a couple that is not similar in levels of emotional development. For instance, an individual who is extremely well-adjusted emotionally would rarely be married to one whose emotional adjustment was borderline.

7. As a relationship progresses over the years, men tend to become more assertive, while women become more mellow.

False. Research suggests just the opposite. Women are less dominant in the early stages of a relationship, when men are more "in charge." But women become more assertive as the years pass—just as men become less dominant and more mellow.

8. Women tend to be more interested in the relationship during the early years of marriage, while men become more interested as they grow older.

True. When couples first marry, the woman usually is more interested in the relationship while the man focuses attention on his work. In later years, women become less interested in the relationship and more concerned with other accomplishments.

9. People who are highly committed to one another as individuals tend to have the fewest problems in marriage.

True. A high level of commitment to an individual as a person—not just to the marriage institution—makes for fewer problems in the marriage.

Source: *The News and Courier/The Evening Post,* Charleston, S.C., February 16, 1986. Associated Press.

CHAPTER REVIEW

- While definitions are not clear-cut, "middle age" generally refers to the period between the ages of forty-five and sixty-four. The proportion of Americans in mid-life is increasing.
- Whereas primary socialization of children occurs in the family of orientation, secondary socialization tends to occur among peers in the school setting, where students spend seven or eight hours per day.
- Situational adjustment plays a major role in socialization into new settings for adolescents and adults. This is often not an individual process but a collective one.
- As children mature into adolescents, they spend more time with peers and less with parents. Though adolescents are often turned off by their "old fuddy-duddy parents," studies conclude that most adolescents love their parents and seek their advice.
- During the middle years, families typically launch children out into the world. As the child moves toward independence, it is not always easy for parents to relinquish their authority.
- It is within the family setting that some of the most intense emotional experiences of a lifetime occur.
- Studies suggest that the time after the children have left home is a rather positive period in the lives of most parents.
- Becoming grandparents is an event largely occurring in the middle years. Grandparents have a unique role—though not the parents, they have a vested interest in the development of the grandchild.

- Being a grandparent seems to be in vogue in the United States today. Relationships between grandparents and grandchildren seem to be good.
- For some couples, the forties are a time of questioning the marriage, and sometimes the questioning results in one partner or the other seeking new adventures. To begin dating again is an uncomfortable experience for many middle-aged adults.

DISCUSSION QUESTIONS

1. Why is middle age sometimes referred to as a crisis?
2. Defend or refute this statement: "The relationship between parents and their adolescent children is generally very bad."
3. What are some dilemmas faced by adolescents in the tug-of-war between parental precepts and peer influences?
4. How do family and school complement each other in socializing adolescents? How do these two institutions sometimes appear to be at odds in dealing with adolescents?
5. How does Becker's concept of situational adjustment apply to a student going off to college for the first time?
6. What is the "launching phase" in the family? Discuss parent and adolescent relationships during this phase, as described in the research cited in this chapter. Why do mothers tend to be more accepting of the launching phase than fathers?
7. What does research suggest about grandparents' attitudes toward their grandchildren? How do the grandchildren feel about having grandparents?
8. Cite reasons why you think a restlessness in the marital relationship may occur when couples are in their forties.

GLOSSARY

cohort: Persons of a similar age group.

cross-sectional study: A study at a particular point in time, as opposed to a longitudinal study, where two or more points in time are considered.

curvilinearity: The nature of a nonlinear relationship between two variables where at a certain point, associated with the increasing values in the independent variable, the relationship with the dependent variable changes. A scattergram graph of this relationship will look like a U or an inverted U.

dysfunctional: Term used to describe a behavior or action whose consequences are negative.

family of orientation: The family in which one is socialized as a child—consisting of one's parents and siblings.

situational adjustment: The process by which an individual is "molded" by the group into which he or she is seeking acceptance; the person learns from the group how to continue successfully in a situation.

SUGGESTED READINGS

Bengtson, Vern L., and Joan F. Robertson. 1985. *Grandparenthood.* Beverly Hills: Sage Publications. An anthology of up-to-date research on the role of grandparenting.

Block, Marilyn R., Janice L. Davidson, and Jean D. Grambs. 1981. *Women Over Forty: Visions and Realities.* New York: Springer Publishing Company. *A book that challenges myths and stereotypes through a factual presentation of the research about older women.*

Farrell, Michael P., and Stanley D. Rosenberg. 1981. *Men at Midlife.* Boston: Auburn House Publishing Company. *A study begun in 1971 compares men in their late thirties and in their early forties to analyze the "mid-life crisis."*

Nolen, William A. 1984. *Crisis Time! Love, Marriage and the Male at Midlife.* New York: Dodd, Mead and Company. *The author describes his own midlife crisis and suggests ways of coping with specific middle-age problems.*

Youniss, James, and Jacqueline Smollar. 1985. *Adolescent Relations with Mothers, Fathers and Friends.* Chicago: University of Chicago Press. *An analysis of adolescents' own descriptions of interactions with parents and friends, together with theory regarding what these relations are and how they contribute to development.*

The Retirement Years

◆ *Dishonor not the old: we shall all be numbered among them.**

While some have observed that "growing old is hell," others look forward to the autumn of their lives and an opportunity for retirement. Goethe stated, "To grow old is in itself to enter upon a new venture." An aging professional athlete noted that growing old is really mind over matter—as long as you do not mind, it does not matter. Robert Browning asserts the desirability of growing old in the familiar first few lines of "Rabbi Ben Ezra":

> *Grow old along with me!*
> *The best is yet to be,*
> *The last of life, for which the first was made.*

Sooner or later there comes to each of us, sometimes with a stab of surprise and a sudden clutching or regret after the vanished years, the knowledge that we are growing old (MacKenna 1933). A gray hair or two over the temples, a deeper wrinkle around the eyes, less ease in climbing a long-frequented hill, less facility in reading a newspaper in fading light, such little things become our monitors. And there is that sinister column in the daily papers where we begin to see with painful regularity the names of our friends. A Sherlock Holmes might guess the age of any man by watching him read his morning paper, notes Robert MacKenna (1933), an English dermatologist who wrote in the early part of this century.

---

*The Apocrypha, Ecclesiasticus 8:6

Whatever a family's outlook toward aging and retirement, this phase of life represents a new venture when it comes to each of us. Whether the "best is yet to be" may well be dependent upon each individual's health, attitude, and circumstances. This chapter will explore some of the positive and negative aspects of retirement years for families in the United States. Specifically, we will discuss sociological approaches to retirement, life satisfaction in retirement, leisure pursuits and avocations, sexuality in later life, and problems of aging—home, health, and finances.

You're As Old As You Feel

The adage has it that you are only as old as you feel. Charles Cavalier's parents must feel pretty young. As does he.

A magazine for retired persons referred to those over 62 as "aged." So Cavalier wrote a letter to the editor: "I resent, and I'm sure others do, being classified as 'aged' just because I am over 62. I am 67 years old, run a $2 million business with 30 employees. I work seven days a week and average 10 hours a day.

"If you are not careful, my 92-year-old dad or my 91-year-old mother will kick the hell out of you."

Source: *The Washington Evening Star* (Washington, D.C., December 18, 1972), p. D-9.

SOCIOLOGICAL APPROACHES TO RETIREMENT

Between World War I and World War II many people believed that the biological and social sciences had produced empirical evidence to confirm the gerontological theories developed at the end of the nineteenth century. These theories held that the aging process brought inevitable physical decay, mental decline, unpleasant and sometimes deviant psychological and behavioral traits, economic problems, personal isolation, and social segregation. By emphasizing these negative themes, the mass media generally increased family anxiety and a dread of the aging process (Achenbaum 1978:109). A 1926 issue of *Ladies Home Journal* depicted well the plight of the elderly (Harris 1926:35):

> *Old people are not so much prisoners of their years and their infirmities as they are of their circumstances, after they are*

no longer able to produce their own circumstances, but are obliged to adjust themselves to conditions made for them by people who belong to a later generation in a new world. It is worse than if they became foreigners in their old age because they are in the midst of familiar scenes, but obsolete, like fine old words erased from the epic of living.

Sociologists looking at families in the retirement years may take several approaches (Streib and Schneider 1971:3). Retirement may be considered in relation to the values pivotal in the society, such as progress, humanitarianism, work, or achievement. Retirement may be observed in terms of **membership groups** and **reference groups** (groups one aspires toward) significant for work and retirement, such as cliques at work or families. Retirement may be studied as it relates to roles interwoven with the experiences and conditions of working and not working.

Disengagement Theory

A popular explanation of adjustment to retirement has been *social disengagement*, or a withdrawal from certain roles in life. **Social disengagement** is usually selective—the family member withdraws from some roles but not others. For example, one might resign from some civic or religious groups but stay active in others. Or the individual might retire from full-time work and continue to remain in the labor force on a part-time basis. The result is decreased interaction between the aging person and others in the society. When the disengagement process is complete, the equilibrium that existed between the individual and society in middle life has given way to a new equilibrium characterized by a greater distance. Disengagement is one possible response to shrinking life space and reduced energy. Disengagement is withdrawing from the world rather than adjusting to it (Atchley 1977:209–10).

Societal disengagement is another component of disengagement: the process whereby society withdraws from, or no longer seeks, the individual's efforts (Atchley 1977:227). Organizations may no longer seek out older people for leadership; their employers may no longer require their labor; their children may no longer want their involvement in decisions; and their government may no longer be responsive to their needs.

Elaine Cumming and William Henry (1961:15), who initiated disengagement theory, argue that with disengagement changes occur at three levels: (1) changes in the number of people with whom the individual interacts and the amount and intensity of that interaction; (2) qualitative changes in the patterns of interaction; and (3) changes in the personality of the individual. They argue that mutual withdrawal is "inevitable" with aging. Robert Butler (1975:8) disagrees with Cumming and Henry, however; he states that no evidence exists to support the theory that mutual separation of the aged person from society is a natural part of the aging experience. He refers to disengagement as a myth and asserts that disengagement is only one of many possible patterns of reaction to old age. Likewise, Robert Atchley (1977:209) notes that after fifteen years of research, it seems clear that disengagement is neither a universal nor an inevitable response to aging. For example, an older person's interaction with family members is likely to increase since he or she has more time away from the responsibilities of a job. Besides disengagement from roles, other approaches to adjusting to the older person's new stage of life are noted below.

The Professor Emeritus: A Test of the Continuity Approach to Aging

Paul Roman and Philip Taietz (1967) studied an occupational role that allows for continued engagement after retirement—the role of the "emeritus professor." Unlike most organizations, American colleges and universities, instead of removing retired faculty from the organization, make available a formalized postretirement position with a flexible role, whose definition is a function of the individual's preretirement position as well as of his or her own choice of postretirement activity. This system allows the *opportunity* for role continuity between full-time employment and retirement.

The amount of continuity possible varied. The research professors had the most, since they could generally continue to get research grants through the university. Those involved in teaching, public service, or administration still had opportunities for involvement, but for them the emeritus role was quite different from their preretirement role. They often ended up writing books, consulting, or becoming administrators. In no case, however, was the continuity complete. The emeritus professor always gave up a measure of involvement. Roman and Taietz assumed that disengagement was the product of *particular* social systems, not of systems in general, and that opportunity structures would greatly influence the individual's "readiness to disengage."

Based on their assumptions about opportunity structures, they predicted that a significant proportion of emeritus professors would remain engaged, and that those allowed role continuity would exhibit a higher degree of continued engagement than those required to adopt new roles. They found that 41 percent of the emeritus professors were still engaged within the same university, 13 percent had taken employment in their profession elsewhere, 24 percent were in ill health, and 22 percent were disengaged from both the university and their profession. Excluding from analysis those who were in ill health, we find that 71 percent of the emeritus professors were still engaged. In addition, Roman and Taietz found that those emeritus professors who had had a research role were still engaged significantly more often than the others. Thus, all of their predictions were supported by their findings that the frequency of disengagement is very much a product of the opportunity for continued engagement. This finding is all the more revealing since almost half of the sample was over seventy-five years old.

Sources: Paul Roman and Philip Taietz, "Organizational Structure and Disengagement: The Emeritus Professor," *Gerontologist* 7:147–52 and Robert Atchley, *The Social Forces in Later Life*, 2d ed. (Belmont, California: Wadsworth Publishing Company, 1977). © 1977 by Wadsworth Publishing Company, Inc. Used by permission.

Activity Approaches

R. S. Havinghurst and R. Albrecht (1953) view adjustment to retirement years through an *activity approach.* They suggest that maintaining the activity level of middle age is the best way to cope with aging. Since this criterion would lead most elderly persons to define themselves as failures, however, it is not very realistic.

Continuity Approach

The *continuity approach* to aging in the family assumes that during the socialization process toward adulthood individuals develop habits, commitments, and preferences that become part of their personalities (Atchley 1977:27). As individuals grow older, they are

Many retired people take up new hobbies or devote more time to favorite activities. Being active can help the elderly maintain good health and a positive outlook on life.

predisposed toward maintaining continuity in their personality characteristics.

Substitution and Accommodation Approaches

Other ways of looking at adjustment to retirement are in terms of *substitution* and *accommodation* (Shanas 1972:224—35). The substitution theory of adjustment states that for good adjustment in retirement an individual must substitute for work other activities that will give him or her the satisfaction of work. Accommodation theory states that the person experiencing retirement undergoes a period of change in which the self seeks to adapt to a new social role, to a position in the family of being around most of the time, to a new rhythm of activity, to a new body awareness, and often to a different level of living. An individual's adjustment to retirement then is dependent upon his or her accommodation to these life changes. Not only is the retired person having to make adjustments, but family members are having to adjust to having this "former worker" around the house both day and night. This can be difficult for all parties involved. Perhaps the reading here has some good suggestions for adjusting to aging.

I Shall Wear Purple When I Am Old

When I am an old woman, I shall wear purple with a red hat which doesn't go, and doesn't suit me, and I will spend my pension on brandy and summer gloves and satin sandals, and say we've no money for butter.

I shall sit down on the pavement when I'm tired and gobble up samples in shops and press alarm bells and run my stick along public railings and make up for the sobriety of my youth.

I shall go out in my slippers in the rain and pick the flowers in other people's gardens and learn to spit.

I can wear terrible shorts and grow more fat and eat three pounds of sausage at a go or only bread and pickles for a week and hoard pens and pencils and beernuts and things in boxes.

But now we must have clothes that keep us dry and pay the rent and not swear in the street and set a good example for children. We must have friends to dinner and read the papers.

But maybe I ought to practice a little now, so people who know me are not too shocked and surprised when suddenly I am old and start to wear purple.

Source: Anonymous.

Whatever approach to this "new venture in life" offers the most helpful insights into adjustments to retirement, retirement of a family member represents more than just a change in an aspect of social life (Donahue, Orbach, and Pollack 1960:334)—retirement is itself a relatively new form of social life which is striving to achieve specific institutional integration. Past societies have had aged persons, but only recently have they had *retired persons*—it was not until 1935 that Congress created the Social Security System, which officially established sixty-five as the retirement age in the United States. Previously, older Americans remained institutionally integrated within the social structure through work and kinship relationships. As a result, until the establishment of Social Security, the retired did not have any institutionalized reference groups or clearly defined roles with which they could identify. This meant that with the general culture's rejection of old age, and with the belief in the United States that retirement and old age are unpleasant experiences, anticipatory socialization for the retirement role was not part of the American experience.

Fortunately, the establishment of a formal retirement age has brought about an awareness among members of American society that the retired are a distinct and important social category with special needs that demand recognition. This has led to extensive changes in U.S. social policy as well as in the plans and lifestyles of individuals who are anticipating their own retirement.

LIFE SATISFACTION IN RETIREMENT

What effects does retirement have on family members who have left the work force? One of the early **longitudinal studies** (long-term studies) on retirement attitudes (Streib and Schneider 1971) indicated that most retirees are relatively satisfied with retirement. Another research project, a ten-year longitudinal study of older men in Iowa (Goudy et al. 1980) confirmed this earlier finding. More recently, a national longitudinal survey (Palmore, Fillenbaum, and George 1984) demonstrated that retirement creates more favorable attitudes toward being retired. Overall, Americans seem to have positive attitudes concerning retirement, and these attitudes become even more favorable once they have left the work force.

> Old age, believe me, is a good and pleasant time. It is true that you are gently shouldered off the stage, but you are given such a comfortable front stall as a spectator, and, if you have really played your part, you are more content to sit down and watch.
>
> Source: Jane Ellen Harrison (1850–1928).

Research on life satisfaction conducted over the past twenty years indicates that older people's outlook on life is remarkably positive (Foner 1986:70). Comparing younger and older adults, Anne Foner (1986) observes that an apparent sense of tranquillity is more likely to characterize older people while a sense of discontent is more typically found among the young.

Surveys of job satisfaction (Foner 1986:70–71) report that workers over fifty are more satisfied with their jobs than younger workers. Work is also more important to the older workers, and they are more committed to their jobs than younger workers. However, Foner (1986:71) notes that retired persons profess they are glad they retired when they did, that retirement has lived up to their expectations, and that they feel good about their lives since retirement.

Older people view their parental roles positively. Little evidence exists to suggest that the postparental stage is an unhappy one for most older parents. As noted in Chapter 12, the so-called empty-nest phase of married life appears to be a particularly happy one (Foner 1986:70–72).

We suspect that what makes many men look forward eagerly to an early retirement from their regular labours, is not so much the craving for time to devote to other pursuits than that of their main calling, as the vague hope that in greater quietness of life they may gain a tranquillity and clearness of spirit to which English practical life is a stranger, —nay, for which in the hurry of petty engagements and a constant necessity for a close packing of small endeavours, there is no room left. In the crowding of our duties, we lose the distinction between the means and the ends of our life, and hardly discriminate between the success gained at the cost of qualities which we once valued, and those which we have gained by the steady use and discipline of those qualities.

We suspect that what is needed for most men is not an early retirement from practical life, under the illusion that leisure will give a new clearness to the mind's vision, but not unfrequent intervals of real retirement throughout the busiest part; that instead of aiming at a mere "holiday," and what is called change and recreation, we should aim at securing intervals which will enable us more or less to understand ourselves, and to weigh our aims, as well as the means we are pursuing to gain those aims; in short, that instead of the constant strain, some of our vacations should be retreats from life to enable us to see how it would appear to us, were it really the end, and how, if a new term of it begins, we should try to remold it anew. That would be infinitely more fruitful than the somewhat hopeless retirement at the real close of active exertion, when all our blunders have been made, and few or none can be, in this life at least, practically repaired. Not even the business of life itself needs more reiterated preparation for it to make it sound and good, than does the retirement from active duties at the close. Indeed, to a considerable extent, preparation for the one is, we suppose, preparation for the other also.

Source: Anonymous, *Littell's Living Age*, 1875.

Friends

Friends and neighbors are important sources of primary relationships in later life. In addition to children and other relatives, friends and neighbors provide older family members with assistance and contact with the outside world. Regardless of how many friends they have, evidence suggests that older people are fairly restrictive in terms of their friends. Age peers and persons of the same sex, marital status, and socioeconomic class have priority as potential friends (Atchley 1977:308–11).

Stephen Crystal (1982:59) cites studies that document that peer contacts make an important difference in morale in the elderly. However, these studies were unable to demonstrate a relationship between frequent contact with children and positive morale. Crystal also noted that research shows that living with children had a small negative effect on life satisfaction, while another study found that seeing children had a small positive effect.

The conclusion that seems to be supported by all these studies is that the number and intensity of interaction with friends has a

Friendships are important at all ages. After retirement, the elderly may have more time to spend with friends and kin and more freedom to travel.

much larger effect upon life satisfaction than the patterns of inter-action with children. There are also indications (Crystal 1982) that the elderly—especially those living alone—have higher morale when their housing circumstances encourage convenient and informal interaction with friends and neighbors. Lewis Aiken (1982:219) and Arlie Hochschild (1973) have demonstrated that people who continue to interact with others and pursue outside activities seem to adjust better to old age than those who isolate themselves.

Health, Income, and Marital Status

Another important factor associated with older people's sense of well-being is their health. Good health is associated with high morale, while poor health appears to undermine morale. Income is also related to life satisfaction, as elderly people with high incomes have higher levels of satisfaction than low-income elderly.

Likewise, being married contributes to older persons' sense of well-being—married elderly have higher levels of life satisfaction than widowed or divorced older persons (Foner 1986:73). A recent study by Colleen Johnson (1985) on the impact of illness on late-life marriages concluded that the marital dyad bears up well when social support must be provided on a long-term basis. Johnson notes old age is a time when being married provides a significant dyadic relationship for which there are few substitutes. The many years of shared experience—hardships as well as successes—are usually viewed as a source of cohesion; thus, the interdependence developed over the years appears to provide the means to meet various needs in old age.

All in all, then, the autumn of our lives seems to hold much satisfaction, contrary to the stereotype of the aged held by many.

LEISURE PURSUITS AND AVOCATIONS

For many individuals, work is something one does for pay and leisure is time spent away from work. While a universal definition of leisure may be difficult to find, gerontologist Robert Atchley (1976) defines leisure as activities pursued as ends in themselves—unplanned and unrequired. Leisure in his view is action directed primarily toward self-satisfaction.

Another definition of leisure comes from Talcott Parsons (1951), who described two basic types of activity of individuals. *Instrumental activity* (work and its routine preparations) is concerned with future gratification of goals and objectives, while *expressive activity* (symbolic and pleasurable material interchanges with the environment) emphasizes rewards and gratifications within the work itself. Leisure activity can be conceptualized as choosing expressive meanings over instrumental themes and giving present desires and wishes precedence over practical preparation for later gratification.

Possible leisure roles for the elderly are very diverse, yet rarely is an older person able to select from the entire range of possibilities. The needs of older families in relation to leisure programs do not differ significantly from those of younger adults. Max Kaplan (1960:409) lists the following leisure-oriented needs and drives of the elderly:

1. Need to render some socially useful service.
2. Need to be considered a part of the community.
3. Need to occupy increased leisure time in satisfying ways.
4. Need to enjoy normal companionship.
5. Need for recognition as an individual.
6. Need for opportunity for self-expression and a sense of achievement.
7. Need for health protection and care.
8. Need for suitable mental stimulation.
9. Need for suitable living arrangements and family relationships.
10. Need for spiritual satisfaction.

Objectives of Leisure Activities

Five major objectives of leisure activities can be described (Gordon, Gaitz, and Scott 1976:314–15) on a continuum of the intensity of expressive involvement. *Relaxation* includes low-intensity activities such as sleeping, resting, and daydreaming. *Diversion* provides a change of pace and relief from mental tension or boredom with activities like sedentary hobbies, light reading, or mass media entertainment. *Developmental activities* result in an appreciable increase in physical capacity and cognitive knowledge; these kinds of activities include learning about a subject of interest or learning to sing, dance, paint, play an instrument, or act. *Creative activities* involve performing actively in a contributory or independent fashion to create new cultural productions; for example, amusing guests by playing the piano or performing a role in a theater production. *Sensual transcendence* lies at the high end of the continuum of intensity of personal involvement and includes the activation of any of the senses by stimuli and actions that provide intense levels of pleasure, excitement, and joy, such as sexual relationships and intense religious experiences.

Types of Leisure Activities

The leisure activities a person has engaged in during middle age can expand to help fill time during retirement. For some retirees, having to learn leisure skills in an environment developed to teach children can be a source of embarrassment; but having developed leisure skills earlier in life can help a person avoid potential embarrassment later on. Though there is a physical element in leisure competence that changes between age forty and age seventy-five, the physical mobility limits on leisure options often change very little, though overall energy may decline (Atchley 1977:159–75). Only 15 percent of noninstitutionalized retirees are seriously restricted in their activities, and retirement activities need not be limited to nonstrenuous pastimes such as fishing, pool, golf, and shuffleboard (Aiken 1982:219). Such activities as dancing, exercise, traveling, reading, and performing in cultural productions are reportedly less frequent in older than younger adults. But other activities like television viewing, discussion, spectator sports, cultural consumption, entertaining, and participation in organizations reveal about the same frequencies in older people as in other adult age groups (Aiken 1982:220). Differences in age groups' activities are probably due more to differential patterns of

For the elderly in the United States, hobbies are an important means of staying active and involved. As sociologist C. Wright Mills noted, the craftsperson is among the least alienated members of society. Woodworking is evidently a peaceful pastime for this elderly man. Communing with nature is another way to enjoy the world around us.

socialization and cultural conditioning between generations than to chronological age per se.

For those who can afford them, **elderhostel** programs, sponsored by colleges throughout the United States, are popular educational programs for older couples and singles. In addition, more elderly are returning to college (or going for the first time) as many colleges and universities are offering scholarships.

Most of elderly Americans' leisure time is spent at home alone. The leisure activity most frequently engaged in by both men and women on weekdays is watching television. On weekends, the main leisure activities are visiting and entertaining, followed by watching television. The next most prevalent activities are visiting, reading, gardening, going for walks, and handiwork. Idleness does not become an important part of life until very advanced ages (Atchley 1977:195–96).

The Working Retiree

To move from full-time work to partial work or complete retirement is not always an easy transition. For some, this change may result in an identity crisis due to the social stigma of implied inability to perform.

Today, however, an increasing number of companies across the country are filling temporary positions with a new source of labor— retirees. Many of the employers are hiring part-timers from the ranks of their own retirees. Labor experts say the trend is a reflection of the aging of the country's population. At the same time that the percentage of the population over sixty-five is growing, it is predicted that by the end of this century the number of people under sixty-five available to work will level off (Brooke 1986).

Retirees say part-time employment keeps them in better physical, mental, and financial shape than full retirement. Company officials say returning retirees are more motivated and better trained than temporary workers provided by outside agencies. Older workers often imbue young workers with good work habits. Sometimes, too, they have unique qualifications.

Older family members continuing to work miss fewer days from work than younger workers (Shanas and Maddox 1976:604). Studies of workers' performance in industry reveal that older employees can keep up with younger people in terms of their attendance, continuity of service, and output per hour (Achenbaum 1978:154). An elderly worker's ability, therefore, should be judged on its individual merits and not on the basis of age.

Thus, not all elderly people in the United States opt for complete retirement from work. Some choose to continue working either full or part time after the traditional retirement age. Some older individuals' choice to continue working after "retirement age" may reflect values prevalent before 1935 (Donahue, Orbach, and Pollak 1960:349). These value elements produced a basic philosophical orientation opposed to social welfare of the kind essential to establishing a system of institutionalized retirement—that is, an orientation toward laissez-faire federal government, states' rights, individualism, the pioneer vision of unlimited opportunity, and the Protestant ethic of success through work. Thus, government-administered retirement plans were opposed by many as socialistic and un-American.

For the 4.4 million individuals who continue to work full or part time after age sixty-five, the problem of how to use leisure time is probably not serious (Aiken 1982:218–19). Whether working for pay or as volunteers, these individuals usually find things to do. Other elderly family members facing retirement, however, often worry about how they will use their time. Without hobbies or other interests they may become anxious about a succession of empty days. Developing interests, hobbies, and leisure activities before retirement is a wise stratagem for everyone.

SEXUALITY IN LATER LIFE

A strong resistance to the acceptance of sexuality in older people exists in our society. Just as it is difficult for many children to accept the fact of parental sexual intercourse, it is even more difficult to accept grandparental sexual activity. Several reasons have been cited (Block, Davidson, and Grambs 1981:31–32) for the strong disapproval of sexual activity in older men and women in our society. First, many Americans tend to see aging as a disease rather than a normal process—and "sick" people are not supposed to exhibit any desire for sex. Unfortunately, research literature and popular articles tend to highlight the small minority of elderly who are sick and inactive rather than the majority who are healthy and sexually involved. Second, the view that sex should be primarily procreative (rather than recreative) leads some people to disapprove of sexual intercourse among the elderly—since, of course, older women are no longer capable of bearing children. According to this view, there is no need for the elderly to be sexually active. Third, since television and the motion picture industry portray only younger individuals involved in romantic and sexually intimate situations, sex, love, and romance have become equated in popular culture with the young and not the old. This has created a situation where there is not much social support for sexual activity among the elderly.

Nursing homes apparently subscribe to the notion that old age is sexless and disapprove of sexually active residents. Because of a lack of privacy (and often of a partner), opportunities for sexual activity for the institutionalized elderly are indeed limited.

In addition to failing to accept sexuality as a normal aspect of aging, there is a tendency to exaggerate the sexual behavior of older men and to characterize them as potential sexual deviants and child molesters—the "dirty old man" stereotype. One elderly man commented that he is hesitant to show affection toward his own grandchildren for fear that his behavior may be misunderstood by others. Research, however, demonstrates that the elderly have the lowest incidence of child molesting (Mohr, Turner, and Jerry 1964). Child molesters mainly come from the following age groups: adolescence, middle to late thirties, and late fifties. Furthermore, the peak of exhibitionism occurs in the mid-twenties and is rare after forty.

Research on sexuality and aging has been somewhat limited. In recent years, however, studies of the sexual behavior of the elderly have been gaining popularity. Ahmed Mobarak and Charles Shamoian (1985:291) concluded the following from longitudinal studies of sexual behavior and the aging process. (1) Sex continues to play an important role in the lives of many elderly persons. (2) Sexual activity declines gradually over time for both men and women. (3) Sexual interest also declines over time, though more slowly than sexual activity. (4) Men are more sexually active than women at any given age. (5) Sexual activity among women is dependent on the availability of a functionally capable male partner.

Timothy Brubaker (1985:39–40) encourages us to remember two important observations when reflecting on the research dealing with sexuality in later life. First, sexual expression is not limited to

Sexual expression takes many forms. The elderly continue to have and express sexual feelings.

sexual intercourse. Older couples are sexually active in ways that may or may not culminate in coitus. Touching, caressing, and massaging can be expressions of sexual desires. Just being in bed together can be a rewarding sexual experience. Second, the patterns of sexual expression in later life can be predicted from the patterns established in the middle years. Couples who have an active sexual relationship in the middle years can be expected to continue this relationship into later life. A middle-aged couple who have discontinued or who seldom have sexual intercourse are not likely to increase their involvement in sexual behavior as they age. A survey of 4,246 men and women over fifty in the United States (Brecher 1984:404) found, on the other hand, that respondents most likely to be happily married are those who enjoy having sex with their spouse.

William Masters and Virginia Johnson's research (1966) confirmed that sexual capacity can continue into advanced old age. When a partner is not available, for many older persons the practice of masturbation apparently continues to serve as a satisfactory form of sexual release (Rubin 1963). Sexual responsiveness for males may be lost in the later years because of one or more of the following factors (Masters and Johnson 1966): (1) monotony of a repetitious sexual relationship (boredom with the partner); (2) preoccupation with career or economic pursuits; (3) mental or physical fatigue; (4) overindulgence in food and/or drink; (5) physical or mental infirmities of the individual or his spouse; and (6) inability to perform at previous level.

Several illnesses that can occur in old age may also have an adverse effect on the sexuality of males and females (Mobarak and Shamoian 1985:300–301). And drugs taken to cure or control these diseases may affect the sexual response cycle. Some alter sexual desire, while others affect erection, orgasm, and/or ejaculation.

For some individuals in the retirement years, dating activities may begin again. To return to dating may not be an easy assignment for an elderly person. Some of the pros and cons of dating after sixty are discussed in this reading.

Love in the "Afternoon" of Life

"Is there dating after the age of 60? Can one fall in love and find romance in the later years of life?" These were the questions we set out to answer when we began interviewing people age 60-plus who agreed to be part of our study of later life dating behaviors.

At first we were not certain that the older adult could define dating. Perhaps it was merely "friendship" they were experiencing, and they would feel uncomfortable with the classification of "dating" as it related to their cross-gender interactions. But the majority of our sixty respondents could clearly define dating as a "going steady type of relationship." They felt that dating was much more than friendship. It provided them with emotional and physical intimacy, and they could communicate to the dating partner in ways unlike their friendships.

Most of our older daters were sexually active with their dating partners, although sexual intercourse was often described as "frosting on the cake" and not the primary reason for continuation of the dating relationship. The older men and women in our sample reported difficulty in telling their adult children about their sexual relationships and often kept the sexual dimension of their dating lives well hidden from family members. As one 61-year-old dater said in reference to her 68-year-old boyfriend's frequent "overnighters," "Even now I have a tendency to hide his shoes when my grandchildren are coming over."

Several senior citizens reported that their adult children would not permit them to sleep with their dating partner when visiting from afar. Reportedly, the middle-age offspring stated "Well, how would this look to the grandchildren?" There is certainly much to support the notion that it is the middle generation that serves as watchdog on the moral values of the older and younger generations.

While most older daters were sexually active, companionship appeared to be one of the strongest motivations for later life dating. There was less emphasis on the passionate side of relationships and greater appreciation for the companionate nature of cross-sex interactions. However, a great many of our respondents reported "falling in love" in later life. It seems that those feelings of romance do not change much over the life course. In the words of one 72-year-old dater, "I knew I was in love with her (his 70-year-old dating partner) when I looked across the room and my heart went pitter-pat." Most of the symbols of romantic love remain consistent, as well, with reports of candlelight dinners and long walks by the lake frequently cited as gestures of romantic affection in later life.

Source: Article by Kris Bulcroft (University of Washington) and Margaret O'Connor. Reprinted by permission.

PROBLEMS OF AGING: HOME, HEALTH, AND FINANCES

The expression "graying of America" certainly holds much truth. For instance, the percentage of persons over age sixty-five in the U.S. population (Cox 1988:3) has gone from slightly over 4 percent in 1900 to approximately 10 percent in 1970 to nearly 12 percent in 1990. By the year 2000 demographers estimate that more than 13 percent of the population will be elderly. This trend calls for new social awareness and policies in such areas as housing, health, and finances. The following section will examine some of these current needs of the elderly in the United States.

Housing

After retirement, many elderly families move into a smaller home and/or to a warmer climate. The move from one environment to another may produce severe stress. Morton Liberman and Sheldon Tobin (1983:3) studied 639 elderly people who changed their living arrangements and found that after one year, 50 percent were dead, physically impaired, or psychologically deteriorated. Relocation produces stress in that it disrupts normal modes of behavior and imposes a need for strenuous psychological work. That is, a change in life space makes heavy demands on an individual for new adaptive efforts in the new environment.

Most older people live in single-family homes, apartments, or rooms in their communities. Though newly constructed retirement communities for the elderly have been created, few can afford such luxurious living. Only 3 or 4 percent of those over sixty-five live in retirement villages, while 60 percent of the elderly are mortgage-free homeowners, and another 12 percent have homes with mortgages (Aiken 1982:213). The majority of the elderly who rent live in apartments (Carp 1976:251).

Contrary to popular belief, few of the elderly in the United States live in nursing homes. Approximately 5 percent of the older population reside in nursing homes at any one time, although 25 percent of all older persons will eventually do so at some point (Cox 1988:216). Among the very old, eighty-five years of age or older, only 17 percent are institutionalized (Atchley 1977:116). Of that number, most are in nursing and personal care homes.

Most people look at nursing homes in a very negative way. We tend to perceive life in a nursing home as a loss of independence, rejection by society, and a place "where one goes to die." Independence is highly prized in the United States. We are socialized as children to make it on our own. As adults we highly esteem physical, financial and social independence. To become partially or completely dependent on others in old age becomes a very negative situation. The loss of independence, with its perceived rejection by society, is feared by most elderly.

Health

How healthy are elderly family members in today's society? While some individuals remain remarkably healthy in their eighties and even into their nineties, others are mentally and physically old at age forty. In the 1970s and 1980s Americans became aware of changes in lifestyles, dietary habits, exercise patterns, and new life-prolonging medical interventions that have the potential to change the health picture for older Americans. Life expectancy has increased. Many older people are enjoying better health than in the past (Rosen and Jerdee 1985:25), and many more may do so in the future.

Perhaps we can learn a lesson from the Abkhasians' longevity. As the reading shows, these long-living people seem to practice all those good rules of which we are aware, but seem to shun.

Abkhasians—the Long-living People

Over 125,000 native Abkhasians live mostly in rural areas on the coast of the Black Sea in Abkhasia, a country about half the size of New Jersey. These people do not have a phrase for "old people." Those over 100 years of age are called "long-living people." Most of the aged work regularly performing light household tasks, working in the orchards and gardens and caring for the animals.

While a large percent of Abkhasians live a very long time, they also seem to be in fairly good health in their "old age." Close to 40 percent of the aged men (over 90) and 30 percent of aged women have good vision—do not need glasses for any sort of work. Nearly half have "reasonably good hearing." Most have their own teeth. Their posture is unusually erect.

Why do these people live so long? First, they have no retirement status but simply decrease their expected work load as they grow older. Second, they do not set deadlines for themselves, thus, no sense of urgency is accepted in emergencies. Third, overeating is considered dangerous; fat people are regarded as sick. Milk and vegetables make up 74 percent of their diet. The aged average 1,900 calories per day—500 less than the U.S. National Academy of Science recommends for those over 55. They do not use refined sugars; they drink water and honey before retiring in the evening. They eat a lot of fruit, and meat is eaten only once or twice per week. They usually cook without salt or spices. The wine they drink is a dry red wine not fortified with sugar and has a low alcohol content. Few of them smoke, and they do not drink coffee or tea. Their main meal is at lunch (between 2 and 3 pm), and their supper is light. Between meals they eat fruit or drink a glass of fermented milk (which is like buttermilk) with a high food value and useful for intestinal disorders. They have a relaxed mood at mealtimes and, when eating, take small bites and chew slowly, thus insuring proper digestion.

Fourth, they avoid stress by reducing competition. Fifth, they exercise daily. Sixth, their behavior is fairly uniform and predictable. Seventh, moderation is practiced in everything they do.

Much of the above is advice we have often heard but failed to put into practice. Perhaps we should adhere to some of the Abkhasians' practices. Who knows, we might even live longer and be more healthy—if that is a goal to be sought.

Source: Adapted from Sula Benet, *Abkhasians: The Long-Living People of the Caucasus* (New York: Holt, Rinehart, and Winston, 1974).

Research findings on the relationship between health and retirement are inconclusive. In a review of these findings, Thomas Wan (1985:7,28) notes that research on the retirement process has concluded that the decision to retire is strongly influenced by the age, perceived health status, and economic well-being of the retiree. However, the research has failed to document the exact way in which retirement is associated with these conditions. While Wan observed that some studies found that poor health frequently precedes retirement, others indicated that retirement itself may lead to poor health. Other research (Wan 1985:7,28) has reported that retirement has little effect on health, while still other studies have documented improved health after retirement.

In his longitudinal study of over 6,000 elderly persons, Wan (1985:17) identified widowhood as the most important predictor of poor health. When widowhood and retirement occur at the same time, the health status of an elderly person is at special risk. Measures of the health status of aged family members become increasingly important as the American health care system attempts to forecast the demand for health services and facilities. Because of the increasing proportion of elderly in the population (Shanas and Maddox 1976:598), the health care system will be experiencing more demands for physicians' care, added space in hospitals and nursing homes, and additional home health services.

To Be Old and Poor and Female

Poverty among the elderly in the United States will increasingly affect women, many of them widowed and living alone, a new report predicts. By the year 2020, of 2 million elderly poor people living alone, 1.5 million will be widows, the report said.

"Elderly poverty in America is becoming widows' poverty," said Thomas W. Moloney, senior vice president of the Commonwealth Fund, a not-for-profit philanthropy specializing in health and medical issues.

The study, which will be released today, was compiled by the fund's Commission on Elderly People Living Alone, a national panel of 12 business people, scholars and health-care experts.

The number of people 65 and older who live alone will rise from 8.8 million to 13.3 million by 2020, the report said. The projections, using March 1985 census data, were made by ICF Incorporated, a research company in Washington.

"In the 1950s, living alone was a statistical curiosity," Mr. Moloney said. "In 1950, only 15 percent of the elderly lived alone. Now, in 1987, 33 percent live alone, and this percentage is likely to stay consistent through the year 2020."

The new study estimated that 80 percent of the elderly now living alone are women, and two-thirds of all elderly people living alone are widows. Among poor elderly people, 67 percent are widows. That statistic will rise to 75 percent by the year 2000, the report projected.

Of the 26 million elderly people who do not live in nursing homes or other institutions, 10 percent, or 2.6 million, are poor, earning less than $5,393 annually, the report said. Of this group, 1.1 million are widows living alone.

For elderly people living alone, poverty is highest among minority groups: 43 percent for blacks and 35 percent for Hispanic people, compared with 16 percent for whites. Approximately 220,000 poor black women who are widows now live alone.

The commission predicted that the economic well-being of elderly people in general will improve in coming years because of increased Social Security and pension benefits and income from individual retirement accounts. But the economic status of men will improve more substantially than that of women; men, earning higher wages over a longer period than women, are likely to receive larger Social Security and pension benefits. However, the commission predicted that the income gap between elderly people living alone and other older people is likely to widen. Especially hard hit economically will be widows, whose numbers will increase by 1.5 million to 7.4 million in the year 2020.

"There will be two worlds of aging," Mr. Maloney said. "There will be a large number of couples age 65 to 74 in relatively good health who have substantial income. But on the other hand, we will have a group of older people, many of whom have health problems, who are poor and living alone. They are more likely to be women, and most likely to be widowed."

It also advocated an increase in Federal Supplementary Security Income payments, the cash-assistance program for low-income elderly and disabled people. Recipients should be brought up to the poverty level—$104 a week for a single elderly person—compared with the current rate of $78 a week, the commission concluded.

To raise the money to increase these payments, the commission suggested raising employers' Social Security tax payments. Other options would "redistribute wealth among elderly people themselves," said the commission's chairwoman, Dr. Karen Davis, a professor of health policy and management at the Johns Hopkins School of Public Health in Baltimore.

One such plan would increase the taxable amount of Social Security benefits from 50 to 85 percent.

"We could give poor people 25 percent more income if the rest of the elderly people would give, on average, 32 cents a day," Mr. Moloney said.

Asked if such revenue-raising proposals are feasible, Mr. Moloney pointed to an earlier study, conducted by Louis Harris & Associates, that measured the attitudes and preferences of the elderly regarding their own health care, living arrangements and finances.

To the question, "Would you be willing to have your Social Security benefits reduced by $20 to $30 a month to guarantee that no elderly person will live in poverty?" over half of those with incomes over $10,000 answered "yes."

Source: Glenn Collins, *New York Times* (New York, April 16, 1987), p. 15. Copyright © 1987 by The New York Times Company. Reprinted by permission.

Despite the influx of nursing homes in recent years, the family is the typical caretaker for the sick elderly person. From two to three times as many persons are bedfast and housebound at home as are in institutions of all kinds (Shanas and Maddox 1976:610–11). Adult daughters are the major social support of the elderly sick, while other relatives arrange for medical care where there are no children. Just how long the family can continue to serve as the major support for the infirm elderly is questionable, however. With the increasing proportion of women in the labor force, the decline in family size, and increased urbanization, family efforts to care for the needy elderly are coming under increasing strain.

The recent development of geriatric day care centers in the United States may help adult children with elderly living in the home. Though these centers are not widespread, for those who can afford them and have them available, geriatric centers serve a very useful purpose. Placement in a day care center during the workday may mean that the elderly family member can continue to live with adult children and avoid moving to a retirement home or nursing home. Adult children can drop off an elderly family member at the day care center on the way to work in the morning and pick him or her up again in the evening after working hours. A geriatric day care center usually employs a nurse who can give medication if needed and conduct other routine checks, such as blood pressure, throughout the day.

Elderly Americans whose sole source of income is Social Security may find themselves unable to satisfy even their most basic needs.

The center staff plans activities, field trips, and crafts. The elderly often engage in community service projects at the center, and making a valuable contribution to the community boosts their self-esteem.

The psychological status of the elderly has an unfortunate stereotype of deterioration. The generalization that old people are "typically senile" is simply inaccurate. Without comprehensive diagnoses for various symptoms, it is currently impossible to know the precise extent to which various cognitive and emotional disorders are a function of treatable disease or affective states rather than of true brain disorders (Hickey 1980:9–10). The health implications of a generalized lack of stimulation in the lives of many older people are beginning to be recognized. Behavioral manifestations of confusion, stress, anxiety, and depression can result from the absence of meaningful stimuli; yet these "symptoms" are often seen as evidence of brain deterioration. In addition, the inability or unwillingness of medical personnel to deal with multiple causes of health problems has not helped the plight of infirm elderly family members.

Finances

The loss of an occupational role may mean a decrease in regular income or support. What is the financial situation of the elderly in retirement?

The retirement system in the United States has the dual character of providing both insurance and a social reward, but it has steadily moved in a more insurance-oriented direction. Social Security is the biggest source of income for most older Americans, with over 90 percent of them receiving some benefits (Cox 1988:251). These benefits account for only 39 percent of the total income of older Americans, however. In addition, earnings account for 23 percent, asset income for 18 percent, private pensions for 7 percent, government pensions for 6 percent, and other sources for 7 percent. Thus, rather than fulfilling the total financial need of the older American, the Social Security system tends to provide basic subsistence at best. With the federal government allowing Individual Retirement Accounts (IRAs) and Keogh plans for those who can afford them, Social Security has become only a supplement to retirement income. However, those on limited incomes cannot afford to put away money each month for retirement, unless their employer does it for them— not usually the case.

Inflation has had a definite impact on elderly family members on fixed incomes. Social Security is the *main* source of income for *two-thirds* of single older people and *half* the married couples in the United States. On the average, the income of a retired man is only about half that of a working man, and that of an elderly woman is half that of a retired man (Aiken 1982:208). Other than Social Security, many Americans have a private pension plan from their earlier employment.

Overall, the financial situation for the elderly in the United States, especially for those below middle class, is difficult. Only about 40 percent of older people have incomes at or above the modest-but-adequate level, and only one-half have the use of an automobile (Atchley 1977: 201). Some approaching the retirement years may find these years to be "the best" if they are healthy and financially secure. For others, with limited resources and failing health, growing old may not be so pleasant.

Despite the "ravages of time," growing older has a happy side (Cunningham and Brookbank 1988:123). Although many bodily systems are on the decline, it remains possible for most elderly to preserve some degree of physical fitness through exercise. If the body remains tuned, the mind may retain much of the mental sharpness of younger years. Combining the richness of experience and wisdom, natural rewards of longevity, life after sixty can be enjoyable and fulfilling. Most elderly do not finish out their years in institutions for the frail. It is likely that many older Americans will enjoy active lives that should contain sexual activity and romance as major factors. Indeed, for many, "the best *is* yet to be."

CHAPTER
REVIEW

- Sooner or later, it will dawn on each of us that we are growing older. Sometimes the signs are not too subtle. The percentage of persons over sixty-five years of age has increased from 4 percent in 1900 to 12 percent in 1990—the "graying of America" is on.
- Social disengagement is the process wherein a family member withdraws from some roles but not others. Societal disengagement is the process of society's withdrawing from, or no longer seeking, an individual's efforts.
- Disengagement theory is refuted by some, who suggest that an older person's interaction with family members is likely to increase, since more time is available for family responsibilities after retirement. Activity theory states that one should try to maintain the activity level of middle age in retirement.
- The continuity approach to aging suggests that individuals are predisposed toward maintaining continuity in their personality characteristics as they grow older.
- The substitution theory of adjustment in retirement states that an individual should substitute for work other activities that will give the satisfaction of work.
- The accommodation theory of adjustment to retirement points out the

need for a retired person to adapt to new social roles and for family members to adjust to his or her being home more often.

- *Aged persons* have been around for a long time, but *retired persons* are fairly recent on the American scene. Studies indicate that most retirees are relatively satisfied with retirement. Older family members tend to have a remarkably positive outlook on life.
- In addition to extended family members, friends and neighbors are important sources of social relationships in later life.
- Leisure roles are diverse for elderly family members. Most of the elderly in the United States spend their leisure at home alone—television tends to be a primary "companion."
- Many Americans continue to work full or part time after age sixty-five.
- Sexuality in later life is viewed negatively by many in the United States.
- After retirement, many elderly families move into less spacious housing facilities. Approximately 5 percent of the older population in the United States live in a nursing home at any one time.

DISCUSSION QUESTIONS

1. Contrast social disengagement with societal disengagement.
2. How does substitution differ from accommodation as an adjustment to retirement?
3. What is satisfying about retirement for the elderly?
4. Refute or support the following statement: Sexuality and old age do not go together.
5. How do the leisure needs of the elderly differ from other adults' leisure needs? How are they similar?
6. Why would the myth develop that in the United States most persons over age sixty-five reside in nursing homes?
7. What solutions would you suggest for solving the problems of housing, health, and finance for the elderly?

GLOSSARY

Elderhostel: A program, usually of one week's duration, for the elderly in the United States and other countries designed as educational and social—typically run by and located within a college or university.

longitudinal study: A study that looks at two or more points in time (studying the attitudes or behavior of a particular group in 1980 and looking at the same situation in 1985).

membership group: A group to which a person actually belongs. He or she is accepted by that group and participates in the group's events.

reference group: A particular group toward which one aspires, and which one tries to "act like"—unlike a membership group, to which one actually belongs and in which one is an accepted participant.

social disengagement: An individual's withdrawal from certain roles in life.

SUGGESTED READINGS

Cicirelli, Victor G. 1981. *Helping Elderly Parents: The Role of Adult Children.* Boston: Auburn House Publishing Company. *Written to give a better understanding about the nature of caring relationships between elderly parents and adult children.*

Cox, Harold G. 1988. *Later Life: The Realities of Aging.* Englewood Cliffs, N.J.: Prentice-Hall. *A good sociological approach to gerontology.*

de Beauvoir, Simone. 1972. *The Coming of Age.* New York: G. P. Putnam's Sons. An excellent cultural and historical account of aging.

Fischer, David H. 1977. *Growing Old in America.* New York: Oxford University Press. Aging in America from an historical perspective.

Keith, Pat M. 1989. *The Unmarried in Later Life.* New York. Praeger. *A study of singleness in later life of males and females—some formerly married and others never married.*

Taylor, Charles. 1984. *Growing On: Ideas About Aging.* New York: Van Nostrand Reinhold Company. *An excellent collection of insights into the experience of growing older.*

PART FIVE

Crises in Families

Divorce and Remarriage

◆ *Marriage is the chief cause of divorce.**

Why do I feel a sense of guilt every time I see a divorce lawyer's commercial claiming that "divorce doesn't have to be a difficult process and can be less expensive than most Americans think"? The popular press would have me believe that half of all marriages in the United States end in divorce—in 1988 there were 2,409,000 marriages and 1,158,000 divorces (National Center for Health Statistics 1989). Some preachers and television evangelists have jumped to the conclusion that the days of the American family are numbered if we do not radically change our ways.

Why do so many marriages end in divorce? And have I contributed to marital problems that many are experiencing in the United States? Maybe my feelings of guilt are caused by the fact that I am asking the wrong questions. If I begin with the assumption that a high rate of divorce is indicative of social pathology, then Americans may be facing significant social problems calling for social policy solutions. But what is the meaning of a high divorce rate? Is it possible that the problem is the American marriage system—too many people getting married? Maybe the meanings of both marriage and divorce have changed in recent history.

In this chapter we will attempt to provide an historical perspective on terminating and reentering marriage. We will also con-

---

*Groucho Marx

sider the effects of divorce and remarriage on those who are involved in the process—the couple, their children, and members of their friendship and kinship groups.

MARRIAGE AND DIVORCE IN A SOCIAL CONTEXT

At the present time approximately 95 percent of all Americans will marry before reaching the age of 45 (U.S. Bureau of Census, 1986). Americans marry at a higher rate than almost all other cultures of the world. Why are Americans more inclined to marry? Are all people in the United States equally suited for marriage? Sociologists try to answer these questions by discussing the process of socialization to adult roles.

First, consider the fact that we have come to believe that adulthood means marrying and raising children. In establishing adult status, it is sometimes even more important to have dependents than it is to become independent of one's family of orientation. Consequently, many Americans may be motivated to marry for reasons that do not promote long-term commitments. If there is truth to the estimate that 10 percent of the population is homosexual, then heterosexual marital relationships should appeal to fewer than 90 percent of the population. Such is not the case. Furthermore, many people would seem to have either personalities or personal goals and objectives for their lives that would render them unlikely candidates for marriage. If you have lived in a dormitory for any period of time, you have probably discovered that the world is filled with people who should not marry. If you search your inner self, you may discover that you fall into this group of people. Yet I once saw a Phil Donahue Show that featured six bright, attractive, and articulate never-married women in their forties and proceeded to give the impression that these were a rare, strange, and perhaps even deviant group of people.

Maybe the burden of proof should be on the people who marry, rather than on those who have chosen not to marry. Older single people are often asked, "Why didn't you ever marry?" or "Haven't you ever met someone who might make a good spouse?" The apostle Paul proclaimed that being single was a more desirable state for the Christian (I Corinthians 7:8–9). Yet in the contemporary Christian church, single people are almost viewed as social deviants. American divorce rates might be lower if there were not so many pressures to marry. This could be especially true for people who realize that they are unlikely candidates for marriage.

Second, the meaning of contemporary American marriages has changed. Historically, Americans married for practical reasons—a man and a woman needed each other to meet the subsistence requirements of life. A sexual division of labor within the home insured the survival of the family. Women attended to domestic chores and cared for children, while men provided the economic means for survival and protected their families against the outside world. Today, with more egalitarian family structures and increased androgynous divisions of labor, couples marry for "affective" reasons—that is, love, affection, encouragement, social support, and emotional well-being. These affective criteria for marital success are much more difficult to achieve. Consider the couple who come to their parents explaining their decision to divorce with the following statements: "We don't love each other any more, we have nothing in common, and we have grown apart." Many members of earlier generations would have said, "So what were you expecting from marriage?"

Third, perhaps each of us expects either too much or too little from marriage. Contemporary Americans tend to enter marriage with one of two sets of assumptions regarding their spouse. The first is that their partner is their perfect complement—the person who will help them fulfill their human potential, their sole partner in dialogue, their total means of sexual fulfillment and personal intimacy, their primary source of security, comfort, and stability, and their place of respite from a depersonalized, cold, and competitive world. The second set of assumptions is that one's marriage partner is merely the present fellow traveler on one's road to developing personal potential. If one's life goals change or one perceives that the marriage relationship is no longer fulfilling and beneficial, one should then disengage from the present relationship and consider affiliating with another traveler, or travel unaccompanied.

Both sets of assumptions make divorce more likely. The first is unrealistic—no marriage can meet all these requirements. Yet because people believe that personal fulfillment is possible in marriage, they find it more difficult to justify remaining in an unsatisfactory marriage (Weitzman 1985:xviii). The second set of assumptions practically amounts to a self-fulfilling prophecy, because leaving open the option of disengagement takes away any motivation for self-sacrifice or unconditional commitment.

Fourth, because our life expectancies have greatly increased since the turn of the century, divorce is assisting death in bringing marriages to a premature close. A comparison of infants born in 1900 with those born in 1950 shows an increase in life expectancy from forty-seven to sixty-eight years. This twenty-one-year increase in fifty years equals the previous increase over the past two thousand years (Phipps 1987:31). According to William Phipps (1987:34), "Before the nineteenth century the average marriage lasted only a dozen years before one spouse died. Now partners who do not divorce have marriages that average four times that long."

Service for the Dissolution of a Marriage

In an attempt to create an amicable divorce, Matthew and Anne Surrey (fictitious) wished to dissolve their marriage in the context of their Christian commitment by solemnizing it with a religious ceremony. Recognizing that rituals associated with marriage—parties before the wedding, the ceremony in the presence of families and friends, the official announcements—are unnecessary, but enriching psychologically and sociologically as couples take on a new marital status, the Surreys improvised their own rite of passage in order to give public recognition and legitimacy to the end of their marriage.

Because they could not find a denomination which would sanctify a divorce, they held this ceremony in a home and invited 30 of their closest friends to attend. When all of the guests were inwardly quiet, the Service for the Dissolution of a Marriage began.

Officient: Let us stand in a circle. (As the guest arranged themselves in a circle the minister stood between Anne and Matt.)

All: Oh Lord, our Lord, how excellent is thy Name in all the earth.

Officient: Dearly beloved, we have gathered here to solemnize the end of one time in Matthew's and Anne's lives, and the beginning of another. We are so made that we cannot live in isolation from our fellow men, but neither can we live too closely joined with them. We are social beings, but also individual selves, and it is the rhythm of union and separation that enables us to live in the communion which sustains our selves, and in the solitude which nourishes our community. As it is written: (Here the officient reads Ecclesiastes 3:1–8, 11–14.)

Officient continues: Thirteen years ago, the time was right for Matthew and Anne to be joined in holy matrimony. Then they needed for their growth in grace and truth the visible bond of marriage. Now the time has come when that bond is hampering both their growth as individual persons and their common life. They have resolved, therefore, to sever the ties of their marriage, though not of their mutual love and honor, and have asked us, their friends, to witness that affirmation of their new lives, and to uphold them in their new undertakings.

Matthew Surrey, do you now relinquish your status as husband of Anne, freeing her from all claims upon and responsibilities to you except those that you willingly give to all other children of God?

Matthew: I do.

Officient: Do you forgive her any sins she has committed against you, and do you accept her forgiveness, thus freeing her from the burdens of guilt and sterile remorse?

Matthew: I do.

Officient: Do you release her with your love and blessing, in gratitude for the part she has played in your life, in knowledge that her part in you will never be forgotten or despised, and in faith that in separation as in union, you both are held in the grace and unity of God?

Matthew: I do.

(The same questions were then asked of Anne, and she replied in the same way.) ...

Officient: Let us pray. Almighty and loving God, who has ordered that the seasons shall change and that human lives shall proceed by change, we ask thy blessing upon thy children who now, in their commitment to thee, have severed their commitment to each other. Send them forth in the bond of peace. When they meet, sustain them in their liberty. Keep them both reminded that thy love flows upon and through them both. Sanctify them in their lives, deaths, and resurrections, by the power of thy Holy Spirit, and for the sake of thy Son, Jesus Christ, our Lord.

All: Amen.

The high point of the party was the cutting of a wedding cake, complete with figures of a bride and groom on top. The company gathered around the table. Anne took the knife and Matt laid his hand on hers. They brought the knife down accurately *between* the dolls, so that one fell over on each side. The noisy chatter started again, not quite drowning Anne's announcement that it was a spice cake, the flavor chosen for its symbolic meaning.

Two days later, after the guests returned home, the mail brought the last of Anne and Matthew's symbolic expressions, the notification printed in Gothic type:

Matthew and Anne Surrey
Announce an Amicable Divorce

Source: Mary McDermott Shideler, "An Amicable Divorce," *The Christian Century* (May 5, 1971). Copyright 1971 Christian Century Foundation. Reprinted by permission.

Finally, as each of us has more and more friends, acquaintances, and relatives who have been divorced, we increasingly view divorce as an acceptable alternative to an unhappy marriage. In the past, even though divorce was an option, people perceived that they were trapped in poor marriages. Many people feared the social stigma of being a divorced person. Others believed that their present marriage was their only opportunity to be married and that even a bad marriage was better than no marriage at all. Dependent women often felt that their lives, and the lives of their children, depended solely upon the economic tie to their husband—divorce appeared to be a certain trip to the poor house.

Today, by contrast, almost everyone knows at least one person who has been divorced and remarried. Divorced people have higher marriage rates than do single people of the same age (Leslie and Korman 1985:541). In addition, women as a group are more self-sufficient than ever before. Despite continuing salary inequities, employment opportunities for women have never been greater—the majority of women are in the labor force. Given the decrease in stigma assigned to divorced persons and the increased opportunities for self-determination, self-sufficiency, and remarriage, perhaps it is unrealistic to expect that 95 percent of members of our geographically mobile society will be able to sustain a committed relationship for fifty years.

WHO GETS DIVORCED AND WHY?

In 1988 there were approximately 2.4 million marriages and 1.2 million divorces—Americans were almost twice as likely to marry as to divorce in this year. Does this mean that one half of all marriages end in divorce? While many have assumed that these figures indicate that 50 percent of all marriages end in divorce, we know that most of the divorces in 1988 involved marriages contracted in prior years. Consequently, based upon this information, it is not accurate to say that 50 percent of all marriages end in divorce.

Ross Eshleman (1985:579–80) points out how confusing numerical comparisons of marriages and divorces in a given year can be. He notes that 40 percent of all marriages occurring in a given year are remarriages of one or both spouses. Persons who divorce and remarry in the same year contribute to both the number of marriages and the number of divorces—giving the ratio of 1 to 1. Eshleman also points out that by combining each year's numbers of deaths and divorces—the two primary causes of marriage dissolution—statisticians can show more marriages ending in a given year than beginning.

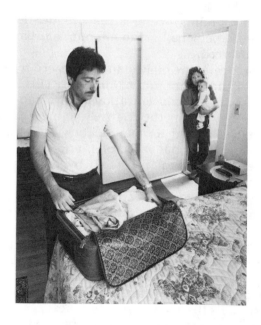

Even though divorce is increasingly viewed as preferable to an unhappy marriage, for many families divorce is an even more difficult crisis than the death of a family member.

Therefore, what are the facts? In 1989 the divorce rate was 4.8 per 1,000 persons in the U.S. population. This was slightly down from 1984, when the rate was 4.9—the same as 1983 and 1982. Since the turn of the century, the divorce rate had been 2.0 or less until 1946, when it jumped to 4.3 per 1,000 people. After this peak year, it sharply declined to approximate prewar rates, then slowly increased until a rapid surge began in the 1970s. Divorces peaked again in 1979 and 1981 at 5.3 per 1,000 (National Center for Health Statistics 1989 and Eshleman 1985). The 1989 divorce rate is the lowest rate since 1975 (National Center for Health Statistics 1989). Much of the increase in divorce rates during the 1970s can be attributed to the "me" decade's change in divorce laws making divorce more affordable and accessible. In reality, the divorce rate is lower and more steady than one might assume from reading commentaries on the contemporary American family. (For an interesting critique of divorce statistics and their interpretation see Crosby 1985:532–43.)

However, the numbers give only a partial picture of contemporary divorce in the United States. The likelihood of divorce is influenced by several factors, including age of the couple, number of years married, number of times previously married, and the couple's race, region of residence, and social class. Gerald Leslie and Sheila Korman (1985:510–16, and 544) have surveyed the effects of the above factors and discovered the following:

1. Divorced persons are more likely to be found in urban areas and underrepresented in rural areas. Two factors contribute

to this finding—rural areas produce less divorces, and divorced persons tend to migrate to urban areas after they are divorced.

2. Divorce rates are highest in the western region of the United States and lowest in the Northeast. This is partially caused by the higher concentrations of Roman Catholics in the northeast and by the relatively younger populations in the west. Leslie and Korman acknowledge that many factors influence regional variations, and most explanations are little more than untested hypotheses and informed speculations.

3. There is an inverse correlation between social class and divorce rates—people from higher social class groups are less likely to divorce than those from the lower social classes. This relationship is constant when either income or education are used as indicators for social class.

4. Race is also related to divorce rates. In general, whites have the lowest divorce rates, but this is due more to social class variations than to racial differences.

5. The divorce rate for previously divorced persons is twice as high as for persons in their first marriage. In contrast, remarried widows have a lower divorce rate than persons in their first marriage. At the other extreme, the divorce rates for persons married three or more times is the highest of all.

6. Men and women who marry at young ages are more likely to experience divorce than are couples who marry when they are older. According to Spanier and Glick (1981:333), women who marry under age seventeen are three times as likely to divorce as women who marry in their twenties. Women who are eighteen or nineteen when they marry are twice as likely to divorce as women marrying in their twenties. Likewise, men who marry in their teens are twice as likely to divorce as men who marry in their twenties.

7. According to the National Center for Health Statistics, in 1974 the median interval from marriage to divorce was 6.5 years. Based on these data and earlier research studies, Leslie and Korman claim that divorce rates are higher in the early years of marriage—the first year of marriage is the peak year for separations, with the largest number of divorces being granted during the third year. According to Eshleman (1985:584), "4.4 percent of the divorcing couples had been married less than one year. One-third of divorcing couples (33.7 percent) were married one to four years, and about one-fourth (27.8 percent) were married five to nine years.

The remaining third of divorcing couples had been married ten years or more with 15 percent married ten to fourteen years and 19 percent married fifteen years or more."

DIVORCE AND THE LAW

In the United States, marriage is regarded as a civil contract between two individuals, and the laws that pertain to these relationships are under the jurisdiction of the fifty state legislatures. To fully understand divorce in U.S. society, one would have to study all fifty individual states. However, the state laws do have many common features.

Historically, the law treated marriage as a nondissolvable union involving lifelong rights and obligations. While divorce was possible, the states allowed for divorce mainly on three very limited grounds: desertion, adultery, and cruelty. (Until the 1960s, the only legal ground for divorce in New York was adultery.) According to Lenore Weitzman (1985:4), however, even though spouses were separated, divorce did not end the obligations of the marriage contract—a husband was responsible for the financial support of his family, and the wife was required to provide care for their dependent children.

Until 1970, when California passed its "no-fault" divorce legislation, all states required that at least one of the spouses had to be in violation of the marriage contract before a divorce would be granted. This **"fault-based" divorce** system required that the "innocent party" had to produce evidence in court that the "guilty party" had violated the contract. If a couple could not qualify for divorce, their only option was legal separation.

If you have ever watched television's "Divorce Court," you have observed that the fault-based system often leads couples to become involved in deception, embarrassment, and **acrimony,** or bitterness. Since one party has to be guilty, even couples who desire an **amicable divorce**—a divorce by mutual agreement—must provide evidence of misconduct.

Since 1970, all states, with the exception of South Dakota, have adopted some form of **"no-fault" divorce.** Under this more permissive system, "marital breakdown" is the only required justification for divorce—making issues of guilt, innocence, and blame irrelevant (Weitzman 1985:20). This system also makes it possible for divorce to be a one-sided decision or **unilateral action**—which means that if one wishes to divorce, there is nothing the spouse can do to stop this action. Under the old system, the "innocent" party was typically awarded a greater share in property settlement. In 1968 wives were awarded 60 percent or more of the property, on average, in cases in both San Francisco and Los Angeles. Most of these awards allowed the wife to keep the family home and its furnishings, which often constituted the single most valuable family asset (Weitzman 1985:30). With the no-fault system, joint or community property is divided equally—usually requiring the family home to be sold, displacing both spouses and any children.

According to Lenore Weitzman (1985:29), under the no-fault system, there are no financial rewards for good behavior. She cites the following example to illustrate the point:

> *A fifty-five-year-old Los Angeles surgeon, explaining that he never took time off to go to the symphony orchestra or to spend a carefree summer at the beach with his wife and children because he thought his job was to "be there to earn the money so that my kids and wife could have everything they wanted," expressed his feelings of outrage this way: "Now, she walked out on me, and what do I get? Nothing. And what does she get? She gets half of my house, half of my pension. . . . For what, I ask you? For running off with a jerk psychologist. That's my reward?"*

Furthermore, under no-fault the divorce court cannot take into consideration the misbehavior of a spouse in determining awards of spouse or child support. Truly, the no-fault divorce system eliminates any moral framework for making legal decisions regarding marriage dissolution.

Finally, the no-fault system eliminates gender biases in divorce proceedings. This means that the laws do not assume that men should pay **spousal support**—support for their ex-wives after divorce—or that women should be given preference in decisions regarding child-custody.

If All Else Fails, There's Always the Option of Divorce

Even when couples do everything humanly possible to keep the fire of romance burning in their relationship, something comes along to quench the passion. Sometimes you find that the two of you, no matter how much you might once have cared for each other, are starting to drift apart. Hey, it happens. People change. They get older. They get larger, and sometimes they start to smell. Maybe the time has come to think about—let's come right out and say it— divorce.

Today, fortunately, it is easier to get divorced in most states than to get a transmission repaired properly. The only requirement is that you have a legal reason, which is technically known as "grounds." If you have no grounds of your own, you can probably get some from your lawyer; or you can select some from this convenient list:

1. Wearing shorts and black knee socks at the same time.
2. Calling you "Sweetie Beancakes" in front of strangers.
3. Forgetting to buy beer.
4. Repeatedly putting the ice-cube tray back in the refrigerator with two or fewer ice cubes in it.
5. Bringing the car home with just enough gas in it so that, if you shut the engine off and coast on the downhill slopes, you can get as far as the end of the driveway.
6. Any cigar-related activity.
7. Standing next to you with a sour facial expression at a party while you tell a really terrific joke and then loudly announcing the punch line three-tenths of a second before you get to it and then saying: "Isn't that awful?" (Note: In some states this is grounds not only for divorce, but also for murder.)
8. Golf.
9. One day, with no warning, bringing home:
   a. a cat, or
   b. an Amway representative.
10. Leaving his or her toenails in a prominent location as though they were decorative art objects.
11. Operating a loud household appliance during the Super Bowl.

Eventually the divorce will become final, and you can start picking up the broken pieces of your life and selling them to pay your legal bills. But also you must think about the future and, yes, meeting someone new. You must not be afraid. Oh, sure, you got burned and you got hurt. But that is no reason to give up. You must not be afraid. You must show the same kind of gumption as the cowboy who, if he gets thrown off a horse, climbs right back on, and if he gets thrown off again, climbs right back on again, and so on, until virtually all of his brain cells are dead.

Source: Dave Barry, "Little Things Mean A Lot To A Marriage's Vitality," *Minneapolis Star and Tribune* (November 4, 1987), p. 1C.

Increasingly, men are being awarded child custody as a result of the "no-fault" divorce system.

A study (Albrecht, Bahr, and Goodman 1983:100) of divorced persons living in Utah, Idaho, and Nevada (all no-fault divorce states) showed that the following, in descending order of importance, were the ten leading self-reported causes for marriage failure:

1. Infidelity
2. No longer loved each other
3. Emotional problems
4. Financial problems
5. Sexual problems
6. Problems with in-laws
7. Neglect of children
8. Physical abuse
9. Alcohol problems
10. Job conflicts

In 1985, after investigating the effects of the no-fault system for ten years, Stanford sociologist Lenore Weitzman wrote an important treatise on the subject—*The Divorce Revolution: The Unexpected Social and Economic Consequences for Women and Children in America.* Her research is based largely on 2,500 California court cases before and after 1970, when that state instituted the country's first no-fault divorce law. She also interviewed hundreds of judges, lawyers, and divorced men and women in Los Angeles and San Francisco. In this study, Weitzman comes to the following conclusions:

1. Contemporary divorce settlements dividing property equally often overlook new forms of property, including the major wage earner's salary, pension, medical insurance, education, license, the goodwill value of a business or profession, entitlements to company goods and services, and future earning power (page xiii).

2. No-fault divorce took away a bargaining tool lawyers used to get women better financial settlements. Women are disadvantaged by legal changes because courts, in dividing property, typically disregard economic inequities created during the marriage.

3. Divorce courts do not typically take into consideration the investment of one spouse in the career of another. If a woman sacrifices her own career in order to stay at home and care for minor children, she is not compensated for her investment. Even if she supports her husband as he earns a law or medical degree, she is unlikely to be adequately compensated in most states (page 133).

4. Courts tend to assume that able-bodied wives will become independent and self-sufficient after divorce (regardless of their age). Consequently, spousal support is either denied altogether or given for only a short period of time (page 33).

5. In more than 80 percent of the cases women are still awarded physical custody of minor children. The change in the law in California did not significantly increase either the requests for or the awards of **physical custody** (care and housing of) minor children. This same lack of change was also observed regarding **legal custody**—the responsibility for the education and welfare of the child (pages 225–28).

6. On the average, child support amounts to only 25 percent of the husband's net income (page 267).

7. On the average, divorced women and the minor children in their households experience a 73 percent decline in their standard of living in the first year after divorce. Their former husbands, in contrast, experience a 42 percent rise in their standard of living (page xii).

8. In summary, no-fault divorce laws were designed to create a system which would be less acrimonious and more humane, fair, and gender-neutral. In reality, the no-fault system is much less likely to stimulate and encourage antagonistic and hostile divorces (page 40), but children and women are financially disadvantaged in the process.

Professor Weitzman's Recommendations for Changes in the "No-Fault" Divorce Laws

While not advocating a return to faultfinding, Weitzman proposes far reaching remedies to make divorce more equitable. Some of them, such as viewing pensions and retirement benefits as marital property, have been recognized by courts in some states. But few states permit older homemakers once covered by group or family health and hospital insurance policies to convert to individual policies without new proof of eligibility, as she advocates. Nor do they guarantee such women an interest in a former husband's income for the rest of their lives, a provision of the "grandmother clause" Weitzman would create.

Another provision is that older homemakers be allowed to continue living in the family home, if it is the only major asset, rather than having to sell and share the proceeds with the former spouse. The parent with the major responsibility for minor children should also be allowed continued use of the home, she says, adding that the use should be seen as part of the child-support award rather than an unequal division of property.

In general, Weitzman recommends that child-support awards be based on an income sharing approach because this formula is most likely to equalize standards of living in both households after divorce. To enforce these awards, she favors such techniques as wage assignments, national location services, property liens and bonds, and, where necessary, jail.

One broad implication of her findings is that changes in divorce laws have changed the marriage rules. "In the past," she said, "the economic contract was she'd be the homemaker and he'd be the breadwinner. Now we've redefined terms so that a homemaker and mother is up a creek at divorce because no court is going to tell him to keep supporting her."

Moreover, the laws reward individual achievement rather than commitment to the family. "What we've really said," Weitzman said, "is you're going to be independent after divorce. If you invest in your husband, if you invest in your children, it doesn't pay under the new rules."

Source: Georgia Dullea, *Minneapolis Star and Tribune* (November 14, 1985), pp. 1C and 11C. Reprinted with permission of Star Tribune, Minneapolis–St. Paul.

RESINGLING—THE ADJUSTMENT TO BEING A DIVORCED PERSON

As an ex-spouse returns to a single marital status, or "resingles," a process of personal adjustment must obviously take place. From a social-psychological point of view, this process is both an individual and a social experience. From a personal perspective, there is a sense of loss—not unlike the experience of bereavement associated with the death of a spouse. In bereavement, or in divorce, people experience many of the following feelings identified by Robert Kavanaugh (1972): shock and denial, disorganization, anger or volatile emotions, guilt, loss and loneliness, and finally relief.

These emotions are normal for people who are attempting to cope with the stress involved in the changing status of a relationship. While some have suggested that there is an inherent order to the experience of these feelings, divorced persons will attest to the fact that they have experienced many of these feelings at the same time and that they go back and forth between them. For example, guilt and anger are related feelings—anger may be directed at a spouse, mistress, or former in-laws; guilt is typically anger turned inward. I have known many divorced people who have vacillated between feelings of anger and relief—on the one hand, they are relieved to be free of an adulterous and dishonest spouse; on the other, they are understandably angry and resentful at this person for violating their trust and commitment.

Recent research (Bloom, White, and Asher 1979) concluded that divorced persons have a higher probability than married people of becoming admitted to psychiatric facilities, are three times as likely to have motor vehicle accidents, experience more drinking-related problems, and are at greater risk of dying from suicide, homicide, and illnesses. It is also possible, however, that some of these problems (e.g., alcoholism or mental illness) influenced the decision to divorce in the first place. Furthermore, socioeconomic status is highly correlated with each of these problems. If these findings were controlled for social class, it is possible that many of these relationships would prove to be spurious.

Obviously, the newly divorced will experience some personal stress involving disorganization, loneliness, unhappiness, and anxiety. Just what are the long-term personal effects of divorce? In a major study of 485 divorced persons (Albrecht, Bahr, and Goodman 1983) 37 percent of the respondents said their divorce was either easier than anticipated or relatively painless. Seventy-five percent of the respondents felt that the most difficult period of their marriage was either before the decision to divorce or just before the final divorce decree. Eighty-one percent claimed that the best time for self and children was at the present time or just after the decree. This evidence provides support for the following conclusion (Albrecht, Bahr, and Goodman 1983:123):

While much has been said and written about the trauma of divorce, and while it is generally accepted that going through a divorce is extremely difficult no matter how bad the marriage was, for most of our respondents the price paid in terminating the marriage appears to have been worth it.

Grin and Bear Lover's Wedding Duties

Dear Abby:

Please, am I being too sensitive, or is it just plain rudeness on the bride's part? I am about to marry a man who has three daughters—all grown. Several months ago, his eldest daughter was married. He took me to the wedding. His daughter insisted that her father be in the group pictures—standing next to his ex-wife. Not only that, but he had to have the first dance with her and stand in the receiving line next to her, which I thought was rather tacky since he had nothing to do with the wedding.

Also, I resented being left alone while all this was going on. I thought once a man is divorced, he doesn't have to play the part of a "husband."

Do I have to go through this with the other two daughters when they get married?

Teed Off in N.J.

Abby says:

When a divorced man has daughters, he is usually expected to play "father of the bride" in order to keep the peace with his first family. It matters not how "Dad"—or the new lady in his life—feels about it; it's the bride's day, and she wants to preserve the illusion of Mom and Dad together (for the bridal book) no matter how lousy the marriage was.

Grin and bear it. That's part of the price you pay for loving a man with a first family. It's only one day out of the year for you. It's his daughter's wedding day.

Source: "Dear Abby," *Minneapolis Star and Tribune* (November 30, 1987), p. 11C. Universal Press Syndicate.

From a sociological perspective, divorce changes family and social interaction patterns. Family and social gatherings are never the same after a divorce. If the divorce has not been amicable, former spouses will want to avoid each other, they will experience discomfort in each other's presence, and they may display acrimony when they get together. Even if they are able to be civil with one another, family and friends may not feel comfortable when both are present at social occasions.

Consider the wedding of a woman whose parents are divorced. When she is ushered down the aisle by her father and the minister says, "Who gives this woman to be married to this man?" the audience will feel uncomfortable if he replies, "her mother and I." Meanwhile, in the first row there may be three sets of grandparents, the mother, the stepfather, and the stepmother. For the guests, this is an awkward social experience par excellence.

Another social problem for divorced people is that as they are resingled, they must readjust to an adult world where most are married. Like other single people, they do not fit into a coupled environment; but unlike other single people, they have a social history dominated by couple-oriented social experiences. Furthermore, many divorced people feel so much discomfort in the social situations in which they formerly participated as married persons that they find it necessary to make new friendships with other people. For example, a friend of mine changed churches and friendship groups after each of her two divorces. She did so because she claimed that the social discomfort (her friends' as well as her own) disrupted the normal spontaneity of her interaction patterns. For this reason, many divorced people create new social lives in order to avoid the burden of the symbolic presence of a former spouse.

Becoming single again often causes people to be thrust into a social world for which they are unprepared. (Francie. Reprinted by permission of UFS, Inc.)

Divorce Does Not Mean Goodbye

A new and more complex portrait of the continuing relationships of divorced spouses has emerged from a meeting of therapists who treat many of the nation's couples and families. Researchers from several disciplines emphasized not only the power of persistent family connections that bind couples together after divorce, but also the role of the parents and extended families of divorcing couples in the adjustment process. They also focused on a new view of single-parent families as part of larger family networks.

A comprehensive study of divorced partners was presented by psychologist Constance R. Ahrons. Preliminary findings of her five-year study—entitled the Binuclear Family Project—tracked the post-divorce history of 98 pairs of former spouses with children. Her findings divided the divorced spouses into four groups—nicknamed "perfect pals," "cooperative colleagues," "angry associates," and "fiery foes."

The "perfect pals" (12 percent of couples studied) had not remarried and still got along very well. They tended to be joint-custody parents who spent time together frequently and reported that they enjoyed one another's company.

The "cooperative colleagues" (38 percent of the couples) had a more moderate level of interaction that was nevertheless cordial, despite occasional conflict, and that focused mostly on the children. These former spouses were more likely to have remarried.

The "angry associates" (25 percent of the couples) were able to cooperate well enough on issues related to their children, but their interactions were fraught with conflict.

The fourth group, the "fiery foes" (25 percent of the couples) never interacted and commonly expressed hostility toward their former partners. They often communicated only through their children. Much of the early clinical data on divorce was based on this fourth group.

Half the couples studied fit the first two categories and displayed relationships that were respectful and friendly. This counters stereotyped notions that divorce relationships are composed of warring partners or that there is no relationship at all. The ages of the couples ranged from 19 to 60, and the average duration of marriages was 10.5 years. The sample of 196 subjects was drawn from the divorce records of Wisconsin's Dane County in 1978.

Of the 196 spouses interviewed in 1979, a year after divorcing, 175 were interviewed again in 1982. About 83 percent of the husbands had remarried or were living with new partners, as were 64

Of all the difficult social adjustments related to divorce, the one of greatest concern for most couples is the adjustment of children. In this next section we will consider the effects of divorce on children.

CHILDREN AND DIVORCE

Only 40 percent of children in the United States will spend their childhood with both birth parents (Weitzman 1985:xvii), and half of all divorces involve minor children. Like the death of a parent, divorce affects all family members, and children experience—among other effects—a loss similar to bereavement at the death of a parent. Like death, divorce disrupts the everyday order of children's lives and changes the interaction patterns within their homes. Like their parents, in coping with these changes children will encounter feelings of denial, anger, disorganization, guilt, loneliness, and relief.

Although in some ways divorce is similar to death, it is also very different. In most situations children still have the opportunity to interact with both parents. They can express their feelings and ask questions of their parents in the process of adjusting to new family relationships. If they have lived in a home with open marital conflict and hostility, after the divorce they may experience a release of family tension. But divorce can also be more problematic than death for children, because divorce is often perceived as a conscious and willful choice made by the parents—a choice that (the child may feel) could have been prevented.

Consequently, divorce is a very confusing time for children. They may feel responsible for their parents' divorce; they may also feel emotionally abandoned by one or both parents as one parent physically leaves the home and both parents become preoccupied with the process of personal adjustment to divorce. Furthermore, according to Karen Appel (1985:12), the emotional demands created by divorce often make parents less aware of their children's pain and stress and insensitive to their children's emotional needs. As a form of compensation, it is common for parents to indulge their children by placing fewer demands on them—creating a sense of marginality for many children.

In American society, the family is expected to fulfill the emotional needs of its members. The family is primarily responsible for nurturing social and personal growth of children and providing a supportive place of respite in a sometimes depersonalized society. Because of these idealized expectations for family life, reunions and get-togethers for families broken by divorce may always be less than fulfilling. Typically, there is a glorified remembrance of the *way things were* and an unrealistic image of *how things might be.*

As noted above, divorce often turns families into battlegrounds rife with intense arguments and hostilities. Sometimes in-laws and extended family members feel free to join the fight, and occasionally children are used by the participants to inflict pain upon the enemy— the former spouse and/or grandparents.

As a consequence of no-fault divorce laws, the financial situation of children of divorcing couples has gone dramatically downhill. As noted earlier, children now experience a 73 percent decline in their standard of living during the first year after divorce. With equal property settlements often requiring the sale of the family residence, many children are also displaced from their physical surroundings— the home that was a source of stability in an ever-changing social world. Moving from the family residence can create a change of schools, churches, and friendship groups. Thus, the entire social world of a child can change as a result of divorce.

Karen Appel (1985:17) has identified three social roles that many children from divorced homes assume in their adjustment process— placater, adjuster, or troublemaker. The *placater* attempts to hold the family together by acting like an adult. This child often provides guidance and nurturing for siblings and sometimes even for the custodial parent. It is generally assumed that this child is coping well with the divorce because he or she tries to be perfect at home and school—masking all feelings of guilt, anger, fear, and/or sorrow related to the divorce. The *adjuster* is an other-directed child and will do whatever is needed to cope with the stress caused by the divorce. If social support for working hard is received, the child will work hard. However, if attention can only be gained by bad behavior, the child will act out for his or her peers and play the part of the clown. Finally, the *troublemaker* consistently misbehaves as a means

This child is in the process of visiting his non-custodial parent. This type of vacation requires adjustment for both parents and children.

of seeking attention from others. This child has discovered that anti-social behavior is a sure method for gaining attention and recognition.

Each of these roles indicates that the child is attempting to cope with loss and at the same time adjust to changes in family living. Adults can assist children in this process by validating their feelings. Open discussion of the reality of the divorce, with assurances that the child was not the cause of the separation, will help. Children also need to be reassured by both parents and told that they are loved and that divorce does not mean they are being rejected by either parent. Finally, when children may be tempted to withdraw from society, they need to be encouraged to develop other social relationships.

In her study of children's social adjustment following divorce, Marjorie Pett (1982) discovered that children from homes perceived to be happy before divorce either experienced no change or less familial security and happiness after the divorce. On the other hand, children from unhappy homes felt more secure and happy. After surveying the limited empirical research on the long-range effects of divorce on children, Andrew Cherlin (1981:79) reached the following conclusions:

1. Almost all children experience an initial period of great emotional upset following separation.

2. Most children return to normal development within one or two years following the separation.
3. A minority of children experience some long-term psychological problems as a result of the separation.

In a clinical study of 131 children from sixty upper-middle-class California families, Judith Wallerstein (Wallerstein and Blakeslee 1989) interviewed all members of families at three intervals following the parents' divorce—eighteen months, five years, and ten years. She discovered that while divorce may improve the family experience for adults, it can have traumatic long-term effects upon the well-being of children.

According to Wallerstein, children seem to adjust to divorce in the short term only to experience a decade later problems of anger, depression, promiscuity, and/or fears of betrayal and abandonment. Furthermore, clinical interviews revealed that more than one-third of the children were clinically depressed after only five years; after ten years 75 percent felt rejected by their fathers, and 35 percent had bad relationships with both parents.

While this research does not provide comparisons with a control group of children from families with intact marriages, it does seem that the long-term effects of divorce upon children may be more problematic than earlier research efforts had lead us to believe. Obviously, the effects of divorce on children are not uniform, but Pett's (1982) conclusion is worth noting: "The adjustment of children to divorce is best facilitated by a custodial parent who is adjusting well." This advice is similar to that given by Michael Leming and George Dickinson (1985:134) on helping children to cope with dying and death:

> *The best thing adults can do for children is to be well-adjusted, secure, and loving people. Who one is is basic to what one does. One's mental, emotional, physical, and spiritual well-being undergirds all our actions in helping the child.*

Friendship and Co-Parenting after Remarriage

According to a study by Eleanor Macklin and Carolyn Weston of Syracuse University, friendship between ex-spouses is not necessarily bad and can even be beneficial to a second marriage. Macklin and Weston interviewed members of 60 stepfather families; none of the stepfathers had any of their children living in the household. They found that the more contact a woman had with her former husband, the happier the new marriage, as long as both she and her new husband agreed about the nature and frequency of contact.

Why did frequent contact make for happier second marriages? First of all, Macklin said, "It works both ways. A happier new marriage may allow more contact with the ex-spouse." But the main reason, she explains, is parenting. Regular contact between former spouses usually ensures that the father will be financially supportive and involved in routine co-parenting. And new husbands are usually happier when they do not end up shouldering the entire burden of raising their stepchildren.

Couples said contact not involving their children mostly consisted of phone conversations about extended family members, mutual friends, and new experiences. Almost *none* of the people in this study had "dated" or had physical contact or sex with their former spouse. The few who had lunch or dinner together said that they arranged these meetings to talk about the children. But it was not unusual for these meetings to include discussions of mutual friends and family or personal issues.

Remarriage can cause a great deal of conflict between ex-spouses. The most conflict occurs when the husband has remarried and the wife has not—the most likely scenario after divorce. According to numerous studies, divorced men remarry more often and sooner than divorced women.

In the rarer situations, when only the woman remarries, the relationship with the former husband is more likely to remain strong. One reason for this gender difference is that new husbands are less threatened than new wives are by a former spouse and are therefore less likely to discourage contact. The issue, again, revolves around parenting. Stepmothers often are very stressed and confused about their role as parent to their stepchildren, who rarely live with them, visiting only on occasional weekends and holidays.

Certain factors can predict whether a divorced couple will be likely to maintain a friendly relationship, according to Macklin. The quality of the relationship before the divorce is one. In addition, a couple's attitude toward divorce is important. "There are some people who believe that complete separation is the only answer," Macklin said. Emotional issues are another factor. Those who are not happy in a current relationship are not good candidates for a friendly divorce.

The circumstances under which the marriage ended usually will affect whether a friendship develops. If it was not a mutual decision, or if there is still a great deal of lingering pain or resentment, the friendship is unlikely. The quality of the new marriage and the self-confidence of the new spouse also are extremely important, as is the attitude of the family in general. Some parents will imply to their children, "You have to choose; you can't be loyal to two people," Macklin said. If spouses are especially close to their in-laws, it will encourage contact between former spouses.

Surprisingly, neither the time that has elapsed since the divorce, geographic distance from relatives, nor the presence of children predicts whether former spouses will remain friends.

Source: Elizabeth Stark, *Minneapolis Star and Tribune* (May 20, 1986), pp. 1C and 9C. Reprinted with permission from Psychology Today Magazine. Copyright © 1986 (PT Partners, L.P.).

REMARRIAGE

In chapter 2 we discussed different forms of composite families, including composite families created by conjugal (marriage) ties. For most of the world these "larger families" come into existence as a result of polygamous marriages (both polygyny and polyandry). In the United States, with high rates of both divorce and remarriage **(sequential monogamy),** we now have a large number of **blended** or **reconstituted families:** composite families created by marriages of formerly married persons, some of whom have children.

In 1980, remarriages accounted for 44 percent of all marriages in the United States (National Center for Health Statistics 1980). In every adult age cohort, persons who have previously been married have a higher probability of remarrying than single persons marrying for the first time (Leslie and Korman 1985:541). At the present time, 80 percent of all divorced persons will eventually remarry, and most of these remarriages will be to persons who have also previously been married (Leslie and Korman 1985:539–40). According to Frank Furstenberg and Graham Spanier (1984:41), 25 percent of American children will grow up having more than two parents. These reconstituted or blended families have been exemplified and legitimated by such television shows as "The Brady Bunch," "Silver Spoons," "Who's the Boss," "Different Strokes," and "One Day at a Time."

An important and not easily answered question is, "How successful are remarriages?" The answers are equivocal at best—comparative success depends upon the group to whom the comparisons are made. If we compare the divorce rates of remarriages to first marriages, first marriages tend to be more stable. Furstenberg and Spanier (1985:45) estimate that approximately 55 percent of remarriages can be expected to terminate. Yet it is clear that there are no equivalent groups by which to compare people in first marriages with those who have remarried one or more times. Furstenberg and Spanier (1984:191—92) contend that people who remarry are more willing to accept divorce as an alternative to an unhappy marriage—"having endured a first marriage to the breaking point, they were unwilling to be miserable again simply for the sake of preserving the union."

On the other hand, if we compare the first and second marriages of given individuals, most people report a more favorable evaluation of the second marriage (Albrecht et al. 1983 and Goode 1956). It should be remembered, however, that most people report greater well-being three or four years after their divorce regardless of whether or not they remarry (Furstenberg and Spanier 1984:176).

When we probe the effects of remarriage upon children, we encounter similar methodological problems. Remarriage can involve significant adjustment problems and/or opportunities for children. For example, with the addition of a stepfather, the financial resources of the family may be increased. However, if this man has major financial responsibilities to a former spouse and/or children, the economic base of the blended family can be jeopardized.

Remarriage creates a new set of relationships with stepparents and their kin. Adjusting to these new family structures and role definitions can be problematic for both children and stepparents. Paul Bohannan (cited by Albrecht et al. 1983:143) suggests that the absence of clearly defined social role relationships in the reconstituted family can be a source of many difficulties. Andrew Cherlin (1981:84) suggests, however, that remarriages can benefit children because they provide additional kin (stepparents, stepsiblings, and stepgrandparents) for individuals who have experienced weakened kinship ties as a result of divorce. Yet when Wilson et al. (1975) compared children who lived with their own parents and those who lived in reconstituted or blended families they discovered both positive and negative effects of reconstituted families.

Most research demonstrates that the adjustment of children following divorce and remarriage is strongly influenced by the nature and quality of the relationship that remains between the parents (Lutz 1983). If parents can cooperate in **co-parenting,** or sharing parental responsibility, the negative effects upon children can be significantly reduced. Conversely, if one parent uses children to hurt the other, or if parents force children to choose sides in disputes, the results of divorce and remarriage can be detrimental.

CONCLUSION

Americans have high rates of marriage, divorce, and remarriage. They believe in marriage, and like the cowboy, if they get thrown off, they'll climb back on again and again until they wear out. When I think about Elizabeth Taylor and Mickey Rooney, I'm apt to assume that they have fairly weak commitments to marriage to have failed so many times. In actuality, these two oft-married stars may be more committed to marriage than I am—they continue trying, when I would have quit after the second or third marriage.

In the United States we have changed the way we think about marriage. We have tremendous expectations of our spouses, which may be unrealistic. My wife is supposed to be my best friend, lover, co-parent, and intellectual sparring partner. Over time my interests, goals, abilities, and talents will change, and she will experience changes as well. Based on the experience of others, the distance to the fiftieth wedding anniversary is a long one that relatively few are able to traverse.

For those who divorce, the process of adjustment is difficult. In the divorce process, it's important to avoid fault finding, blaming, and acrimony, which can lead only to bitterness, guilt, and self-depreciation in the adjustment period. Cooperation with a former spouse and in-laws is not easy, but will lead to greater emotional well-being in the future for oneself and one's children.

Divorce does not have to mean failure. The relationship may have ended, but human growth can emerge from personal crisis. While children should not be forced to take sides in marital problems, they should be included in discussions of the pain involved in coping. Support groups of caring friends will help, but only time can provide the necessary perspective on past experiences, personal changes, and future opportunities.

CHAPTER REVIEW

- Perhaps it is unrealistic to expect that 95 percent of the citizens in such a geographically mobile society will be able to sustain a committed relationship for fifty years.
- Many Americans expect too much or too little from marriage. These expectations contribute to high divorce rates.
- Partly because Americans are increasingly viewing divorce as an acceptable alternative to an unhappy marriage, divorce is assisting death in bringing marriages to premature closure.
- The divorce rate is lower and more steady than what one might assume from reading commentaries on the contemporary family.
- The likelihood of divorce is influenced by a number of factors, including a couple's age, number of years married, number of times previously married, race, region of residence, and social class.
- In the United States, marriage is regarded as a civil contract between two individuals, and the laws pertaining to these relationships are under the jurisdiction of the fifty state legislatures.
- Until 1970, when California passed its "no-fault" divorce legislation, all states required that at least one of the spouses had to be in violation

of the marriage contract before a divorce would be granted. All states except South Dakota have adopted some form of no-fault divorce. Under this more permissive system, "marital breakdown" is the only necessary justification for divorce—making issues of guilt, innocence, and blame irrelevant.

- On the average, divorced women and the minor children in their households experience a 73 percent decline in their standard of living in the first year after divorce. Their former husbands, in contrast, experience a 42 percent rise in their standard of living.
- From the perspective of adults and children, divorce involves a sense of loss—not unlike the experience of bereavement associated with death.
- Divorce is a very confusing time for children. They may feel responsible for their parents' divorce, and they may also feel emotionally abandoned by one or both parents. Twenty-five percent of children in the United States will grow up having more than two parents.
- Moving from the family residence can create a change of schools, churches, and friendship groups. As a result, the entire social world of a child can change after divorce.
- Most research demonstrates that the adjustment of children following divorce and remarriage is strongly influenced by the nature and quality of the relationship which remains between the natural parents.
- In every adult age cohort, persons who have been married before have a higher probability of remarrying than single persons have of getting married for the first time.
- If we compare the divorce rates of remarriages to first marriages, first marriages tend to be more stable. On the other hand, if we compare the first and second marriages of given individuals, most people report a more favorable evaluation of the second marriage.

DISCUSSION QUESTIONS

1. Do 50 percent of all marriages end in divorce? Explain some of the problems in determining the percentage of marriages that end in divorce.

2. What are the factors associated with divorce? Why have we experienced an increase in divorce rates since 1970? Based on your reading of the news, what changes, if any, do you see in divorce rates since 1989?

3. How do our expectations influence marital satisfaction and divorce?

4. What is an amicable divorce? Do you think that amicable divorces are possible? If you belong to a religious group, do you think it would adopt a service for the dissolution of a marriage? Why or why not?

5. What is the difference between a "no-fault" divorce system and a fault-based system of divorce? What are the advantages of each? What are the disadvantages of our present no-fault system?

6. How are divorce and death alike? How does the bereavement process

related to death differ from adjustment to divorce? Explore these questions from the perspectives of adults *and* children.

7. What are adults' and children's major adjustment problems relative to divorce? How can adults help children to cope with divorce?

8. What factors affect the relationship between ex-spouses after divorce? How do these factors affect successful co-parenting?

9. Why do you think divorced people have a greater probability of remarrying than single people have of marrying for the first time? How successful are remarriages? What factors will affect the happiness of these marriages?

10. What are the potential problems and opportunities of blended families from the perspective of stepparents and stepchildren?

GLOSSARY

acrimony: Fighting, bickering, hostility, and bitterness between spouses, often increased as a result of divorce proceedings.

amicable divorce: A divorce in which the former spouses treat each other in a civil and/or friendly manner.

blended families: The composite families created by the marriages of formerly married persons, some of whom have children. A blended family includes stepparents, stepchildren, and natural parents.

co-parenting: Cooperation between two formerly married natural parents in the process of parenting their children.

fault-based divorce: A divorce where evidence is presented that at least one spouse has violated the marriage contract. The most common grounds for fault-based divorce are desertion, adultery, and cruelty.

legal custody: Court-mandated responsibility for the education and welfare of the child—the parent with legal custody is the child's legal guardian.

no-fault divorce: Divorce granted in all states, with the exception of South Dakota; "marriage breakdown" is the only requirement for divorce.

physical custody: Custody granted to the parent with whom the child lives.

reconstituted families: Same as blended families.

sequential monogamy: Marriage to more than one person, but only one at a time—the sequence of marriage, divorce, remarriage, divorce, and so on.

spousal support: Alimony or financial support paid to one spouse after the dissolution of the marriage. Currently spousal support is usually offered for a limited period of time or until the spouse remarries.

unilateral action: One-sided action, as is possible, under no-fault divorce laws, where one spouse can end the marriage even if the other spouse opposes this action.

SUGGESTED READINGS

Albrecht, Stan L., Howard M. Bahr, and Kristen L. Goodman. 1983. *Divorce and Remarriage: Problems, Adaptations, and Adjustments.* Westport, Conn.: Greenwood Press. *An outstanding empirical study of divorce and its effects upon families in western (intermountain) states of the United States.*

Appel, Karen W. 1985. *America's Changing Families: A Guide for Educators.* Bloomington, Ind.: Phi Delta Kappa Educational Foundation. *An excellent resource for people working with children whose parents are either divorced or remarried.*

Cherlin, Andrew J. 1981. *Marriage, Divorce, and Remarriage.* Cambridge: Harvard University Press. *A comprehensive treatment of issues related to divorce and remarriage.*

Crosby, John F. 1985. *Reply to Myth: Perspectives on Intimacy.* New York: John Wiley and Sons. *An excellent resource for those wishing to make sense out of marriage and divorce statistics provided by the U.S. government.*

Furstenberg, Frank F., Jr., and Graham B. Spanier. 1984. *Recycling the Family: Remarriage after Divorce.* Beverly Hills, Sage Publications. *A comprehensive study of the effects of remarriage following divorce.*

Wallerstein, Judith S., and Sandra Blakeslee. 1989. *Second Chances: Men, Women, and Children a Decade After Divorce.* New York: Ticknor and Fields. *A very important ten-year clinical study of the long-term effects of divorce on children and their parents.*

Weitzman, Lenore J. 1985. *The Divorce Revolution: The Unexpected Social and Economic Consequences for Women and Children in America.* New York: The Free Press. *An important study of the effects of California's no-fault divorce law on the lifestyles of parents and children following divorce.*

Death in Families

◆ *Death presents society with a formidable problem not only because of its obvious threat to the continuity of human relationships, but because it threatens the basic assumptions of order on which society rests.**

You may have noticed that every textbook concerned with marriage and the family has at least one chapter on divorce and presents it as *the* crisis in the American family, yet that few textbooks devote even as much as a few pages to the topic of death. In reality, not all families will experience divorce; yet every family will experience death. In this chapter, therefore, we will discuss the way American families respond to death, the dying process, funeral rituals, and the bereavement process. While dying is one of the most individual things that can happen to a person, with reference to the *meaning* of dying, the dying process is also one of the most profoundly social experiences undergone by individuals and their families.

DEATH IN AMERICAN CULTURE

Consider the following facts:

1. Seventy percent of all deaths take place in institutional settings—hospitals and nursing homes. Dying in the United States occurs "offstage," away from the arena of familiar surroundings of kin and friends.

---

*Peter Berger, *The Sacred Canopy* (1967): p. 23.

2. With less than 10 percent of the United States population living on farms, birth and death scenes have largely been confined to television or to the worlds of health care professionals and removed from the personal observation of most individuals.
3. The average life expectancy has increased more than twenty years since 1920.
4. The average attendance at funerals and wakes has decreased significantly during the past twenty years.

Is it any wonder that Richard Dumont and Dennis Foss (1972:2) questioned the abilities of modern Americans to cope with death, when it is experienced infrequently, is highly impersonal, and is viewed as virtually abnormal. U.S. society has done little formally to socialize its members to deal with dying and death on the personal and emotional levels.

For most of us, our most frequent experience with death comes from the evening news, as reporters attempt to bring us as close to scenes of death as availability and "good taste" will allow. However, since we are unlikely to know the people who have died, the effect of this death news upon us is minimal. Robert Kavanaugh (1972:13) makes the following observation demonstrating this problem.

> *Over a two-week period of nighttime [television] viewing, I counted an average of 34 deaths at close range, countless more at a distance. Not one death raised as much as a slight tremor in me. Television feeds our fantasy of forever being a spectator. Even a bloody nose or a fainting spell by a fellow viewer would have aroused more emotion in me than a hundred deaths on the tube.*

In the 1970s and 1980s many Americans began to look anew at death as a normal part of the life cycle. Just as the prepared childbirth movement made it possible for fathers and siblings to become helpful observers, if not active participants, in the birthing process, so too the contemporary hospice movement is attempting to promote a more human and humane approach to the dying process.

Hospice, or nonhospital terminal care, as a modern social movement began in 1967 when Dr. Cicely Saunders founded the St. Christopher's Hospice in London to care for dying patients. The contemporary hospice movement in the United States began in the early 1970s and sought the following as its primary objectives:

1. Provide medical care when medical cure is not possible.
2. Provide a social context that promotes dignity and autonomy for the dying patient and his or her family.

3. Promote open and honest communication between medical personnel, family members, and patients relative to issues of dying and death.
4. Provide pain control for patients suffering from terminal illness.
5. Provide the necessary resources for families and patients so that death can take place in the home.
6. Provide a competent professional presence so that the dying patient need not be alone when death occurs.

The hospice movement is not the only agent of socialization attempting to prepare Americans to view dying as a normal part of living. Death education in schools and religious institutions is assisting Americans to understand that a knowledge of the certainty of their death can help them live life more fully.

Explaining Death to Children

With a note of irony, Edna St. Vincent Millay (1969) calls childhood "the kingdom where nobody dies," referring to the reluctance of many adults to be open in talking to children about death. Children can and do, however, think about death and often need to talk about it. As when adults have difficulties in talking about sex with children, many adults project onto the child their own reluctance to deal openly with death. Whenever a child asks a question about death—whether of animals, other people, or himself or herself—an adult should be ready to respond in a natural and matter-of-fact way. As Robert Kastenbaum (1977) suggests, do not wait or plan "one big tell-all." Parents should be good observers of the discussion and behaviors of children related to death. They should become partners in a continuing dialogue in which death is just one of the many topics that adults and children can discuss together.

Helene Galen (1972) suggests that a parent capitalize on "the teachable moment" whenever it arises with children. It's helpful to encourage children to express fear, doubt, and curiosity, as well as to express one's own feelings concerning death. Galen lists four guidelines:

1. Ask yourself: "How would I treat this action, comment, or question if it were not about death?" The answer would usually be, "Matter-of-factly."
2. Ask: "What is this child really seeking by this action, comment, or question?" Recognize that children often act out their feelings rather than verbalizing them clearly.

3. Take care to present only basic truths about what is being asked. Total comprehension will be achieved only gradually. Give the child time to grasp the broader implications of the subject.
4. With children younger than eleven or twelve, use concrete terms such as "died, death, buried." Abstract or metaphorical terminology such as "sleep," "passed on," or "God wanted another angel" are simply confusing to the child. Euphemisms may meet the needs of adults, but can cause untold problems for children.

Ruth Formanek (1974) adds some helpful ideas. She urges teachers to explore the thoughts, associations, and feelings that the child attaches to death. We should have the following concerns: "What does the child really want to know?" "Does the child's question represent a need for reassurance, a need for information about the possibility of dying, being separated from loved ones, or being abandoned?"

Robert Kastenbaum (1977) encourages parents to remember that children are part of the family and should not be removed from the scene when the family confronts death. It may be more damaging to the child to be "protected" from death, to have to deal with the imagination's construction of what's going on, than to be given the opportunity to participate in the family's response to death. A child's sense of comfort will be strengthened by the very fact that family members are available for discussion. Kastenbaum (1977) notes that

Excluding their participation in death-related events does not protect children from death anxiety.

the expression of feelings natural to the situation (worry, sorrow, and even anger) will not harm a child but provide the child with a basis for expressing his or her own feelings and emotions.

Ruth Formanek (1974) points out that young children having difficulty dealing with the anxiety aroused by the subject or event of death may manifest the following behavioral changes: anger, regressive infantile attitudes and actions, aggression, hostility, withdrawal, or euphoria. School-age children who have lost a loved one through death may manifest the following normal bereavement responses: preoccupation with images of the deceased, a drop in school performance, guilt, strong anger, feelings of uselessness, numbness, withdrawal, and bodily distress.

The behaviors listed above are to be considered "normal" child responses to death and bereavement. However, if symptoms increase in intensity and continue over an extended period of time, the child may not have found a place or person with whom to vent his or her feelings about the subject or event of death. Some children may also need professional help.

In conclusion, Robert Kavanaugh's (1972) advice deserves consideration:

> The best and final answer lies in the abiding security of loving folks and family in an understanding and supportive home. In this atmosphere inordinate fears will usually recede or be outgrown. Only those few whose fears are prolonged and paralyzing will need professional therapy.

Death Attitudes and Death Fears

Death per se has no meaning other than that which people give it. If this is true, why is it that most of us believe that death is something that intrinsically engenders fear? Anthropologists would be quick to respond that not all cultures in the world hold that death is necessarily something to be feared. However, there seem to be a large number of cultures, including our own, which attach fearful meanings to death and death-related situations. Why is it that so many people have less than positive views of death?

Death universally calls into question the order upon which most societies are based. As a **marginal situation** (unusual event), death not only disrupts normal patterns of interaction but causes one to reflect upon the ultimate meaning of life. With the exception of those societies where death is treated as a routine event in the lives of the people (e.g., Uganda, Sudan, Cambodia, and New Guinea), death in most parts of the world is a stressful event because it brings disorder to those whose lives it touches. Any change in ordinary patterns of social interaction requires that the individual adjust. Most of us prefer the security of situations that are predictable, stable, and routine. The disorder created by changes in everyday life, such as death, can make for a stressful situation as individuals attempt to adjust to these changes (Holmes and Rahe 1967).

In the United States, too, we are systematically taught to fear death. Horror movies portray death, ghosts, skeletons, goblins, bogymen, and ghoulish morticians as things or people to be feared. "Sesame Street" tries to create a more positive image of monsters as children are befriended by Grover, Harry, Oscar, and Cookie Monster. But with the exception of Casper, "the friendly ghost," other death-related fantasy figures have not received the same positive images. Instead, our culture has chosen to reinforce fearful meanings of death. Cemeteries are portrayed as eerie, funeral homes are to be avoided, and morgues are scary places where you wouldn't be caught dead.

One of the reasons death education courses incorporate field trips to hospices, funeral homes, crematories, and cemeteries is to confront negative death meanings and fantasies with first-hand objective observations. The preparation room at the mortuary is a good example. If you have never been in one, think about the mental image that comes to your mind. For many people, the idea of the preparation room conjures up images of something not unlike Dr. Frankenstein's laboratory (complete with bats, strange lighting, body parts, and naked dead bodies). The great disappointment for most students as they walk through the door is that they find a room that looks like a physician's examination room. "Is that all there is?" is the comment often heard after visiting the preparation room.

The sociologist Erving Goffman (1959) has observed that first impressions are unlikely to change and tend to dominate the meanings related to subsequent social interaction patterns and experiences. And indeed most of us want to retain untrue fearful meanings of death, even when confronted by positive images.

In some individuals, too, fearful meanings attributed to death can arise from a traumatic death-related experience. Being a witness to a fatal car accident, discovering someone who has committed suicide, or attending a funeral where emotional outbursts create an uncomfortable environment for mourners can all increase death anxiety for individuals. Such occurrences are, however, rather uncommon for most people and do not account for the prevalence of our society's preoccupation with death fears. In a survey of college students, Robert Kavanaugh (1972) found that 78 percent had yet to see a dead person up close and more than 92 percent had yet to witness a death.

In summary, death fears are not instinctive, they exist because

U.S. culture has created and perpetuated fearful meanings and ascribed them to death. They are also a function of the fact that death is a nonordinary experience challenging the order of everyday life in society. And in some people death fears are a function of occasional first-hand encounters that—because death has become so unusual—become traumatic.

References to death fear or death anxiety can seem to suggest that death fear is unidimensional and that consensus exists relative to its meaning. Such is not the case—two persons may say that they fear death, but the content of their respective fears may be quite different.

Death anxiety (or death fear) is a multidimensional concept based upon the following four foci: (1) concern with the death of self; (2) concern with the deaths of significant others; (3) concern with the process of dying; and (4) concern with the state of being dead. Elaborating upon this model, the following eight facets of death anxiety can be applied to the death of self and the deaths of others: (1) fear of dependency; (2) fear of the pain in the dying process; (3) fear of the indignity of the dying process; (4) fear of the isolation, separation, and rejection that can be part of the dying process; (5) fear of leaving loved ones; (6) fear of what the afterlife may hold; (7) fear of the finality of death; and (8) fear of the fate of the body.

Table 15.1 shows that the content of fear will be influenced by whose death the individual is considering. From a personal death perspective, one may have anxiety over the effect that one's dying (or being dead) will have on others. There may also be private worries about how one may be treated by others—and even by God. From the perspective of the survivor, the individual may be concerned about the financial, emotional, and social problems related to the death of a significant other.

Since many factors related to the experience of death and death-related situations can engender fear, we might expect to find differences between persons with respect to the type and intensity of death fear they experience. The social circumstances and past experiences of individuals will also have differential effects upon the type and intensity of fears the persons ascribe to death. With all of the potential sources for differences, however, it is interesting that a study of over one thousand individuals yielded consistently high anxiety scores for fears of dependency and pain related to the process of dying and relatively low anxiety scores for fears related to the afterlife and the fate of the body. Approximately 65 percent of the respondents had high anxiety concerning dependency and pain, whereas only 15 percent experienced the same level of anxiety about the afterlife and the fate of the body (Leming 1979–80). Thus, it is the *process* of dying—not the *event* of death—that causes the most concern.

TABLE 15.1   The Eight Dimensions of Death Anxiety as They Relate to the Deaths of Self and Others

Self	*Others*
Process of Dying	
1. Fear of dependency	Fear of financial burdens
2. Fear of pain in dying process	Fear of going through the painful experience of others
3. Fear of the indignity in dying process	Fear of being unable to cope with the physical problems of others
4. Fear of loneliness, rejection, and isolation	Fear of being unable to cope emotionally with problems of others
5. Fear of leaving loved ones	Fear of losing loved ones
State of Being Dead	
6. Afterlife concerns	Afterlife concerns
Fear of an unknown situation	Fear of the judgment of others— "What are they thinking?"
Fear of divine judgment	
Fear of the spirit world	Fear of ghosts, spirits, devils, etc.
Fear of nothingness	Fear of never seeing the person again
7. Fear of the finality of death	Fear of the end of a relationship
Fear of not being able to achieve one's goals	Guilt related to not having done enough for the deceased
Fear of the possible end of physical and symbolic identity	Fear of not seeing the person again
Fear of the end of all social relationships	Fear of losing the social relationship
8. Fear of the fate of the body	Fear of death objects
Fear of body decomposition	Fear of dead bodies
Fear of being buried	Fear of being in cemeteries
Fear of not being treated with respect	Fear of not knowing how to act in death-related situations

THE AMERICAN WAY OF DYING

Most Americans, then, fear the process of dying much more than they do the fact that at some point in time they will be dead. Woody Allen once said, "I'm not afraid of dying. I just don't want to be there when it happens." The nature of our dying will depend to a great extent upon the nature of the cause of the death and the social context in which the dying takes place.

Ask a few people the following question: "When your time comes, how would you wish to die?" With the exception of comics who will reply, "When I am ninety-two, at the hands of a jealous lover," most people will respond, "At home, unexpectedly, in my own bed, when I am asleep, and when I am very old—but with my full mental and physical capabilities." Unfortunately, most of us will not die as we would like, and for some this may be a source of apprehension and anxiety. Most Americans will die in institutionalized settings and not at home as they would like. A small percentage of persons die of **acute illnesses** (rapid-onset diseases like scarlet fever), while most (76 percent) will die of one of the following **chronic illnesses,** or long-term conditions: cardiovascular disease, cancer, AIDS, diabetes, or diseases of the liver, kidney, or lung. With these chronic diseases, deaths are usually prolonged and are anything but sudden and unexpected as most people desire.

Human beings do not respond to all deaths in the same manner; humans ascribe meanings to death and then respond to these meanings. The American way of dying places higher values on some causes of deaths and ascribes less status to other causes. Likewise, a person's ability to cope with the death of a loved one will be influenced by the cause of the death.

While there are some special problems associated with deaths caused by a chronic disease (e.g., heart disease, cancer, or diabetes), there are some real advantages also. The following is a partial list of the opportunities provided by a slow death from chronic disease:

1. The dying person is given an opportunity to attend to unfinished business—make out a will, finish up projects.
2. The dying person and his or her family can attempt to heal broken family relationships, they can say their final farewells, and they can all participate in preparing for a meaningful and dignified death.
3. Funeral and other arrangements can be made with the consent and participation of the person who is dying.
4. Anticipatory grief on the part of the survivors and dying patient can take place.

Deaths due to acute diseases (e.g., pneumonia), accidents, and suicide also provide special problems and advantages to survivors. In a quick death there is the problem that both the dying person and the survivors are unprepared for the death. Some of the grieving preceding the death due to a chronic disease cannot be expressed in deaths of this type. Consequently, grief is usually more intense when the dying takes place in a short period of time. Survivors may also experience more intense guilt—"If only I had done something, she wouldn't have died." Suicide creates special problems for survivors because in addition to feeling guilt they often fear being stigmatized by having a relative commit suicide—"They drove him to it." Finally, when people die without warning, survivors often are troubled because they did not have a chance to mend a broken relationship or say goodbye.

On the other hand, survivors of deaths due to acute diseases, accidents, and suicide are spared the following problems associated with chronic diseases:

1. Dying persons may not be willing to accept death, and when learning of their fates, may act in unacceptable ways.
2. Families may also be unwilling to accept the impending death of a loved one and may respond inappropriately.
3. The dying process may be long and painful, not only for the dying patient, but for the family as well.
4. The cost of dying from a chronic disease can be, and usually is, very high. The entire assets of a family can be wiped out by the medical bills of a chronically ill patient.

The Dying Process

When we think about someone who is dying, the first thing that comes to our awareness is the concept of time. We are confronted with the fact that time, for the terminal patient, is running out. Yet when does the dying process begin? From the moment of our births, we are approaching the end of our lives. We assume that terminal patients will experience death before nondying individuals, although this is not always the case. Still, since it is possible to diagnose diseases from which most people die, we assume that patients with these diseases are "more terminal" than individuals without them. The terminal patient is very much concerned with the time dimension of his or her physical existence. Many surveys (see Glaser and Strauss 1965) have demonstrated that as many as 80 percent of patients want to be told if their illness is terminal. However, doctors are not always prepared to tell their patients of a terminal diagnosis.

Even when the patient has not been told of a terminal condition, he or she will eventually become aware of it. Many times factors related to social space will give the patient clues that the condition is terminal. Within the hospital, for instance, there are areas where the very ill are treated. When a patient is placed in the intensive care unit or on an oncology (cancer) ward, it becomes obvious that all is not well and that death is a real possibility.

Confinement to a health care institution conveys a tremendous amount of meaning to the patient. For the most part, he or she is alone. The spatial setting tells the patient that he or she is removed from the things giving life meaning and purpose—family, friends, and job. For the terminally ill patient, this is the first stage of social disengagement.

Some of the most beautiful human interactions I have witnessed have occurred between dying patients and supportive families. Sometimes the quality of human interactions in the terminal phase far exceeds anything the patient or family experienced prior to diagnosis.

I strongly feel the dying patient should be told as much as he or she wants to know. The family should also be encouraged to share feelings with the patient in an open manner. *Nothing* is worse than dying alone. The terminal patient whose family won't broach the subject, or who is afraid to upset his or her family or doctors with fears and feelings, *does* die alone.

Source: George E. Dickinson and A. A. Pearson, "Sex Differences of Physicians in Relating to Dying Patients," *Journal of the American Medical Women's Association* 34 (1979), physician's comment.

Social space is very important in the process of patient **disengagement,** or withdrawal. This disengagement can come about through two avenues—the patient can withdraw from others and others can withdraw from the patient. If the patient is debilitated by illness, he or she may not have the energy to continue normal patterns of social interaction. The loss of physical attractiveness can also cause the patient to withdraw. Some patients, knowing that they are terminal, may disengage as a coping strategy to avoid having to see all that their death will take from them. They may also disengage as a sign of their acceptance of social death—"I'm as good as dead" (anticipatory death).

The primary way individuals disengage themselves from society is by relinquishing social **roles,** or expected behaviors. Role disengagement has many consequences for the patient as well as for his or her family members. N. J. Gaspard (1970:78) notes:

> *If the father is ill, the mother must generally become the breadwinner, and children who are able often must take over household tasks sooner than they otherwise might. Each person in such a situation may feel both guilt and resentment at such a change whereby they can no longer adequately fulfill the expectations they have had of themselves. Conversely, if the mother is ill, household help may be hired, and problems may arise with regard to the mother's maintaining, in so far as is possible, her self-image in relation to caring for her family.*

Patient disengagement will also take place when persons significant to the patient withdraw. In this situation the process of disengagement is something beyond the patient's control. Family members and friends can refrain from visiting the patient as a sign of their acceptance of social death. The "terminal" label can stigmatize the patient, and others may treat the individual differently.

In addition to entering into the disengagement process, patients are expected to acquire the sick role (Parsons 1951). As part of this role they are expected to want to get better—to want to seek more treatment—even though everyone realizes that such treatment only prolongs death and not life. This role can create conflict within the family, especially when the patient has accepted his or her death (and even longs for it), while family members are unwilling to let the patient go. As Elizabeth Kubler-Ross, in her best-selling book *On Death and Dying* (1969), documents, families often cannot comprehend that a patient reaches a point when death comes as a great relief, and that patients die more easily if they are allowed and helped to detach themselves slowly from all the responsibilities and meaningful relationships in their lives.

Many patients defined as having a terminal condition begin to view themselves as being "as good as dead." They have accepted the terminal label, have applied it to their understanding of who they are, and have experienced anticipatory death. Families also come to see themselves as being in bereavement. This symbolic definition of the patient is reinforced by the role disengagement process, the spatial isolation of the dying patient, and the terminal label placed upon the patient by the physician and other medical personnel. The patient

When I say I feel as comfortable with a dying patient as with any other, and that I do not find treating a dying patient unpleasant, I do not mean that I am anaesthetized to the fact that they are dying, and do not have feelings about that patient which are different from my feelings about a patient whom I know will get well. Anaesthesion of feeling is the method which we physicians employ initially in dealing with the pain—ours and theirs—involved in treating a dying patient. But this passes, and when one accepts the patient as part of life, and not someone who is no longer a real part of the world (or a frightening part of the world), then caring for the dying patient becomes (though often sad) neither unpleasant nor something one wishes to avoid. To abandon the dying patient is the *worst* thing that can be done—both for the patient and the doctor.

Source: A physician's comment on a survey of 1,093 physicians conducted by George E. Dickinson and A. A. Pearson, 1980–81.

seems to take on a status somewhere between the living and the dead.

Kubler-Ross (1969:116) says that the terminally ill have a need to detach themselves from the living to make dying easier. The following example illustrates this point:

> *She asked to be allowed to die in peace, wished to be left alone—even asked for less involvement on the part of her husband. She said that the only reason that kept her still alive was her husband's inability to accept the fact that she had to die. She was angry at him for not facing it and for so desperately clinging on to something that she was willing and ready to give up. I translated to her that she wished to detach herself from this world, and she nodded gratefully as I left her alone.*

When an individual's condition has been defined by self and others as terminal, all other self meanings take on less importance. While a given patient may be a lawyer, Democrat, mother, wife, Episcopalian, etc., she tends to think of herself primarily as a terminal patient. The terminal label, in this instance, is what sociologists refer to as a **master status** because it dominates all other status indicators. Consequently, most of the symbolic meanings we have previously explored become incorporated into the individual's self-meaning.

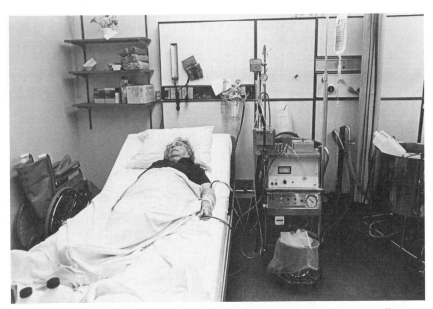

Sometimes it is difficult to remember that a terminal patient is also a mother, worker, and community volunteer.

Acquiring the terminal label as part of the self-definition is not an easy task for the individual. Elizabeth Kubler-Ross (1969) delineated the following five stages patients go through in accepting their terminal self-meaning: *denial, anger, bargaining, depression, and acceptance.*

In the first stage the patient attempts to deny that his or her condition is fatal. The patient may seek additional medical advice in hope that the terminal diagnosis will be proven false. When the diagnosis is verified, the patient may often retreat into self-imposed isolation. The second stage—anger—is a natural reaction for most patients. The patient may vent anger at various individuals—at the doctor because he or she is not doing enough, at relatives because they will outlive the patient, at other patients because their condition is not terminal, and at God for allowing the patient to die.

When the individual has begun to incorporate the terminal label into his or her self-meaning, he or she may attempt to bargain for a little more time. There may be promises made to God in exchange for an extension of life, followed by the wish for a few days without pain or physical discomfort. This bargaining always includes an implicit promise that the patient will not ask for more if the one postponement is granted. That promise is very rarely if ever kept, according to Kubler-Ross (1969:84).

The fourth stage is one of depression. The patient begins to realize that with death approaching he or she will lose the valued things of life—family, physical appearance, personal accomplishments, and often a sense of dignity.

In the final stage, the patient accepts death as a sure outcome. This acceptance, while not happy, is not terribly sad either. The patient is able to say, "I have said all of the words that have to be said. I am ready to go."

The Care of the Dying Patient

No matter how we measure his or her worth, a dying human being deserves more than efficient care from strangers, more than machines and septic hands, more than a mouth full of pills, arms full of tubes and a rump full of needles. Simple dignity as a human should merit more than furtive eyes, reluctant hugs, medical jargon, ritual sacraments or tired Bible quotes, more than all the phony promises for a tomorrow that will never come. We have become lost in the jungle of ritual surrounding death.

Source: Robert E. Kavanaugh, *Facing Death* (Baltimore: Penguin Books, 1972), p. 6.

As the dying patient comes to grips with the terminal condition, the way he or she defines the social situation will have a tremendous impact upon the process of dying. If the patient views the hospital as a supportive environment, he or she may cope better. On the other hand, if the patient feels all alone in this place of confinement and defines the hospital as a foreign place, personal adjustment to dying and death will be hindered.

Like all other meaning systems, the definition of the social situation is an attempt by the individual to bring order to his or her world. Since situational meaning always involves selective perception, the terminal patient creates the meaning for the social environment and responds to this meaning and not to the environment itself. Each terminal patient, then, not only experiences death in a different environment but has a unique interpretation of the social situation. This accounts for the different experiences of dying patients. The hospice movement is an attempt to create a positive and supportive social situation in which dying can take place.

THE CONTEMPORARY FUNERAL

Most anthropologists agree that no civilization yet discovered has not in some form given evidence of a **funeralization** process. This process varies greatly from culture to culture, but the basic elements of the recognition of the death—a rite or ritual and the final **disposition** or placement of the body—have their manifestations in every culture. Funeral **rituals,** or culturally prescribed sets of actions, allow individuals of every culture to maintain relations with ancestors while uniting family members, reinforcing social status, fostering group cohesiveness, and restoring the social structure of the society.

Since in the United States most deaths occur in hospitals or institutions for the care of the sick and infirm, the contemporary process of body disposition begins at the time of death when the body is removed from the institutional setting. Most frequently the body is taken to a funeral home. There, the body is bathed and undergoes an **embalming** or preserving treatment. It is then dressed and placed in a casket selected by the family. Typically, arrangements are made for the ceremony, assuming a ceremony is to follow. The funeral director, in consultation with the family, determines the type, time, place, and day of the ceremony. In most instances, this is a public rite or ceremony with a religious content (Pine 1971). The procedure described above is followed in approximately 75 percent of funerals in the United States.

Following the funeral ceremony, final disposition of the body occurs: burial (85 percent), **cremation** or burning (10 percent), or

entombment or placement in a crypt (5 percent). These percentages are approximate national averages and vary by geographical region.

Paul Irion (1954) has described the following needs of the bereaved: the need for reality, the need for expression of grief, the need for social support, and the need to place the death in a context of meaning. For Irion, the funeral is an experience of significant personal value insofar as it meets the religious, social, and psychological needs of the mourners. Fulfillment of each of these needs is necessary to help bereaved individuals return to everyday living and, in the process, resolve their grief.

Alternatives to the Funeral

People often ask if there are less costly alternatives to the typical conventional, traditional funeral described above. There are primarily three alternatives to the funeral: the immediate disposition of the body of the deceased, the bequest of the deceased to a medical institution for anatomical study and research, and the memorial service.

In immediate disposition, the body of the deceased is removed from the place of death, proper certificates are filed and permits received, and the body is disposed of by cremation or earth burial without any ceremony. In these instances, the family is not present, usually does not view the deceased after death, and is not concerned with any further type of memorialization. Disposition is immediate in that it takes place as quickly after death as is possible. In this situation, the body will probably not be embalmed, and the only preparation will consist of washing the body.

Body bequest programs have become more well known since about 1960 and permit the deceased (prior to death) or the family (after the death) to donate the body to a medical institution. A "Compendium on Body Donation" (National Funeral Directors Association 1981) indicates that when the family desires, 75 percent of donee institutions permit a funeral to be held prior to the delivery of the body to the institution for study or research. Some medical schools will also pay the cost of transporting the body to the medical school; others will not. This is the least expensive way of disposition of the body, especially if a memorial service is conducted without the body present. The "Compendium" also indicates that in almost every instance the family may request that either the residue of the body or the cremated remains be returned when the body is of no further benefit to the donee. Or if the family does not desire to have the body or the cremated remains returned, the donee institution will arrange for cremation and/or earth burial—often with an appropriate ceremony. People who are considering donating their bodies should be

The Vietnam memorial is visited by more Americans than any other national monument in Washington, D.C. It is a place where people can go to remember loved ones who have given their lives for their country.

aware of the fact that at the time of death a specified donee institution may not have need of a body. If this does happen, the family will have to find another institution or make other arrangements for the disposition of the body.

The memorial service is defined as a service without the body present. In one sense, of course, every funeral is a memorial service—inasmuch as it is in memory of someone—but a memorial service as such is an alternative to the typical funeral with casket and burial. A memorial service may be conducted on the day of the death, within two or three days of the death, or sometimes as much as weeks or months following the death. The content of the service places little or no emphasis on the death. Instead, it is often a service of acclamation of philosophical concepts or celebration of the life of the deceased. These services may be religious or nonreligious in content. It is obvious that this type of service can meet the needs of the bereaved.

There are consumer organizations called **memorial societies.** An example of a memorial society is the one in Ithaca, New York. The by-laws of this particular nonprofit and nonsectarian organization state the following as the purposes of the society:

1. To promote the dignity, simplicity, and spiritual values of funeral rites and memorial services.

2. To facilitate simple disposal of deceased persons at reasonable costs, but with adequate allowances to funeral directors for high quality services.
3. To increase the opportunity for each person to determine the type of funeral or memorial service he or she desires.
4. To aid its members and promote their interests in achieving the above.

THE BEREAVEMENT PROCESS

If at the conclusion of the funeral service grief work were finished, the process of reintegration of the bereaved into society would be completed. The funeral service and the final disposition of the dead only mark the end of public mourning; however, private mourning continues for some time, involving a period of postfuneral adjustment for the family. While it certainly will vary with individual cases, Glen Davidson (1975) suggests that the grief process will take from eighteen to twenty-four months. The grief process will likely last at least one year, since the bereaved have to experience every anniversary, holiday, and special event once without the person who has died. However, Davidson would point out that grief is never completely resolved but remains with an individual throughout his or her lifetime.

Folk wisdom would contend that "time heals"—with the intensity of grief diminishing over time. A more accurate picture of mourning, however, would indicate that while time intervals between intense experiences of grief increase with the passing of time, it is not abnormal to experience periods of mourning for losses that occurred many years before. What is abnormal behavior, from the perspective of the American bereavement role, is preoccupation with the death of the loved one and refusal to make attempts to return to normal social functioning. Examples of deviant behavior of this type include the following:

1. Malingering in the bereavement role and memorializing the deceased by refusing to dispose of articles of clothing or personal effects and living as if one expected the dead to reappear.
2. Rejecting attempts from others who offer social and emotional support, refusing to seek professional counseling, and taking up permanent residence in "Pity City."
3. Rejecting public funeral rituals and requesting that the funeral functionaries merely pick up the body and dispose of it through cremation without any public acknowledgment of the death that has occurred.

Behaviors such as these are usually sanctioned by others through social avoidance, ostracism, and criticism. As a consequence, most people are not only encouraged but forced to move through the grieving process.

The grieving process, like the dying process, is essentially a series of behaviors and attitudes related to coping with the stress of changing the status of a relationship. Not only Kubler-Ross but many other psychologists have attempted to understand coping as a series of universal, mutually exclusive, and linear stages. However, since most observers acknowledge that not all people progress through the

The Loss of a Significant Person

The loss of a significant person can be one of life's most devastating experiences. Yet, every human relationship is destined to end in loss. Loss is the price paid for relationships that insure survival and participation in the human experience.

The death of a loved one is, of course, the ultimate loss. Death is final and complete. But many little deaths are suffered by all of us along the way. Divorce, desertion, separation, abortion, stillbirth, and rejection mean losses of significant people. Jobs, military service, travel, and geographic moves also take us away from important others. So does placing the aged, mentally retarded, emotionally ill, criminal and delinquent, and putting dependent and neglected children up for adoption or foster care. Further, illness, accidents, and aging can change a loved one so drastically that the person we once knew is gone.

From infancy on our lives are bound up with those of others. We are social beings whose very existence depends on attachment to others. The loss of such an attachment can feel like a threat to life itself. That is not to say that all close ties are ties of love. Love and hate are closely interwoven, and every relationship has some of both. Ambivalence is the essence of every relationship. Whether the relationship is weighted toward positive or negative feelings, however, it has to end. No matter how much we love someone we cannot keep that person alive forever or at our side forever. So loved ones die or go away, and those who are more hated than loved do also, and sometimes we get rid of those whom we do not love in other ways. Such losses bring their own kind of pain because we have had a say in them.

Source: Bertha G. Simos, *A Time to Grieve: Loss as a Universal Human Experience* (New York: Family Service Association of America, 1979), pp. 10 and 11.

Bereavement behavior involves a process of adjustment including denial, disorganization, anger, guilt, loneliness, and reestablishment.

stages in the same order or in the same manner, it might be more appropriate to list a range of coping strategies used to resolve the pain caused by the loss of a personally significant relationship. For example, as mentioned in chapter 14, Robert Kavanaugh (1972) identifies seven behaviors and feelings as part of the coping process: shock and denial, disorganization, volatile emotions, guilt, loss and loneliness, relief, and reestablishment. It is not difficult to see similarities between these behaviors and Elizabeth Kubler-Ross's five stages of the dying process.

As a grieving person moves toward reestablishment of a life without the deceased, it is obvious that the process involves extensive adjustment and time, especially if the relationship was one of deep emotional involvement. It is likely that in bereavement feelings of loneliness, guilt, and disorganization may all come at the same time, and that just when a person begins to experience a sense of relief, something may happen to trigger a denial of the death which has occurred.

Knowing that bereavement and adjustment are normal to the coping process facilitates the experience of these feelings. Ultimately, hope (holding the person together in fantasy at first) provides the survivor with the promise of a new life filled with order, purpose, and meaning.

CHAPTER REVIEW

- The American way of dying is typically confined to institutional settings and removed from usual patterns of social interaction.
- American society has done little formally to socialize its members to deal with dying and death on the personal and emotional levels.
- The manner in which an individual dies will influence the way in which his or her survivors cope with the death. Chronic and acute diseases have advantages and disadvantages for the coping abilities of dying patients and their families.
- Death fears exist because cultures create and perpetuate fearful meanings and ascribe them to death.
- Death anxiety is a multidimensional concept with the *process* of dying rather than the *event* of death causing the most concern.
- A dying patient may go through stages in accepting his or her terminal self-meaning.
- The meaning of dying is dependent upon the social context in which it takes place.
- Within the contemporary funeralization process, final disposition of the body is made by either burial (85 percent), cremation (10 percent), or entombment (5 percent). These percentages are approximate national averages.
- Alternatives to funerals include immediate disposition, body donation, and memorial services.
- The grieving process is similar to the dying process in that it is a series of behaviors and attitudes related to coping with the stress of changing the status of a relationship.
- Abnormal bereavement behavior includes preoccupation with the death of the loved one and refusal to attempt returning to normal social functioning.
- It is important in grieving to let feelings emerge into consciousness and not to be afraid to express feelings of sadness.

DISCUSSION QUESTIONS

1. How do most Americans die and how has the experience of dying contributed to the American avoidance of death and dying?
2. In what ways can children be prepared for death?
3. Should children be told that someday they will die?

4. List some of the guidelines discussed in this chapter on how to talk to children about death. Do you agree or disagree with these guidelines?
5. Compare and contrast the relative advantages and disadvantages of dying from acute and chronic diseases. What effects do each of these causes have on the abilities of families to cope with the death of a family member?
6. What is meant by death fear or death anxiety? Why is this concept multidimensional rather than unidimensional?
7. What types of death fears are the most salient for Americans? How might you explain why these fears are more intense than some other fears?
8. What does it mean to you to say that for an individual the meaning of dying depends upon the social context in which his or her dying takes place?
9. You have just been told that you have inoperable cancer. Discuss how you think you would react. In what ways might you change your life?
10. What would be your choice of final disposition of your body? Why would you choose this method, and what effects might this choice have upon your survivors (if any)?
11. Describe how the funeralization process can assist survivors in coping with grief and facilitate the bereavement process.

GLOSSARY

acute illness: A disease caused by any of a number of microorganisms including viruses, fungi, and bacteria. Acute illnesses last for a relatively short period of time and result in either a cure or death. Examples of acute illnesses include smallpox, malaria, cholera, influenza, and pneumonia.

chronic illness: A disease from which the individual rarely recovers, even though the symptoms of the disease can often be alleviated. Chronic illnesses usually result in deterioration of organs and tissues, making the individual vulnerable to other diseases, often leading to serious impairment and even death. Examples of chronic illnesses include cancer, heart disease, arthritis, emphysema, and asthma.

cremation: The reduction of human remains by means of heat or direct flame. The cremated remains of an adult are called "cremains" or "ashes" and weigh between six and eight pounds. "Ashes" is a very poor description of the cremated remains because they look more like crushed rock or pumice.

death anxiety: A learned emotional response to death-related phenomena, characterized by extreme apprehension. In this chapter the term "death anxiety" is used synonymously with "death fear."

disengagement: The process by which an individual withdraws from society or by which society withdraws from or no longer seeks the individual's participation.

disposition: Final placement or disposal of the body of a dead person.

embalming: A process that temporarily preserves the deceased by means of displacing body fluids with preserving chemicals.

entombment: Opening and closing of a crypt, including the placement and sealing of a casket within.

funeralization: A process involving activities, rites, and rituals associated with the final disposition of the deceased's body.

hospice: An alternative care program that serves patients with illnesses such as cancer during the last days of their lives.

marginal situations: Unusual events or social circumstances not occurring in normal patterns of social interaction.

master status: The status (position) that dominates all other statuses in the mind of an individual.

memorial society: A group of people joined together to promote dignity, simplicity, and economy in funeral arrangements through advance planning.

rituals: A set of culturally prescribed actions or behaviors.

role: Specified behavior expected of persons occupying specific social positions.

SUGGESTED READINGS

Kavanaugh, Robert E. 1972. *Facing Death.* Baltimore: Penguin Books. *An important early book in the thanatology movement, which suggests that a realistic consciousness of death can contribute to a more meaningful and peaceful life.*

Kubler-Ross, Elizabeth. 1969. *On Death and Dying.* New York: Macmillan. *Kubler-Ross elaborates on the five common emotional stages observed in her work with terminal patients. She concludes that if relatives and hospital personnel are unable to deal with death in their own lives, they will be unable to face death calmly and helpfully with the patient.*

Leming, Michael R., and George E. Dickinson. 1990. *Understanding Dying, Death, and Bereavement.* (Second Edition) Ft. Worth, Tex. Holt, Rinehart, and Winston. *Provides readers with information necessary both to understand and to cope with the social and psychological impact of dying, death, and bereavement.*

Le Shan, Eda. 1976. *Learning to Say Good-By: When a Parent Dies.* New York: Macmillan. *An excellent book with a very helpful reading list for children, parents, and teachers. Aimed at a teen audience, yet helpful even for young adults and parents as a model for explaining death to teenagers.*

Maryland Center for Public Broadcasting. 1977. *The Last Rights: Funerals.* Owings Mills: Maryland Center for Public Broadcasting. *A detailed report describing funerals, burials, and alternatives, including memorial societies, cremations, and organ donations. Discusses issues of cost and specific steps to be considered in burying the dead.*

Worden, J. William. 1982. *Grief Counseling and Grief Therapy.* New York: Springer Publishing Company. *A great practical guide for lay and professional people dealing with the needs of bereaved family members. The book discusses four tasks of mourning and how to assist people in accomplishing them.*

16

Family Violence

♦ *Family violence. . . can be likened to a cancer, which is part of an organism but which at the same time fatally corrupts and destroys its host.* *

Family violence is not new to the scene of American families. Since the early 1970s, however, much has been said and written about this topic. We now have nationwide task forces on domestic violence and over seven hundred shelters for abused women. Legislation exists to protect abused children, battered spouses, and vulnerable adults; a growing number of states also have marital rape, elder abuse, and warrantless arrest laws (Steinmetz 1986:51).

If one accepts the definition of violence as an act carried out with the intention of physically hurting another person, then such actions as spanking a child for a violation of a cultural norm is a form of violence. The intent to hurt stems from sources ranging from concern for a child's safety—as when a parent spanks a child for running in front of a car—to hostility so great that death is desired (Steinmetz 1986:52).

Corporal punishment (physical punishment) of a child through spanking, pinching, thumping, hitting, or slapping may not be considered "violence" by some, but if the intent is to hurt the person physically, such action fits the definition of violence offered above. As we noted in Chapter 11, some societies simply do not tolerate such behavior.

Determining the frequency of **family violence**, or violence directed at family members, is not an easy assignment because of

---

*William A. Stacey and Anson Shupe, *The Family Secret: Domestic Violence in America* (Boston: Beacon Press, 1983), p. xv.

the variable and frequently imprecise definitions used and because of statistical reporting of data that leaves much to be desired. Richard Gelles (1985:2) studied 2,143 American families in 1976 to determine the extent of violence in these families. The interviewers first discussed the issue calmly, gradually worked into more "difficult" questions like asking if the respondents slapped or spanked, then finally inquired about how often a knife or a gun was threatened or used on the individual. From the responses obtained in the survey sample, it was projected that in the United States approximately 50,000 parents use knives or guns on their children each year. Nearly half a million parents have used knives or guns on their children while raising them. A knife or gun was used by 175,000 individuals against a sibling in the previous year. Some 100,000 husbands and wives use guns and knives against one another in a year.

From a feminist perspective, it is not surprising that violence exists in the family, since patterns of inequality and conflict exist between husbands and wives. Shulamith Firestone (1970:130) argued that love between the sexes is "complicated, corrupted, or obstructed by an unequal balance of power." The least powerful members of families—children and women—are the most likely victims of violence.

As Barrie Thorne (1982:14) notes, however, women are not passive victims. They often resist men's control and develop their own forms of power and means of struggle. Like members of dominant races or social classes in racial or class conflict, men are often unaware of how much the social structure yields advantages for them in the battle of the sexes. Therefore, even though there's no real threat to their power, men often view women's efforts at resistance as a major menace—and often react with still more violence.

Violence in families is an expression of the stresses latent in the heterogeneity within families. Family members in individual families experience family violence in different ways. This chapter will consider violence in American families. We will specifically look at child abuse, parent abuse, spouse abuse, elder abuse, and sexual abuse. We will also examine some of the sociological explanations for these forms of abuse.

CHILD ABUSE

While **infanticide** (the intentional killing of newborn children) is fairly uncommon in the world today, in earlier times such behavior was widely accepted and practiced (Radbill 1980:3). Infants could be killed because they cried too much, because the family was getting too large, because a child was sickly or deformed, because of some perceived imperfection, because of illegitimacy, because the mother was unable to produce enough milk if an older child was still suckling at the breast, or because the father wanted a boy but the newborn was female. For cultures historically practicing infanticide, for example the Yanomamo in South America and the Bushmen in Africa, these were "practical" reasons, and death normally occurred very soon after birth.

Violence and abuse of children has not been limited to infanticide, however (Gelles and Cornell 1985:28). From ancient times to colonial America, mutilation, violence, and abuse were not only condoned but frequently mandated as appropriate ways of raising children. Puritan parents in colonial America were exhorted to "beat the devil" out of their children. By the end of the 1960s, however, all fifty states had passed laws requiring health care professionals to report suspected cases of child abuse. In 1974 the federal government passed the Child Abuse Prevention Act establishing the National Center on Child Abuse and Neglect (Gelles and Cornell 1985:30).

Spanking children is probably the most common form of family violence in the United States. Spanking has been reported to occur in 84 to 97 percent of all families (Lystad 1986:56). Main objectives of spanking or hitting a child are to teach a lesson, to discipline the child, or perhaps to relieve a parent's own pent-up frustration. As noted in chapter 11, a spanking in public is often the result of parental embarrassment because of a child's behavior; spanking the child in front of others tells the world that the parent does not condone such behavior. Thus, the perceived social pressure is such that it is "okay" to spank a child in public; by extension, according to this line of thought, physical violence is an acceptable way to correct a child and keep him or her in line.

As for spankings administered to relieve a parent's pent-up frustrations, there are certainly more constructive forms of tension release than hitting children—for example, working out with a punching bag, jogging or running, taking a very cold or very hot shower, or simply going for a long walk. Such behavior is much better for the adult's health, to say nothing of the physical and mental health of the child.

The Extent of Child Abuse

Determining the extent of child abuse and violence toward children in the United States is a difficult task, as such behavior often goes unreported. A national survey (Straus, Gelles, and Steinmetz 1980) of family violence toward children between ages three and seventeen revealed that more than 80 percent of the three- to nine-year-olds,

67 percent of the preteens and young teenagers, and more than 33 percent of fifteen- to seventeen-year-olds were hit at least once in the course of each year. Within the year preceding the survey, 58 percent of the parents slapped or spanked their child, 32 percent pushed, grabbed, or shoved their child, 19 percent hit their child with something or threw something at their child, and 3 percent kicked, bit, or punched their child. A small child has more chance of being killed or severely injured by his or her parents than by anyone else. Consequently, the home is likely to be one of the most dangerous places for children.

Child Abusers

Just who are these child abusers? Mothers are more likely to abuse their children than fathers (Gelles and Cornell 1985:55–57). Mothers are more likely to be the abusers of young children, whereas fathers are more likely to be the abusers of children in their teen years. The differences by sex are not great, however, and factors other than gender are likely to contribute. For example, mothers tend to spend more time with children, especially younger children. Mothers have traditionally been considered more responsible for the children's behavior than fathers.

Young adults are more likely to abuse their children than older parents. Stressful situations such as the birth of a new baby, illness, and/or death are all linked to higher rates of abuse and violence. Abusive parents tend to be socially isolated from both formal and informal social networks. Persons who were abused as children tend to be abusers themselves. Abusive families are likely, too, to have the following characteristics (Garbarino and Gilliam 1980:31): (1) stress in the parents' lives, such as economic problems; (2) especially needy or demanding children; (3) parents with unrealistic expectations about their role; and (4) parents with limited opportunities to learn the role of caretaker.

Reports of Abuse of Children on Rise

From broken hearts to broken bones, more than 2 million children were abused and neglected across the United States last year. Three died every day. Even more alarming, reports of child abuse have increased by 223 percent over 10 years, according to the National Committee for the Prevention of Child Abuse, a non-profit, Chicago-based organization with 67 chapters.

The case numbers rose from 669,000 in 1976 to 2,160,000 in 1986, although some experts say some part of the increase is due to heightened public awareness and state laws that make reporting mandatory. Tragically, too many abuse cases slip past the social agencies meant to protect such children.

Two recent cases in Massachusetts underscore the agencies' limitations: In one, a toddler who had already survived two fractured skulls was returned to her parents because an agency had not told the hearing judge that assault charges were pending against them; in the other, despite the best efforts of social workers, an alcoholic mother allowed her twin daughters to starve to death.

Child abuse ranges from a lack of affection to death. Based on incomplete surveys and projections, the National Committee for the Prevention of Child Abuse estimated that 1,132 children died of abuse last year. But Cindy Moelis, a research analyst for the committee, said the number could be as high as 5,000. "Many deaths are often attributed to other causes such as sudden infant death syndrome but are suspected to have been caused by child abuse," said Ms. Moelis.

According to recent committee findings, at least 25 percent of the fatal cases had previously been referred to authorities but fell through the cracks because there wasn't enough coordination between agencies. Ms. Moelis said authorities are so overwhelmed by their workload that "it's very difficult to assess which families are most at risk of seriously harming their child."

In about half the cases, abuse takes the form of physical neglect, according to a 1984 report from the American Association for Protecting Children, based in Denver. Children are not properly fed, clothed or given medical care. An additional 25 percent are physically abused, 14 percent are sexually assaulted and 10 percent suffer emotional abuse such as unreasonable parental demands or lack of caring. In 85 percent of the cases, the abusers are the parents.

Many states are trying to deal more effectively with child abuse. Thirty-two states have review committees to examine child abuse deaths. Fifteen states are trying to find better ways to flag the greatest risk cases. Six states have passed or proposed legislation to toughen sentences for abusers who kill children.

Source: Associated Press, *News and Courier* (Charleston, S.C., May 1, 1988), p. 40-G.

The Abused Child

Who are the abused? The very youngest children seem to be at the greatest risk of being abused (Gelles and Cornell 1985:54). Social workers have evoked the typical scene—a tired and headachy young mother in a cramped apartment, a hot day, a whining three-year-old, and now the new baby cries and cries until she starts hitting it and can't stop. Young children are physically more fragile and their vulnerability makes them more likely to be reported and diagnosed as abused when injured. Older children are underreported as victims of abuse; they may be considered delinquent and thus thought of as contributing to their own victimization. Younger boys are more likely to be abused than older boys, but older girls are more likely to be victimized than younger girls. Also, premature, handicapped, retarded, or developmentally disabled children are all at greater risk of being abused by their parents or caretakers.

Thus, from spanking to homicide, children in America seem to experience much physical abuse, and this abuse overwhelmingly comes from the child's family, not from strangers. We need to remember that children are people too. They happen to be smaller and more vulnerable than adults, but nonetheless they are people. As my daughter reminded me when she was about eight years old, "kid power" is something to respect. Kids too have rights, and need to receive humane treatment like other members of the human race.

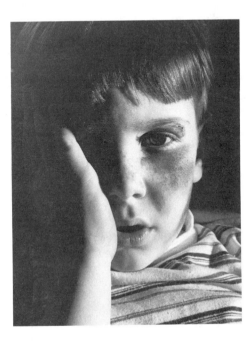

Statistics on child abuse within the family are often difficult to determine since such behavior often goes unreported.

PARENT ABUSE

Most researchers agree that about 10 percent of children abuse their parents (Gelles and Cornell 1985:98). With parents being in a position of control of family resources and generally larger in physical size than their children, and with greater social disapproval of children using violence against a parent than of a parent using violence against their children, one does not typically think that children are in a position to injure their parents. Since many parents are ashamed of their own victimization, reporting of children abusing their parents is also very rare. But every year about 750,000 to one million teenagers commit violent acts against their parents, and each year about 2,000 parents are killed by their children (Gelles 1980).

The majority of children who attack a parent are between the ages of thirteen and twenty-four (Harbin and Madden 1979). Sons are slightly more likely to be violent and abusive than daughters. The sons' rates of severe violence against a parent increase with age, while the daughters' rates decline with age (Gelles and Cornell 1985:99). Perhaps the increase for males is due to their taking advantage of increased size and strength as they grow older.

Mothers are more likely to be abused than fathers, and the typical situation appears to be older sons abusing their mothers. Two possible reasons why mothers appear to be the primary targets of violence (Gelles and Cornell, 1985:99–100) are: (1) Mothers may lack the physical strength to retaliate against their abusive boys, and (2) boys may learn that their mothers are an acceptable target for their violence.

Children are more likely to abuse their mothers in homes where the mother is also a victim of spouse abuse. Families viewing violence as a legitimate way to resolve conflict run a greater risk of experiencing all forms of family violence, including parent abuse. Indeed, abuse tends to breed abuse.

SPOUSE ABUSE

Like child abuse, wife abuse is very frequent in the United States. Husband abuse, however, like parent abuse, is somewhat infrequent.

Abused Women

Numerous studies document that in the United States between 50 and 75 percent of all women probably experience physical violence from their partners at some time (Lystad 1986:55). Violence toward women is not limited to any one social class; wife or partner beating occurs in all strata of our society, among the rich and the poor and the well-educated and the uneducated (Thorman 1980:106–7).

While a high correlation exists between the husband's drinking of alcohol and his beating his wife or partner, there is some doubt that alcohol is the real trigger of the husband's attack (Thorman 1980:108). Do men drink, lose control, and then abuse, or does alcohol become a convenient excuse for violent behavior that would have happened anyway?

Wife beating may sexually arouse some husbands, since some husbands demand sexual intercourse immediately following the assault. Some investigators indicate that the typical abusive husband is an extremely insecure man and that his need to assert his masculinity and his strong drive to show his power over the woman may be related to the impulses that cause men to commit rape. Terry Davidson (1978) also notes that wife beaters are often rigid and uncompromising. Attacks on their wives seem to compensate for their feelings of being powerless and ineffectual.

It may surprise you to learn that women are more likely to be abused when pregnant. Richard Gelles (1975) offers five reasons why pregnancy tends to increase the frequency of abuse toward women: (1) There may be sexual frustration due to some couples' abstinence from sex during this period; (2) biochemical changes in the woman can lead to greater irritability and dependency; (3) the pregnant woman is relatively defenseless; (4) the family is in a period of transition, stress, and strain brought on by the pregnancy; and (5) beatings during the pregnancy can represent prenatal child abuse or abortion attempts.

The Shattered Dreams and Self-Esteem of the Battered Wife

Charlotte O'Donnell was a girl sheltered by her upper middle-class Baltimore family. Her father, a physician, provided the devoutly Catholic family with worldly goods as well as security. But for some reason, as Charlotte grew, she became stuck in that stage of low self-esteem most teenagers merely pass through on their way to grown-up poise.

That's why, when she caught the eye and heart of the handsome, brilliant John Fedders, she was so flattered she fell blindly in love, so much so that even during the courtship she couldn't see his faults or the cruelty behind his barbs and criticism.

They married, and almost immediately his professional star soared. By age 39, he was the chief enforcement officer at the Securities and Exchange Commission. By then, they'd been married 15 years, and John Fedders had become a tyrant—sometimes violent, but almost all of the time, mean. And by then, Charlotte was a frightened mass of insecurity, sometimes hiding huddled in the nursery closet.

Most of us no longer scorn a woman who has allowed herself to be treated so badly by a man. Most of us understand that a woman's view of her own situation can become so distorted by fear, intimidation and shame that she sees no outlet.

Sometimes, as in the case of Charlotte Fedders, when a woman does seek help, she can't find it. The police made her feel like a tattle tale, while her physician and psychiatrist did little more than shake their heads in disapproval. "That's inappropriate behavior" was as strong an indictment as they offered, as they treated the damage done to her body and her mind. Only when she felt her children were in danger did she finally file for divorce.

A year or so ago, *Washingtonian* magazine reporter Laura Elliott wrote about the Fedders and the tragedy their marriage became. That story has now been expanded into "Shattered Dreams," an exploration of how this horrible behavior pattern existed in not only a "respectable" family but a public one.

Some readers might question Charlotte Fedders' judgment, if not her intentions. This is a family matter, they'll say, and shouldn't be turned into a personal vendetta. But her story offers the clearest explanation I've ever read of how the battered-woman syndrome nourishes itself.

It's more than a description of those women and children who live in terror or who have found their own homes places of fear rather than refuge. It's a guarantee that most readers will not say again, "I'd never sink that low."

If you were Charlotte Fedders you might have. If you had loved the wrong person or loved for the wrong reasons or even loved at the wrong time, you might have been the victim of one kind of tyranny or another.

Charlotte, calling herself a reluctant advocate, says her mission is to help other wives understand that no person has the right to make another afraid.

I'll say amen to that.

Source: Sheila Taylor, *Fort Worth Star-Telegram,* 1988. Reprint courtesy of the Fort Worth Star-Telegram.

The overall profile of the violent man is described by Shupe, Stacey, and Hazelwood (1987:42–43). He is not violent in any other areas of his life outside the home. Typically, he is in his late twenties, married for several years or living with a woman. Arguments usually are minor, but escalate in rapid fashion to physical violence. Apart from these outbursts of anger and violence, the man is described by his wife as a good husband and father and is usually a dependable and stable employee. As a child, he probably witnessed his father beat up his mother and attempted to intervene in the violence at least once to protect his mother.

In other words, in a great many respects the violent man is similar to the average husband and father. That, in fact, is typical of a violent man—on the surface, he seems perfectly harmless, but in the privacy of the home, he asserts himself and overpowers his wife or children to assert his masculinity. The wife is not likely to tell others about his outbursts for fear of her own physical safety.

Abused Men

What about wives who physically abuse their husbands? To many people, the idea of a woman beating up on her husband is a joke. While limited research exists on women abusing husbands, however, it does happen—although many women who abuse their husbands are likely to do so in self-defense or as a result of an argument. Richard Gelles (1979) found numerous cases of wives using violence exclusively for self-defense. If a wife believes she is about to be abused again by her husband, she may strike first to protect herself. Many women engage in husband abuse to protect themselves from potential harm or from other degrading or humiliating experiences.

In seeking explanations as to why women are violent, Anson Shupe et al. (1987:56–60) identify four crucial dimensions. First is reverse sexism. For example, under certain circumstances society considers it okay for a woman to slap a man, and custom requires the man to accept the slap without resistance as a reminder of his responsibility—to retaliate is unfair.

Second is the inheritance of violence—generational transfer. As we've noted in the cases of child abuse and wife abuse, experiencing violence in the home while growing up affects women by showing them when to use violence themselves and often produces dependent women with low self-esteem and hostility.

Third is the lack of social skills. Many violent women lack the skills to deal with problems arising in intimate relationships with men or to control their anger. They are often the products of traditional cultural values prizing passive female behavior; they may have little or no experience in taking the initiative to express their own ideas, yet find themselves in situations where they are pressured to communicate in some way. Violence thus can become the end result of the lack of effective communicative skills among women who have never learned to negotiate openly as equals with their partners.

Fourth is the exposure to **stressor events**—points in every person's life that make it more difficult. Stressors do not cause the violence but become the bases of arguments and disagreements between men and women. The resulting mounting tension is analogous to steam in a boiler with no safety valve. Often, when a woman is unable to find nonviolent ways to deal with the stress, the boiler explodes, and the violence becomes a mechanism for coping.

Thus, the wife can be the abuser, though in most cases the husband is the abuser and the wife the victim. However, when the wife is the abuser, she does so most often in self-defense.

ELDER ABUSE

The most recent research area related to family abuse is concerned with the aged family member who is vulnerable to abuse, neglect, or exploitation by other family members. While many societies revere the elderly and believe that "with age comes wisdom," recent studies have shown that the elderly in America are often not treated with the greatest respect by their families. Journalistic descriptions have produced a number of labels for violence toward the aged family member such as "battered elder syndrome," "battered parent syndrome," "grandparent abuse," "granny bashing," "granny battering," and "family violence unto elders" (Rathbone-McCuan and Voyles 1982).

Abuse of the elderly can be defined as any action on the part of an elderly person's family taking advantage of his or her person, property, or emotional being through threat of violence, use of violence, or use of disciplinary restraints. Types of abuse repeatedly mentioned are (1) active physical assault; (2) verbal and psychological abuse, including provision of inadequate living environments, inadequate grooming, or abuse by neglect; (3) theft or misuse of money or property, such as trust fund embezzlement or failure to notify the state of a patient's death; (4) misuse or abuse of drugs, (5) withholding basic life resources; and (6) not providing care to the physically dependent.

It has been estimated that 500,000 persons sixty-five or older who live with younger family members are being physically abused by relatives, neighbors, and/or friends—and evidence suggests that this abuse is repetitive rather than a single occurrence (Kimsey, Tarbox, and Bragg 1981:466). Adult children or other informal caretakers who become neglectful or abusive tend to do so when the burdens of providing care for a frail, elderly person interact with stress, alcohol abuse, financial difficulties, and other situational factors (Douglass 1983). An aging parent's moving into an adult child's

Incidence of Elder Abuse Increasing Across the Country

As many as one in ten Americans over age 65 may suffer from some type of abuse, and one in 25 likely will be the victim of a moderate to severe incident, according to an American Medical Association report. The most common form of abuse of the elderly was simply neglect—leaving an elderly person at home while the caregiver goes to work. But the number of moderate to severe incidents of abuse has climbed by nearly 100,000 annually each year since 1981, the report concluded. That is a particularly worrisome trend because researchers estimate only one in five cases of elderly abuse is reported, compared with one in three cases of child abuse.

According to E. Harvey Estes, a member of the AMA's Council on Scientific Affairs which prepared the report, there is a consensus in categorizing abuse of the elderly as physical, psychological, and financial, and/or material. The experts also generally agree on the causes of abuse. Typically, the individual is no longer able to take care of him/herself financially and moves in with a relative. The situation may eat into the caregiver's time, add to the responsibilities, and put a strain on the family's budget. Estes notes that a situation like this can begin with the family neglecting the older person more and more, and in some situations, the severity of the abuse escalates.

The report says abuse was a recurring incident in 80 percent of the cases reported and that a typical victim was likely to be a 75-year-old widow whose economic situation dictates her moving to a younger family member's home. In 86 percent of the incidents, the abuser is a relative. In 75 percent of these cases, the relative lives with the elderly person. About half of the abusers are children or grandchildren of the victims and about 40 percent are spouses. This last finding contradicts the results of a study by two University of New Hampshire sociologists who concluded that 65 percent of elderly victims were physically or verbally abused by their husbands or wives and 23 percent by their children.

Source: Adapted from *News and Courier* (Charleston, S.C., February 7, 1988), p. 9-F. Associated Press.

In the United States, abuse or neglect of the elderly within the family is an increasing problem. Their physical, mental, or financial weaknesses may make elderly family members particularly susceptible to ill treatment. (© 1976 Ron Cobb. All rights reserved. From *Cobb Again*. Wild & Woolley, Sydney Australia.)

household may produce new conflicts based on the dependency of the parent on the child—role reversal from earlier days when the child was living with and dependent on the parent.

Many working men and women find it difficult, both physically and financially, to care for their aged parents. Such care is not only expensive but sometimes exhausting. To find competent in-home help, however, is difficult and costly. It is often hard for people who have not cared for an older person to comprehend the helplessness and frustration sometimes involved (Lezak 1978).

Eloise Rathbone-McCuan and Barbara Voyles (1982:192) note that the elderly in the United States have long been victims of societal neglect and blatant discrimination—and family life reflects the norms and values of the larger society. Family life is also, in many cases, characterized by violence. There is now mounting evidence that the elderly are the next category of hidden victims of intrafamily violence to emerge before an alarmed but passive citizenry.

SEXUAL ABUSE

Up to this point, we have largely dealt with physical abuse. We now turn to sexual abuse. As with physical abuse in families, data on sexual abuse within families are difficult to obtain. The victimized person, be it a child or an adult, is usually too intimidated or upset by the experience to report it.

Child Sexual Abuse

Though more cases of incest are probably being reported today, the majority of such cases go unreported. Since sexual abuse of children is usually committed by males and is usually heterosexual, girls are more likely than boys to experience it. An especially difficult area of information on sexual abuse in families is that involving younger children with older siblings. Most states have laws defining sex with persons under eighteen years of age as statutory rape, since these persons may be easily pressured into such behavior; but if both partners are under eighteen, statutory rape laws usually do not apply. And since both parents of the victim and the offender are likely to cover up this behavior, it is not likely to be reported to the police.

Chances are that many readers of this book will have memories of sexual abuse or incest from their childhoods—an uncle fondling you for several seconds, a sibling forcing you to the ground to examine your genitals, or possibly sexual intercourse with a parent or stepparent. Sexual abuse invariably involves exploitation and harm to a child. We doubt that any documented cases exist of a child enjoying being molested and feeling positively about the experience as an adult.

The American Psychological Association estimates that between 12 and 15 million American women have been the victims of incest. About 25 percent of these cases are father-daughter and 25 percent stepfather-stepdaughter; the rest are attributed to grandfathers, brothers, uncles, cousins, adoptive fathers, half brothers, and brothers-in-law (Brozan 1984).

Very little attention has historically been paid to the sexual abuse of boys, which is now known to be more widespread than was previously believed. Sexual abuse of boys by women is thought to occur in as many as 5 percent of all families (Lindsey 1984).

Child molestation crosses all social, economic, and racial boundaries and affects a wide range of people and family situations. Stereotypes portraying the offenders as neurotic, lecherous, dirty old men are inaccurate. Strangers represent about 25 percent of the offenders, thus the majority of sex offenders are family members or someone known to the victim (Gordon and Snyder 1986:117–19). The child needs to understand that no one—strangers, neighbors, relatives, or family members—has the right to touch or fondle their private parts—penis, vulva, vagina, breasts, and anus.

Parents often incorrectly believe that their children are really in little danger of being sexually abused. Findings from a 1981 study of 521 parents by David Finkelhor (Brody 1987) revealed that most parents believe their children face little danger of sexual abuse, that they are too young to be told of the possibility, and that discussions of the subject will frighten the children unnecessarily. The facts con-

Like child abuse, sexual abuse within the family often goes unreported. Lasting psychological and physical harm can result from familial relationships such as incest.

tradict such parental attitudes and beliefs, as an estimated one in four girls and at least one in seven boys is sexually abused one or more times before age eighteen. Abuse can start when a child is as young as two months, with the most vulnerable years between six and eight. Yet parents in the study picked nine as the best age to talk about sexual abuse.

Children's lack of knowledge and uncertainty about behavior often lead to their victimization. Children often believe offenders who tell them the sexual activity is all right. Unexpected behavior of an adult can throw them off guard.

Adult Sexual Abuse

Adult sexual abuse within the family, or **marital rape,** has probably been around as long as marriage but has just recently begun to exist in a legal sense. Traditional marriage contracts held that husbands had sexual access to their wives at will. Thus, marital rape in the past was legally impossible. But in 1974 a case of marital rape was prosecuted in the United States. Today all but ten states allow prosecution of estranged or divorced husbands for raping their wives;

twenty-four states have laws permitting prosecution of actively co-habiting husbands for marital rape (Okun 1986:52).

Not only does the law often not recognize marital rape, but the victim herself may not recognize the possibility of rape in a conjugal relationship. One-third of the battered women studied by Barbara Star et al. (1979) believed that they did not have a right to refuse sex with their husbands/mates. Ten to 20 percent of marriages are estimated to involve marital rape.

Many people fail to be alarmed about the problem of marital rape because they think it is a rather less traumatic form of rape (Finkelhor and Yllo 1983:126). Women raped by their husbands, however, are often traumatized at a more basic level than being afraid about their physical safety; they are often traumatized in their ability to trust. A woman's basic confidence in forming relationships and trusting intimates is affected. She may even be left feeling much more powerless and isolated than if raped by a stranger.

SOCIOLOGICAL EXPLANATIONS OF FAMILY ABUSE

Thus, whether the victims are children, women, or older people, the picture of what is happening in some American families is not pleasant. In the "security" of their own homes, many individuals are apparently not very secure. Why do some individuals abuse others both physically and sexually? Though family situations vary and no two families are the same, patterns of family violence do tend to prevail. Sociological paradigms and theories, as discussed in chapter 3, offer numerous possible ways of understanding the roots of violence in the family. (See Linda Phillips 1986 for a more detailed discussion of these theoretical approaches, especially as they pertain to the elderly.)

One explanation of abuse in the family is *social exchange theory*. Social exchange theory sees the aggressor and the victim as having few alternatives to continuing the exchange, and views the aggressor as having a monopoly on rewards and thus little to lose by being unjust. When the aggressor determines that the personal rewards arising from a situation are not proportional to the personal costs being incurred, there is a violation of the law of distributive justice (that which one is giving does not equal the return), which may result in violence. For example, a father may be having sexual relations with a daughter (against her will). Since he is financially supporting her, he resents her unwillingness to be cooperative. Therefore, he punishes her by beating her. The victims—mainly children, wives, and the elderly—are more powerless, dependent, and vulnerable, and thus have few alternatives to continued interaction.

Another sociological approach to explaining family violence is the *situational model*. As the stress associated with certain situational and/or structural factors increases for the abuser, the likelihood increases of abusive acts directed at a vulnerable individual who is seen as being associated with the stress. In other words, the "scapegoat" for frustrations becomes the child, wife, or elderly member of the family.

Closely related to the situational model is *conflict theory*, which suggests that unequal power is a key cause of violence. Families generally powerless because of poverty face special difficulties that make them especially vulnerable to violence. Families with unequal power distribution, such as an authoritarian, male-dominated family, are at high risk for family violence. In many such cases, the husband/father is deprived of power outside the family and so abuses his power within the family out of frustration over his lack of clout in the larger society. Thus, the conflict perspective suggests that social inequality, within and outside the family, plays an important part in family violence.

Another theoretical explanation for family abuse is offered by *symbolic interactionism*. The individual's definition of the situation determines his or her expectations and provides the background against which actions are planned; behavior is then based on perceived images of the self rather than on true reality. A social construction of reality occurs: the individual "builds" what to him or her is reality and then acts accordingly. A woman tells herself that she deserves to be beaten because she is not living up to her husband's expectations. Being beaten to her becomes a normal part of their relationship. The same with the child or the elderly member of the family—they begin to believe that they deserve their abusive treatment. The abuser, on the other hand, defines the abused as needing to be beaten and put in his or her place by the more dominant member of the relationship.

The *functionalist perspective* gives a different slant on family violence. This approach believes that social integration is a necessary element of social life. It is important for each of us to be part of a group with rules about behavior and to have relationships that make us feel wanted and included. According to French sociologist Emile Durkheim, not to be socially integrated creates a situation of **anomie**—isolation and lack of effective norms. Socially isolated families have high risks of violence, according to the functionalist perspective, because they have nobody to help enforce societal rules and because they suffer feelings of being unwanted.

While not new to the family scene in the United States, family violence has been a focus for research and the media since the early 1970s. Since most children experience violence when growing up (spanking is probably the most common form of family violence) and the practice seems to meet the approval of society in general, it is no wonder that family violence is as prevalent as is suggested in this chapter. Thus, child abuse, parent abuse, spouse abuse, and elderly abuse continue to prevail in American society.

CHAPTER
REVIEW

- Violence is an act carried out with the intention of physically hurting another person. While infanticide is fairly uncommon in the world today, it is an extreme form of violence.
- Spanking children is probably the most common form of family violence in the United States today. In spanking children, adults are often taking out their frustrations.
- Parents should teach their children how to recognize and cope with unsafe situations.
- Though parent abuse by children is rarely reported, sons are more likely to be abusive than daughters, and mothers are more likely to be abused than fathers.
- The majority of women probably experience physical abuse from their partners at some time in their marriage or relationship.
- Marital rape has only recently begun legally to exist. Up to 20 percent of marriages are estimated to involve marital rape.
- Pregnancy tends to increase the frequency of abuse toward women. A violent man in the home generally is not violent outside the home.
- Women who abuse their husbands are likely to do so in self-defense, as a result of an argument.
- Abuse of the elderly involves taking advantage of the person's property or emotional being through threat of, or use of, violence or neglect.
- Exchange theory suggests that the aggressor and the victim have few alternatives to their abusive situation.
- The situational model of family violence states that the perceived "weaker" member of the relationship becomes the scapegoat.
- Symbolic interactionism argues that the definition of the situation determines an individual's expectations and thus his or her perception of the self and the situation.

DISCUSSION
QUESTIONS

1. Why has the topic of family violence become popular since the early 1970s? For background material see Suggested Readings.
2. Why or why not should children be spanked? How does your opinion relate to your own parents/guardians' behavior toward you regarding spanking?
3. Why is child abuse difficult to detect?

4. Characterize child abusers and explain the persistence of child abuse using the social exchange theory.
5. Discuss why parent abuse is seldom reported.
6. Explain why marital rape is often played down in our society by using the symbolic interactionist perspective.
7. Characterize the violent husband.
8. Why do women abuse their husbands?
9. Compile as full a list as possible of the reasons why the elderly are abused by family members.
10. Why are girls and women sexually abused in the family more than boys and men?

GLOSSARY

anomie: A condition characterized by the relative absence or confusion of values within a group or society.

corporal punishment: Punishment inflicted directly on the body.

familiy violence: An act carried out with the intention of physically hurting another family member.

infanticide: The intentional killing of a baby.

marital rape: Forcible or coerced sex between conjugal partners that would always be recognized as rape if they were unmarried or noncohabitant.

stressor event: An event producing change in the family social system.

SUGGESTED READINGS

Lystad, Mary. 1986. *Violence in the Home: Interdisciplinary Perspectives.* New York: Brunner/Mazel Publishers. *Eighteen contributers write about causes of family violence, clinical intervention programs, and community intervention programs.*

McCubbin, Hamilton I., A. Elizabeth Cauble, and Joan M. Patterson, eds. 1982. *Family Stress, Coping and Social Support.* Springfield, Ill.: Charles C. Thomas. *An anthology of various stressful family situations with an emphasis on coping with stress.*

Pillemer, Karl A., and Rosalie S. Wolf, eds. 1986. *Elder Abuse: Conflict in the Family.* Dover, Mass.: Auburn House Publishing Co. *An anthology covering the following topics on elderly abuse: family conflict in later life, empirical and theoretical perspectives on elder abuse, and treatment and prevention of family conflict and elder abuse.*

Stacey, William A., and Anson Shupe. 1983. *The Family Secret: Domestic Violence in America.* Boston: Beacon Press. *A sociological study of domestic violence—a look at wives, children, and husbands.*

Thorman, George. 1980. *Family Violence*. Springfield, Ill.: Charles C. Thomas. *A good description of violent families with suggestions for treatment and prevention.*

Thorne, Barrie, ed. 1982. *Rethinking the Family: Some Feminist Questions.* New York: Longman. *An excellent anthology about the family from a feminist perspective.*

PART SIX

Epilogue

Epilogue

◆ *Snow White married the Prince and they lived happily ever after.*

The above statement concerning Snow White refers to the time in the story when they would have you believe that all of the conflicts and tensions throughout the book have been resolved and that the heros live their lives undisturbed by the problems of everyday life that we routinely encounter. We are smart enough, however, to know that such is not the case.

We know that for Snow White and her prince, life was no less interesting after the end of the story. Maybe the couple returned to the prince's castle to discover that his parents had already prearranged a marriage between the prince and the daughter of another king—a political ally. Perhaps the prince then renounced his birthright and married Snow White without the blessing of his parents. They then left the kingdom and moved into a small house owned by the seven dwarfs.

Perhaps Snow White developed a successful business cleaning houses for the dwarfs, their friends, and other people of the village. The prince also found prominence as a hunter and fur trader. Within a couple of years, Snow White gave birth to twin sons—Snappy and Dappy—and hired Doc and Sleepy to care for her children while she and her husband were involved in career-related activities.

Sadly, a few years later, it was discovered that Dopey had Alzheimer's disease and had to be put into a nursing home, Bashful and Sneezy died in a mine disaster, and Grumpy became really nasty and brought legal suit against the couple for physical abuse. During the court proceedings, the prince "came out of the closet" and announced to the world that he was in love with his lawyer. Snow White and the prince were later divorced and both were awarded joint custody of Snappy and Dappy.

We have now reached the end of this book, but the remainder of the story of American families in social context will be written by all of us and our descendants. We will build upon the social customs and traditions which we have inherited. But we will also lay new foundations in our own family lifestyles, and our lifestyles in turn will be replicated and modified by our children and grandchildren. Your study of family sociology will be helpful to you in this process, if you have learned something that will help you to adjust to changing social circumstances and future family experiences.

WHAT HAVE WE LEARNED?

We have explored many topics in working toward a sociological understanding of American families. In our analysis, we have consistently demonstrated that there are many different forms of family structures in the United States and each, to be properly understood, must be viewed within its social context.

We have primarily employed the following four theoretical perspectives in providing a sociological explanation for familial behavior: structural-functional theory, conflict theory, symbolic interactionist theory, and exchange theory. Each of these theoretical orientations offers a method for summarizing behavioral science research findings regarding human behavior within families.

We have approached the sociological analysis of families from historical, cross-cultural, and subcultural perspectives. We have discussed variations in family structures, norms, and values resulting from social class, ethnic, and gender differences. Furthermore, we have emphasized that as family institutions are created by human beings as practical ways of meeting their basic needs, social order emerges, providing stability not only for the group or society, but for the lives of individuals as well.

In Parts Three and Four of this book we followed a life-cycle approach to the understanding of family life within the United States. We began with the mate selection process and emphasized that it is very similar to a market system where individuals and families barter with symbolic and nonsymbolic rewards in arranging a marriage. Within this process, people of similar social backgrounds and relatively "equal value" (as evaluated by their respective subcultures) find and marry each other. Unlike people in many other cultures (where love is seen as undermining the stratification system, parental authority, and loyalties to the extended family), Americans are expected to employ love as *the* primary criterion in the free choice of marriage partners.

Marriage is extremely popular in the United States—95 percent of all Americans will marry at least once in their life. Furthermore, the majority of married people in the United States consider themselves to be happily married—even though in a given year there are half as many divorces as there are marriages. This fact has made most married couples aware that they must work together to make their relationship succeed. As couples attempt to enhance their relationship, they must develop an appreciation for each other's differences and an ability to communicate in an open, comfortable, and reassuring manner.

While many believe that having children can strengthen a marriage relationship, research has demonstrated that marital happiness and satisfaction often increase after the children have left home. Furthermore, couples tend to have more favorable evaluations of their relationships before having children than at other stages in the family life cycle. The reasons for this are many—some of which are the economic costs and time investment involved in raising children, the role conflicts created by adding parental responsibilities to career and marriage commitments, and inherent social problems and personal jealousies created when groups change from dyads to triads. As a result, today many couples are deciding to have smaller families, and childlessness is becoming increasingly popular in the United States.

Those couples who do opt for raising children are assisted by many other social agents in socializing their offspring. While the family is the location where primary socialization occurs, secondary socialization takes place within the neighborhood (as children interact with their peers), at day care centers and preschool programs, and within educational institutions. As children mature into adolescents, they spend more time with peers and other members of society and less time with parents and other family members. However, even though many non–family members become significant reference groups for adolescents, research studies have demonstrated that most adolescents love their parents and seek their advice.

The "empty nest" period can be, and often is, a very positive stage in the family life cycle for parents—it is a time characterized by relatively high life satisfaction and marital happiness. Research on retired individuals has similarly documented that most retirees and older family members are satisfied with retirement and have a remarkably positive outlook on life. Leisure roles are diverse for elderly family members, but relationships with extended family members, friends, and neighbors are important sources for emotional satisfaction in later life. For the healthy and financially secure elderly, the retirement years can be among the best in the family life cycle; however, failing health and limited resources can make the retirement years seem like a "living hell."

In the fifth section of the book we discussed three major crises experienced within families—divorce, death, and family violence. Since 1970, when the first no-fault divorce legislation was written, the incidence of divorce has greatly increased. In prior times couples had to demonstrate that there had been a violation of the marriage contract before a divorce would be granted. With the exception of South Dakota, all states now have adopted some form of no-fault divorce. Under this more permissive system, "marital breakdown" is the only required justification for divorce. Consequently, divorces are being granted and child custody is being determined independently of guilt or innocence. Furthermore, property is being equally divided without any considerations for gender differences or any attempt to compensate blameless victims. As a result, on average, divorced women and the minor children in their households experience a 73 percent decline in their standard of living in the first year after divorce, while former husbands experience a 42 percent rise in their standard of living.

Today, only 40 percent of children will spend their entire childhood with both natural parents. However, this situation is not that dissimilar from earlier periods in history when death brought marriages to premature closure. For couples and their children, the adjustment to divorce is similar in some ways to that experienced by families having a parent die. From a sociological perspective, both death and divorce create changes in family and social interaction patterns. In these situations, family members encounter feelings of denial, anger, disorganization, guilt, loneliness, and relief. Yet unlike death, divorce does provide the opportunity for children and other family members to continue to interact with both parents, expressing their feelings as they adjust to new family relationships.

Physical, emotional, and sexual abuse are family crises that have become quite prevalent in the 1980s. Spanking children is probably the most common form of family violence in the United States, but parent and elderly abuse are not uncommon—even though rarely reported. Research suggests that the majority of women will experience some form of physical abuse from their partners at some point in their marriage. Many husbands also experience physical abuse from their wives, but most of this violence is a defensive action.

The family may be viewed as both the cause and cure for the social stress of its members. It is in the family where Americans experience the most tender and emotionally supporting intimate experiences, as well as the most brutal of all physical acts of violence. Unfortunately, it is the latter that daily fill our newspapers and broadcast media. But stress is an inevitable part of contemporary life in the United States. The family, for many, is a sanctuary from the world's pressures and tensions. However, many two-career families experience tremendous stress and strain caused by role conflicts and the overloads of multiple commitments to family, work, and marriage relationships.

WHAT CHANGES WILL THE FUTURE BRING TO FAMILIES?

In the remainder of this chapter we will examine three major social problems that will greatly influence the lifestyles of American families in the coming years. These problems are the AIDS crisis, the expanding size of the elderly population, and the day care crisis for children of working parents.

From what you have learned while reading this book, it is obvious that social phenomena like these will affect American families in many different ways. The structures, values, and norms of some families will be modified greatly. Other families will continue their present family lifestyles, appearing to be unaffected by changes in the larger society. Many different coping strategies will be employed, and various structural forms will be initiated by families as they attempt to satisfy group needs and individual goals and objectives.

The AIDS Crisis

At present more than 102,621 Americans have AIDS, and for every case of AIDS there are 2 to 3 cases of AIDS-Related Complex (ARC). Already 59,391 have died with AIDS (Center for Disease Control, July 31, 1989). Yet we know that the AIDS future in the United States is even more bleak. Currently there are approximately 4 million people in our nation already infected with the AIDS virus, and in two years approximately 360,000 people will develop full-blown AIDS. Each of these persons will be terminally ill—with no hope of a cure.

According to the Center for Disease Control, it is expected that by 1992 the leading cause for death for males between the ages of twenty-two and sixty-five will be AIDS. In that same year it is expected that one-fifth (20 percent) of all hospital admissions will be AIDS cases or AIDS-related illnesses. The total economic impact of AIDS in the United States by 1990 is projected at 44 to 84 billion dollars; these costs include direct health care costs as well as lost income and productivity from both illness and death. On an individual level, the cost per patient will range from $30,000 to $150,000, depending upon the availability of less-expensive community-based health services.

There are primarily three methods by which AIDS is transmitted from infected individuals—sexual contacts, the mixing of blood (particularly through the use of shared intravenous drug needles), and the transmission of the virus from a mother to her unborn child. Yet because we have learned that the AIDS virus is not spread by casual contact, Americans are somewhat ambivalent about this disease and its victims.

At the present time 90 percent of U.S. AIDS patients are homosexual/bisexual men and/or are intravenous drug users. These are persons who have violated traditional standards of conduct proscribed by Jewish and Christian moral teachings. They are also persons who are in all probability the most marginal to most social institutions. Hence our ambivalence—why do these people deserve our attention and concern?

The answer to this question is that these infected persons are members of our families or friendship groups. Furthermore, the cost of institutional care for treating all these patients not only could

It wasn't until the 1980s that AIDS became recognized as a national health problem in the United States.

bankrupt its victims and U.S. insurance companies, but could create a financial disaster for the nation as well. Consequently, families will become increasingly responsible for the care of persons with AIDS. As has been the case with the hospice movement in the treatment of persons with terminal illnesses (e.g., cancer and leukemia), home health care for the dying AIDS patient will make death a more routine aspect of family living.

Furthermore, as Americans become aware of the AIDS epidemic and the tremendous proliferation of sexually transmitted diseases, we may begin to see major changes in sexual behaviors. Already, there is evidence in the gay community of San Francisco that the per capita number of sexual partners has been significantly reduced. Anonymous sex and other unsafe sexual practices have undergone major changes. There may be similar modifications in the extramarital and premarital behaviors of heterosexuals in the United States.

The Expanding Size of the Elderly Population

In chapter 13 we discussed life in the retirement years. Issues raised in that chapter are becoming increasingly important for society as the number and percentage of older persons in the United States grows. At the present time, persons aged sixty-five and older account for 12 percent of the U.S. population and are the fastest growing age cohort (U.S. Department of Commerce 1986:23). By the year 2111, when the "baby boomers" (individuals born between 1946 and 1964) begin joining the ranks of the retired, approximately forty million Americans (or 13 percent) will be sixty-five years of age or older (U.S. Department of Commerce 1986:16).

Then, as now, the major problems faced by these older Americans will be issues of health care, financial resources, and housing. Today many working people are concerned that when they reach the age of retirement the Social Security System (into which they and their employers have contributed 14 percent of their income) may be defunct. At present, Medicare and other benefits tied to Social Security are threatening the stability of the system. As a result, the federal government must subsidize the Social Security system in order to protect the well-being of older people. However, these subsidies, added to other federal expenditures (e.g., military spending), are creating tremendous budget deficits, thus increasing the national debt (now approaching three trillion dollars).

Americans are currently spending $425 billion a year on health care (U.S. Department of Commerce 1986:85). Through Medicare, Medicaid, and Veterans Administration benefits, the federal and state governments pay for more health care than any group in the society.

The increasing number of elderly people and the high cost of health care they require threatens the future of the Social Security system in the United States.

More than 40 percent of health care expenditures are from public funds (U.S. Department of Commerce 1986:85).

In the United States the leading causes of death are the chronic diseases (e.g., heart disease, cancer, leukemia, and AIDS). Because of the nature and treatment of these chronic diseases, most of us can expect to spend one-half of our lifetime expenditures for health care during the last year of our lives. Older people account for 21.7 percent of all health-related expenditures in the United States, even though they make up only 12 percent of the population. Persons over seventy-four years of age account for 4.8 percent of the population in the United States but 13.3 percent of all money spent on health care (U.S. Department of Commerce, 1986:14 and 88). Between 1970 and 1985 expenditures for nursing home care have increased from $6.7 billion to $52 billion.

What do these facts mean to the future of families in the United States? Many people believe that national spending priorities must be readjusted by Congress to deal with the impending needs facing older Americans and their families. We must answer a number of significant questions. Should Medicare benefits continue, even if the Social Security system collapses under this financial burden? Should families be responsible for the cost of caring for their older members when they are unable to pay? Do the elderly in our country deserve a minimum standard of living based upon their past societal contributions? Does the entire medical system need to be changed to a

Day Care for Elderly Would Offer Dignity and Hope

I was called to the emergency room the other day to see an 82-year-old widow, a victim of a mild stroke. For the last 12 years, I have seen her transformed from an active and independent woman, enjoying retirement with her husband, to a person who depends on others. She developed complications from diabetes, heart disease, and anemia. When she fell and broke her hip, she agreed to live with her son's family.

With the advancement in public health and medicine, Americans are living longer—the number of people over the age of 80 will rise from 6.2 million today to 12.1 million in 2010. Thus, in time, almost every family will have to care for an aged relative with a similar medical history. How are we going to afford the care they will need without sacrificing quality? The key is *adult day care*.

The costs of nursing homes was $21 billion in 1980 and has become $70 billion in 1990. Adult day care provides an alternative to institutionalization. It relieves the family members of 24-hour responsibility, especially when they have full-time jobs. It should be emphasized that this is not just a "sitting service." Properly conceived, adult day care includes medical care, nursing, rehabilitation, and social services.

Nurses play a central role, but social workers also are important. Old people often come to my office with bundles of papers, overwhelmed with bills and computer printouts from the doctors, hospitals, Medicare, and insurance companies. A social worker untangles the complexities and relieves the anxieties. Psychological support for the aged is of no use unless such matters are resolved.

To date, adult day-care centers are community projects supported mostly by local resources. Churches, voluntary organizations, and private foundations partially fund our program in San Angelo, Texas. But expanding federal and state aid through Medicare and Medicaid would make sense—on average, it costs about half as much to maintain a patient in day care as in a nursing home. Society has to help the debilitated elderly live with dignity and hope. Day care would do just that.

Source: Fazlur Rahman, *Minneapolis Star and Tribune* (September 6, 1988), p. 15A. Copyright © 1988 by The New York Times Company. Reprinted by permission.

socialized model, where all Americans have the right to health care, regardless of their ability to pay? These and other questions will be answered in the context of the political process.

As a beginning, Jule M. Sugarman (1987:1), an architect of the successful Head Start Program, has recommended that the government provide tax incentives to help families maintain older relatives in their homes and that the government provide community in-home nursing services, respite care, and chore services for the elderly of our nation. Such family and community-based services would be more cost efficient and dignifying than the more expensive institutionalized care.

Rather than taking a "Band-Aid" approach to modifying domestic policy dealing with the needs of the elderly, older Americans will need to work within the political process to become change agents in society. In the past, it has been difficult to mobilize older people as a political force to facilitate legislation. At the present time, however, the AARP (American Association of Retired Persons) has 27 million members, and with the election of 1988 "gray power" became a reality. According to Margot Hornblower (1988:36),

> AARP is the nation's largest special-interest group. This elderly behemoth, nearly twice the size of the AFL-CIO, continues to grow by about 8,000 new dues payers a day. One out of nine Americans belongs, paying a $5 annual fee. AARP offers drug and travel discounts, runs the nation's largest group-health-insurance program and a credit union. In addition, its savvy media operation includes Modern Maturity, the nation's third highest circulation magazine, a wire service that provides newspapers with "unbiased reporting" on elderly issues, and a weekly television series.

In the 1988 election AARP spent $8 million in get-out-the-vote efforts and ad campaigns favoring Social Security programs and government-sponsored long-term health care as top federal priorities (Hornblower 1988:36). Given the political facts that voters over sixty-five are three times as likely to vote as persons under twenty-four, and that it is now possible to mobilize the older voter, it becomes obvious that older Americans are a political force that neither the Democrats nor the Republicans can ignore (Hornblower 1988:36). As a result, we can expect to see a definite "graying" of domestic policies dealing with family issues.

The Day Care Crisis

Whether or not Americans are pleased with the situation, most children in the United States have and will continue to have employed parents. Single parents must work, and most two-parent families

Presently there is no day care system in the United States that adequately serves the needs of employed persons and their children.

believe that the stay-at-home parent is either a luxury or not a contemporary option for their family.

Yet the United States has not adequately built the social infrastructure to support the dual-earner family. Many women are not guaranteed employment after a pregnancy leave, and quality day care is either hard to find or unaffordable, or both. At the time of this writing there are two bills before the United States Senate. The first is the $2.5 billion legislation submitted by Senators Christopher Dodd (Democrat from Connecticut) and John Chafee (Republican from Rhode Island) and cosponsored by twenty-three other senators. This bill is known as the Alliance for Better Child Care Bill (S.1885) and has as its goal the improvement of the entire day care industry—including the establishment of federal standards for safety and quality, improvement of staff salaries, and consumer access to affordable quality child care. The second bill is Senator Orin Hatch's (Republican from Utah) $250 million legislation (S.1678), which would provide funds to states to award grants to eligible entities such as local governments, nonprofits, small business consortia, and educational institutions for projects to improve child care (Herendeen 1987:6). This bill would provide only for start-up costs and would attempt to make day care a matter of state and local initiatives.

The issues related to the passage of either of these bills will revolve around the appropriate role of the federal government in dealing with family issues. Should the government establish quality standards? Is it desirable for the federal government to encourage the proliferation of institutionalized care for infants and preschool children? Should low-income families' day care be subsidized?

Another major concern will be the level of funding needed to create a comprehensive system of child care in the United States. Can the federal budget afford a major investment in day care provisions? What are the long-term federal costs incurred by continuing the present federal policies related to the inadequate provision of quality child care programs? If the national debt must be increased to cover this legislation, in effect will not children be forced to pay for their own day care? To these financial concerns Senator Patricia Shroeder (Democrat from Colorado) has said that even the more expensive Dodd/Chafee bill is less costly than one military aircraft carrier.

Whatever course the federal government will take will not be enough to deal with the present day care crisis in the United States. Dr. Edward Zigler (cited by *American Family* 1987), a Yale University psychologist and one of the architects of the Head Start program, believes that local schools should coordinate child care services in the community. He believes schools can and should provide services to infants and preschoolers, and to elementary school students whose parents work when school is not in session. While this approach is opposed by many on the grounds that the schools are already overburdened, both conservatives and liberals see promise in this approach because it provides local control of a potentially comprehensive system of child care.

CONCLUSION

As you consider the three family issues of the AIDS crisis, the increase in the elderly population, and the U.S. day care crisis, you can see that your life will be affected. Understanding these problems will not be enough. If you want to live your life "happily ever after," you will have to become a part of the social process attempting to find a solution to these and other social problems facing American families.

As one individual in society, you may find comfort in the discovery that the United States is a pluralistic society—there are many legitimate ways to organize families and experience personal fulfillment. Unfortunately (or fortunately, depending upon your perspective), you will be responsible for working with others to create a mutually satisfying family lifestyle. For Americans, life may not always be lived happily ever after, but it can be interesting, challenging, and fulfilling for those willing to commit themselves to family relationships in a social context.

Appendix
A Research Example Illustrating the Conduct of Inquiry in the Sociology of the Family

Appendix Figure 1 on page 416 illustrates the stages in the process of conducting social research. The research process is illustrated as having the form of a circle or ellipse. One can enter the research process either by beginning with the body of knowledge (theory) or by starting with an untested research hypothesis or an intuitive hunch. If one begins with theory, research becomes a deductive exercise; to being with a research hypothesis involves an inductive procedure.

If we arbitrarily begin the research process by formulating a research hypothesis, our second step will be to provide both theoretical and operational definitions for the concepts of the hypothesis. After this has been accomplished, it is now possible to state the hypothesis in the form of an empirical proposition. It is at this point that we enter into the process of empirical verification. Sampling and research design procedures will enable us to select a population for study and a method by which data will be collected. After these procedures have been determined, data will be collected and analyzed. As the final step, the research conclusions will be used to build or modify the theoretical body of sociological knowledge.

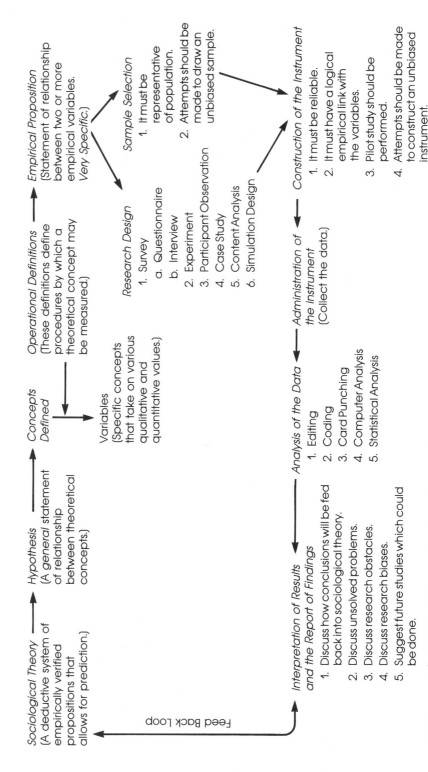

FIGURE A.1 The Process of Conducting Social Research

To illustrate the process of social science research on the family, we will use a research example involving the effects of geographical mobility upon extended family cohesiveness. Because Americans emphasize achieved rather than ascribed status, they favor geographic mobility as one means for acquiring an elevated status position in the society. According to Talcott Parsons, this has left the American family socially isolated, lonely, and separated from kin networks. He sees this isolation as part of the general trend of differentiation in U.S. society. Increasing specialization has taken place, so that certain functions formerly carried out by one unit are taken over by other specialized units. Thus, the original unit concentrates upon fewer functions. For example, economic production and certain financial and educational responsibilities have been taken over from the family by other organizations. As a result, the family has become a more specialized group, concentrating on the functions of socialization of the child and the exchange of affection and emotional support. Parsons sees the nuclear family as residentially and economically isolated from its extended family.

A number of critics have disagreed with the emphasis Parsons placed upon the "isolated" nuclear family. Eugene Litwak (1960) has argued that extended family relations do take place without interfering with occupational or geographic mobility. He therefore prefers to speak of a "modified extended family" rather than an isolated nuclear family. According to Litwak, a modified form of the extended family (once characterized by geographic propinquity, occupational nepotism, and strict authority relations) exists in the United States, with personal relationships being maintained even though the extended family as an economic and occupational unit has disappeared.

THE HYPOTHESIS

As we read these two perspectives, we were left with the following research questions:

1. What is the relationship between geographic mobility of the nuclear family and extended family cohesiveness?
2. Does the number of times the nuclear family moves affect extended family cohesiveness?
3. Is geographic distance a significant factor in weakening kinship ties?

In order to formulate the research hypotheses, we assumed that Litwak is correct and that the kinship structure in the United States is organized around a "modified extended family" rather than an isolated nuclear family structure. Given this assumption, our research hypotheses were as follows:

Extended family cohesiveness will not be affected by a nuclear family's geographic mobility. More specifically . . .

Extended family cohesiveness will not be affected by the number of times a nuclear family moves.

Extended family cohesiveness will not be affected by the distance a nuclear family lives from extended family members.

OPERATIONALIZATION OF VARIABLES

In operationalizing the dependent variable, extended family cohesiveness, we utilized questions from Peter Heller's (1976) "familism" scale. These questions measured attitudes toward family cohesion. We also used questions pertaining to frequency of telephoning, visiting, writing, and engaging in activities in operationalizing extended family cohesiveness. In total, there were thirteen items, which collectively formed a scale measuring extended family cohesiveness.

We operationalized the first independent variable, geographic mobility, by asking the question: "How many times have you and your family moved?" We measured the second independent variable, distance from extended family members, by taking the average distance from all kin members (paternal and maternal lineage groups).

RESEARCH AND SAMPLING DESIGNS

In this project we selected the survey research design and employed a questionnaire method for collecting data. We had a fixed number of response options for each question on the questionnaire. In assessing the dependent variable, extended family cohesiveness, thirteen items created a Likert (or summated) scale where the numerical values assigned to each response category were added together. Later, we divided the total respondent group into four groups (Low, Moderately Low, Moderately High, and High Cohesiveness) based upon their relative scale scores.

The sample population was selected by a systematic random sample of the entire student body of St. Olaf College in Minnesota.

The procedure included employing a table of random numbers to select one of the first seven students listed in the student directory. After selecting this first student as a beginning point, we then systematically selected every seventh student—which yielded a total sample of 435 students. We then mailed each of these students a questionnaire encouraging participation. Of the 435 students, 297 returned their questionnaire (a response rate of 68 percent).

THE QUESTIONNAIRE

The following were the questions used in operationalizing the concepts of extended family cohesiveness, number of times moved, and distance from kin:

Dependent Variable—Extended Family Cohesiveness

Instructions: For each question please circle the number beside the answer that best applies to you.

1. How often do you visit in the homes of your relatives?
   1. Less often than once a year
   2. At least once a year but less than once a month
   3. At least once a month but less than once a week
   4. At least once a week
2. When you do visit relatives, what is the average length of your stay?
   1. Less than one day
   2. One day
   3. More than one day but less than a week
   4. One week or more
   5. I do not visit relatives
3. How often do you engage in activities (such as bowling, movies, etc.) with your relatives?
   1. Less often than once a year
   2. At least once a year but less than once a month
   3. At least once a month but less than once a week
   4. At least once a week
4. How often do you borrow things from or lend things to your relatives?

1. Less often than once a year
2. At least once a year but less than once a month
3. At least once a month but less than once a week
4. At least once a week

5. How often do you do favors (other than lending) for your relatives?
   1. Less often than once a year
   2. At least once a year but less than once a month
   3. At least once a month but less than once a week
   4. At least once a week

6. How often do you write to your relatives?
   1. Less often than once a year
   2. At least once a year but less than once a month
   3. At least once a month but less than once a week
   4. At least once a week

7. How often do you telephone your relatives?
   1. Less often than once a year
   2. At least once a year but less than once a month
   3. At least once a month but less than once a week
   4. At least once a week

8. On occasions, such as birthdays, weddings, funerals, or holidays, is it a practice to get together with your relatives?
   1. Never
   2. Sometimes
   3. Often
   4. Always

9. Do you feel comfortable or relaxed in the presence of your relatives?
   1. Uncomfortable
   2. Somewhat comfortable
   3. Comfortable
   4. Very comfortable

10. Do you visit your relatives more than your friends?
    1. Yes
    2. No

11. Have any of your relatives ever given you financial assistance ($100 or more)?
    1. Yes
    2. No

12. At any time have you helped with a sick relative?
    1. Yes
    2. No

13. Have any relatives lived in your home for an extended period of time (a month or more)?
    1. Yes
    2. No

Independent Variables—Number of Times Moved and Distance from Kin

How many times have you and your family moved? _____

Please place the appropriate number from the key into the blank, indicating the approximate distance your immediate family lives from other relatives *presently*.

KEY

1. Under 10 miles
2. 10 to 50 miles
3. 51 to 150 miles
4. 151 to 300 miles
5. More than 300 miles

_____ Paternal Grandparents (father's side)
_____ Maternal Grandparents (mother's side)
_____ Aunts and Uncles (father's side)
_____ Aunts and Uncles (mother's side)

INTERPRETATION OF FINDINGS AND RESEARCH CONCLUSIONS

In Table 1 we observe that the number of times moved does not seem to have an influence upon the strength of extended family ties. The distribution of families characterized by high and low extended family cohesiveness does not seem to be associated with the number of times that a nuclear family has moved. However, from Table 2 we learn that the distance from relatives does have an influence upon extended family cohesiveness—living closer to relatives is associated with higher extended family cohesiveness.

Collectively, Tables 1 and 2 tend to provide evidence leading us to reject our first research hypothesis and accept the alternative conclusion that geographic mobility (involving physical separation) does affect extended family cohesiveness. Yet Table 1 indicates support for our second hypothesis—the number of moves does not affect extended family cohesiveness. However, Table 2 leads us to reject our third hypothesis, that extended family cohesiveness will not be affected by distance from extended family members. In general this evidence tends to support Talcott Parsons's contention that the contemporary American nuclear family, which is geographically mobile and lives a great distance from the larger kinship group, tends to be rather isolated from its extended family members.

THE RESEARCH FINDINGS

Appendix Tables 1 and 2 present our research findings.

APPENDIX TABLE 1   Strength of Extended Family Cohesiveness by Number of Times Moved

Strength of extended family cohesiveness	Number of Times Moved				
	0 moves	1 move	2 moves	3 or 4 moves	5+ moves
Low	13 23.21%	15 26.32%	15 25.42%	15 21.43%	16 29.09%
Moderately low	11 26.32%	18 31.58%	14 23.73%	18 25.71%	14 25.45%
Moderately high	16 28.57%	12 21.05%	14 23.73%	20 28.57%	10 18.18%
High	16 28.57%	12 21.05%	16 27.12%	17 24.29%	15 27.27%
TOTALS	56 100%	57 100%	59 100%	70 100%	55 100%

Chi square = 5.37
Not statistically significant at .05 Level

APPENDIX TABLE 2   Strength of Extended Family Cohesiveness by Distance from Relatives

Strength of extended family cohesiveness	Distance from Relatives			
	50 miles or less	51–150 miles	151–300 miles	More than 300 miles
Low	5 15.63%	14 17.28%	38 29.01%	17 32.08%
Moderately low	6 18.75%	17 20.99%	38 29.01%	14 26.42%
Moderately high	7 21.88%	24 29.63%	31 23.66%	10 18.87%
High	14 43.75%	26 32.10%	24 18.32%	12 22.64%
TOTALS	32 100%	81 100%	131 100%	53 100%

Chi square = 16.89
Not statistically significant at .05 Level

References

CHAPTER 1

Baumrind, Diana. 1967. "Child-care Practices Anteceding Three Patterns of Preschool Behavior." *Genetic Psychology Monographs*, volume 75, 43–88.

Becker, Gary S. 1981. *A Treatise on the Family.* Cambridge, Mass.: Harvard University Press.

Elshtain, Jean Bethke. 1981. *Public Man, Private Woman: Women in Social and Political Thought.* Princeton, N.J.: Princeton University Press.

Eshleman, J. Ross. 1985. *The Family: An Introduction.* 4th ed. Boston: Allyn and Bacon.

Gouldner, Alvin W., and Helen P. Gouldner. 1963. *Modern Sociology: An Introduction to the Study of Human Interaction.* New York: Harcourt, Brace and World.

Himes, Joseph S. 1968. *The Study of Sociology.* Glenview, Ill.: Scott, Foresman.

Homans, George C. 1967. *The Nature of Social Science.* New York: Harcourt, Brace, and World.

Irwin, Michael. 1988. Letter to the authors, December 7.

Krutch, Joseph W. 1929. "Genesis of Mood." *The Modern Temper.*

Morgan, Edmund S. 1966. *The Puritan Family: Essays on Religion and Domestic Relations in Seventeenth-Century New England.* New York: Harper & Row.

Rudner, Richard S. 1966. *Philosophy of Social Science.* Englewood, Cliffs, N.J.: Prentice-Hall Publishing Company.

Sorokin, Pitirim A. 1947. *Society, Culture, and Personality.* New York: Harper & Row.

Stack, Carol B. 1974. *All Our Kin: Strategies for Survival in a Black Community.* New York: Harper & Row.

Theodorson, George A., and Achilles G. Theodorson. 1969. *Modern Dictionary of Sociology.* New York: Thomas Y. Crowell Company.

Will, George F. 1983. *Statecraft as Soulcraft: What Government Does.* New York: Simon and Schuster.

CHAPTER 2

Bakinikana, Isaya K. M. 1972. "The Structure and Function of the Family in Bukoba, Tanzania." Unpublished paper written at St. Olaf College, Northfield, Minn.

Berger, Peter L. 1969. *The Sacred Canopy.* New York: Doubleday.

Eshleman, J. Ross. 1985. *The Family: An Introduction.* 4th ed. Boston: Allyn and Bacon.

Huber, Joan. 1981. "From Sugar and Spice to Professor." In *Down to Earth Sociology,* ed. James M. Henslin, pages 234–45. New York: The Free Press.

Leslie, Gerald R., and Sheila K. Korman. 1985. *The Family in Social Context.* 6th ed. New York: Oxford University Press.

Mead, Margaret. 1935. *Sex and Temperament in Three Primitive Societies.* New York: William Morrow and Company.

Murdock, George. 1957. "World Ethnographic Sample." *American Anthropologist* 59 (August): 680ff.

Queen, Stuart A., and Robert W. Habenstein. 1967. *The Family in Various Cultures.* 3d ed. Philadelphia: J. B. Lippincott Company.

Stephens, William N. 1963. *The Family in Cross-Cultural Perspective.* New York: Holt, Rinehart, and Winston.

CHAPTER 3

Blau, Peter M. 1964. *Exchange and Power in Social Life.* New York: John Wiley and Sons, Publishers.

Braithwaite, Richard B. 1964. *Scientific Explanation.* New York: Harper and Brothers.

Chafetz, Janet S. 1978. *A Primer on the Construction and Testing of Theories in Sociology.* Itasca, Ill.: F. E. Peacock Publishers.

Collins, Randall. 1985. *Three Sociological Traditions.* New York: Oxford University Press.

Durkheim, Emile. 1964. *The Rules of the Sociological Method.* New York: The Free Press.

Eshleman, J. Ross. 1985. *The Family: An Introduction.* 4th ed. Boston: Allyn and Bacon.

Merton, Robert K. 1967. *On Theoretical Sociology.* New York: The Free Press.

Parsons, Talcott. 1938. "The Role of Theory in Social Research." *American Sociological Review* 3, no. 1 (February): 13–20.

Ritzer, George. 1975. *Sociology: A Multiple Paradigm Science.* Boston: Allyn and Bacon.

Turner, Jonathan H. 1985. *Sociology: A Student Handbook.* New York: Random House.

Vernon, Glenn M. and Jerry D. Cardwell. 1981. *Social Psychology: Shared, Symboled, and Situated Behavior.* Washington, D.C.: University Press of America.

Waller, Willard. 1951. *The Family: A Dynamic Interpretation.* New York: Holt, Rinehart, and Winston.

Weber, Max. 1966. *The Theory of Social and Economic Organization.* Reprint. New York: The Free Press.

Willer, David, and Murray Webster Jr. 1970. "Theoretical Concepts and Observables." *American Sociological Review* 35, no. 4 (August): 748–57.

Winch, Robert F. 1958. *Mate Selection: A Study of Complementary Needs.* New York: Harper.

CHAPTER 4

Barbeau, Clayton C. 1971. *Future of the Family.* New York: Bruce Publishing Company.

Blau, Francine D., and Marianne A. Ferber. 1986. *The Economics of Women, Men and Work.* Englewood Cliffs, N.J.: Prentice-Hall.

Calhoun, Arthur W. 1973. *A Social History of the American Family.* Vol. 1. New York: Arno Press.

Cavan, Ruth Shonle. 1969. *The American Family.* 4th ed. New York: Thomas Y. Crowell Company.

Demos, John. 1970. *A Little Commonwealth: Family Life in Plymouth.* New York: Oxford University Press.

Enoch, J. Rex, Jerald O. Savells, and George E. Dickinson. 1976. "Disruption or Disorganization." *Phi Kappa Phi Journal* 56 (Summer):27–31.

Eshleman, J. Ross. 1985. *The Family: An Introduction.* 4th ed. Boston: Allyn and Bacon.

Furstenberg, Frank F. 1966. "Industrialization and the American Family: A Look Backward." *American Sociological Review* 31 (June):326–37.

Gittins, Diana. 1986. *The Family in Question: Changing Households and Familiar Ideologies.* Atlantic Highlands, N.J.: Humanities Press.

Goode, William J. 1968. "The Role of the Family in Industrialization." In *Selected Studies in Marriage and the Family,* ed. Robert F. Winch and Louis W. Goodman. New York: Holt, Rinehart, and Winston.

Goode, William J. 1982. *The Family.* 2d ed. Englewood Cliffs, N.J.: Prentice Hall.

Greenfield, Sidney M. 1961. "Industrialization and the Family in Sociological Theory." *American Journal of Sociology* 67:312–22.

Hawley, Amos H. 1971. *Urban Society: An Ecological Approach.* New York: John Wiley and Sons.

Huxley, Aldous. 1932. *Brave New World.* New York: Harper and Brothers Books.

Lasch, Christopher. 1977. *Haven in a Heartless World: The Family Besieged.* New York: Basic Books.

Morgan Edmund S. 1966. *The Puritan Family: Essays on Religion and Domestic Relations in Seventeenth-Century New England.* New York: Harper and Row.

Orwell, George. 1949. *1984*. New York: Harcourt, Brace and Company.

Otto, Arthur. 1970. *The Family in Search of a Future*. New York: Appleton-Century-Crofts.

Pollak, Otto. 1967. "The Outlook for the American Family." *Journal of Marriage and the Family* 29 (February):193–205.

Queen, Stuart A., and Robert W. Habenstein. 1974. *The Family in Various Cultures*. 4th ed. Philadelphia: J. B. Lippincott Company.

Ryan, Mary P. 1983. *Womanhood in America: From Colonial Times to the Present*. 3d ed. New York: Franklin Watts.

Schulz, David A. 1972. *The Changing Family*. Englewood Cliffs, N.J.: Prentice-Hall.

Scott, Donald M., and Bernard Wishy. 1982. *America's Families: A Documentary History*. New York: Harper & Row.

Skinner, B. F. 1948. *Walden Two*. New York: Macmillan Company.

Sorokin, Pitirim A. 1937. *Social and Cultural Dynamics*. New York: American Book Company.

Vanek, Joann. 1974. "Time Spent in Housework." *Scientific American* (November):116–20.

Vincent, Clark E. 1966. "Familia Spongi: The Adaptive Function." *Journal of Marriage and the Family* 28 (February):29–36.

CHAPTER 5

Beckett, Joyce O., and Audrey D. Smith. 1981. "Work and Family Roles: Egalitarian Marriage in Black and White Families." *Social Service Review* 55 (June):321, table 3.

Block, Jeanne H. 1976. "Debatable Conclusions About Sex Differences." *Contemporary Psychology* 21:517–22.

Brown, Rita Mae. 1973. *Rubyfruit Jungle*. New York: Bantam.

Close, Paul, and Rosemary Collins. 1985. *Family and Economy in Modern Society*. London: Macmillan Press.

Collins, Glenn. 1986. "Family: Both Cause of and Cure for Stress." *The New York Times* (June 9):Y15.

Deigh, Robb. 1987. "The Mystery of the Closing Pay Gap." *Insight* (October 19):44.

Dillingham, Susan. 1987. "Cooking and Cleaning Is Still Women's Work." *Insight* (July 13):44.

Ehrenreich, Barbara. 1983. *The Hearts of Men: American Dreams and the Flight from Commitment*. Garden City, N.Y.: Anchor Press.

Filene, Peter G. 1986. *Him/Her/Self: Sex Roles in Modern America*. Baltimore: Johns Hopkins University Press.

Gerson, Kathleen. 1985. *Hard Choices*. Berkeley: University of California Press.

Goldberg, Herb. 1976. *The Hazards of Being Male: Surviving the Myth of Masculine Privilege*. New York: Signet.

Hewlett, Sylvia Ann. 1986. "Feminism's Next Challenge: Support for Motherhood." *The New York Times,* (June 12):Y27.

Haugh, Susan S., Charles Hoffman, and Gloria Cowan. 1980. "The Eye of the Very Young Beholder: Sextyping of Infants by Young Children." *Child Development* 51:598–600.

Hawley, Amos H. 1971. *Urban Society: An Ecological Approach.* New York: John Wiley and Sons.

Holmstrom, Lynda Lytle. 1973. *The Two-Career Family.* Cambridge, Mass.: Schenkman.

Lott, Bernice. 1987. *Women's Lives: Themes and Variations in Gender Learning.* Monterey, Calif.: Brooks/Cole Publishing Company. Copyright © 1987 by Wadsworth, Inc. Reprinted by permission of Brooks/Cole Publishing Company.

Lowe, Marian. 1978. "The Dialectic of Biology and Culture." In *Woman's Nature: Rationalizations of Inequality*, ed., M. Lowe and R. Hubbard, 39–62. New York: Pergamon.

Maccoby, Eleanor E., and Carol N. Jacklin. 1974. *The Psychology of Sex Differences.* Stanford, Calif.: Stanford University Press.

Mortimer, Jeylan T. 1979. "Dual-Career Families: A Sociological Perspective." In *The Two-Career Family: Issues and Alternatives*, ed. Samiha S. Peterson, Judy M. Richardson, and Gretchen V. Kreuter. Washington, D.C.: University Press of America.

National Commission on Working Women. 1983. *Women's Work: Undervalued, Underpaid.* Washington, D.C.: Center for Women and Work.

Rapoport, Rhona, and Robert Rapoport. 1971. *Dual Career Families.* Baltimore: Penguin.

Rothenberg, Paula S. 1988. *Racism and Sexism: An Integrated Study.* New York: St. Martin's Press.

Rubin, Jeffrey A., Frank J. Provenzano, and Zella Lauria. 1974. "The Eye of the Beholder: Parents' Views on Sex of Newborns." *American Journal of Orthopsychiatry* 44:512–19.

Ryan, Mary P. 1983. *Womanhood in America: From Colonial Times to the Present.* 3d ed. New York: Franklin Watts.

Seavey, Carol A., Phyllis A. Katz, and Sue R. Zalk. 1975. "The Effect of Gender Labels on Adult Responses to Infants." *Sex Roles* 1:103–9.

Sidovowicz, Laura S., and G. S. Lunney. 1980. "Baby X Revisited." *Sex Roles* 6:67–73.

Smith, Caroline, and Barbara Lloyd. 1978. "Maternal Behavior and Perceived Sex of Infant: Revisited. *Child Development* 49:1263–65.

Steinem, Gloria. 1978. "If Men Could Menstruate." *Ms* (October):110.

Time. 1987. "The Child-Care Dilemma." June 22:54–63.

Time. 1973. "Brother Becomes Sister." January 8:34.

Trost, Cathy. 1987. "Best Employers for Women and Parents." *Wall Street Journal* (November 30):21.

United States Department of Commerce. 1987. "Women Making Headway in Share of Male-Dominated Occupations, Census Bureau Says." *U.S. Commerce News* (September 4).

Williamson, Nancy E. 1976. "Sex Preferences, Sex Control, and the Status of Women." *Signs* 1:847–62.

CHAPTER 6

Alvirez, David, and Frank D. Bean. 1976. "The Mexican American Family." In *Ethnic Families in America,* ed. Charles Mindel and Robert W. Habenstein, 271–92 New York: Elsevier.

Balswick, Jack. 1966. "Are American-Jewish Families Closely Knit?" *Jewish Social Studies* 28:159–67.

Billingsley, Andrew. 1968. *Black Families in White America.* Englewood Cliffs, N.J.: Prentice-Hall.

Cherlin, Andrew. 1981. *Marriage, Divorce, Remarriage.* Cambridge, Mass.: Harvard University Press.

Corwin, Arthur F. 1973. "Causes of Mexican Emigration to the United States: A Summary View." *Perspectives in American History* 7.

Dickinson, George E. 1975. "Dating Behavior of Black and White Adolescents Before and After Desegregation." *Journal of Marriage and the Family* 37 (August):602–8.

Farber, Bernard, Charles H. Mindel, and Bernard Lazerwitz. 1976. "The Jewish American Family." In *Ethnic Families in America,* ed. Charles Mindel and Robert W. Habenstein, 347–78. New York: Elsevier.

Femminella, Francis X., and Jill S. Quadagno. 1976. "The Italian American Family." In *Ethnic Families in America,* ed. Charles Mindel and Robert W. Habenstein, 61–88. New York: Elsevier.

Frumkin, Robert M. 1954. "Attitudes of Negro College Students Toward Intrafamily Leadership and Control." *Journal of Marriage and the Family* 16 (August):252–53.

Gans, Herbert L. 1962. *The Urban Villagers.* New York: The Free Press.

Gary, L., L. Beatty, G. Berry, and M. Price. 1983. *Stable Black Families.* Washington, D.C.: Institute for Urban Affairs and Research at Howard University.

Giambino, Richard. 1974. *Blood of My Blood.* New York: Doubleday and Company.

Glenn, Norval D., and Michael Supancic. 1984. "The Social and Demographic Correlater of Divorce and Separation in the United States: An Update and Reconsideration." *Journal of Marriage and the Family* 46 (August):563–75.

Greeley, Andrew M. 1969. *Why Can't They Be Like Us?* New York: Institute of Human Relations Press.

Hechter, Michael. 1974. *Internal Colonialism: The Celtic Fringe in British National Development.* Berkeley: University of California Press.

Hill, Robert. 1972. *The Strengths of Black Families.* New York: Emerson Hall.

Horowitz, Ruth. 1983. *Honor and the American Dream: Culture and Identity in a Chicano Community.* New Brunswick, N.J.: Rutgers University Press.

Huang, Lucy Jen. 1976. "The Chinese American Family." In *Ethnic Families in America,* ed. Charles Mindel and Robert W. Habenstein, 124–47. New York: Elsevier.

Hutter, Mark. 1988. *The Changing Family: Comparative Perspectives.* 2d ed. New York: Macmillan Publishing Company.

Johnson, Colleen L. 1985. *Growing Up and Growing Old in Italian-American Families.* New Brunswick, N.J.: Rutgers University Press.

Jones, Jacqueline. 1985. *Labor of Love, Labor of Sorrow.* New York: Basic Books.

Kitano, Harry H. L. 1969. *Japanese Americans: The Evolution of a Subculture.* Englewood Cliffs, N.J.: Prentice-Hall.

Kitano, Harry H. L., and Akemi Kikumura. 1976. "The Japanese American Family." In *Ethnic Families in America,* ed. Charles Mindel and Robert W. Habenstein, 41–60. New York: Elsevier.

Lang, Olga. 1968. *Chinese Family and Society.* New York: Archon Books.

Leslie, Gerald R., and Sheila K. Korman. 1985. *The Family in Social Context.* 6th ed. New York: Oxford University Press.

Mindel, Charles H., and Robert W. Habenstein. 1976. *Ethnic Families in America.* New York: Elsevier.

Moore, Joan W. 1976. *Mexican Americans.* Englewood Cliffs, N.J.: Prentice-Hall.

Moynihan, Daniel P. 1965. *The Negro Family: The Case for National Action.* Washington, D.C.: U.S. Department of Labor, Office of Planning and Research (March).

Nelli, Humbert S. 1983. *From Immigrants to Ethnics: The Italian Americans.* Oxford: Oxford University Press.

Powell, Gloria J. 1973. *Black Monday's Children.* New York: Appleton-Century-Crofts.

Rischin, Moses. 1987. *The Jews of North America.* Detroit: Wayne State University Press.

Scanzoni, John H. 1971. *The Black Family in Modern America.* Boston: Allyn and Bacon.

Simon, Rita J. 1985. *New Lives: The Adjustment of Soviet Jewish Immigrants in the United States and Israel.* Lexington, Mass.: Lexington Books.

Simpson, George E., and J. Milton Yinger. 1965. *Racial and Cultural Minorities.* 3d ed. New York: Harper & Row.

Sowell, Thomas. 1981. *Ethnic America.* New York: Basic Books.

Stack, Carol B. 1974. *All Our Kin: Strategies for Survival in a Black Community.* New York: Harper & Row, Publishers.

Staples, Robert. 1978. "The Black Family Revisited." In *The Black Family: Essays and Studies,* 2d ed. Robert Staples, 13–18. Boston: Allyn and Bacon.

Staples, Robert. 1985. "Changes in Black Family Structure: The Conflict Between Family, Ideology and Structural Conditions." *Journal of Marriage and the Family* 47 (November):1005–13.

U.S. Bureau of the Census. 1985. Percentage of People in Various Groups Below the Poverty Level. Washington, D.C. *Current Population Reports,* ser. p-60, no. 154.

Vogel, Ezra F. 1963. *Japan's New Middle Class.* Berkeley: University of California Press.

Volsky, George. 1985. "Jews Urged to Convert Spouses in Mixed Marriages." *The New York Times,* (November 10).

Weinberg, Sydney S. 1988. *The World of Our Mothers: The Lives of Jewish Immigrant Women.* Chapel Hill, N.C.: The University of North Carolina Press.

Willie, Charles V. 1985. *Black and White Families: A Study in Complementarity.* New York: General Hall, Inc. Publishers.

CHAPTER 7

Bendix, Reinhard, and Seymour M. Lipset. 1966. "Karl Marx's Theory of Social Classes." In *Class, Status, and Power: Social Stratification in Comparative Perspective,* ed. Reinhard Bendix and Seymour M. Lipset, 6–11. 2d ed. New York: The Free Press.

Berger, Bennett. 1960. *The Working Class Suburb.* Berkeley: University of California Press.

Cavan, Ruth S. 1969. *The American Family.* 4th ed. New York: Thomas Y. Crowell.

Curtis, Richard F., and Elton F. Jackson. 1977. *Inequality in American Societies.* New York: Academic Press.

Davis, Kingsley, and Wilbert E. Moore. 1945. "Some Principles of Stratification." *American Sociological Review* 5:242–49.

de Lone, Richard. 1978. *Small Futures.* New York: Harcourt, Brace, and Jovanovich.

Domhoff, G. William. 1983. *Who Rules America Now? A View for the 80s.* Englewood Cliffs, N.J.: Prentice-Hall.

Enos, Darryl D., and Paul Sultan. 1977. *The Sociology of Health Care: Social, Economic and Political Perspectives.* New York: Praeger.

Eshleman, J. Ross. 1985. *The Family: An Introduction.* 4th ed. Boston: Allyn and Bacon.

Goode, William J. 1966. "Family and Mobility." *Class, Status and Power: Social Stratification in Comparative Perspective,* ed. Reinhard Bendix and Seymour M. Lipset, 582–601. 2d ed. New York: The Free Press.

Hodge, Robert W., and Donald J. Treiman. 1968. "Class Identification in the United States." *American Journal of Sociology* 73:535–48.

Hollingshead, A. B., and F. C. Redlich. 1958. *Social Class and Mental Illness.* New York: John Wiley.

Hyman, Herbert H. 1966. "A Social Psychological Contribution to the Analysis of Stratification." In *Class, Status and Power: Social Stratification in Comparative Perspective,* ed. Reinhard Bendix and Seymour Lipset, 488–99. 2d ed. New York: The Free Press.

Jackman, Mary R., and Robert W. Jackman. 1983. *Class Awareness in the United States.* Berkeley: University of California Press.

Leslie, Gerald R., and Sheila K. Korman. 1985. *The Family in Social Context.* 6th ed. New York: Oxford University Press.

Marx, Karl, and Friedrich Engels. 1848. *Communist Manifesto.* Reprint 1967. New York: Pantheon.

Oppenheimer, Valerie K. 1982. *Work and the Family: A Study in Social Demography.* New York: Academic Press.

Ostrander, Susan. 1984. *A Study of Upper Class Women*. Philadelphia: Temple University Press.

Rapp, Rayna. 1982. "Family and Class in Contemporary America: Notes Toward an Understanding of Ideology." In *Rethinking the Family: Some Feminist Questions,* ed. Barrie Thorne and Marilyn Yalom, 168–87. New York: Longman.

Rubin, Lillian B. 1976. *World of Pain: Life in the Working-Class Family*. New York: Basic Books.

Sorokin, Pitirim A. 1964. *Social and Cultural Mobility*. New York: Macmillan Company.

Tischler, Henry L., Phillip Whitten, and David E. K. Hunter. 1986. *Introduction to Sociology*. 2d ed. New York: Holt, Rinehart, and Winston.

Walker, J. A. 1979. *Sacred Cows: Exploring Contemporary Idolatry*. Grand Rapids, Mich.: Zondervan Publishing House.

Walton, John. 1986. *Sociological and Critical Inquiry: The Work, Tradition and Purpose*. Chicago: Dorsey Press.

Warner, W. Lloyd. 1949. *Social Class in America*. New York: Harper & Row Publishers.

Weber, Max. 1946. *Max Weber: Essays in Sociology*. Translated by H. H. Gerth and C. Wright Mills. New York: Oxford University Press.

CHAPTER 8

Associated Press. 1987. *Minneapolis Star and Tribune,* December 7, 2A.

Blazer, J. A. 1963. "Complementary Needs and Marital Happiness." *Marriage and Family Living* 25:89–95.

Cooley, Charles Horton. 1922. *Human Nature and the Social Order*. New York: Charles Scribner's Sons.

Eysenck, H. J., and James A. Wakefield. 1981. "Psychological Factors as Predictors of Marital Satisfaction." *Advanced Behavioral Research Therapy* 3:151–92.

Goode, William. 1964. *The Family*. Englewood Cliffs, N.J.: Prentice-Hall.

Katz, I., S. Glucksberg, and R. Krauss. 1960. "Need Satisfaction and Edwards PPS Scores in Married Couples." *Journal of Consulting Psychology* 34:205–8.

Leslie, Gerald R., and Sheila K. Korman. 1985. *The Family in Social Context*. 6th ed. New York: Oxford University Press.

Lewak, Richard W., James A. Wakefield Jr., and Peter F. Briggs. 1985. "Intelligence and Personality in Mate Choice and Marital Satisfaction." *Personality and Individual Differences* 6 no. 4:471–77.

Macklin, Eleanor. 1978. "Nonmarital Heterosexual Cohabitation." *Marriage and Family Review* 1 (March/April):463–72.

Mathes, Eugene W., and Cheryl L. Moore. 1985. "Reik's Complementarity Theory of Romantic Love." *The Journal of Social Psychology* 125, no. 3:321–27.

Meyer, J. P., and S. Pepper. 1977. "Need Compatibility and Marital Adjustment in Young Married Couples." *Journal of Personality and Social Psychology.* 21:331–42.

Murstein, Bernard I. 1971. "Stimulus-Value-Response—A Theory of Marital Choice." *Journal of Consulting and Clinical Psychology* 37:47–52.

Murstein, Bernard I., and G. D. Beck. 1972. "Person Perception, Marriage Adjustment, and Social Desirability." *Journal of Consulting and Clinical Psychology* 39:396–403.

Queen, Stuart A., and Robert W. Habenstein. 1961. *The Family in Various Cultures.* Philadelphia: J. B. Lippincott Company.

Rubin, Zick. 1973. *Liking and Loving: An Invitation to Social Psychology.* New York: Holt, Rinehart, & Winston.

Safran, Claire. 1985. "Why More People are Making Better Marriages." *Parade* (April 28):14–17.

Solomon, Zahava. 1986. "Self Acceptance and the Selection of Marital Partner—An Assessment of the SVR Model of Murstein." *Social Behavior and Personality* 14, no. 1:1–6.

Tharp, R. G. 1963. "Psychological Patterning in Marriage." *Psychology Bulletin* 60:97–117.

Thelen, Mark H., M. Daniel Fishbein, and Heather A. Tatten. 1985. "Interspousal Similarity: A New Approach to an Old Question." *Journal of Social and Personal Relationships* 2, no. 4:437–46.

U.S. Bureau of the Census. 1984. "Households, Families, Marital Status, and Living Arrangements: March 1984 (Advanced Report)." *Current Population Reports,* ser. P-20, no. 391. Washington, D.C., August.

Waller, Willard. 1937. "The Rating and Dating Complex." *American Sociological Review* 2 (October):727–34.

White, Stephen G., and Chris Hatcher. 1984. "Couple Complementarity and Similarity: A Review of the Literature." *The American Journal of Family Therapy* 12, no. 1:15–25.

Winch, Robert R., Thomas Ktsanes, and Virginia Ktsanes. 1954. "The Theory of Complementary Needs in Mate Selection: An Analytic and Descriptive Study" *American Sociological Review* 19:241–49.

Wolf, Margery. 1968. *The House of Lim.* New York: Appleton-Century-Crofts.

CHAPTER 9

Arar, Yardena. 1987. "Los Angeles Television Station Becomes First to Air Condom Ad." News and Courier (Charleston, S.C., February 12):3.

Berger, Joseph. 1987. "Condoms, AIDS and Morals: New Concern Alters Debate." *New York Times* (February 12):1.

Cates, Willard. 1986. "The First Decade of Legal Abortion in the United States: Effects on Maternal Health." In *Abortion, Medicine, and the Law,* 3d ed., ed. J. Douglas Butler and David F. Walbert, 307–22. New York: Facts on File Publications.

Comfort, Alex. 1972. *The Joy of Sex: A Gourmet Guide to Love Making.* New York: Simon and Schuster.

Dickinson, George E. 1978. "Adolescent Sex Information Sources: 1964–1974." *Adolescence* 13:653–58.

Ehrenreich, Barbara, Elizabeth Hess, and Gloria Jacobs. 1986. *Re-Making Love: The Feminization of Sex.* New York: Anchor Press/Doubleday.

Freedman, R., P. Whelpton, and A. Campbell. 1959. *Family Planning, Stability and Population Growth.* New York: McGraw-Hill.

Gilmartin, Brian G. 1978. *The Gilmartin Report.* Secaucus, N.J.: Citadel.

Gordon, Sol, and Craig W. Snyder. 1986. *Personal Issues in Human Sexuality.* Boston: Allyn and Bacon.

Gross, Michael. 1987. "Among Women, the Talk Is of Condoms." *New York Times* (February 23):18.

Guttmacher, Alan F. 1963. *The Complete Book of Birth Control.* Rev. ed. New York: Ballantine Books.

Harry, Joseph. 1983. "Gay Male and Lesbian Relationships." In *Contemporary Families and Alternative Lifestyles,* ed. Eleanor D. Macklin and Roger H. Rubin, 216–34. Beverly Hills, Calif.: Sage Publications.

Hunt, Morton. 1974. *Sexual Behavior in the 1970s.* New York: Dell.

Hunt, Morton. 1983. "Marital Sex." in *Family in Transition,* 4th ed., ed. Arlene S. Skolnick and Jerome H. Skolnick, 219–33. Boston: Little, Brown and Company.

Hyde, Janet Shibley. 1982. *Understanding Human Sexuality.* New York: McGraw-Hill.

Johnson, Sharon. 1986. "For Sex Education, A New School Phase." New York Times (January 9):15.

Kaplan, Helen S. 1974. *The New Sex Therapy.* New York: Times Books.

Laskin, Daniel. 1982. "The Herpes Syndrome." *The New York Times Magazine* (February 12).

Leslie, Gerald R., and Sheila K. Korman. 1985. *The Family in Social Context.* 6th ed. New York: Oxford University Press.

Luker, Kristin. 1975. *Taking Chances: Abortion and the Decision Not to Contracept.* Berkeley: University of California Press.

Macklin, Eleanor D. 1980. "Nontraditional Family Forms: A Decade of Research." *Journal of Marriage and the Family* 42 (November):905–22.

Masters, William H., and Virginia E. Johnson. 1970. *Human Sexual Inadequacy.* Boston: Little, Brown and Company.

"More Questions Than Answers." 1987. *Post-Courier* (Charleston, S.C., March 1):3-D.

Morganthau, Tom. 1986. "Future Shock: The AIDS Epidemic." *Newsweek* (November 24):30–39.

Perlez, Jane. 1986. "On Teaching About Sex." *New York Times* (June 24):17.

Petchesky, Rosalind P. 1984. *Abortion and Woman's Choice: The State, Sexuality, and Reproductive Freedom.* New York: Longman.

Press, Aric. 1987. "A Victory for AIDS Victims." *Newsweek* (March 16):33.

Rodman, Hyman, Susan H. Lewis, and Saralyn B. Griffith. 1984. *The Sexual Rights of Adolescents.* New York: Columbia University Press.

Shapiro, Thomas M. 1985. *Population Control Politics: Women, Sterilization and Reproductive Choice.* Philadelphia: Temple University Press.

Sussman, Garry. 1986. "Attitudes on Legalized Abortion Have Changed with the Times." *The Washington Post National Weekly Edition* (January 13):37.

Symons, Donald. 1985. "Darwinism and Contemporary Marriage." In *Contemporary Marriage: Comparative Perspectives on a Changing Institution*, ed. Kingsley Davis, 133–55. New York: Russell Sage Foundation.

Tanner, D. 1978. *The Lesbian Couple*. Lexington, Mass.: D. C. Heath.

Tietze, C. 1984. "The Public Health Effect of Legal Abortion in the United States." *Family Planning Perspectives* 16:26–28.

Time Essay. 1967. "On Teaching Children About Sex." *Time* (June 9):36–37.

Weis, David L. 1983. "'Open' Marriage and Multilateral Relationships: The Emergence of Nonexclusive Models of the Marital Relationship." In *Contemporary Families and Alternative Lifestyles*, ed. Eleanor D. Macklin and Roger H. Rubin, 194–215. Beverly Hills, Calif.: Sage Publications.

CHAPTER 10

Aries, Philippe. 1985. "Love in Married Life." In *Western Sexuality*, ed. Philippe Aries and Andre Begin, 130–39. New York: Basil Blackwell.

Bane, Mary Jo. 1976. *Here to Stay: American Families in the Twentieth Century*. New York: Basic Books.

Davis, Kingsley. 1985. "The Meaning and Significance of Marriage in Contemporary Society." In *Contemporary Marriage: Comparative Perspectives on a Changing Institution*, ed. Kingsley Davis, 1–21. New York: Russell Sage Foundation.

Degler, Carl N. 1980. *At Odds: Women and Family in America from the Revolution to the Present*. New York: Oxford University Press.

Firestone, Shulamith. 1970. *The Dialectic of Sex*. New York: William Morrow.

Galvin, Kathleen M., and Bernard J. Brommel. 1982. *Family Communication: Cohesion and Change*. Glenville, Ill.: Scott, Foresman and Company.

Gerstel, Naomi, and Harriet Gross. 1984. *Commuter Marriage: A Study of Work and Family*. New York: The Guilford Press.

Gittins, Diana. 1986. *The Family in Question: Changing Households and Familiar Ideologies*. Atlantic Highlands, N.J.: Humanities Press International.

Glenn, Norval D. 1975. "Psychological Well-Being in the Post-Parental Stage: Some Evidence from National Surveys." *Journal of Marriage and the Family* 37 (February):105–9.

Hastings, Elizabeth H., and Philip K. Hastings. 1984. *Index to International Public Opinion, 1982–1983*. Westport, Conn.: Greenwood Press.

James, E. O. 1965. *Marriage Customs Through the Ages*. New York: Collier Books.

Karlsson, G. 1951. *Adaptability and Communication in Marriage: A Swedish Predictive Study of Marital Satisfaction*. Uppsala, Sweden: Almquist and Wiksells.

Madden, M. E., and R. Janoff-Bulman. 1981. "Blame, Control, and Marital Satisfaction: Wives' Attributions for Conflict in Marriage." *Journal of Marriage and the Family* 43:663–73.

Margolin, Leslie, and Lynn White. 1987. "The Continuing Role of Physical Attractiveness in Marriage." *Journal of Marriage and the Family* 49 (February):21–27.

Navran, L. 1967. "Communication and Adjustment in Marriage." *Family Process* 6:173–184.

Parsons, Talcott. 1965. "The Normal American Family." In *Man and Civilization,* ed. S. M. Farber, P. Mustacchi, and R. H. L. Wilson, 31–50. New York: McGraw-Hill.

Porat, Frieda, and Jacquelyn Carr. 1987. *Equal Partners: The Art of Creative Marriage.* Saratoga, Calif.: R & E Publishers.

Safran, Claire. 1985. "Why More People are Making Better Marriages." *Parade,* April 28, 14–17.

Smart, Laura S., and Mollie S. Smart. 1980. *Families Developing Relationships.* 2d ed. New York: Macmillan Publishing Company.

Tavuchis, Nicholas, and William J. Goode. 1975. *The Family Through Literature.* New York: McGraw-Hill.

Vrazo, Fawn. 1985. "Arrangement Not Without Its Sacrifices." *Lexington Herald-Leader,* Lexington, Ky., June 30, G1.

Winfield, Fairlee E. 1985. *Commuter Marriage: Living Together, Apart.* New York: Columbia University Press.

CHAPTER 11

Aldous, Joan. 1978. *Family Careers: Developmental Change in Families.* New York: John Wiley & Sons.

Bernard, Jessie. 1974. *The Future of Motherhood.* New York: Penguin.

Blau, Francine D., and Marianne A. Ferber. 1986. *The Economics of Women, Men, and Work.* Englewood Cliffs, N.J.: Prentice-Hall.

Brooks, J. B. 1981. *The Process of Parenting.* Palo Alto, Calif.: Mayfield Publishing Company.

Bulatao, R. A. 1981. "Values and Disvalues of Children in Successive Childbearing Decisions." *Demography* 18:1–25.

Cataldo, Christine Z. 1987. *Parent Education for Early Childhood.* New York: Columbia University Teachers College Press.

Chodorow, Nancy, and Susan Contratto. 1982. "The Fantasy of the Perfect Mother." In *Rethinking the Family: Some Feminist Questions,* ed. Barrie Thorne. New York: Longman.

Cooley, Charles H. 1915. *Social Organization.* New York: Charles Scribner's Sons.

Dinnerstein, Dorothy. 1976. *The Mermaid and the Minotaur.* New York: Harper and Row.

Firestone, Shulamith. 1970. *The Dialectic of Sex.* New York: Morrow.

Gallup International. 1981. "Trend to Smaller Families Worldwide." *Gallup Report,* No. 185 (February).

Gerson, Kathleen. 1985. *Hard Choices: How Women Decide about Work Career, and Motherhood.* Berkeley: University of California Press.

Hamner, Tommie J., and Pauline H. Turner. 1985. *Parenting in Contemporary Society.* Englewood Cliffs, N.J.: Prentice-Hall. © 1985. Reprinted by permission of Prentice Hall, Inc.

Hoffman, Lois W., and Jean D. Manis. 1979. "The Value of Children in the United States: A New Approach to the Study of Fertility." *Journal of Marriage and the Family* 41 (August):583–96.

Mead, Margaret. 1966. "Marriage in Two Steps." *Redbook Magazine* (July).

Morrison, G. S. 1978. *Parent Involvement in the Home, School and Community.* Columbus, Ohio: Charles E. Merrill.

Olson, Lawrence. 1983. *Costs of Children.* Lexington, Mass.: Lexington Books.

Polit-O'Hara, Denise, and Judith Berman. 1984. *Just the Right Size: A Guide to Family-Size Planning.* New York: Praeger Publishers. Copyright © 1984 by Praeger Publishers. Used with permission.

Quarm, Daisy. 1984. "Sexual Inequality: The High Cost of Leaving Parenting to Women." In *Women in the Workplace: Effects on Families,* ed. Kathryn M. Borman, Daisy Quarm, and Sarah Gideonse, 187–208. Norwood, N.J.: Ablex Publishing Corporation.

Ritchie, Oscar W., and Marvin R. Koller. 1964. *Sociology of Childhood.* New York: Appleton-Century-Crofts.

Roopnarine, Jaipaul L., and Brent C. Miller. 1985. "Transitions to Fatherhood." In *Dimensions of Fatherhood,* ed. Shirley M. H. Hanson and Frederick W. Bozett, 49–63. Beverly Hills, Calif.: Sage Publications.

Rossi, Alice S. 1968. "Transition to Parenthood." *Journal of Marriage and the Family* 30:26–39.

Satchell, Michael. 1985. "Should Children Be Hit in School?" *Parade,* March 24, 4–5.

Vinocur, John. 1980. "Swedish No-Spanking Law: It Works." *Louisville Courier-Journal,* October 26, G-12.

CHAPTER 12

Aldous, Joan. 1978. *Family Careers: Developmental Change in Families.* New York: John Wiley and Sons.

Atchley, Robert C. 1977. *The Social Forces in Later Life.* Belmont, Calif.: Wadsworth Publishing Company.

Atwater, Eastwood. 1983. *Adolescence.* Englewood Cliffs, N.J.: Prentice-Hall.

Becker, Howard S. 1964. "Personal Change in Adult Life." *Sociometry* 27 (March):4053.

Bronfenbrenner, Urie. 1970. "The Psychological Costs of Quality and Equality in Education." In *Personality and Social Structure,* ed. N. S. Smelser and W. T. Smelser. New York: John Wiley and Sons.

Brown, Judith K., and Virginia Kerns. 1985. *In Her Prime: A New View of Middle Aged Women.* South Hadley, Mass.: Bergin and Garvey Publishers.

Farrell, Michael P. and Stanley D. Rosenberg. 1981. *Men at Midlife.* Boston: Auburn House Publishing Company.

Galvin, Kathleen M., and Bernard J. Brommel. 1982. *Family Communication: Cohesion and Change.* Glenview, Ill.: Scott, Foresman and Company.

George, L. K. 1980. *Role Transitions in Later Life.* Monterey, Calif.: Brooks/Cole.

Glenn, N. D. 1975. "Psychological Well-being in the Postparental Stage: Some Evidence from National Surveys." *Journal of Marriage and the Family* 31:105–10.

Glick, Paul C., and Sung-Ling Lin. 1986. "More Young Adults are Living with Their Parents: Who Are They?" *Journal of Marriage and the Family* 48:107–12.

Hartshorne, T. S., and G. J. Manaster. 1982. "The Relationship with Grandparents: Contact, Importance, Role Conceptions." *International Journal of Aging and Human Development* 15:233–45.

Hughs, G. Carswell. 1987. Lecture entitled "Hope Comes Like a Child," Charleston, S.C., July 19.

Jersild, Arthur T., Judith S. Brook, and David W. Brook. 1978. *The Psychology of Adolescence.* 3rd ed. New York: Macmillan Publishing Company.

Kahana, B., and E. Kahana. 1970. "Grandparenthood from the Perspective of the Developing Grandchild." *Developmental Psychology* 3:98–105.

Kivnick, H. Q. 1982. "Grandparenthood: An Overview of Meaning and Mental Health." *Gerontologist* 22:59–66.

Leslie, Gerald R., and Sheila K. Korman. 1985. *The Family in Social Context.* 6th ed. New York: Oxford University Press.

Levinson, Daniel J. 1978. *The Seasons of a Man's Life.* New York: Alfred A. Knopf.

Lowenthal, Marjorie F., and David Chiriboga. 1972. "Transition to the Empty Nest: Crisis, Challenge, or Relief?" *Archives of General Psychiatry* 26:8–14.

MacKenna, Robert W. 1933. *As Shadows Lengthen: Late Essays.* New York: Dutton.

Neugarten, Bernice L. 1970. "Dynamics of Transition of Middle Age to Old Age." *Journal of Geriatric Psychology* 4:71–87.

New York Times. 1985. "Grandparents Liable if Teen-agers Give Birth," November 14.

Nolen, William A. 1984. *Crisis Time! Love, Marriage and the Male at MidLife.* New York: Dodd, Mead and Company.

Phillips, Richard. 1979. "Exploding the Myths of Adolescence." *Chicago Tribune,* May 6, Section 12, p. 14.

Pineo, Peter C. 1961. "Disenchantment in the Later Years of Marriage." *Marriage and Family Living* 23:3–11.

Rogers, Dorothy. 1981. *Adolescents and Youth.* 4th ed. Englewood Cliffs, N.J.: Prentice-Hall.

Rollins, Boyd C., and Harold Feldman. 1970. "Marital Satisfaction over the Family Life Cycle." *Journal of Marriage and the Family* 32 (February).

Sebald, Hans. 1986. "Adolescents' Shifting Orientation toward Parents and Peers: A Curvilinear Trend over Recent Decades." *Journal of Marriage and the Family* 48 (February):5–13.

Smith, Ken R., and Phyllis Moen. 1988. "Passage Through Midlife: Women's Changing Roles and Economic Well-Being." *The Sociological Quarterly* 29 (4):503–24.

Timberlake, E. M. 1980. "The Value of Grandchildren to Grandmothers." *Journal of Gerontological Social Work* 33:263–90.

Troll, Lillian E. 1971. "The Family of Later Life: A Decade Review." *Journal of Marriage and the Family* 33:263–90.

Troll, Lillian E. 1980. "Grandparenting." In *Aging in the 1980s: Psychological Issues,* ed. L. W. Poon, Washington, D.C.: American Psychological Association.

U.S. Bureau of Census. 1981. "Social and Economic Characteristics of Americans During Midlife." In *Current Population Reports,* ser. P-23, no. 111. Washington, D.C., June.

Youniss, James, and Jacqueline Smoller. 1985. *Adolescent Relations with Mothers, Fathers and Friends.* Chicago: University of Chicago Press.

CHAPTER 13

Achenbaum, W. Andrew. 1978. *Old Age in the New Land: The American Experience Since 1790.* Baltimore: Johns Hopkins Press.

Aiken, Lewis R. 1982. *Later Life.* 2d ed. New York: Holt, Rinehart, and Winston.

Atchley, Robert C. 1976. *The Sociology of Retirement.* Cambridge, Mass.: Schenkman.

Atchley, Robert C. 1977. *The Social Forces in Later Life.* 2d ed. Belmont, Calif.: Wadsworth Publishing Company.

Block, Marilyn R., Janice L. Davidson, and Jean D. Grambs. 1981. *Women Over Forty: Visions and Realities.* New York: Springer Publishing Company.

Brecher, Edward M., and the Editors of Consumer Reports Books. 1984. *Love, Sex and Aging.* Boston: Little, Brown and Company.

Brooke, James. 1986. "Retirees, Many Bored, Try Un-retirement." *The New York Times,* January 19, p. 1.

Brubaker, Timothy H. 1985. *Later Life Families.* Beverly Hills: Sage Publications.

Butler, Robert N. 1975. *Why Survive? Being Old in America.* New York: Harper and Row.

Carp, Frances M. 1976. "Housing and Living Environments of Older People." In *Handbook of Aging and the Social Sciences,* ed. Robert H. Binstock and Ethel Shanas, 244–71. New York: Van Nostrand Reinhold Company.

Cox, Harold G. 1988. *Later Life: The Realities of Aging.* 2d ed. Englewood Cliffs, N.J.: Prentice-Hall.

Crystal, Stephen. 1982. *America's Old Age Crisis.* New York: Basic Books.

Cumming, Elaine, and William E. Henry. 1961. *Growing Old: The Process of Disengagement.* New York: Basic Books.

Cunningham, Walter R., and John W. Brookbank. 1988. *Gerontology: The Psychology, Biology, and Sociology of Aging.* New York: Harper and Row, Publishers.

Donahue, Wilma, Harold L. Orbach, and Otto Pollak. 1960. "Retirement: The Emerging Social Pattern." In *Handbook of Social Gerontology: Societal Aspects of Aging,* ed. Clark Tibbitts, 330–406. Chicago: University of Chicago Press.

Foner, Anne. 1986. *Aging and Old Age: New Perspectives.* Englewood Cliffs, N.J.: Prentice-Hall.

Gordon, Chad, Charles M. Gaitz, and Judith Scott. 1976. "Leisure and Lives: Personal Expressivity Across the Life Span." In *Handbook of Aging and the Social Sciences,* ed. Robert H. Binstock and Ethel Shanas, 310–41. New York: Van Nostrand Reinhold Company.

Goudy, W. J., E. A. Powers, P. M. Keith, and R. A. Reges. 1980. "Panel Study of Older Males." *Journal of Gerontology* 35:942–48.

Harris, Corra. 1926. "The Borrowed Timers." *Ladies Home Journal* 43 (September):35.

Havinghurst, R. J., and R. Albrecht. 1953. *Older People.* New York: Longmans, Green.

Hickey, Tom. 1980. *Health and Aging.* Monterey, Calif.: Brooks/Cole Publishing Company.

Hochschild, Arlie Russell. 1973. *The Unexpected Community: Portrait of an Old Age Subculture.* Berkeley: University of California Press.

Johnson, Colleen L. 1985. "The Impact of Illness on Late-life Marriages." *Journal of Marriage and the Family* 47:165–72.

Kaplan, Max. 1960. "The Uses of Leisure." In *Handbook of Social Gerontology: Societal Aspects of Aging,* ed. Clark Tibbitts. Chicago: University of Chicago Press.

Liberman, Morton A., and Sheldon S. Tobin. 1983. *The Experience of Old Age: Stress, Coping, and Survival.* New York: Basic Books.

MacKenna, Robert W. 1933. *As Shadows Lengthen: Late Essays.* New York: Dutton.

Masters, W. H., and V. E. Johnson. 1966. *Human Sexual Response.* Boston: Little, Brown.

Mobarak, Ahmed, and Charles A. Shamoian. 1985. "Aging and Sexuality." In *Sexuality: New Perspectives,* ed. Zira DeFries, Richard C. Friedman, and Ruth Corn, 288–309. Westport, Conn.: Greenwood Press.

Mohr, J. W., R. E. Turner, and M. B. Jerry. 1964. *Pedophilia and Exhibitionism.* Toronto: University of Toronto Press.

Palmore, E. B., G. G. Fillenbaum, and L. K. George. 1984. "Consequences of Retirement." *Journal of Gerontology* 39:109–16.

Parsons, Talcott. 1951. *Toward a General Theory of Action.* Cambridge, Mass.: Harvard University Press.

Rosen, Benson, and Thomas H. Jerdee. 1985. *Older Employees: New Roles for Valued Resources.* Homewood, Ill.: Dow-Jones-Irwin.

Rubin, Isadore. 1963. "Sex Over Sixty-five." In *Advances in Sex Research,* ed. H. G. Beigel. New York: Hoeber-Harper.

Shanas, Ethel. 1972. "Adjustment to Retirement: Substitution or Accommodation?" In Retirement, ed. Frances M. Carp, 219–43. New York: Behavioral Publications.

Shanas, Ethel, and George L. Maddox. 1976. "Aging, Health, and the Organization of Health Resources." In *Handbook of Aging and the Social Sciences,* ed. Robert H. Binstock and Ethel Shanas, 592–618. New York: Van Nostrand Reinhold Company.

Streib, Gordon F., and Clement J. Schneider. 1971. *Retirement in American Society.* Ithaca, N.Y.: Cornell University Press.

Wan, Thomas T. H. 1985. *Well-Being for the Elderly.* Lexington, Mass.: D. C. Heath and Company.

CHAPTER 14

Albrecht, Stan L., Howard M. Bahr, and Kristen L. Goodman. 1983. *Divorce and Remarriage: Problems, Adaptations, and Adjustments.* Westport, Conn.: Greenwood Press.

Appel, Karen W. 1985. *America's Changing Families: A Guide for Educators.* Bloomington, Ind.: Phi Delta Kappa Educational Foundation.

Barry, Dave. 1987. "Little Things Mean A Lot To A Marriage's Vitality." *Minneapolis Star and Tribune,* November 4, 1C.

Bloom, Bernard L., Stephen W. White, and Shirley J. Asher. 1979. "Marital Disruption as a Stressful Life Event." In *Divorce and Separation: Context, Causes, and Consequences,* ed. George Levinger and Oliver C. Moles. New York: Basic Books.

Cherlin, Andrew J. 1981. *Marriage, Divorce, and Remarriage.* Cambridge: Harvard University Press.

Collins, Glenn. 1985. *Minneapolis Star and Tribune,* October 30, 1985, 1C and 9C.

Crosby, John F. 1985. *Reply to Myth: Perspectives on Intimacy.* New York: John Wiley and Sons.

Dullea, Georgia. 1985. *Minneapolis Star and Tribune,* November 14, 1985, 1C and 11C.

Eshleman, J. Ross. 1985. *The Family: An Introduction.* 4th ed. Boston: Allyn and Bacon.

Furstenberg, Frank F., Jr., and Graham B. Spanier. 1984. *Recycling the Family: Remarriage after Divorce.* Beverly Hills: Sage Publications.

Goode, William J. 1956. *After Divorce.* Glencoe, Ill.: The Free Press.

Kavanaugh, Robert E. 1972. *Facing Death.* Baltimore: Penguin Books.

Leming, Michael R., and George E. Dickinson. 1985. *Understanding Dying, Death, and Bereavement.* New York: Holt, Rinehart, and Winston.

Leslie, Gerald R., and Sheila K. Korman. 1985. *The Family in Social Context.* 6th ed. New York: Oxford University Press.

Lutz, Patricia. 1983. "The Stepfamily: An Adolescent Perspective." *Family Relations* 32 (July):367–75.

National Center for Health Statistics. 1980. *Monthly Vital Statistics Report,* March 14, 2.

National Center for Health Statistics. 1989. *Monthly Vital Statistics Report,* May 1, 1–3.

Pett, Marjorie G. 1982. "Correlates of Children's Social Adjustment Following Divorce." *Journal of Divorce* 5, (Summer):25–39.

Phipps, William E. 1987. *Death: Confronting the Reality.* Atlanta: John Knox Press.

Shideler, Mary McDermott. 1971. "An Amicable Divorce." *The Christian Century,* May 5.

Spanier, Graham B., and Paul C. Glick. 1981. *Journal of Marriage and the Family* 44 (November):1032ff.

U.S. Bureau of the Census. 1986. Marital Status and Living Arrangements: March 1985. *Current Population Reports,* ser. P-20, no. 410, table 1, p. 17. Washington, D.C.

Wallerstein, Judith S., and Sandra Blakeslee. 1989. *Second Chances: Men, Women, and Children a Decade After Divorce.* New York: Ticknor and Fields.

Weitzman, Lenore J. 1985. *The Divorce Revolution: The Unexpected Social and Economic Consequences for Women and Children in America.* New York: The Free Press. Reprinted with permission of The Free Press, a Division of Macmillan, Inc. Copyright © 1985 by Dr. Lenore J. Weitzman.

Wilson, Kenneth L., Louis A. Zurcher, Diana Claire McAdams, and Russell L. Curtis. 1975. "Stepfathers and Stepchildren: An Exploratory Analysis from Two National Surveys." *Journal of Marriage and the Family* 37 (August):526–36.

CHAPTER 15

Berger, Peter. 1967. *The Sacred Canopy.* New York: Doubleday and Company.

Davidson, Glen W. 1975. *Living with Dying.* Minneapolis: Augsburg Publishing House.

Dickinson, George E., and A. A. Pearson. 1979. "Sex Differences of Physicians in Relating to Dying Patients." *Journal of the American Medical Women's Association* 34:45–47.

Dumont, Richard G., and Dennis C. Foss. 1972. *The American View of Death: Acceptance or Denial?* Cambridge, Mass.: Schenkman.

Formanek, Ruth. 1974. "When Children Ask About Death." *Elementary School Journal* 75, no. 2:92–97.

Galen, Helene. 1972. "A Matter of Life and Death." *Young Children* 27, no. 6 (August):351–56.

Gaspard, N. J. 1970. "The Family of the Patient with Long-Term Illness." *Nursing Clinics of North America* 5, no. 1:77–84.

Glaser, Barney, and Anselm Strauss. 1965. *Awareness of Dying.* Chicago: Aldine.

Goffman, Irving. 1959. *The Presentation of Self in Everyday Life.* New York: Doubleday.

Holmes, T. H., and R. H. Rahe. 1967. "The Social Readjustment Rating Scale." *Journal of Psychosomatic Research* 11 (August):213, table 3–1.

Irion, Paul E. 1954. *The Funeral and the Mourners.* Nashville, Tenn.: Abingdon Press.

Kastenbaum, Robert J. 1977. Death, Society, and Human Experience. St. Louis: C. V. Mosby.

Kavanaugh, Robert E. 1972. *Facing Death.* Baltimore: Penguin Books.

Kubler-Ross, Elizabeth. 1969. *On Death and Dying.* New York: Macmillan.

Leming, Michael R. 1979–80. "Religion and Death: A Test of Homans' Thesis." *Omega* 10, no. 4:347–64.

Leming, Michael R., and George E. Dickinson. 1985. *Understanding Dying, Death, and Bereavement.* New York: Holt, Rinehart, and Winston. Copyright © 1985 by Holt, Rinehart, and Winston, Inc. Material reprinted by permission of the publisher.

Millay, Edna St. Vincent. 1927. "Childhood is the Kingdom Where Nobody Dies." *Collected Lyrics.* New York: Harper and Row, 1969, 203–5.

National Funeral Directors Association. 1981. "Body Donation: A Compendium of Facts Compiled as an Interprofessional Source Book." Produced by the College of Health Sciences (University of Minnesota) and the National Funeral Directors Association.

Parsons, Talcott. 1951. *The Social System.* New York: The Free Press.

Pine, Vanderlyn R. 1971. *Findings of the Professional Census.* Milwaukee: National Funeral Directors Association (June).

CHAPTER 16

Brody, Jane E. 1987. "When A Child Is Molested." *New York Times,* February 18, 18.

Brozan, N. 1984. "Helping to Heal the Scars Left by Incest." *New York Times,* January 9.

Davidson, Terry. 1978. *Conjugal Crime.* New York: Hawthorne.

Douglass, Richard L. 1983. Opportunities for Prevention of Domestic Neglect and Abuse of the Elderly." *Prevention in Human Services* 3 (Fall):135–50.

Finkelhor, David, and Kersti Yllo. 1983. "Rape in Marriage: A Sociological View." In *The Dark Side of Families: Current Family Violence Research,* ed. David Finkelhor, Richard J. Gelles, Gerald T. Hotaling, and Murray A. Straus, 119–30. Beverly Hills: Sage Publications.

Firestone, Shulamith. 1970. *The Dialectic of Sex.* New York: Morrow.

Garbarino, James, and Gwen Gilliam. 1980. *Understanding Abusive Families.* Lexington, Mass.: D. C. Heath.

Gelles, Richard J. 1975. "Violence and Pregnancy." *Family Coordinator* 24 (January):81–86.

Gelles, Richard J. 1979. "The Truth About Husband Abuse." *Ms. Magazine.*

Gelles, Richard J. 1980. "Violence in the Family: A Review of Research in the Seventies." *Journal of Marriage and the Family* 42:873–85.

Gelles, Richard J. 1985. "Family Violence: What We Know and Can Do." In *Unhappy Families,* ed. Eli H. Newberger and Richard Bourne, 1–8. Littleton, Mass.: PSG Publishing Company.

Gelles, Richard J., and Claire P. Cornell. 1985. *Intimate Violence in Families.* Beverly Hills: Sage Publications.

Gordon, Sol, and Craig W. Snyder. 1986. *Personal Issues in Human Sexuality.* Newton, Mass.: Allyn and Bacon.

Harbin, H., and D. Madden. 1979. "Battered Parents: A New Syndrome." *American Journal of Psychiatry* 136 (October):1288–91.

Kimsey, Larry R., Arthur R. Tarbox, and David F. Bragg. 1981. "Abuse of the Elderly: The Hidden Agenda." *Journal of the American Geriatrics Society* 29 (October):465–72.

Lezak, M. D. 1978. "Living with the Characterologically Altered Brain Injured Patient." *Journal of Clinical Psychiatry* 39:592.

Lindsey, R. 1984. "Sexual Abuse of Children Draws Experts' Increasing Concern Nationwide." *New York Times,* April 4, A21.

Lystad, Mary. 1986. *Violence in the Home: Interdisciplinary Perspectives.* New York: Brunner/Mazel Publishers.

Okun, Lewis. 1986. *Woman Abuse: Facts Replacing Myth.* Albany: State University of New York Press.

Phillips, Linda R. 1986. "Theoretical Explanations of Elderly Abuse: Competing Hypotheses and Unresolved Issues." In *Elder Abuse: Conflict in the Family,* ed. Karl A. Pillemer and Rosalie S. Wolf, 197–217. Dover, Mass.: Auburn House Publishing Company.

Radbill, Samuel. 1980. "A History of Child Abuse and Infanticide." In *The Battered Child,* 3d ed., ed. R. Helfer and C. Kempe, 3–20. Chicago: University of Chicago Press.

Rathbone-McCuan, Eloise, and Barbara Voyles. 1982. "Case Detection of Abused Elderly Parents." *American Journal of Psychiatry* 139 (February):189–92.

Shupe, Anson, William A. Stacey, and Lonnie R. Hazlewood. 1987. *Violent Men, Violent Couples: The Dynamics of Domestic Violence.* Lexington, Mass.: Lexington Books.

Star, Barbara, Carol G. Clark, Karen M. Goetz, and Linda O'Malia. 1979. "Psychosocial Aspects of Wife-Battering." *Social Casework* 60:479–87.

Steinmetz, Suzanne M. 1986. "The Violent Family." In *Violence in the Home,* ed. Mary Lystad, 51–67. New York: Brunner/Mazel Publishers.

Straus, Murray, Richard Gelles, and Suzanne Steinmetz. 1980. *Behind Closed Doors: Violence in the American Family.* Garden City, N.Y.: Anchor Press.

Thorman, George. 1980. *Family Violence.* Springfield, Ill.: Charles C. Thomas Publishers.

Thorne, Barrie. 1982. "Feminist Rethinking of the Family: An Overview." In *Rethinking the Family: Some Feminist Questions,* ed. Barrie Thorne, 1–24. New York: Longman.

CHAPTER 17

American Family. 1987. "Child Care: A Crucial Aspect of Family Policy" (editorial), vol. 10, no. 12 (December).

Herendeen, Lisa. 1987. "Child Care No Longer a Partisan Issue in the Senate." *American Family* 10, no. 12 (December):6.

Hornblower, Margot. 1988. "Gray Power!" *Time* 131, no. 1:36–37.

Sugarman, Jule M. 1987. "Family Policy Recommendations." *American Family* 10, no. 12 (December):1.

U.S. Department of Commerce. 1986. *Statistical Abstract of the United States: 1987.* 107th ed. Washington, D.C.

APPENDIX

Heller, Peter L. 1976. "Familism Scale: Revalidation and Revision." *Journal of Marriage and the Family* 38 (August):423–29.

Litwak, Eugene. 1960. "Geographical Mobility and Extended Family Cohesion." *American Sociological Review* 25 (June):385–94.

Name Index

Subject Index

Boldface numbers indicate pages on which glossary definitions are given.

women's sexual
revolution and, 197
Birth control pill, 203, 205
Black Americans, 118–124
change and, 122–123
female-headed families
among, 121–122
interracial marriage and,
123
marriage and, 122, 123
social class and,
120–121
Blended families, 347, **351**
Body bequest programs,
370–371
Bourgeoisie, 148, **162**
Brave New World (Huxley),
79

Career, 103, **115**
two-person, 103, **116**
See also Work
Carnegie Council on
Children, 146
Change
American families'
reaction to, 83–86
in black families,
122–124
future, 405–412
marriage and, 233
Chicanos, 128–130
Child abuse, 380–384
extent of, 381–382, 383
sexual, 392–393
Child Abuse Prevention act
of 1974, 381
Child abusers, 382–383
Childless marriages, 252,
259
Children
adolescent, 271–282
in Chinese American
families, 133
in colonial America,
70–71
corporal punishment of,
262–263, 379
cost of raising, 250–251
custody of, 336, 337,
346–347, 349
discipline of, 261–263
divorce and, 336,
342–346, 349
explaining death to,
357–359
gender-role socialization
of, 93–96
grandparenting of,
282–284
influences of peers vs.
parents on, 273–274
in Italian American
families, 132

in Japanese American
families, 134–135
launching of, 276–282
in Mexican American
families, 129–130
number of, 80, 81–82,
84, 102, 250–253,
263–265
parents as friends,
274–276
sex education for, 201
socialization of, 93–96,
259–263, 271–272
See also Parents
Chinese Americans, 133
Chlamydia, 218
Chronic illness, 363, **376**
Class. *See* Social class
Cohabitation, 187–190
Cohorts, 273, **293**
Colonial life, 68–71,
171–172
Commission on Elderly
People Living Alone,
316
Communication, in
marriage, 233–236
Commuter marriages,
240–244, **245**
Complementarity,
181–182, **192**
Complementary needs,
theory of, 179–181,
192
*Complete Book of Birth
Control, The*
(Guttmacher), 202
Composite family, 22,
28–29; **40**
Conceptual scheme,
44–45, **61**
Concrete propositions,
45–46
Condoms, 204–207, 215
Conflict, in marriage,
237–240
Conflict theory, 51–52
on family abuse, 395
on social inequality, 145
Conformity, 274–275
Conjugal family, 21–22,
40, 75–77, **87**
Consanguinal family, 22,
40, 76, 87
Content conflict, 238
Continuity approach to
aging, 298, 299–300
Contraception. *See* Birth
control
Co-parenting, 346–347,
349, **351**
Corporal punishment,
262–263, **266,** 379,
397

See also Family violence
Creative activities, 306
Cremation, 369–370, **376**
Crisis Time! (Nolen), 270
Cross-cultural perspective,
19–38
on family authority,
35–37
on kinship behaviors,
31–33
on lineage systems,
29–31
on residential groupings,
33–35
on rules of inheritance,
33
on types of families,
21–29
Cross-sectional studies,
284, **293**
Cultural heterogeneity,
118, **138**
Culture, 9, **16**
Curvilinearity, 274, **293**

Dating
mate selection and,
184–187
in middle years,
286–288, 289
Day care
for children, 109–113,
410–412
for elderly, 318–319,
409
Death, 355–375
in American culture,
355–369
attitudes toward,
359–362
bereavement process
and, 372–375
disengagement and,
365–368
dying process and,
364–369
explaining to children,
357–359
fears about, 361–362
funerals, 369–372
statistics on, 355–356
Death anxiety, 361–362,
376
Deductive system, 46–47,
56–57, **62**
Deference, 31, **40**
Dependent variable, 46, **62**
Descent, 29–31, 154
Descriptive concepts, 44,
62
Developmental activities,
306
Dialectic of Sex
(Firestone), 254

Social behavioralist
paradigm, 49
Social class, 141–162
black Americans and,
120–121
determination of,
147–149
inequality and, 143–147
measures of, 149
middle, 150, 153–154
mobility and, 159–161
upper, 150, 151–153
working, 150, 154–159
Social control, 72–73, **87**,
202
Social definitionist
paradigm, 52–56
Social disengagement,
297–298, **321**
Social exchange theory,
54–56, 169–170,
394
Social factist paradigm,
49–52
Social inequality,
143–145, **163**
Socialization, 255–263,
266
of children, 93–96,
259–263
to gender roles, 91–97
in parental roles,
255–259
primary, 259–263
secondary, 271–272
Social mobility, 159–161
horizontal, 159, **162**
vertical, 159, **163**
Social science
disciplines in, 7–14
as science, 6–7
Social science research.
See Research
Social Security, 301, 316,
317, 319–320, 407,
408, 410
Social stratification,
144–147, **163**
Societal disengagement,
297
Society, egalitarian, 143,
162
Sociology, 7–9, **17**
Spanking, 262–263, 381
Spousal support, 336, **352**
Spouse abuse, 385–389,
393–394
Statecraft as Soulcraft
(Will), 12
Status
achieved, 77–78, **87**
ascribed, 77–78, **87**
dating and, 186
distinctions in, 143

master, 367, **377**
of women, 142
See also Social class
Statutory rape, 392
STDs. *See* Sexually
transmitted diseases
Stem family, 27, **42**
Sterilization, 205,
207–208
Stress, and family,
104–105, 107–109
Stressor events, 389, **397**
Structural-functional
theory, 50–51
on family violence, 395
on social inequality,
144–145
Subjective approach to
measuring social
class, 149
Swedish people
on corporal punishment,
262
divorce among, 190
"Swinging," 212–213
Symbiotic relationship, 60,
62
Symbolic interaction
theory, 53–54, 395
Syphilis, 218–219

Taboos. *See* Incest
Taiwan, marriage in, 174,
175
Taking Chances (Luker),
202–203
Television
contraceptive advertising
on, 206–207
deaths on, 356
marital communication
and, 235
Terminally ill, 364–369
Theoretical concepts, 44,
62
Theories, 44–61, **62**
complementary needs,
179–181, **192**
conceptual scheme and,
44–45
conflict, 51–52, 395
deductive approach to,
56–57
disengagement,
297–298
inductive approach to,
56–57
paradigms and, 48–49
propositions and, 45–46
research and, 57–60
social exchange, 54–56,
395
structural-functional,
50–51, 395

symbolic interaction,
53–54, 395
verification of, 46–47
Theory inference, 46–47,
62
Toda society, 25–26
Transactional Analysis
(TA), 257
Treatise on the Family, A
(Becker), 12
Triad, 258, **266**
Trial marriage, 189
Tubal ligation, 207
Two-career family,
102–113, **116,**
240–244
Two-person career, 103,
116
Two-step marriage,
187–188

Ultimogeniture, 33, **42**
Unilateral action, 333, **352**
Unilineal descent, 29, 30,
42
Upper class, 150, 151–153
Urban families
conjugal system in,
75–77
rural vs., 72–75

Vaginal foam, 205
Vaginal sponge, 205
Vaginismus, 220
Value conflict, 238
Variables, **63**
dependent, 46, **62**
operationalization of,
418
Vasectomy, 207
Verification, 46–47
Verstehen, 53
Vertical social mobility,
159, **163**
Village settlement pattern,
68, **87**
Violence. *See* Family
violence

Walden Two (Skinner),
79–80
War on Poverty, 256
*Webster v. Reproductive
Health Services of
Missouri*, 209
Weddings
cost of, 178
Japanese, 177
See also Marriage
Welfare, 121
West, history of family in,
71–72
Widowhood, 315,
316–317, 390

Wife abuse, 385–388, 393–394
Withdrawal method of birth control, 203, 205
Women
abuse of, 384–388, 393–394
biological differences in, 90–91
child abuse by, 382–383
in colonial America, 69–70
as head of family, 121–122
in historical West, 72
housework and, 109, 110
income of, 99–101, 270, 316–317
marital rape of, 393–394

motherhood and, 253–255
in polyandrous cultures, 24–26
in polygynous cultures, 23–24
responsibility for birth control and, 202–203
retirement and, 316–317
sexual dysfunctions in, 197, 220
sexual revolution and, 196–197
status of, 142
in workforce, 98–99, 101
see also Gender roles
Women's Lives: Themes and Variations in

Gender Learning (Lott), 94–95
Women's movement
on motherhood, 253–255
sexual revolution and, 196–197
Work, 97–113
commuter marriages and, 240–244
day care and, 109–113
gender roles and, 97–102
parental leave from, 112–113, 255
retirees and, 308–309
satisfaction in, 302–303
two-career family and, 102–109
Working class, 150, 154–159